"*Onward* reveals Elena Aguilar's wisdom and humanity in helping educators find the power within themselves to realize their aspirations, despite the pervasive challenges. It is truly an amazing book, full of brilliant strategies and advice and rooted in her own vulnerable, honest, beautiful experience and stories. Anyone who makes the time to read and sit with this incredible resource will be stronger, happier, and better for it, and, I predict, forever grateful."

—*Wendy Kopp, founder, Teach For America; CEO, Teach For All*

"*Onward* will change your life! Elena Aguilar provides a thoughtful, moving, and timely framework for how to increase the resilience of the adults who serve our students. It provides a clear path using science, research, and the compelling experiences of one who has been down this path herself. This book is a gift to every teacher, from novice to veteran, and should be required reading for anyone in school leadership."

—*Ron Severson, superintendent of the Roseville (CA) Joint Union High School District*

"Elena Aguilar offers a hopeful message to stressed-out educators—resilience is something that you *can* cultivate through your habits and dispositions. There is no magic wand to sweep away all stress and weariness, but this book offers good guidance for fostering a sustainable approach to the meaningful but arduous work of educating the young minds entrusted to our care."

—*Megan Tschannen-Moran, professor of educational policy, planning, and leadership, William & Mary School of Education*

"Elena Aguilar's writing is the antidote every teacher needs to fight burnout and meet challenging students with fresh set of eyes. *Onward* is empowering, specific, and makes it seem possible to bring your best self to the classroom every day. When you feel the need to hit the reset button, pick up this book!"

—*Celine Coggins, lecturer and entrepreneur-in-residence, Harvard Graduate School of Education*

"I invite every educator to keep a copy of this book by your nightstand. Each month a new chapter provides you new opportunities for exploring how you will build your resilience and commitment to great teaching."

—*Stephanie Hirsh, executive director, Learning Forward*

"*Onward* is not a feel-good, theoretical guide to enhancing resilience. It's a tough, look-in-the-mirror-and-do-it set of practical strategies for all educators to be their personal and professional best in this inherently stressful profession."

> —*Colin Seale, founder and CEO, thinkLaw*

"Leaders, in schools big and small, will use this book every year! *Onward* guides you through the best strategies to bring out the leaders in your staff and students. It acknowledges the ebbs and flows of a school year and how to keep your organization and you moving forward!"

> —*Michelle Carpenter, principal, Berney Elementary, Walla Walla, WA*

"We educators owe it to ourselves and our students to cultivate resilience so we can continue to inspire, teach, and lead. Read this book. Grow your resiliency. Stay in this work to transform education."

> —*Christine Carlson, instructional coach, KIPP Northeast Denver Middle School*

"*Onward* opens up the real conversation about *how* to support teachers and leaders. Each page addresses essential, but often overlooked, ways we can all thrive as educators. Every new teacher and administrator needs this book."

> —*Cheryl Lana Agrawal, San Mateo (CA) County Office of Education*

"We know that for teachers, symbolic violence within this work is a natural reaction to being silenced, but *Onward* helps us to create a world where there isn't such a heavy weight behind us while at the same time cultivating the resistance needed for the freedoms within ourselves to be felt by the nature of our very own existence and relationship to resilience."

> —*Mario Benabe, STEM educator*

Onward

Cultivating Emotional Resilience in Educators

Elena Aguilar

A Wiley Brand

Published by Jossey-Bass
A Wiley Brand
One Montgomery Street, Suite 1000, San Francisco, CA 94104-4594—www.josseybass.com

Jossey-Bass books and products are available through most bookstores. To contact Jossey-Bass directly call our Customer Care Department within the U.S. at 800-956-7739, outside the U.S. at 317-572-3986, or fax 317-572-4002.

Wiley publishes in a variety of print and electronic formats and by print-on-demand. Some material included with standard print versions of this book may not be included in e-books or in print-on-demand. If this book refers to media such as a CD or DVD that is not included in the version you purchased, you may download this material at http://booksupport.wiley.com. For more information about Wiley products, visit www.wiley.com.

Many of the names of the educators that I reference throughout this book are indeed their real names. To the very best of my abilities, I've depicted them and shared their words with as much accuracy as possible. When appropriate, I've used pseudonyms. To protect privacy, I've also changed identity markers and some aspects of the narrative with the hopes that the people about whom I write will be unidentifiable.

Library of Congress Cataloging-in-Publication Data

Names: Aguilar, Elena, 1969- author.
Title: Onward : cultivating emotional resilience in educators / by Elena
  Aguilar.
Description: San Francisco, CA : Jossey-Bass, 2018. | Includes
  bibliographical references and index.
Identifiers: LCCN 2017057676 (print) | LCCN 2017061590 (ebook) | ISBN
  9781119364924 (pdf) | ISBN 9781119364900 (epub) | ISBN 9781119364894 (pbk.)
Subjects: LCSH: Teachers--Psychology. | Teacher morale. | Educators. |
  Resilience (Personality trait)
Classification: LCC LB2840 (ebook) | LCC LB2840 .A38 2018 (print) | DDC
  371.102--dc23
LC record available at https://lccn.loc.gov/2017057676

Cover image: © Erick Joyner / EyeEm / Getty Images
Cover design by Wiley

Printed in the United States of America

FIRST EDITION

PB printing   C10011078_061119

CONTENTS

PREFACE

You're on a rugged trek in an arid land. Thirsty and dusty, you concentrate on putting one foot in front of the other. The heat makes your head pound, and you wonder whether you're lost. Just as you reach your limit, you come to a clearing. Hummingbirds appear, darting back and forth, dipping into and then emerging from what you see is a huge hole in the ground.

Stepping to the rim, you peer into a deep cave, at the bottom of which lies a pool of sublime turquoise water. Here, the foliage is lush and green, refreshing and inviting. An old wooden ladder beckons you, and you descend tentatively toward the pool.

Your apprehension begins to dissipate. The air is cool. You hear only water dripping off the ends of stalactites as your eyes adjust to the light. You drink from an underground stream that flows into the pool.

You wade in, submerge your body, and allow the translucent water to envelop you. As you float on your back, the layers of dust, exhaustion, and fear wash away.

Cradled by these blue-green spring waters, you know you can do anything. You will continue the trek, and, even though you'll face thirst and fatigue again, you'll be able to go on. You know now. You remember the way.

❧❧

In Mexico's Yucatan Peninsula, as well as in other parts of the world, just meters below ground lie *cenotes*, water holes formed millions of years ago by the collapse of limestone. That's the image on the cover of this book. These natural springs, filled by underground rivers and rainwater, have been a resource for people for thousands of years. The ancient Mayans built villages around these pools and believed them to be a portal to speak with the gods—*cenote* means "sacred well."

Today, Mayans continue to care for these places and enjoy the relief of the waters in the long, hot days of summer.

When you float in a cenote, you feel—I can assure you—that anything is possible.

The cenote offers a beautiful metaphor for resilience. Within you and outside you is a wellspring of life-giving energy that you can access and cultivate. The cenote provides relief on a scorching day. It already exists. Our task is to find our way back to it, understand what it offers, care for it, and then float. Resilience is within us. Let's start the journey.

In memory of my grandparents, Lil and Frank, who personified resilience, fought the good fight, and loved me fiercely

With our lives we make our answers all the time, to this ravenous, beautiful, mutilated, gorgeous world.

VICTORIA SAFFORD

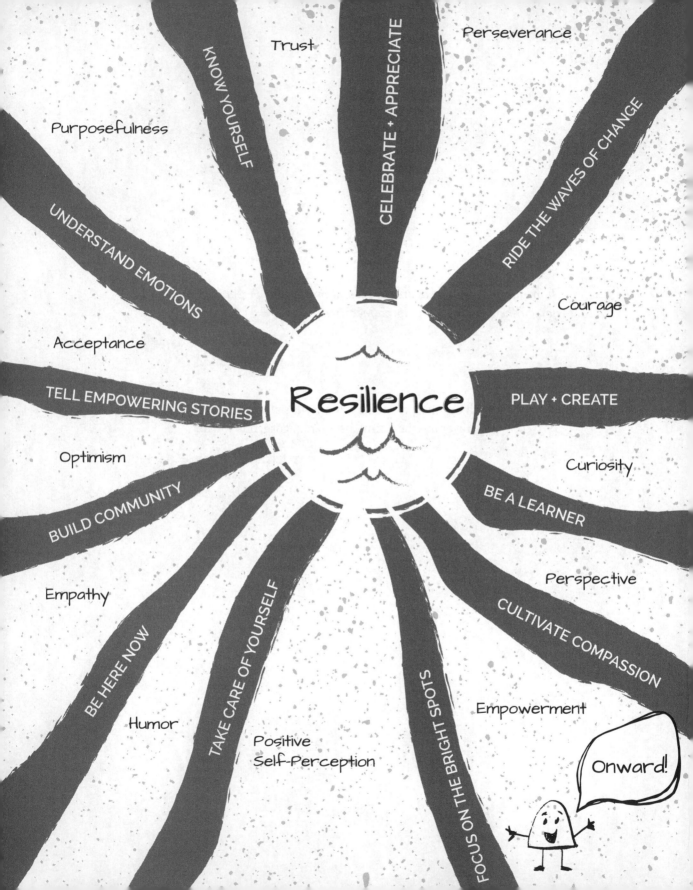

INTRODUCTION

Imagine it's the end of a rainy Friday when kids didn't get time outside and you had to supervise indoor recess. You had only 10 minutes for lunch, during which you inhaled a bag of chips and a soda; and during the final few minutes of cleanup, a student who often pushes your buttons says something disrespectful to you. You had only asked the student to pick up a piece of trash. Other kids giggle and watch to see what you'll do.

Freeze this scene.

This moment between something that happens and how we respond is what this book is about. This is the moment when we cultivate resilience. This is the moment that is referenced in this quote (erroneously attributed to Viktor Frankl but actually of unknown origin): "Between stimulus and response there is a space. In that space is our power to choose our response. In our response lies our growth and our freedom."

Educators encounter hundreds of moments like these every day. We are challenged over and over and over by things that students do, or the unplanned fire drill, or the announcement of a mandatory meeting on Wednesday afternoon, or an upset parent showing up at our door five minutes before school starts, or the broken copy machine, or a request that we cover someone else's class during our prep because their sub didn't show, or any number of other things. Alone, these are minor inconveniences, but the sum total of these moments feels exhausting, depletes our resilience, and contributes to burnout. There is no moment more important for educators to attend to than this one between stimulus and response. If we slow down and examine these moments, if we cultivate new responses, we might just transform our schools into places where we all thrive.

Change is the only thing we can count on. It will rain when we wish it wouldn't, kids will say obnoxious things when we're exhausted, leaders will come and go. However, we have tremendous power in *how we interpret* what happens and, therefore, in how we respond to big and little incidents that we didn't anticipate, don't want, or don't like. The opportunity for resilience originates in how we make sense of the things that happen, because interpretation dictates actions. There are many ways to interpret a student's obnoxious comment at the end of a rainy Friday, and each of those interpretations will lead us to act in a different way. Each of those actions will have intended and unintended consequences, ripples of impact on ourselves, our class, and our relationship to that individual student. We can make a choice in these moments.

Let this sink in: We can pinpoint the exact moment when resilience can be cultivated. You can actually do something about how you experience every day; you don't have to be a victim of the turmoil and unpredictability of the world. Change is a given in life; how you respond is within your control.

I have no doubt that we all enter this field of work because we want to positively impact young people. The key to achieving our purpose lies in the moment between stimulus and response. We can meet our commitment to educational equity when we examine this moment and cultivate behaviors different than those in which we habitually engage. By cultivating resilience, we can fulfill the intentions that brought us into this profession. In addition, with this knowledge, we can do something about the exodus of teachers who quit because of burnout. We can offer our students more stability and continuity, as well as role models for managing the inevitable challenges of life.

Resilience: The What, Why, and How

Simply put, resilience is how we weather the storms in our lives and rebound after something difficult. The most important thing to know is that you can increase your resilience; it's a set of adaptive behaviors. In this book, I hope to guide you in a journey to discover the resilience that already exists within you, and to discover many ways to cultivate your resilience.

Resilience is in great part about our attitude and behaviors; that's what we'll focus on in this book. However, it's also important to acknowledge that our ability to be resilient is also connected to our circumstances, which we may have only limited ability to influence. Furthermore, researchers have found that there are neurobiological underpinnings of emotional resilience (Osório, Probert, Jones, Young, and Robbins, 2017). This research seeks to understand why there's such variation in the way people respond to adversity: Some people overcome unbelievable hardship, whereas others' lives are completely derailed by intense levels of stress. Various mechanisms in our bodies, and specifically our brains, work in concert to make us more or less stress resilient across our life span. Our genetic makeup may play a role: We may actually be born with a set amount of resilience. The emerging field of epigenetics is exploring this question of how stressors that our ancestors experienced might impact our level of resilience.

Although this research is interesting and someday may point to very useful implications, we'll focus on this fact: A substantial amount of our ability to be resilient is fostered in our daily habits. This is good news. Here's an expanded definition of resilience, which forms that basis for this book. Resilience is

- A *way of being* that allows us to bounce back quickly from adversity, and stronger than before, so that we can fulfill our purpose in life.
- An adaptive, dynamic process that includes an individual's interactions over time in a complex environment. Context plays a role; resilience is not simply a function of one individual's behavior. Who we are and where we are impact our ability to cultivate resilience.
- Cultivated through engaging in specific habits and by fostering specific dispositions.
- What enables us to thrive, not just survive.

Why We Must Focus on Resilience

Schools are stressful places. Regardless of whether you teach in an established, well-resourced private or suburban school or in an underfunded school in an underserved community, teaching is emotional work and is inherently stressful. In part, this is the nature of being in a helping profession and serving young people in complex organizations. Healthy stress can be okay; it can challenge us and help us develop. However, in many of our schools, healthy stress is frequently displaced by toxic stress. Toxic stress occurs when demands consistently outpace our ability to cope. Toxic stress first manifests as decreased productivity, and escalates to more serious symptoms such as anxiety, dissociation, frustration, and, eventually, burnout. Roughly half a million US teachers leave the profession each year—a turnover rate of over 20% (Alliance for Excellent Education, 2014).

School leaders—both site leaders and central office leaders—must focus on boosting the resilience of staff as a lever for school transformation. Teacher attrition among first-year teachers has increased about 40% in the past two decades (Ingersoll, Merrill, and Stuckey, 2014). A range of factors, such as morale, accountability expectations, and salaries, certainly contribute to the attrition problems, but stress and poor management of stressors are also rated as a top reason why teachers leave the profession (Carver-Thomas and Darling-Hammond, 2017).

Burnout is physical and emotional fatigue—and surely we can do something about that. This rate is much higher in urban areas, in secondary classrooms, and in hard-to-staff content areas such special education, math, science, and foreign languages (Carver-Thomas and Darling-Hammond, 2017). It is estimated that teacher turnover costs school districts upwards of $2.2 billion per year (Alliance for Excellent Education, 2014) and the cost of replacing a teacher in an urban district exceeds $20,000 per teacher (Carver-Thomas and Darling-Hammond, 2017). For site administrators, turnover rates may be comparable, particularly in urban areas, but the data is not systematically collected as it is for teacher attrition.

Lack of resilience, therefore, has a financial cost and contributes to staff instability, which in turn negatively impacts student learning and experience. High turnover rates at schools make it hard to accumulate professional capital, hinder the implementation of programs, contribute to low levels of trust among stakeholders, and make staff and student culture fragile. It would simply make good sense, from a financial perspective, to focus on increasing staff resilience.

The end goal, of course, is not just to retain warm adult bodies in classrooms but to meet the needs of our students. Kids need passionate, effective, committed educators. In order to retain such people, school leaders need to provide teachers with resources to meet the challenges they'll encounter in their work so that they can learn from those challenges, surmount them, and fulfill their purpose. And our purpose is to ensure that we are working in, teaching in, and leading organizations *where every single child thrives*—academically, socially, and emotionally. We must cultivate resilience so that all children feel that they belong to a resilient community, so that all children graduate and are eligible for the college or career of their choice, and so that all children have an expansive tool set to contribute to our society.

Over the last decade or two, in many schools across the United States and in other countries, there has been increased attention to the social and emotional learning (SEL) needs of children. Curricula and standards have been developed, resources have been allocated to SEL programs, and staff have been trained. This is a tremendous advancement in acknowledging children as complex, multifaceted beings, and it is our responsibility, as adults committed to guiding children in acquiring the massive set of skills they'll need in order to have productive lives, to attend to children's social and emotional skills.

It's now time to look at teachers and all the adults working in and with schools through this same lens—as people whose learning needs include the social and emotional realm of existence. In the majority of schools, what's needed isn't more professional development on deconstructing standards or academic discourse or using data to drive instruction. What's needed is time, space, and attention to managing stress and cultivating resilience. Whether you're a teacher reading this intent on boosting your capacities in these areas or you're a positional leader concerned about the flood of teachers leaving your schools, this book, and the companion workbook, offer a way to begin this learning. We must focus on cultivating our own resilience because it'll help us manage physical and emotional stressors, enjoy life more, and fulfill our purpose as educators.

The Three Conversations We Must Have

There are three conversations in which we must simultaneously engage to consider how cultivating resilience can transform our schools. These three, depicted in Figure I.1, are

1. **Individual resilience.** We can do a lot to boost our own individual resilience, improve our well-being, and prevent burnout. Ultimately, this is what we have the most influence and control over: What we think, how we engage with our emotions, and the actions we take every day to cultivate resilience. It is incumbent on each of us to attend to our resilience.

2. **Organizational conditions.** Focusing on individual well-being and action is not enough. If the conditions and context in which teachers work are suboptimal, it is not enough to tell teachers to sleep more, check their attitude, and be grateful. Conditions in many organizations don't foster well-being. These

Figure I.1   Three Conversations We Need to Have to Transform Schools

include the adult culture, the strength of leadership, and basic operational routines and systems. To address burnout and turnover, leaders in organizations must take responsibility for substantially improving the conditions in which people work. Until then, we'll still see teachers leaving in droves—even those with high levels of individual resilience.

3. **Systemic conditions.** We must address the macro, political, and economic context of our education system. Teachers must be paid more, and they must be treated as people who can think and who can learn. Teacher and administrator preparation must improve. We must address the racism, classism, and sexism that exists in our institutions, including in our schools. We'll need to talk about testing and publishing scores and performance pay. Until we dig down to the structural and systemic roots of the dysfunctions in our education system, we'll still see high levels of teacher turnover. This may open a Pandora's box, because we'll need to talk about capitalism and the legacy of colonialism and property taxes and who votes and for whom we vote. We'll need to talk about patriarchy and the dehumanization of some groups of people. We must have these conversations, however; our resilience and well-being are connected to them. And if our true goal is school transformation, we'll need to have them.

Here's my theory of action: If we boost our individual resilience, then we will have more energy to address organizational and systemic conditions—to elect officials who will fund public education, organize against policies that dehumanize educators, and push back on punitive assessment policies and scripted curriculum that turn teachers into robots and students into depositories to be filled. With more energy and more resilience, we can build and strengthen the kinds of communities in which we can thrive, where we can engage in professional development that allows us to reflect on our own biases, and where we can observe and learn from each other.

I wrote this book, and *The Onward Workbook,* to begin addressing the first of these conversations: To offer strategies to boost our individual resilience. But I know that this book will contribute to the second and third conversations, because in acquiring the individual strategies, resilient educators can then transform their entire classroom as a subset of society, their school as a larger subset, and even the larger school district and system. Resilient educators may also have the energy to engage in conversation about the macro context and to take action to change it.

In order to create the just and equitable society that I know so many of us yearn for, we need tremendous reserves of resilience. We must change the macro conditions in which we live and work, and to do that, we'll need all the physical and emotional resources we can muster. As Frederick Douglass said, "Power concedes nothing without demand," and we'll need a lot of energy to make our demands.

A Conceptual Framework for Resilience

This book is anchored in a four-part conceptual framework, based on the key components of resilience and how it is developed. The four parts are *who we are, where we are, what we do,* and *how we are.* Figure I.2 represents this framework.

Figure I.2   The Resilience Pie

 What you can most influence; the content of ONWARD.

Who We Are: What We Start With

A great deal of who we are is somewhat fixed in our genetics, personality, identities, and so on. However, we can cultivate resilience through deep understanding of these dimensions of who we are—which can also help us understand where we can influence or even change aspects of ourselves that we consider fixed. Who we are includes

- Genetics
- Personality traits
- Values and beliefs
- Aptitudes and strengths
- Sociopolitical identities (including gender, race, ethnicity, age, ability, sexual orientation, and socioeconomic status)
- Our psyche (including the physiological components of emotion)

Where We Are: Context Matters

Context matters, even though we may have limited ability to change or impact it. Context includes

- Circumstances and situation
- Sociopolitical, cultural, and economic context
- Stage of life and phase of career

Who we are intersects in a number of ways with where we are, in time and space. Our context includes personal life circumstances, such as whether we are parents caring for young children or are living far from home. In addition, there's professional context, which includes the nature of and challenges in the district, school, or organization in which we work. The context for our resilience is different if we work in a small, suburban, well-resourced school that's had the same effective principal for 14 years, as opposed to, for example, a large, urban, underfunded high school that sees new administrators every year. Context matters.

The sociopolitical, cultural, and economic context in which we all work affects our resilience. Context is the school's funding, education policy, and shifting demographics. The social, cultural, political, and economic systems in which we live also deeply influence our beliefs and ways of thinking. We must recognize and name these; otherwise they exist in the shadows, from which they wield too much control.

Finally, context is career stage. At different stages, we deal with different factors that affect our resilience: New teachers struggle with feeling effective, for example, whereas experienced teachers struggle more with challenges of motivation and commitment (Day, Sammons, and Gu, 2008). Context matters, and we'll keep it within our peripheral vision in order to clarify our sphere of influence and hone our awareness of our thoughts and feelings.

What We Do: The Habits of Resilient Educators

Habits and behaviors are the third component of this framework—and this is what *Onward* focuses on. This is where resilience can be intentionally, strategically, methodically, and systematically cultivated. I have identified 12 habits in my research that are the highest leverage in building resilience in educators. They form the basis for this book and its companion, *The Onward Workbook*. The Habits and Dispositions of Resilient Educators, following this introduction, summarizes the 12 habits of resilient educators.

How We Are: The Dispositions of Resilient Educators

Think about people you know who have faced adversity and continue to move forward in life, pursuing their dreams and passions. How would you describe these people's attitude and character? Optimistic? Tenacious? Humorous? These are *dispositions*. A disposition is

- A descriptor of someone's temperament, character, constitution, attitude, mindset, or mood
- A way of being
- Demonstrated through a behavior or a habit
- A reflection of a person's beliefs and thinking

Dispositions are not fixed; they can be learned. We can learn to be more optimistic. Habits pave the way for acquiring new dispositions. That's why this book emphasizes the *habits* that build resilience and less so the dispositions. Practicing the habits, ideally on a daily basis, helps us develop resilient dispositions.

Researchers from various fields have identified many dispositions of resilient people. I've sorted through those findings and grouped the dispositions into those that are most relevant to the context of education and most evident in resilient educators.

You can see the 12 dispositions in The Habits and Dispositions of Resilient Educators, which follows this introduction. How do you think your days in the classroom might be different if your mood and temperament reflected these dispositions? How might your experience be different if your principal demonstrated the majority of these dispositions? If your superintendent did? The dispositions of the resilient can be strengthened by engaging in the habits described in this book and through the exercises in *The Onward Workbook*.

What Informs This Book?

I've been interested in resilience since I was eight, when my mother married a Chilean exile who had been imprisoned and tortured in his country under General Pinochet. The community in which I was raised included South African freedom fighters, exiled South American teachers, and aging Jewish immigrants who had experienced anti-Semitism in more than one place in the world. I learned of more details about their experiences than may have been appropriate for a child. However, I also watched these people sing, celebrate, dance, and love in a way that embodied *joie de vivre*. They had a selfless and unique sense of humor that they used as a weapon against the suffering they had experienced, and I saw them build meaningful lives for themselves, form communities, and fiercely charge onward to change the world. They didn't see themselves as victims, and the struggles they'd endured didn't end their lives.

I've long been fascinated by how people have not only survived adversity but emerged as stronger, more compassionate and resolved people with energy and commitment to transform society. In addition, like all of us, I've had my share of personal hardships, which include being the child of divorced parents, being an immigrant, and losing my mother to cancer. These personal experiences of adversity also inform this book.

This is a book about cultivating resilience *in educators,* and although all of the habits described here are relevant to building resilience in anyone, and any reader could benefit from the contents of this book, I write specifically for those in the field of education. There are particular implications for resilience building when working in the field of service, spending your days with children, on a school-year calendar, and in complex and dynamic (and often dysfunctional) systems. This book addresses those particularities.

The 25 years I've spent working in education are the foundation for this book. These years include many in the classroom in the Oakland (California) Unified School District, as well as in other roles in this district. My experience over the last decade as an instructional and leadership coach, a trainer of coaches, and an author of two books about coaching and team development (*The Art of Coaching* and *The Art of Coaching Teams*) informs how I've chosen to write this book. Coaching is, at its essence, about helping people change habits and strengthen dispositions. You may not notice all my "coaching moves," but in this book and *The Onward Workbook,* I employ my skills as a coach to facilitate growth.

Personal and professional curiosity led me to research emotional resilience, psychology, systems thinking, and change management. I've scoured literature from the fields of positive psychology and neurobiology, listened to experts and

The Onward Workbook

The Onward Workbook contains some thirty activities for each chapter to help you explore the concepts in this book and put them into practice. My vision is that you'll engage in an activity every day, because resilience is cultivated one day at a time.

The workbook contains the questions I'd ask you if I was coaching you or facilitating your team's weekly meetings. It will guide you to practice, internalize, and apply these resilience-boosting habits. I hope that you'll read a chapter of this book and then reach for the workbook.

sages speak on mindfulness and Eastern philosophy, and devoured self-help books for insights and instructions on how to cultivate resilience. I've also read everything I could find specifically on resilience in teachers.

The strategies in this book and *The Onward Workbook* have been personally tried and tested in schools, offices, and training centers across the United States. I've spent a decade piloting them with individual teachers and leaders and in group settings with teams of educators, and now they're ready for you.

Who Is This Book For?

Whether you're in your 1st or 15th or 30th year of teaching, this book is for you. Life brings constant change and challenges, and I haven't yet met anyone who feels as though he or she couldn't use more tools to manage the ups and downs. New and novice teachers were front and foremost on my mind as I wrote this book, as well as educators who embark on new endeavors—be that starting a school, teaching a new grade level or subject, or moving into a new role. Moments of change bring increased stressors, calling us to intentionally boost our resilience.

If you picked up this book because you are concerned about the well-being and attrition of teachers from your school or district, I'm thrilled. I hope that this book will end up in the hands of those who can make decisions and who coach, supervise, and lead others, and I hope you'll be convinced to cultivate the resilience of your staff. If you are reading this book intent on boosting the resilience of your coachees, mentees, or staff, you will gain a lot of skills and knowledge to do so. However, also know that you'll need to explore this topic and experience the strategies personally in order to help others. To lead transformational efforts, begin by attending to your own transformation.

This book, along with the accompanying workbook, is designed as a curriculum for professional development for a school staff or a central office team, for coaches and site administrators—essentially, for any group that operates in or with our education system. I envision groups gathering for weekly or monthly professional development (PD) sessions, taking up the habit of the month and engaging in the workbook activities together. I hope that this book might help leaders reenvision PD—how, where, when, and why we do it.

Specifically for Leaders

I'm committed to helping you build your resilience and the resilience of others. Toward that end, you'll notice sections of this book titled "Implications for Leaders," which provide strategies and tips for implementing these ideas. My advice and suggestions for you are informed by my years of coaching leaders and my understanding of your role and context.

How Is This Book Organized?

Here's a brief overview of the structure of chapters.

Contents

Each chapter focuses on a habit and how it builds resilience. It contains the following sections:

- A "dive into an emotion," which explores a specific emotion, such as anger or shame, and how it is connected to that chapter's habit.
- "Dispositions," which discusses 1 of the 12 dispositions and how it connects to the habit of the month.

Some chapters have a section called "Acknowledging Context," in which our social, political, historic, cultural context is recognized, and the connections are drawn between the context and our work in schools.

The content of this entire book is about making big and little changes in your behaviors, habits, and routines. Appendix B, How to Make Lasting Change, offers a primer for how to effectively and even painlessly build and maintain new habits.

You might want to read that before you continue, or explore it later. It's treated as an appendix so that you can easily find it and frequently reference it.

Sequence

I've sequenced the habits of resilience to build on each other and map onto the rhythms of the school year. *Onward* could be read all at once, but the strategies in *The Onward Workbook* will be internalized best if they are digested, discussed, and practiced over the course of a year.

Each habit correlates to the month that best aligns to that particular theme. Ideally you could begin your study of this book in June, when you can focus on the habit of self-knowledge. In November, when most educators are exhausted from the launch of the school year, *Onward* offers a chapter on self-care, and then in May, a chapter on celebration—obviously an appropriate topic for the end of the school year. A Calendar of Learning, a table that follows this introduction, connects each habit to a month.

The first three chapters of this book should be read in order. They offer foundational approaches for building resilience. After that, if you want to jump to Chapter 9 because that's the one you feel would help you the most, or because it maps onto the current month, then go ahead! Appendix A, The Habits and Dispositions of Resilient Educators: A Self-Assessment, can help you make decisions about the order in which you might read this book.

An Invitation to a Journey

Resilience is not a magical elixir that will eliminate *all* of the physical, emotional, or cognitive demands of teaching, but resilience can substantially and dramatically increase our ability to manage the daily stressors and rebound from inevitable setbacks. Resilience allows us to listen to students and their families and take in painful information, because resilience ensures that we can keep our hearts open to what we see and hear. Resilience makes us confident in our ability to manage our own, and others', intense emotions. Resilience also enables us to have difficult conversations—and if we aren't having difficult conversations in our efforts to transform schools, we're probably not making meaningful progress. Resilience will bring communities and educators out of our silos and into healthy camaraderie. As we strengthen our resilience, we'll have more energy to direct toward participating in transformational school change.

With this book, I'm inviting you to join a movement toward self-knowledge, understanding, and acceptance; toward embracing emotions and creating space for them in our public, professional spaces; and toward authentic community among adults, between adults and children, and for youth, so that we may create spaces where young people can acquire the skills to thrive. I hope you will be a part of this movement. You can join others on the website, www.onwardthebook.com. The Resilience Manifesto, which follows this introduction, offers a platform for this movement.

And now, let's start our journey. Cultivating resilience is easier than you might think. Within you, you already have a spring to drink from and rest in—your own internal *cenote.* You are already resilient. In this book, and in *The Onward Workbook,* I hope to guide you back to this pool of strength and resources, help you find ways to fill it, and offer new ideas for how you might rest in it more often. And so onward, ever onward, because really, what other option do we have?

For online resources please visit www.onwardthebook.com.

The Habits and Dispositions of Emotionally Resilient Educators

Chapter Month	HABIT *Your behaviors*	DISPOSITION *Your attitude, character, or way of being*
1 June	**Know Yourself**	**Purposefulness**
	When you know yourself well—when you understand your emotions, social identities, core values, and personality—you gain clarity on your purpose in life and in work. Being anchored in purpose makes you able to deal with setbacks and challenges.	
2 July	**Understand Emotions**	**Acceptance**
	Understanding emotions—accepting them and having strategies to respond to them—is essential to cultivate resilience. With an understanding of emotions, you can accept their existence, recognize where you can influence a situation, and let go of what is outside your control.	
3 August	**Tell Empowering Stories**	**Optimism**
	How you interpret and make sense of events is a juncture point where emotional resilience increases or depletes. You make the choice about what story to tell. When you tell empowering stories, your optimism may expand, and optimism is a key trait of resilient people.	
4 September	**Build Community**	**Empathy**
	We are social beings, and we need each other to thrive. A strong, healthy community can bolster us through challenging moments and bring joy to our lives. When we build community, we can build empathy for each other; and building empathy for each other helps us build community.	
5 October	**Be Here Now**	**Humor**
	Learning to be in the present moment, without judging it, boosts our resilience. It can allow us to feel accepting and clearheaded about our options for response. When we're fully present, we're more likely to find appropriate levity in moments of challenge and to relieve stress by finding humor in a situation.	
6 November	**Take Care of Yourself**	**Positive Self-Perception**
	Physical self-care and well-being are foundational for many other habits. When your body is cared for, you're better able to deal with emotions. Resilient people have a healthy self-perception, are committed to taking care of themselves, and accept themselves more or less as they are.	

Chapter Month	HABIT *Your behaviors*	DISPOSITION *Your attitude, character, or way of being*
7 December	**Focus on the Bright Spots**	**Empowerment**
	We can hone our attention to focus on our strengths, assets, and skills. This helps us generally feel better and enables us to respond to challenges more effectively. Focusing on strengths also boosts our levels of self-efficacy, and we feel more empowered to influence our surroundings.	
8 January	**Cultivate Compassion**	**Perspective**
	Compassion for ourselves, as well as for others, helps us deal with the interpersonal challenges we face on a daily basis. Perspective allows us to recognize the complexity of a situation. Perspective allows us to empathize with others, see the long view, extricate ourselves from the drama of a moment, and identify a wider range of responses to an event.	
9 February	**Be a Learner**	**Curiosity**
	If we see challenges as opportunities for learning, if we engage our curiosity whenever we're presented with an obstacle, we're more likely to find solutions. This habit and disposition help us not just survive adversity but thrive in the aftermath.	
10 March	**Play and Create**	**Courage**
	Creativity and play unlock inner resources for dealing with stress, solving problems, and enjoying life. When we are creative, we are resourceful, and we problem-solve in new and original ways, which fuels our courage. Our thinking expands, and our connection with ourselves and others deepens.	
11 April	**Ride the Waves of Change**	**Perseverance**
	Change is one thing we can count on, and when we encounter it, we can harness our physical, emotional, mental, and spiritual energies, and direct them where they will make the biggest difference. Perseverance, patience, and courage help us manage change.	
12 May	**Celebrate and Appreciate**	**Trust**
	Individual and collective celebrations, as well as the practice of gratitude, is the capstone to the habits in this book. Even during hard moments, if we can shift into a stance of appreciation, we'll build our resilience. Appreciation cultivates our trust in ourselves, in a process, and perhaps in something greater, which helps us respond to the inevitable challenges of life.	

A Calendar of Learning

Chapter	Habit	Month
1	Know Yourself	**June:** This habit is foundational for all the others. In June you can reflect on last year, transition into summer, and contemplate next year while gaining deeper self-understanding.
2	Understand Emotions	**July:** Summer is an ideal time to reflect on your emotions because hopefully you can sleep a little more, enjoy warm evenings, and find a few minutes for contemplation.
3	Tell Empowering Stories	**August:** Your thoughts are the keys to unlocking reserves of resilience. Start the year with this key habit.
4	Build Community	**September:** During the month when we're surrounded by new people, building strong relationships must be our primary goal. The community we build is foundational for our resilience.
5	Be Here Now	**October:** As we move into the fall, our energy wanes, and we're triggered more easily. Learning to be in the present moment enables us to cultivate awareness of our emotions and make choices that foster our resilience.
6	Take Care of Yourself	**November:** Self-care is the root of resilience when you're dragging yourself toward winter break and your emotions are raw.
7	Focus on the Bright Spots	**December:** When the days are short and you haven't recovered from the exhaustion of late fall, look for the light.
8	Cultivate Compassion	**January:** Start the new year by strengthening your compassion for yourself and others, and unlock another resource for resilience.
9	Be a Learner	**February:** Around midyear, you may have the bandwidth to reflect on how you learn and to return to your beginner's mind, because learning is a path to growth and resilience.

Chapter	Habit	Month
10	Play and Create	**March:** Spring break brings an opportunity to explore play and creativity so that you can integrate these activities into daily life. Resilience arises from creation.
11	Ride the Waves of Change	**April:** Although change is constant, spring brings especially high levels of change to schools. Learn to ride those waves of change with focus, patience, persistence, and courage.
12	Celebrate and Appreciate	**May:** Endings are times for celebration and appreciation, which lay the foundation for resilience in the days ahead.

The Resilience Manifesto

A manifesto is a public declaration of principles and intentions. May these principles guide our individual and collective commitment to resilience.

1. A wellspring of resilience is inside us. We are stronger than we think.
2. We were born with individual and collective resilience. Our quest is to find our way to these internal springs and nurture them.
3. We cultivate resilience so that we can thrive, not simply to prevent burnout or survive.
4. Resilience is cultivated through daily habits and thoughts that strengthen dispositions.
5. It is a human right to explore and express emotions.
6. To help children build their emotional intelligence and resilience, we must simultaneously tend to our own emotional intelligence and resilience.
7. Powerful and effective educators talk about emotions at work.
8. How we interpret events and tell our story matters most. In our interpretation, we exercise the freedom to choose our attitude.
9. We are all connected and responsible for each other: Caring for the other is caring for the self.
10. We cultivate our resilience and become stronger so that we can help others become stronger; we cultivate our resilience so that we have energy to heal and transform the world.

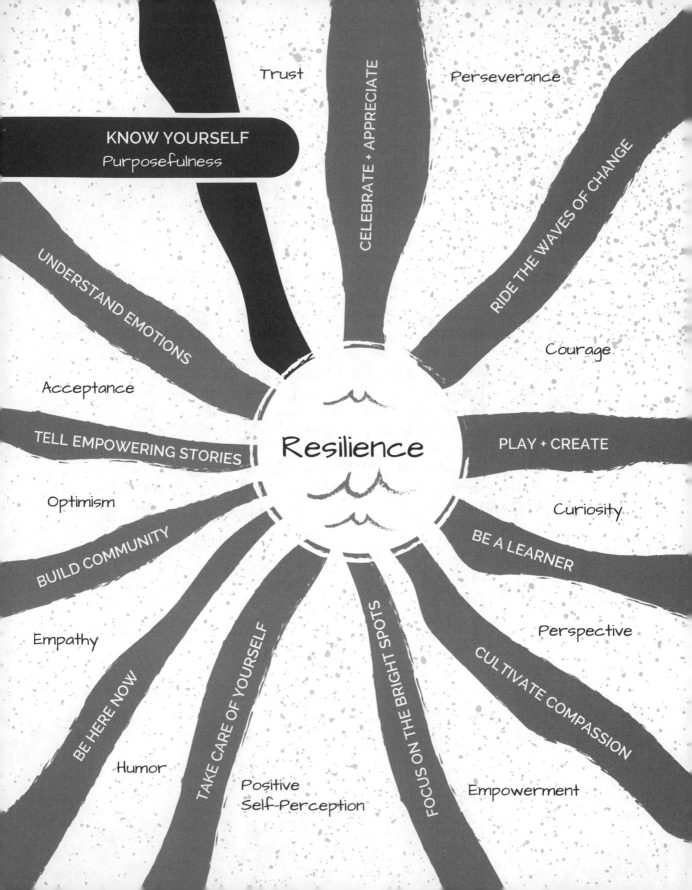

CHAPTER 1

Know Yourself

When you know yourself well—when you understand your emotions, social identities, core values, and personality—you gain clarity on your purpose in life and in work. Being anchored in purpose makes you able to deal with setbacks and challenges.

June: This habit is foundational for all the others. In June you can reflect on last year, transition into summer, and contemplate next year while gaining deeper self-understanding.

❧❧❧

It was late spring during my first year of teaching, and I stood sobbing in front of my principal, and not just regular sobbing but that uncontrollable kind during which strange sounds you didn't know your body was capable of making burst out of you. I was furious.

There'd been a breakdown in communication; if I gave you all the details, you'd probably think, *Elena, that's really not a big deal.* But when I learned about the communication glitch, I felt wronged. I felt disrespected. I felt unappreciated. I sobbed and argued and then bolted from the room, but I wasn't so far down my emotional vortex that I didn't register the look of surprise on her face. My principal was a veteran educator who wore a skirt, nylons, and heels every day and whom I never once called by her first name. She was always steady, focused, and calm. But surely, in her decades as a principal, Mrs. Cooke had witnessed other worn-out young teachers unravel into hysterics? Yet as I replayed her surprised expression, I couldn't help but wonder whether perhaps I really *had* been the first one.

Although it's been decades since this incident, I remember it vividly. I'd felt excruciating embarrassment and then avoided my principal at all costs during the last few weeks before summer. Although part of me wanted to lock the memory away, once I had a few weeks of rest and perspective available to me, my meltdown in front of Mrs. Cooke pushed me to greater self-understanding.

That summer, as I reflected on the previous school year, I recognized why I was so upset. I felt as though values I held around respect and appreciation had been violated. I'd also received no feedback during the year. I wanted Mrs. Cooke's approval, or at least an indicator that I was on the right track as a teacher. I didn't know how schools worked or how communication between staff operated. Generational and cultural differences were also among the many factors that contributed to how I experienced the communication glitch and how I responded. I can see all of this now, in retrospect, but at the moment of the incident, I wasn't aware of these elements. My gaps in self-awareness set my distress in motion. By contrast, if I'd had more self-awareness in Mrs. Cooke's office that day, I would've been better positioned to take a deep breath and show up differently. Self-knowledge helps us to be more confident about our actions and clear on our decisions. It's what enables us to show up in the way we want to show up.

Fast-forward to a few years later, to a similar miscommunication with a different principal. Following a slight (and private) meltdown, I reflected, applied the self-knowledge I'd amassed, and initiated a conversation. As a result of the learning and growth I'd made in my self-knowledge, our relationship became stronger, I felt both heard and respected, and I was pleased with how I handled the situation.

Self-Knowledge Is True Power

A teacher who really knows herself is keenly aware of her values and beliefs, and her behaviors consistently reflect those; she understands how aspects of her personality affect how she works and lives. She uses that knowledge to make decisions about her life, and she accepts her personality traits; she has a sharp sense of her sociopolitical self and can see the role that dominant culture plays in her experiences; she knows what she's good at and what she likes doing. She understands her own emotions and has tools to engage with them.

With this kind of deep self-knowledge, a teacher can deftly navigate the thousands of challenges that she faces every day, playing to her strengths and innate resources and drawing on her assets to help her manage rough moments. When an upset happens, she's unlikely to "take it personally," because she knows who she is, and she can distinguish between the external event and herself. In other words, she's resilient.

Your *self:* your essential being that distinguishes you from others; includes your values, personality, character, aptitudes, interests, identity, mind, and psyche

Resilience is cultivated through hundreds of little choices every day. In order to make the best choice, you need to know yourself. With self-knowledge, you can anticipate moments that might trigger you. Self-knowledge enables you to build stronger relationships with others. With knowledge of your unique talents, aptitudes, and interests, you play to your strengths and wisely direct your energy. When you're clear on your values, you align your skills, time, and energy to your purpose—and *purposefulness* is a key trait of the resilient.

In this chapter, we'll explore how self-awareness is the foundation for the decisions crucial to boosting your resilience. We'll explore the following elements of self: Values, personality type, sociopolitical identities, and strengths and aptitudes. Because the psyche, our emotional self, is at the core of emotional resilience, Chapter 2 is devoted entirely to it. Figure 1.1, Elements of Self, reflects the aspects of ourselves that we'll explore in this chapter and in Chapter 2.

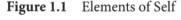

Figure 1.1   Elements of Self

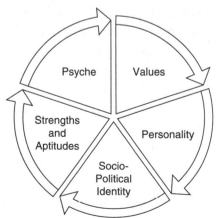

Values: What We Believe

If you followed Leo around for a day, you'd observe a principal consistently acting on his values. His three core values are family, kindness, and equity, and whether he's interacting with a student, an office staff member, his boss, or a teacher, you'll see evidence of these. When he makes decisions about allocating resources, he does so from a lens of equity. He listens to students with patience and respect, and holds them to high expectations, "Because I know what they're capable of," he says. When he gives hard feedback, he's kind. I've coached Leo for several years. I've heard his innermost thoughts and am inspired to know an educator like Leo who lives his values so consistently. His staff members also appreciate this, as is evidenced by their annual feedback raving about his leadership, and by the exceptionally high retention of teachers at his school. Finally, Leo cites the alignment between his values and his behaviors as a source of inner strength: "I know who I am," he says, "and that helps me manage the challenges of this job. As long as I honor who I am, I'm good." In spite of unrelenting pressures and stressors, Leo really is doing well most of the time and research on resilient school leaders confirms that thriving leaders are grounded in their values (Patterson and Kelleher, 2005).

A value is a tightly held belief from which we act. Our *core values* are often enduring beliefs that can be traced back to our families of origin or religious traditions. Examples of values include compassion, responsibility, hard work, justice, and community. Sometimes we use the terms *values* and *beliefs* interchangeably; they are aspects of the same idea. Core values can change over time. You may have had different values as a young adult. Values are essentially beliefs, and beliefs are strongly held opinions. It's useful to remember that beliefs can change—our own beliefs, as well as those of others. For some, values may remain the same for many years, and that's okay too.

What are your core values? If you aren't aware of them, there's an activity in the workbook to help you identify them. You might also just consider what comes first to mind in response to these questions: What do you value most? Which behaviors and values in others do you most appreciate?

Our values orient us, drive us, and anchor us. We experience integrity when we act in alignment with them. When our actions are not aligned with our values, it doesn't feel good. We might say to ourselves, *This isn't me,* which can indicate that our actions don't reflect a core value. When an inner voice says something like that, listen closely. Interestingly, psycho-neuroimmunologists find that our immune systems are strengthened or depleted by the degree of integrity with which we live our lives. When we act in ways that are out of alignment with our values, we physically don't feel good. This is why, when you are asked to do something you don't believe in, you might say, "It makes me feel sick to my stomach to have to do this," because your body literally feels unwell.

Can you recall a time recently when you felt that you acted in alignment with your values? Or another time when you did something that conflicted with a value? What might it feel like to work with the same degree of conviction that a superhero has about her values? Your values can be a source of strength when you're aware of them. I know you have them, even if you're not crystal clear right now on what they are. We can also forget what our values are and find ourselves operating on autopilot, sometimes not in alignment with our values. This is why we need time to reflect on who we are and what we value, and also to talk with others about our values. Now might be a good time to take a break from reading and engage in some of the activities in the workbook!

Implications for Leaders

- A great way to start the year is to have staff identify their core values and share those with each other. (See activities in the workbook for how to do this.)
- When a teacher is distraught or confused, ask about his or her core values, or if you know what they are, remind him or her of those.
- Organizations thrive when they have clear, shared values and where practices align to those values. Schools need articulated, lived values.
- People want to feel connected to values, and connected to each other through values. When shared values aren't strong, people resort to their own individual values, which weakens the school's overall mission. Invite your team to do an integrity scan. Review your organization's mission or vision statements. Do they include clearly stated values that are instructive and that compel people to take action?

Personality: The Way We Are

Whereas our values develop and change throughout our lives, our personalities don't change much. Respond to these statements with a quick true or false:

- Finding out, a week before school starts, that our schedule has changed really upsets me and throws me for a loop.

- In order for me to get on board with a new initiative, don't start by telling me about the details. I need to first understand the big picture.
- If you want me to implement a new program, show me the data proving that it works. I want to know where it's been tried and tested with kids like ours.
- Deadlines help me stay focused and motivated. When I have a clear due date, I block out time on my calendar and then stick to it.
- If I start teaching a unit and then I hear about a different approach that sounds more effective, it makes sense to stop and change course. Why would you continue doing something one way if there's a better way?

Your responses to these statements have to do with your personality—your unique patterned body of habits, traits, attitudes, thoughts, and preferences. Psychologists agree that for most of us, our personalities become fixed as young children and rarely change as we get older (unless we experience severe trauma). A great deal of the way we work, live, socialize, and perhaps even feel has to do with our personality—yet many of us don't have this awareness and can't draw connections between our personalities and our preferences for how to spend a sunny Sunday or how we like to get information from our principal.

There are different approaches within the field of psychology to explain personality types. I find the easiest to understand and apply is the Myers-Briggs Type Indicator (MBTI), which is based on Jungian psychology and is used widely in the public and private sectors (Briggs Myers and Briggs, 1995). This model presents four domains of personality, each with two tendencies. There's a more extensive overview of these domains in the workbook, but here's a quick overview of the Myers-Briggs personality types:

Domain	Tendencies
1. Energy	Extroversion (E) or Introversion (I)
2. Perception of Information	Sensing (S) or Intuitive (N)
3. Decision Making	Thinking (T) or Feeling (F)
4. External Structure	Judging (J) or Perceiving (P)

In each personality tendency, we all fall along a continuum. For example, each of us is more or less introverted or extroverted, and some people fall so close to the center that they think of themselves as "ambiverts." If you take a Myers-Briggs personality test (the best free one is www.16personalities.com), you'll be given a combination of four letters; for example, I'm an INFJ. The different combinations of these letters represent different personality types, so although I am an introvert, in combination with the Intuitive and Feeling aspect of my personality, I sometimes seem extroverted. There's a great deal of nuance and complexity to this framework, and it's meant to provide insight and to provoke questions about yourself. It's not a hard science or a determinant of what you can do—which some personality types have a hard time with!

One of the most useful aspects of personality to understand is your tendency toward introversion or extroversion, which is about how you get energy. Introverts replenish their energy reserves from time spent alone or in small groups; by contrast, introverts are drained by being in large groups, constantly switching partners in a PD session, and lots of new social interactions. Extroverts, however, are energized by large groups and numerous social interactions. Whereas introverts prefer quiet time to process information, working independently, and collaborating with the same partner over a period of time, extroverts prefer lots of time for verbal processing and like to frequently mix up the configuration of groups and pairs. When you think about yourself in the context of school, what role do you suspect your tendency toward introversion or extroversion plays?

Self-knowledge and understanding contribute to your emotional intelligence, which we'll explore in Chapter 2. Understanding personality traits has made me more accepting of myself—of my strong introverted tendency—as well as more effective and kinder as a coach. For example, when I supported a ninth-grade team in selecting a new advisory curriculum, I used my knowledge of the teachers' personality types to present the different options. Some teachers wanted data on where different programs had been used and what impact they'd had. Other teachers wanted to hear anecdotes about how the programs had been implemented. As they browsed through the curriculum and said things like, "I have a feeling that this one would be best for our kids" or "There's great data on how this impacted a population similar to ours," I saw that they took in the information according to their tendencies of Thinking or Intuiting. Rather than getting annoyed with the people who wanted data (given that that's not my tendency), I could just accept them and meet their needs. This awareness also helped me understand why I could be triggered by leaders who focused a great deal on data and seemed to be uninterested in the stories behind the data. Understanding your own personality and that of others helps cultivate empathy and self-compassion—and anything we can do that cultivates those states is a priority.

If we understand our personality tendencies, we can also identify spots where we can grow and learn. For example, if you're a Perceiving type, then external structure may not feel comfortable or make sense. You may think, *I don't need to write a lesson plan using this format—it's all in my head; I know what I'm teaching.* And even though this might work for you, there are some shortcomings to teaching without a lesson plan. Maybe with more understanding of how you like to organize things, you could find your way into lesson planning that doesn't feel incongruous with who you are. Judging types, by contrast, might get too attached to their lesson plans and thus miss "teachable moments" when they arise. Some of the conflict we experience has to do with this mismatch between what we're asked to do and who we feel we are.

Implications for Leaders

- Know your own personality type and how it impacts how you coach, manage, and lead. We tend to engage with others in the way that we feel most comfortable and familiar—in other words, in the way that works for our personality. That doesn't always work for others. You may find you have the most conflict with people whose personalities are the most opposite to your own.

- Ask staff to take a MBTI personality test and give them a chance to share those results with each other and with you. Keep a list of your people and their types somewhere accessible and, when you're struggling with a particular person, look for connections between his type and how you're engaging him.

- Design meetings and PD sessions that account for the tendencies on your team toward introversion and extroversion. Offer activities that meet the needs of both introverts and extroverts. What kinds of back-to-school staff bonding experiences can you offer that allow introverts to feel comfortable?

- With knowledge of how your staff members perceive information and make decisions, be strategic and intentional when presenting new information or trying to get them on board with something new.

Sociopolitical Identity: Social Affiliation and Group Belonging

What aspect of your sociopolitical identity might have the biggest impact on your interactions with your students: Your age? Your cultural background? Your gender?

This aspect of your self plays a key role in how you experience your work as a teacher or leader, but we don't think or talk about it much.

What Is Sociopolitical Identity?

Let's begin by getting clear on the definition of the term *sociopolitical identity*. Your sociopolitical identity refers to the social groups to which you belong—which may align to your race or ethnicity, gender, class background, and sexual orientation—and the complex way that these intersect and influence the amount of power you have in different social spaces. These elements of your identity may be inseparable from other aspects of self (such as beliefs and values, personality, and psyche) because those are so deeply influenced by your sociopolitical identity, which has been a part of you since birth or childhood. For example, it's likely that your values were shaped by your cultural heritage and that your personality may have been influenced by social constructions of gender. It's hard to really know who you are without an understanding of the social, political, and cultural construction of self.

These elements of who you are play a role in how you relate to students and how you experience stress. You may find yourself feeling more or less stressed in one environment or another because of your sociopolitical identity. Your understanding of yourself can help you gain insight into where you may need to build your resilience. For example, if you work in a school in which there are few others of your cultural group, you may want to seek out community outside of school where you feel a greater sense of belonging.

Furthermore, awareness of your sociopolitical identity can help you see how your values and beliefs are *cultural constructs*. If we hold *our* way as better, we'll struggle to work effectively in environments with people from other cultures. It doesn't mean that our values are wrong or that there's anything bad about them; it just means that we need to know that they aren't universally shared, and we don't have a right to ask that they be. This kind of self-knowledge can also help you uncover potential bias, and this awareness is a strength. We'll explore this deeper in Chapter 4—because if we are to build truly strong, healthy, and resilient communities, we'll need heightened self-awareness about sociopolitical identity.

Sociopolitical Self-Awareness Helps Improve Relationships with Students

Ling was a young woman whom I coached during her first two years teaching. She struggled to build relationships with her high school students, particularly with the boys. She had unattainably high expectations for ninth graders, was often angry with students for their behavior, and was set off by little things. Halfway through

Defining Race and Ethnicity

There is a great deal of confusion about these terms, so let's define them:

- **Race:** Groups of people who have differences and similarities in biological traits deemed by society to be socially significant; people are treated differently because of these traits.
- **Ethnicity:** Shared cultural practices, perspectives, and distinctions that set one group of people apart from another; a shared cultural heritage. The most common characteristics distinguishing various ethnic groups are ancestry, a sense of history, language, religion, and forms of dress. Ethnic differences are learned, not inherited.

her first year, she considered quitting. "I can't stand how they disrespect me," she said when she told me that she was contemplating resigning.

In our conversations, as we untangled the knots of her experience, a number of elements relating to sociopolitical identity surfaced: Ling was a Chinese immigrant, and during her childhood her family had been destitute. Her family communicated strong beliefs around authority and respect, relationships between males and females, and how young people should treat their elders. Ling felt that because she knew what her students were going through, she was justified in "not coddling them." As she uncovered this connection between her upbringing and her practice, she recognized that she had tremendous empathy for her students—many whom were also immigrants from low-income families, trying to navigate a different culture.

Ling recognized that she was often unconsciously imposing her own cultural values on her students and viewing them through her unique experiences. This prevented her from getting to know her students and building strong relationships with them. As Ling cultivated awareness of how her sociopolitical identities showed up in the classroom, she made better real-time decisions. When a boy shouted out of turn, she would say to herself: *That's a trigger for me because in my culture, in my house, boys would never think of doing that.* This awareness allowed her to respond by saying, "I'll need you to raise your hand if you want to contribute to the discussion," and the incident would pass without escalation—neither with her students nor internally. It was just a quick redirect, and Ling didn't feel the slightest bit disrespected.

For Ling, it was critical that she recognize the role her own sociopolitical identity played in her experience in the classroom. It wasn't that she needed to be any different or that her ethnicity and experiences were an obstacle. In fact, there were many times when her background facilitated understanding and connection with her students. But when Ling could distinguish, in a particular interaction, how her identity affected her experience, she made clearer choices about how to respond.

Can you think of a time when you might have been triggered by a student, colleague, or supervisor in some way that connected to your sociopolitical identity? Perhaps you felt as though someone didn't listen to you because of your age or gender. Perhaps you felt that a student didn't respect you because of your ethnicity.

As we cultivate self-awareness of our sociopolitical identity, we better understand why we are triggered, as well as our strengths and assets. This can help us not take things personally and recognize that some of the ways that we think about things are not a fact of life, but rather patterns of thought that can be changed. With an awareness of sociopolitical identity, we can also see how who we are can be leveraged for building relationships with others.

Like awareness of other elements of self, awareness of who you are sociopolitically is ultimately empowering. Identity can be a source of strength, an anchor, a way to connect with others. It can also help you understand how to further boost your resilience: How to strengthen trust with others, how to uncover and understand your unconscious bias, and how to form deeper, more nourishing connections with students, colleagues, and supervisors.

Implications for Leaders

- It's critical that you have self-knowledge of your sociopolitical identity, because your identity is core to how you lead. Ideally, you might engage in this learning and reflection with the support of a skilled leadership coach, and also perhaps in the company of colleagues. Appendix F, Resources for Further Learning, might also be helpful.
- Likewise, it is of critical importance that your staff have an opportunity to understand who they are sociopolitically and to recognize the implications of that identity at work. Whether your staff reflect the demographics of your students or not, this awareness of self is foundational to being culturally competent. Thoughtfully designed and skillfully executed PD sessions that explore identity can have a powerful impact on staff resilience and on student success.

- Reflections and conversations around these aspects of self are likely to raise uncomfortable feelings. As a leader, you are responsible for creating the conditions in which people can productively engage in these reflections. As you may know or suspect, this is hard work to lead, and you may wonder whether you are ready or able to do it. Do some learning and preparation, consult and collaborate with others, and open the conversation. Be aware of your fear, and get curious about where it's coming from, but don't let your fear hold you back from initiating important conversations.

Aptitudes and Skills: Doing What We Love and Are Good At

What did you love doing as a child? What have people always told you you're really good at? What have you learned that came easily or even naturally? Your responses to these questions provide insight into your unique aptitudes—your innate and acquired capacities, skills, and abilities. There are also activities in the workbook to help you figure out these answers.

Start with Strengths

Knowing what we can do, as well as being really clear about what we love to do, is another component of self-knowledge. Many of us are well aware of our shortcomings and areas for growth, and we know what we don't like doing. However, we tend to spend less time cultivating an understanding and appreciation of our skills and capacities, as well as our interests and passions. If we were aware of our skills, we'd be positioned to make better decisions. Start this cultivation by identifying your strengths. Then consider your current role: How often do you have the opportunity to tap into your strengths? What impact does that have on your energy and resiliency in your work? What if you held a role in which, at least 50% of the time, you were using *and* building on your strengths, rather than focusing on growing in your weaker areas or managing your deficits?

Working from a strengths-based approach doesn't mean that you ignore areas for growth. Part of what happens when you work from strengths is that you have more energy to get through the rough waters of new challenges. As a novice teacher, I was keenly aware of everything I didn't know. In fact, a few months into my first year, I sat down and listed all of those things. There were so many skills that I hadn't realized I'd need before I stepped into the classroom, so much knowledge I didn't have. The list was long, and when I finished, I felt daunted by it. *I should just quit right now,* the dramatic, tired part of me said.

Then a wiser part of myself suggested making a list of what I knew and could do. That list, though not as long, helped me see that I could read a picture book, I could create a basic but engaging science lesson, I knew what to do when a child was crying, I knew how to calm a distressed parent, and I could speak Spanish. I knew I needed to make curriculum culturally relevant, and I knew, with absolute conviction, that I loved my students. When I got to that point on the list (which I still have because I can't throw anything out), I dropped the pen and lay back in relief. My love for my students meant that I must learn the things I didn't know (and on that list was "teach reading"), but I also knew that love was crucial. I intuited that my love for my students would motivate my learning.

The act of writing this list was just the start of the hunt for my growing knowledge and skills. When there was an unscheduled fire drill, I said to myself, *Ah, in September's drill, I did not know what to do, and it was chaos. Now, I more or less know.* I knew more than I thought I knew.

As you might recognize, I was cultivating a growth mindset (see Chapter 9 for a description of the growth mindset). I knew I was *capable* of learning, that *I had* learned, and that my challenges were problems of learning. This awareness was liberating. I wasn't a bad teacher, as I sometimes told myself. I could see my skill set growing.

We must know our strengths to have the emotional fortitude to confront the long list of things we need to learn. There is not a single new teacher who doesn't bring some skills and knowledge into his or her classroom on day one, nor is there a single "resistant" veteran teacher who doesn't have strengths. We can both build resilience and enjoy moments of respite in the midst of our crazy days when we're able to stop and recognize that we have good stuff to build on and that there's *a lot* we already know how to do.

What are you good at? Take a moment to think about that question.

Find a Place Where You Might Thrive

Identifying our aptitudes boosts our resilience and provides more options for where we work and what we do. As you increase your awareness of your skills, strengths, passions, values, personality, and sociopolitical identity, you might find that although you're struggling and burning out in your current role, there could be a different role in which you can directly or indirectly better serve children.

Mitch was an eighth-grade math teacher who struggled to form strong relationships with students and manage his classroom. He had tremendous aptitude for understanding numbers and wanted to work in education. After two years of tumultuous teaching, he moved into a central office role in the data analysis department, where his skills were needed and appreciated.

Rachelle, who taught fifth grade, was overwhelmed by the energy and rambunctiousness of her students. Her desire for a quiet classroom was at odds with what students needed in order to learn best. She thrived when working one-on-one and with small groups, and she was especially skilled with students who struggled academically. She had an uncanny knack for identifying creative tricks to help kids learn. When she became a special education teacher, Rachelle found her place.

Many new teachers, as well as seasoned educators, see limited options for roles in education. Sometimes this is because we don't know much about other roles. Other times it's because we aren't clear enough about what we *are* good at and what we love doing. With clear understanding of your aptitudes, you'll be more likely to recognize a role that's a better fit or to validate that the role you're in *is* the right role for you after all.

Implications for Leaders

- As your staff clarify their aptitudes, make sure to hear what they have learned about themselves. You may gain insight into why they thrive or struggle in certain areas that could affect staffing decisions. Figuring out how to guide people into the *right* roles is a worthy leadership puzzle.
- Cultivate empathy among your staff by creating space for them to share their values and personality types. Your staff will also appreciate learning about you.

Acknowledging Context: Dominant Culture

Mike was a coach who described himself as "a big softie." When we first met, he said, "I get so emotional sometimes when a teacher is distressed. I'm trying to toughen up." Mike's sense of self was influenced by his internalization of the values that dominant culture holds around men and emotions. It can be hard to know who you are outside the values of dominant culture.

Dominant culture is the most powerful, widespread, or influential culture within a social group, organization, or society that may have multiple cultures present. Culture is the way we do things—our values, customs, and communication styles. In schools, culture finds its way into how we collaborate with each other, into power dynamics between administrators and staff, into how we give and receive feedback, into how we make decisions—and much more. These ways of doing things are seen as the norm—they aren't questioned, and they become the standard. For example, the notion that men should restrain their emotions, especially in the workplace, is so widely accepted that we've forgotten that it's a socially constructed notion. In the United States, and in much of the Western world, dominant culture is male, white/European, Christian, middle class, and heterosexual. Centralizing these identities creates definitions around what we think is "normal" and what we value and respect. If we feel uncomfortable when a grown man cries, it's because we've internalized beliefs about how men express emotions.

Context is the stuff we feel we have little influence over, that feels outside our control. Sometimes we can influence it more than we think, and sometimes it's important just to name and acknowledge it.

Dominant culture can make it hard for us to know ourselves. We're constantly seen by others through dominant views about our gender, race or ethnicity, sexual orientation, ability, and economic class status—and the many places in which these identities intersect. Furthermore, we buy into those views and adopt them as our own. Mike believed that as a man, he needed to be less emotional; he'd bought into this dominant cultural value.

Let's consider some more examples. Mohammed, an instructional coach in his early 60s, was of Pakistani decent and a practicing Muslim. He was dark skinned and wore a cap every day. He described feeling worried that teachers would be afraid of him because he was Muslim and said that because of this, he found himself smiling all the time—often forcefully. "I am burning out from all the smiling," he told me.

Mohammed's fear was not irrational. For hundreds of years, the Western world has put forth dehumanizing societal messages about dark-skinned men and Muslims. These messages have been upheld by those in power. For centuries, race has been a determinant of who had freedom, who could vote, who could buy houses in which areas, who could get certain jobs, and even who is more likely to be shot by police. When Mohammed sat down to meet with a coachee, especially a female coachee, he was aware of the distorted construction dominant culture has created of him, and he felt pressure to alleviate what he suspected was her fear of Muslim men.

Tiffany was an older, Caucasian principal in a rural community. She was from that same community, but many younger members of her staff were not. Tiffany grew up on the "wrong side of the tracks," she explained to me. She felt that because of her class background, several members of her staff didn't respect her. "I feel like they don't believe that I'm capable, and I feel like I have to prove that I deserve to be in this role every day."

Like Mohammed's, Tiffany's resilience was depleted. Their identities—gender, class, race, culture, religion—aren't the problem. The problem is a society that undervalues their identities and normalizes a dominant culture to which they do not belong. Dominant culture is a complicated, sticky web with invisible threads that can bind us. As Tiffany and Mohammed cultivated self-knowledge along with building their knowledge of the role that dominant culture was playing in their experience, they emerged with greater clarity, and that clarity cultivated resilience.

Here's how to loosen the binds of dominant culture: Learn to recognize and identify the webs of dominant culture, name them and their power, place them in a historical context, and identify the nuances of how they impact mundane social interactions. Recognizing these can be painful as we acknowledge how many of us have been hurt by dominant cultural notions. And recognition alone doesn't mean that the systems of oppression don't exist or will go away; they are very real, and they will continue to affect the lives of the majority of people. But recognizing them allows us to define ourselves outside of dominant culture. There are some moments when we can act outside the constraints of dominant culture, and by doing so, we cultivate our own resilience. Furthermore, recognizing dominant culture allows us to depersonalize what we're experiencing and to address dominant culture as the problem—and to have the energy to change it.

I coached Mohammed and Tiffany on recognizing the web of culture and power to explore their own social identities. We practiced conversations they could have to respond when they saw dominant culture at play. After a number of coaching sessions, Tiffany reported on a conversation that previously would have left her angry, but this time, left her feeling empowered. A male teacher who was finishing his first year in the classroom had stopped by her office with opinions on the master schedule for the following year. "His words and tone were authoritative," Tiffany said. "At one point he actually suggested I take notes on his ideas. First, I asked myself, *Is this young man telling me how I should build our master schedule because he thinks I don't know how? Is this because of his internalization of our culture's views of older women and people from low-income backgrounds?* But I know what I'm doing, and I don't need his input. So I said, 'I suspect you're trying to help, and I appreciate that, but I'm curious to understand why you think I need help with this? I've been a principal here for 12 years.' In that moment, I felt so clear and energized. Understanding the webs of culture made what happened feel both more and less personal, which was okay."

Although Tiffany's question made the teacher uncomfortable for a moment, she persisted and raised her concerns about not being respected because of who she was. Tiffany explained: "I just kept telling myself, *His assumptions are problematic and need to be surfaced and addressed. In order for me to be a good leader here, that's what I need to do right now.*" As Tiffany told me this story, her posture shifted dramatically from its usual slumped position. "And after he left, I felt good," she said, leaning back and smiling. "In fact, it might have been one of my best days this year."

Mohammed, by contrast, tried a different approach. "I just stopped smiling as much," he said. "And it was okay. I decided I have a right to feel like a normal human being." Mohammed also found other male educators of color with whom to discuss these experiences. Between the camaraderie and some reading about racism, he felt renewed energy. "It's not that I wasn't aware of all of this," he said. "After all, I'm a 62-year-old, dark-skinned Muslim man who has lived in the US for most of my life. But I now have more language to name what I see; I have greater intellectual understanding. That's felt energizing. It makes some of what I experience feel less personal, and I also feel clearer about the many ways I can respond."

As Tiffany's and Mohammed's understanding of their sociopolitical identities grew, so did their commitment and confidence to address dominant culture, implicit bias, and racism. Both leaders designed and facilitated PD sessions around sociopolitical identity and dominant culture, sessions that were well received and powerful learning experiences for all. They had many one-on-one conversations in which they discussed the issues that were coming to the surface.

When my work with Tiffany came to an end, she sent me an email that included this passage:

> I wanted coaching because I was burning out. I just wanted to run my school efficiently and I was tired of these young'uns judging me. Now a whole can of worms has opened up and I've become an equity leader. We've made progress in how teachers think of people from low-income backgrounds, and we've all made growth in other areas. Now things feel like they're really changing and I'm doing it. This feels more important than just running an efficient school. I'm more energized than I was fifteen years ago.

Understanding your self as it is constructed socially and politically is empowering. Regardless of your race or gender, your age or ethnicity, or any of the other social identities that you claim, you'll have greater insight into how you move through the world, how others respond to you, and your options for action. It will also help you understand others better—your colleagues, students, and their parents. This understanding is essential for building healthy communities, which we'll consider in Chapter 4.

Before you continue reading, perhaps take a moment to reflect on what this section has raised for you. What role do you see dominant culture playing in your sense of self? Which of your values, beliefs, or behaviors reflect the dominant culture that you're in? Where do you feel a disconnect between dominant culture and how you think of yourself?

There's much more exploration for us to do into how dominant culture impacts our sense of self and our resilience. The intent of this section was to acknowledge this context, raise some questions, and, I hope, provoke further inquiry—which you can do through the exercises in the workbook as well as by following the recommendations in Appendix F.

A Dive into Vulnerability

In the summer of 2017, I delivered a keynote address to some two thousand strangers, during which I spoke about a moment as an educator when I felt tremendous shame, a moment when I became aware of my own unconscious bias. Three African American boys from my second period said they felt as though I singled them out and that I treated them more harshly than others. This in spite of the fact that I'm married to an African American man and am the mother of a black boy. I felt almost more shame because of these facts; I should have known better.

I'd never written or talked about this incident before this keynote. But as I wrote the speech about how to build equitable schools, I decided to include this story. My overall message in this keynote was that most of us unconsciously perpetuate inequities because the roots of bias run deep, that we all need to honor and accept our emotions, *and* that we need to take responsibility for our conscious and unconscious actions. I'm committed to doing what I ask others to do—so it felt right to share the story of those three boys.

During the speech, I felt focused and enjoyed myself. (This introvert has no fear of public speaking.) It helped that the huge room was dark, so I couldn't see a single face. But when I was finished, I bolted from the stage and left the building.

I felt a wave of intense vulnerability. I couldn't make eye contact with the many people I passed in the halls. I felt so exposed. *What were people thinking?*

This wasn't the first time I had shared a story that made me feel vulnerable, however. In my writing and workshops, I tell other stories about how I've messed up as a teacher and coach. I'm often nervous when I tell these; my heart races, my palms perspire, and a part of me thinks, *What the hell are you doing, Elena?* But I tell my stories anyway. I've learned that the part of me that avoids the telling is the part that feels ashamed—and that part doesn't serve me. My commitment to truth and equity and community is greater than the little, scared part of me that fears judgment and rejection. What I've also learned is that my truth telling and vulnerability are appreciated. By sharing my stories, I give others permission to share theirs. I communicate the message that we're all human, we all mess up—that we need to take responsibility for what we did, learn from it, and move on. If we're going to talk about the injustices we've perpetuated in schools, we'll need to harness our courage, face some pain, and be uncomfortable. Vulnerability will be a regular emotional experience on this journey.

What makes you feel vulnerable? What do you do when you feel vulnerable? When do you choose to be vulnerable? What motivates you to make that choice?

Sociologist Brené Brown, perhaps the world's expert on vulnerability, defines vulnerability as the courage to be yourself. You cannot know yourself, she says, unless you can be vulnerable with yourself. You have to be willing to feel your tender places, acknowledge your unique gifts and talents, and see your shadow self—the parts of yourself that you don't know well and that you may not like. Being vulnerable with others includes, and begins with, being vulnerable when we're alone, with our thoughts and feelings and reflections.

I imagine that the content of this chapter and of this whole book (and the workbook) may make you feel vulnerable. After all, I'm encouraging you to look closely at yourself, and any time we hold up a mirror to ourselves, we are likely to feel vulnerable. I'm asking you to be vulnerable because I think it'll be worth it. You'll learn about yourself by doing so, and you'll emerge stronger, more empowered, more courageous, and more accepting of yourself. You might also form deeper connections with others.

If you're reading this book with colleagues and engaging in the workbook activities together, then I anticipate that you'll feel even more vulnerable. Vulnerability is a path toward wholeness and connection. At the same time, you can be thoughtful about sharing your stories. You don't have to plunge headfirst into the deep end of the pool. Practice managing your discomfort as you push the edges of your vulnerability with yourself and with others. Push gently out of your comfort zone. You're stronger than you think.

Implications for Leaders

- Being vulnerable with staff is being powerful. If you think you need to always project an image of confidence, competence, and authority, you might be undermining your own leadership. That image is inauthentic, and people pick up on inauthenticity immediately. It erodes trust. In order to be authentic, you need to know who you are and to act in alignment with that understanding of yourself.
- When was the last time you admitted to your staff that you didn't know the answer? Could you share your professional goals and what you're learning about yourself as a leader? This is one way to be vulnerable.

Disposition: Purposefulness

Self-knowledge is the portal through which we cultivate our disposition of purposefulness. When you feel purposeful, you'll sense it in every confident stride you take, in the words you speak, and in the way you dust off your knees and stand up tall again after you've fallen down.

The habit we've focused on in this chapter, Know Yourself—a habit ideally reflected upon in the summer months when you've got a little extra time and space in your life—cultivates one of the core dispositions of a resilient person: Your *why*. Your purpose. Your reason for getting up in the morning. The better you know yourself, the clearer your purpose becomes. When you are firmly grounded in your intrinsic motivation, when you know why you are getting out of bed and heading off to teach those 120 people, you'll have a symbolic spring in your step as you make your way toward that day. When the hard moments come, your eyes will be on the prize—on fulfilling your sense of purpose. When you need to make decisions and pick your battles, you'll be anchored in and emboldened by purpose. All the research on resilience has found that resilient people are firm and clear on their purpose.

Why are you doing what you're doing? Why are you teaching or leading or coaching? You must have answers to these questions, and you must feel them in the marrow of your bones if you are to embody this disposition.

If Your Purpose Is Unclear, Discover It

Carmela was a kindergarten teacher who disliked teaching most of the curriculum (which she made well known) and described herself as usually cranky (which I observed). She was sick a lot, and her administrators perceived her as resistant. When I began coaching her, I asked her to write a mission statement. Her first draft was generic and general. As I probed, I learned that Carmela's love and appreciation for the arts was what drove her. She felt that her mission was to provide children with opportunities to create their own art and appreciate that of others. Given the current kindergarten curriculum, she was unable to fulfill this purpose. Two years later, she took a position as an art teacher at a neighboring school and became, according to her reports, "a different person." When I visited her at her new school, she was joyful and energetic with students, her classroom was plastered with amazing student artwork, and her principal couldn't stop telling me about how lucky he was to have her.

Sometimes it might be this easy. When we are in a place or doing something that feels disconnected from our sense of mission or purpose, it can be, on the level of psyche and soul, excruciating. That's what makes us cranky, resistant, disengaged, sick, drained, and ineffective. I have seen this many times: Teachers who are working in a community that they don't perceive as reflecting their sense of purpose; teachers teaching a subject or grade level that doesn't align with their mission; leaders in a district in which it feels impossible to act on their sense of mission. Clarity can help us make decisions.

But clarity doesn't mean we necessarily have to quit our jobs or change schools. Having a sense of purpose helps us persevere through tough moments, and it keeps our perspective on something bigger and beyond the routine, tedious aspects of our job. Clarity about our purpose can motivate us to cope with the difficult challenges of our work.

Identifying your purpose can take some digging. (You'll find activities in the workbook to help you do this.) Sometimes we might be reluctant to explore our purpose because we fear that we'll uncover a truth that could be hard to accept—that our mission is to travel around the world collecting seeds or to dance on Broadway. If so, explore anyway. It's much better to know what you feel called to do than to wander in a haze. If you discover that you're in the wrong profession, at least you'll recognize that it's not your principal's fault that you're miserable teaching the new curriculum; it's just that you're being asked to do something that's a total mismatch with why you feel you're on earth. With this clarity comes potential empowerment, because where you are and what you're doing are within your sphere of influence.

Stay Anchored in Purpose

Clarity of purpose allows us to access deep reserves of energy. Recall a day that went really well at school. Identify what made it go so well. Now see if any of those elements connect with your sense of your purpose.

My best days as a teacher were the ones in which my students grappled with new ideas that I knew they'd continue to talk about on the yard, as they walked home, and with their families in the evening. By the end of those days, I was often tired; I may have delivered a lesson that took a long time to craft or managed complicated structures and routines, but I often left school also feeling energized because I was living my purpose. The awareness of this was critical. I could tell myself, *I'm exhausted, and I'm doing what I was born to do.* Without self-awareness, we can't make such connections.

When the Earth Shakes Under Your Feet

When I recall the hardest times and the lowest points during the 19 years I worked in the Oakland Unified School District, they were moments when big changes happened and I felt powerless. In those moments, what guided me to make decisions was my knowledge of who I am. The clearer I was, the more firmly I stood in my values and purpose, and the more I accepted and embraced my skill sets and personality, the easier it was to make decisions.

I resigned from the district when a supervisor informed me that I'd have to take a set of actions to which I felt deeply opposed. When she told me, I thought, *That's not who I am.* The clarity was liberating. I was sad and upset about the direction the district was going, but I wasn't confused—and confusion is excruciating. I knew where I stood in relationship to the district's direction, and I knew what I had to do. In that moment, I drew on my reserves of resilience to get me through what felt like a painful separation—I really didn't want to leave the school district—but in the process, I cultivated more resilience.

Self-knowledge is critical in times of turmoil and helps us manage the onslaught of emotions that arise during change or when we want to lead change. Self-knowledge is foundational for any superhero, which is not to say that a teacher needs to aspire to be Wonder Woman, but we can take a lesson from her book because Wonder Woman knows who she is. She knows what she values, and she acts in alignment with those values. Authentic confidence comes from self-knowledge. When you know who you are, you feel it in your bones, and when you walk down the hallway, your stride says, *I am here*. It's not the stance of dominance. It's the stance of deep, internal power. Self-knowledge is also a precursor to knowing your purpose—how can you be clear on what you're here to do if you don't know who you are? Wonder Woman knows what she's here to do. She's rarely confused or muddled when she has to make decisions, for her inner compass, informed by her self-knowledge, points the way. Wonder Woman also knows what she's good at; she can use her skills and aptitudes to accomplish her goals. She can accept her innate limitations and acknowledge the areas where she can change and grow.

Superheroes may wear disguises at times, but they always remember who they truly are, and, when necessary, they'll don a cape and do what has to be done, because they know why they're on earth. Perhaps the key for us, because we don't live in a comic book, is to integrate the superhero part of ourselves with our regular, daily self so that we don't need to wear disguises and so that we can be whole. That would be true power.

CHAPTER REFLECTION

- Of the different elements of self in this chapter, which ones do you feel have the greatest impact on your daily experience as an educator?
- Which of these elements of self do you want to learn more about?
- How could you explore your purpose and feel more purposeful?

CHAPTER 2

Understand Emotions

Understanding emotions—accepting them and having strategies to respond to them—is essential to cultivate resilience. With an understanding of emotions, you can accept their existence, recognize where you can influence a situation, and let go of what is outside your control.

July: Summer is an ideal time to reflect on your emotions because hopefully you can sleep a little more, enjoy warm evenings, and find a few minutes for contemplation.

રટ રટ

For years, I tried to be an instructional coach without dealing with emotions—my own or those of others. *Who has the time?* I thought. There is too much to do. Lessons to create. Parents to meet with. Injustices to uproot. Whether in response to my own emotions or those I perceived in others, my mindset was, *I see that you're sad, and I'm sorry, but deal with it. Wipe off those tears. Get to work.* It wasn't that I lacked empathy, but I didn't believe that there was a need to explore the emotions that adults had, or that it was my role. However, this stance prevented me from getting where I wanted to be as a coach, leader, and human being.

I now believe that it's essential that we educators explore our emotions, that unless we do so, we won't be able to make good on our mission to educate children. A series of incidents led to this conviction. There was the time when in response to hearing me rant about problems at school, a wise friend said, "You sound cynical.

Behind every cynic is someone whose heart has been broken." In that moment, it was as if a veil had been lifted and I could see the vast landscape of my sadness. It was scary to see, but also a relief as the murky terrain of emotions came into focus. I also sensed that there might be an alternate way of feeling beyond experiencing low-level anger all the time.

There were also times when I saw emotions in others, and, rather than avoid them or push them away, I cautiously leaned in—with the intent not to steamroll those feelings but rather to acknowledge and honor them. I discovered that with compassion and curiosity, I could explore emotions fairly quickly. In a coaching session with a new teacher, we could both explore her feelings of incompetence and also get some lesson planning done.

In some of the schools in which I worked, students engaged in social emotional learning (SEL). Educators talked about SEL standards, described the importance of SEL, and implemented new curriculum. Sometimes I'd observe an SEL lesson and find myself experiencing it as if I were a student rather than a coach. *I never got this as a kid,* I thought, realizing that I didn't know the basics—neither the names for emotions nor how to define an emotion. Was "tired" an emotion? And what was frustration, anyway? Was cynicism sadness? Where was the SEL curriculum for adults?

As I learned about emotions and integrated new approaches into my work as an instructional coach, I became more effective as a coach. I also felt better at work, had more energy, and, as a side benefit, found myself more skilled at responding to conflict in my personal life. I learned that neither my emotions nor those of others would consume me. I learned that it was easier than I'd assumed to manage my emotions and help others manage theirs. I learned that we deserve to have conversations about our emotions. For the sake of fulfilling our purpose as educators, it is imperative that we be brave enough to have these conversations.

Take a moment to consider these questions:

- How comfortable are you thinking about and talking about emotions?
- How might your professional and personal life be different if you had greater knowledge and understanding of emotions?
- How might your life be different if you had more tools to respond to your emotions when they arise?

What Are Emotions?

Recall a time in recent weeks when you felt a strong emotion. Can you put a name to that feeling? And what was it that happened, anyway? Was the emotion a thought? Or was it triggered by a thought? Was the emotion a physical experience? A bio-chemical impulse? Let's get clear on what these things are.

Emotions Are a Series of Events

An emotion is a reaction you have to an event. Something happens, your mind processes it, your body responds. Then you behave in response to your mind's in-terpretation and your body's response. Emotions are physiological, cognitive, and behavioral experiences.

Let's look at the six-part cycle of an emotion (illustrated in Figure 2.1).

Prompting event. This is the stuff that happens outside you, in your environment, such as an unexpected fire drill, a cancelled meeting, a crying child, finding that your classroom was broken into overnight, and so on. Prompting events can also happen within you; they can be thoughts, memories, or even other emotions.

Interpretation. Your mind makes sense of what happened. The event is filtered through your evaluation, understanding, beliefs, and assumptions, and you explain it to yourself in a particular way. For example, you interpret the un-expected fire drill as evidence, yet again, of your assistant principal's oblivi-ousness to how hard a teacher's job is: Surely, if he'd ever taught first grade, he'd know that Friday after lunch is not the time for a drill. Probably he was supposed to do this drill earlier, and he has to check it off his list by the end of the week. You interpret the event as evidence of your assistant principal's incompetence and lack of respect.

Physical response. The event and your interpretation result in a physical response in your body. Your thoughts about your assistant principal's lack of respect produce stress hormones that make your heart race, your throat constrict, and your hands tremble.

Urge to act. Almost simultaneous to the physical response, you feel an urge to do something. You may or may not act on this impulse, but it's useful to notice what you feel compelled to do in those first moments. As you fume over your assistant principal's incompetence and disrespect, you might start composing mental emails to your principal expressing your frustration.

Figure 2.1 Cycle of an Emotion

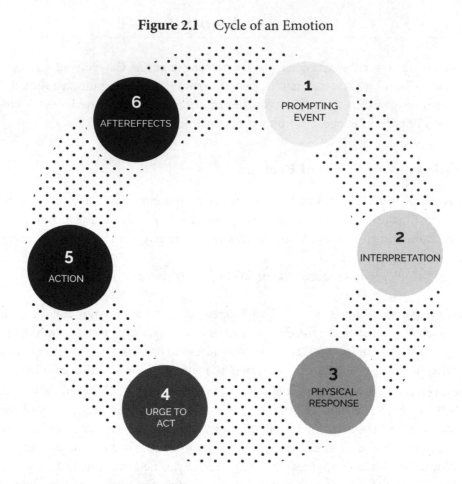

Action. Then there's what you actually do. You may or may not feel as though you're in control of your behavior at this point. As you're herding your students out the door, grabbing your class list and emergency supply backpack, you might yell at someone, slam a door, or shoot a dirty look at your assistant principal when he asks for your attendance list. Later you might send off that angry email or just reach for a bag of cookies.

Aftereffects. Finally, the emotion affects other emotions, thoughts, and behaviors, and your body. The aftereffects can be a prompting event that sets off another emotion cycle. Sometimes the original emotion needs more processing; other times, a secondary emotion is triggered. For example, your anger at your assistant principal can lead to a cycle of anxiety about your job. The aftereffects can include feeling physically exhausted or having regrets about how you behaved.

This is the universal structure of *all* emotional experiences. Learning to identify the parts of the cycle in yourself is freeing because the cycle can be interrupted. You can intervene at any step. At the point where your mind interprets your assistant principal's decision to have an unscheduled fire drill and says, *What an inconsiderate jerk,* you can say to yourself, "Ah, I'm making an assumption right now." And right there, you shift your experience of the cycle. Or perhaps when your hands tremble and your throat constricts with anger (because you had a brilliant lesson planned for the afternoon and now it's all shot to hell), you might recognize where you are in the cycle and do some deep breathing and shift your experience. Or maybe you catch yourself at the action step, and you don't yell, slam, or shoot dirty looks.

Do you see how liberating it could be to spot the steps of an emotion cycle? Take a break from reading and see if you can think of an event from the last week that triggered an emotion cycle. Do you remember how you interpreted the event? Can you recall your physical response? What did you actually do? And what were the aftereffects of the emotion?

Emotions Are Temporary

By recognizing the cycle of emotional experiences, you'll learn one of the most empowering lessons about emotions, which is that they are temporary. We often fear emotions because we incorrectly assume that they are permanent; after all, they feel so strong when we experience them. Resilient people rebound quickly after adversity and rebound stronger than before. In order to rebound when you're down and struggling, you need to know that the emotions you're experiencing are temporary. This belief helps you get back up because you recognize that you're in charge of the cycle of the emotion. You don't need to wait for someone to pick you up or for something in your external world to change; the way to get back up has to do with how you think about what's going on. It has to do with your knowledge about where you can intervene in an emotion cycle and what tools you have available to do so. I'll offer you many tools in this book and in the workbook to intervene in emotion cycles.

How We Think About Emotions Affects How We Experience Them

If you've ever been in the grips of an intense emotion, such as anger or sadness, then you may understand why, throughout history and around the world, emotions have been seen as undesirable and frightening. Dating back to the ancient Greeks, emotions were described as external forces: We are "overcome" by rage, "seized" by pleasure, and "struck" by love. Among the indigenous Maori of New Zealand, fear is a spirit that possesses people. Some cultures embrace and even welcome the temporary presence of strong emotion, whereas others have no tolerance for emotional expression.

Within our dominant Western culture, there are strong opinions about how, where, and when emotions should be expressed, and what is appropriate for boys and girls and men and women. Depending on someone's age, gender, and race or ethnicity, emotions are interpreted differently: A woman in the throes of anger may be seen as "hysterical." The way we describe responding to emotions sometimes implies their undesirability: We must "manage," "control," or "master" emotions, as if they are unruly subordinates or children. A lack of awareness of our emotions and our assumptions about them influence how we relate to and therefore experience our emotions.

Emotions are often talked about as "positive" or "negative." But emotions aren't good or bad; rather, the way we *respond* to our emotions can be positive or problematic. Like it or not, we are pretty much constantly experiencing feelings. Most often these are low-intensity emotions that we may not be aware of. Pause right now in your reading—what are you feeling? Maybe a low level of calmness or contentment? Or maybe slight nervousness? We tend to notice our feelings when they are strong, and we spend a lot of energy trying to block uncomfortable emotions.

Emotions are a reaction to something that happens, and they play an important role in conveying information to our bodies and directing our actions. I prefer the terms "comfortable" and "uncomfortable" or "distressing" emotions. Anger, for example, is uncomfortable, and when we don't respond to it well, it can have a negative impact on us and on others. But anger also has a lot to teach us if we can learn to listen to it.

Here's a key to cultivating resilience: Learn to recognize your emotions as messengers, as potential sources of energy, and as a fact of human existence. This allows you to pause when emotions come barreling in and to understand what they want to tell you. Change how you think about emotions and you'll change how you experience them.

Understanding Emotional Intelligence

In the last century or so, the field of psychology has prompted a cultural shift toward exploring and accepting emotions, turning the tide on cultural attitudes about emotions as things that must be suppressed and denied. Researcher, writer, and

Implications for Leaders

- Learn about how your staff think and feel about emotions. With insight into their mindsets, you'll more effectively lead discussion and exploration around emotions.
- Clarify your own thoughts and beliefs about emotions. You can't lead what you aren't clear on yourself.
- Encourage teacher leaders to provide opportunities for departments and teams to talk about and process emotions.

professor Daniel Goleman (1995), a pioneer in this movement, offers a definition of emotional intelligence with four components: self-awareness, self-management, social awareness, and social management, which are explained in Exhibit 2.1, The Definition of Emotional Intelligence.

Exhibit 2.1 The Definition of Emotional Intelligence

Self-awareness: The ability to recognize your own feelings, know when you're having an emotion, and name it. This awareness allows you to recognize the impact of your emotions and your strengths and limits.

Self-management: The ability to make conscious decisions about how to respond to emotions. This includes self-control, transparency, and adaptability.

Social awareness: The ability to recognize and understand the feelings that others experience. This includes empathy (sensing others' emotions, understanding their perspective, and taking active interest in their concerns) and service (recognizing the needs of others and meeting them).

Social management: The ability to form healthy relationships, manage conflicts with others, collaborate, and motivate and inspire others. The ability to cultivate trust with others is an expression of social management.

These competencies build on each other. You can't manage your emotions if you aren't aware that you're having them, and you will struggle in relationships with others if you are not aware of your emotions and don't have tools to respond to them.

Although I value the work on emotional intelligence, I am uncomfortable with some terminology, beginning with the term *intelligence*. There's a lot of historical baggage in its association with "intellectual intelligence," or IQ, and with the power and privilege connected to IQ. Similarly, the term *management* is problematic. It echoes a technological, industrial approach to responding to something entirely human—the expression of our feelings. However, because these terms are so widespread, I will continue to use them, but I'll also integrate synonyms in the hope that we can transition away from language that reflects an outdated and unhealthy mindset about emotions. Rather than suggesting that you "manage" anger, for example, I may also encourage you to "respond" to your anger or "engage with it." If you think about your feelings as visitors, then when they knock at the door, you don't need to go into a tizzy trying to manage them and force them to sit down in a chair and face forward; you could just access a bank of tools to engage with them.

In recent years, there's been increased interest in the field of emotional intelligence from all sectors of society—from business to the military—as we learn about the connection between emotional intelligence and personal and professional success. In study after study, emotional intelligence is found to be the strongest predictor of successful job performance. In research conducted by Bradberry and Greaves (2009), 90% of top performers were high in emotional intelligence—in all fields, at every level, and in every region of the world. This makes sense when you consider that emotional intelligence is the foundation of trusting relationships, interpersonal communication, flexibility, and assertiveness—not to mention how it helps with regulating stress, engaging with anger, dealing with unexpected change, and collaborating with others.

The most important thing to know about emotional intelligence is this: It is a set of *learned abilities*. We can learn to understand our emotions, and we can acquire strategies to respond to them that leave us feeling happier, stronger, healthier, and more connected to others.

Befriending Emotions

The Pixar movie *Inside Out* is revolutionary in its suggestion of how we relate to emotions. *Inside Out* depicts emotions as characters that reside within us, each identified by a different color and each necessary for our overall emotional wellbeing. If you haven't seen this movie, do so now. It offers a liberating cultural construct for emotions.

Human beings yearn for good relationships. When we struggle with classroom management, our relationships with students are often at the root of the struggle. When children don't feel that they've been listened to, understood, or respected, they act out. This doesn't mean that we don't create clear boundaries or hold them to behavioral expectations; it means that we need to know them and not just lay down the law.

This same thinking applies to emotions. These aspects of ourselves want to be understood, and they also need boundaries. Thinking about your emotions as characters, as demonstrated in the movie *Inside Out*, helps us move toward a healthy way to relate to our emotions.

Implications for Leaders

- Begin a conversation with staff about emotions by watching and discussing *Inside Out*. The workbook offers discussion questions.

Naming Our Emotions

The first element of emotional intelligence is identifying the feelings you're having. But emotions can be hard to pin down because they are often layered and complex. If my principal informs me that the field trip I planned was not approved, I might initially experience disappointment, then anger, then sadness, and perhaps even relief.

Emotions come in waves and degrees of intensity. Frustration is a shade of anger, feeling competitive is a degree of jealousy, and relief is related to happiness. Anger, jealousy, and happiness are what experts call *core emotions*. There's lots of debate among psychologists over how many core emotions there are and how to categorize them. I've landed on an adaptation of Erin Olivo's list (2014), which offers eight core emotions and many words to describe aspects of those emotions. Because I think they'll be a great resource for you, these lists are in Appendix C: The Core Emotions so that you can easily find them.

When I first came across a document like Appendix C, I was fascinated that the wild and opaque terrain of my emotional landscape could be contained in a double-sided sheet of paper. I could literally touch my finger to the words that reflected how I was feeling. I felt relieved. In my work as a coach, I frequently offer educators this document and observe them having similar responses; there's clarity, insight, and, perhaps, a burst of empowerment. When we can identify something, especially elusive emotions, we can make decisions about what to do. We feel the grip of the experience or emotion loosen just a bit.

This entire book, and the workbook, will help you build your emotional intelligence in the four domains outlined by Goleman. Perhaps it's obvious, but it's worth explicitly stating: Emotional intelligence is foundational to your ability to cultivate emotional resilience.

"I'm So Stressed and Overwhelmed"

When I ask educators how they're feeling, the most common phrases I hear are, "I'm so tired," "I'm overwhelmed," and "I'm so stressed." Sound familiar? Tired, overwhelmed, and stressed aren't listed in Appendix C because they aren't specific emotions. Rather, they cross emotion families. They signify an *emotional state,* but not necessarily an emotion. They are symptoms emerging from emotions. Likewise, "fine" and "okay" also reflect emotional states—they aren't emotions themselves. These words could indicate a positive emotion or could mask distress. "Moody," "upset," and "numb" are also emotional states.

Think about the eight core emotions as eight families of related feelings. Each emotion family is unique in when and why it happens; what it feels, looks, and sounds like when you experience it; and how you feel about it afterwards. You may find it difficult to identify whether you are angry or sad or scared, but identifying your emotion is the first step in responding to it. The more you understand these families and their distinguishing characteristics, the more skilled you'll be at managing the emotions you experience.

Burnout

About ten years into teaching, I experienced a stretch of intense burnout. It was an unnerving emotional state because it felt so different from the depression I'd experienced after my mother died that I didn't know what to call it. I felt constantly frustrated by my students, set off by little things that had never bothered me; I couldn't find the joy I had always felt in the classroom; I felt pessimistic about what could be done for children in underserved communities. I would get home from school and want to just lie on the couch and watch TV, which was (and still is) completely out of character for me. Although I recognized that I needed to do something, I didn't know how to address the elements that were contributing to my state. But I got off the couch and started a 6 a.m. exercise boot camp that jolted me back into a place of clearer thinking. It was after that intense bout of burnout that I began to explore the paths that would lead me to coaching, accepting that I needed to make a change in my work life.

As many as half of all workers in high-stress jobs suffer from some form of burnout in their career (Salzberg, 2013, p.106). Stress, anxiety, and depression can coexist with burnout, but burnout is a distinct condition of exhaustion, characterized by apathy, fatigue, frustration, anger, depression, and dissatisfaction. Findings on how to prevent burnout are not surprising: We prevent burnout by strategically renewing ourselves, sleeping more, and taking time off more frequently. We also prevent burnout by boosting our resilience.

Interestingly, introverted teachers might be at greater risk of burnout than extroverted ones (Cano-Garcia, Muñoz, and Carrasco-Ortiz, 2005). This may be because introverts need more quiet and alone time to recharge than extroverts, and teaching is inherently noisy and socially engaging. Many of the introverted teachers I've coached have wanted quieter classrooms than students want and have had a harder time participating in professional communities. Burnout is also more prevalent among teachers who don't feel supported by their administrators or who have dysfunctional relationships with supervisors, and also among teachers who don't have strong relationships with their students (Hirschkorn, 2009; Howard and Johnson, 2004; Yost, 2006).

When to Call the Doctor

Emotions can turn into moods, and if moods hang around long enough, they may become diagnosable emotional problems, such as depression or an anxiety disorder. In Appendix D, you'll find a resource to help you self-assess for depression and anxiety. If you find yourself feeling "overwhelmed" a great deal, this can be a sign of depression. And if you find yourself feeling "stressed" a lot of the time, this can be a sign of anxiety. It's important to know the signs of depression and when to get help or encourage someone else to get help.

Common indicators of depression:

- Changes in sleep, appetite, concentration, energy levels, daily behaviors, and self-esteem
- Excessive crying, agitation, irritability, and social isolation
- Loss of interest in or pleasure in activities that used to bring you joy
- A persistent state of hopelessness, guilt, anxiety, sadness, or apathy

This Body We Live In

Preceding our emotions and thoughts is our physical experience as human beings. In this book, starting here in this chapter, we'll periodically look at what our body experiences and communicates, and how our physical experience can undermine or boost our resilience. Our emotional experience has its roots in our body—it would be irresponsible to skip an inquiry into our physical self.

Tune in to Your Body to Boost Self-Awareness

Here's what happens in our body when an irate parent storms into our classroom just after the bell rings: Our heart rate increases, we breathe faster, and we sweat.

Our blood pressure soars, stress hormones flood our system, and our blood flows to our major muscles. Our central nervous system has responded quickly to what it has perceived as a threat, and all that action makes something else happen: Our higher-order brain functions slow down. Everything not essential for immediate survival is abandoned, including problem solving, the ability to learn, empathy, and flexible thinking. Our attention becomes fixed and narrow.

With emotional intelligence, we can register our physical state and learn strategies to regulate our physiological response so that we can return to a clearer thinking state. In that moment, if we can intervene in the cycle of emotion, we might be able to prevent ourselves from saying something to that irate parent that we'd later regret.

Managing relationships isn't the only reason why we need to learn how to regulate our physiological response. The physical symptoms of uncomfortable emotions don't make us feel well—not in the immediate aftermath or in the long term. We get headaches, indigestion, insomnia, and so on. Distressing emotions can weaken the immune system and may play a role in the development, progression, and outcome of some medical conditions.

How you feel physically is often a map of how you feel emotionally. One of the first steps in regulating emotions is to identify the physical feelings that indicate there's a strong emotion present. Managing our emotions may start with befriending our bodies.

Here are some ways to cultivate body awareness:

- Do a body scan: Sense the physical state of the different parts of your body—your shoulders, jaw, chest, arms. As you notice what's going on in your body, see if you can sense an emotion. Perhaps you notice that your body feels relaxed—are you feeling happy? Or perhaps you notice that your hands are perspiring—are you nervous?
- When you sense a strong emotion and notice that your body has responded, take three deep breaths and imagine that breath going into the part of your body that is reacting to the emotion.
- If you can anticipate that a certain person triggers you—for example, a student's way of communicating is especially annoying—then, as soon as that person shows up or talks to you, tap your index finger to your thumb. Allow this to be a cue for you to bring awareness to your body and to breathe into the areas that get constricted.

Your body provides clues to your emotions. As you pay more attention to it, your understanding of your emotions will expand.

Interrupt the Intensity of Emotions

Breathing is the fastest way to interrupt the havoc of intense emotions and shift the experience. Slowing your breathing slows your heartbeat, normalizes hormone release, and relaxes tense muscles. Breathing is the switch that can turn off the signals of emotional distress, which sometimes feel as though they switch on by themselves.

Here's the key to using your breath: Exhale slowly. Breathe in through your nose, then out through your mouth, counting slowly to five on your exhale. That's it. Next time you catch yourself in the grips of a strong, uncomfortable emotion, breathe. Taking five of these slow, deep breaths changes your physiology and begins to restore your ability to think clearly.

Improve Social Management by Paying Attention to Your Body Language

Although it's important to register the body language of others, it's also crucial that we turn our gaze onto ourselves and explore our own nonverbal communication. This is key to working on the area of emotional intelligence known as social management. When we're feeling certain emotions, our bodies display cues. When we're sad, we might slump over. When we're distressed, our brows might furrow, or we might lean back and cross our arms. When we're ashamed, we might fold in on ourselves, making ourselves small. In our effort to cultivate trust and build relationships, we need to be conscious of our body language.

Sonia, a principal I coached, had a brilliant mind. She was a deep, provocative thinker, and I learned a great deal from the way she led. She read widely, planned methodically, and was a master at creating tools for productivity. One day, she was distressed about an interaction with a teacher, and she asked for advice. Sonia had provided the teacher with carefully planned feedback. Upon hearing Sonia's opening statements, the teacher had burst into tears. Before bolting from her office, the teacher said, "You are always so critical of everything I do! You never tell me anything I'm doing right!"

I noticed that as Sonia relayed the incident, she hunched her shoulders, her breathing was shallow, her hands balled, and her jaw was clenched. I asked what she was sensing in her body. She looked stunned by my question. She sat quietly for a moment. "I have no idea," she said. "I don't live in my body." She glanced down as if taking stock of an alien appendage. "I have no idea," she repeated. I shared what I'd observed about her shoulders, jaw, hands, and so on. "Wow," she said, "I am so disconnected from my body."

What probably happened in Sonia's interaction with the teacher was that her emotional distress—her frustration—had manifested in her body language. I had observed her on many occasions responding to others with words that seemed thoughtful, but with nonverbals that communicated a stew of feelings. On that day, following that distressing interaction, I invited Sonia to engage in an inquiry project on her nonverbal communication. Drawing on her strengths as a planner, she developed an action plan, including goals, to get to know her body.

When I saw Sonia the following week, she said, "Today is shoulders. I'm observing my shoulders all day, focusing on dropping them when I'm talking to others. Yesterday was eyebrows. I videoed myself in a meeting, and afterwards I turned off the sound and just looked at the movement in my eyebrows. Most of the time they were open and expressive, but there were a few times when I frowned and looked scary." Sonia applied her analytical capacities to examining her body language. Her increasing awareness, and the insight she gained into her emotional states, led to more skillful responses to her feelings and more effective communication with her staff.

Explore the Physiology of Moods

Maybe you are reading this book and using the workbook, and you feel that no matter what you try, you can't get out of a funk, or you often feel anxious, or you feel as though you should have (and would like) more energy for life. Perhaps you've even been on prescription medication to address your moods, and maybe they've helped, but you've also had to deal with a host of unpleasant side effects. If you have tried everything to feel emotionally well and you're not where you want to be, I urge you to explore the physiology underlying your emotional state.

Our medical model is in its infancy when it comes to acquiring scientific knowledge on the connection between our bodies and our emotions and mental states. What we eat affects our moods, as does how much we sleep and how much we move our bodies. You could try everything I suggest, yet if your body isn't getting the kind of nutrition, rest, and exercise it needs, you'll hit a big wall as far as your well-being is concerned.

If you've done everything you can think of to feel better, I encourage you to work with a nutritionist, or simply to research the connection between moods, nutrition, and physical well-being. For example, hormones profoundly impact our moods. If you have been under great stress for long periods of time, it may be that your adrenal glands are not working as they should, which affects your hormones and can make you feel tired and down. If you aren't getting amino acids in your diet, you can feel low energy and even depressed. Many of us are vitamin D and B deficient. Many teachers don't drink enough water—and dehydration makes you feel thickheaded and sluggish. There can be many biological reasons for your feeling anxious, sad, or low energy. Do some research, get counsel from experts, try taking supplements, and change your diet. There's more on this topic in Chapter 6.

Examine the Conditions in Which You Work

The conditions in which we work have a huge impact on our emotional well-being. I fantasize about organizations that account for the biological needs and rhythms of our bodies. In these schools, we'll begin teaching at a reasonable hour—say 9:00 a.m. Both the students and teachers will have had enough sleep and will have had time for exercise, and teachers perhaps will have had time for a morning meeting with colleagues. After a couple hours of classes, teachers will have a two-hour break. During this time, they'll sit and eat together, maybe meditate for a little bit, go for a walk, or even take a nap, and then teach for another couple of hours. After school, they'll prep for the next day and be home in time to prepare dinner or go to a dance class.

When I imagine this school that accounts for our biological needs, it's clear that students would benefit not only from having rested, well-fed teachers who take walks but also from having their own biological needs accounted for—their need for rest, food, exercise, and quiet.

Until our working conditions change, you can find ways to take little breaks, get more rest, and have entire weekends off. This can be done. In addition, the hundreds of suggestions in this book and the workbook are intended to counter the endless barrage of stressors. If you are an introverted teacher, be especially diligent in finding times to recharge. As you cultivate your own resilience, you will have more energy to advocate for the structural changes that need to be made for all of us to live and work in better conditions.

 A Dive into Anger

There are few things that would bring me more joy than seeing groups of educators sitting together talking about anger. I'm not joking. Of all the emotions, this is perhaps the one that we're all most afraid of, that has become a nondiscussible. We have good reasons to be wary of anger; it has caused a lot of chaos in our world and homes. Yet we need to befriend it so that we can understand and use it. If we were able to talk candidly about anger, we'd make tremendous headway in improving our schools.

Implications for Leaders

Many factors that lead to burnout are outside your control, but you can provide your staff with opportunities for strategic renewal. Here are some ways to do this:

- The beginning of the year is a period of intense energy output for teachers. There's meeting the new students, of course, and their parents, but then there's the back-to-school BBQ, the new committee meeting, the rollout of the new curriculum adoption, the district's meeting for new teachers, and so on. Consider your options for mitigating the outpouring of energy and how you might balance this with opportunities for renewal. Remember also that all of these social engagements are harder for introverts—both the quantity of engagements and the engagements themselves. Structured interactions help relieve unpredictability and thus minimize the energy drain.
- Limit what you ask staff to do on evenings and weekends. It's hard to say no to your boss: It can appear as if they're "not team players" when really, all they need is downtime.
- When teachers arrive for an afternoon PD session (after teaching all day), begin with reflection, a pair-share conversation, reading a poem, or some kind of activity that allows for quiet introspection or connection with one other person around something meaningful. Create pockets of silence during the session. And feed people something nutritious—even just almonds and apples—because the exhaustion at the end of the day is physical.
- If teachers regularly meet to plan lessons or create assessments together, consider incorporating structures that allow for quiet. Use asynchronous collaborative tools, such as a shared document.
- Consider an optional 10 minutes of mindfulness before school starts (see Chapter 5). I work with one high school where a handful of staff participate in this routine every morning, and even the highly extroverted principal finds it tremendously helpful.
- If you are concerned that a teacher might be exhibiting signs of burnout, talk to her. Listen, express your concern, and together come up with a support plan. Burnout isn't permanent. Some people can recover and remain in their positions, whereas others may choose to explore alternate positions in the field.

The Danger with Anger

First, let's get clear on this: There's a difference between anger and aggression. Anger is an energy that becomes aggression when it manifests as an action or a set of thoughts. Aggression is throwing a plate across the room, belittling someone, shutting down and not speaking, complaining relentlessly, or being hypercritical, resentful, or bitter. Aggression is a maladaptive response to suffering, and that response—not the anger—is the problem. If you are uncomfortable with the way you demonstrate anger, you need to look at the expression of the emotion rather than condemn the anger itself. The anger is trying to tell you something, but its manifestation is taking a toll on you and the people around you. That's not okay. It's your responsibility to investigate your anger and find other ways to express the emotions that fuel aggressive behaviors.

Know Your Anger

You are responsible for knowing your anger. Anger might just be the hardest emotion to deal with, and yet we must. Anger is so uncomfortable that at any sign of it, most of us push back, lash out, shut down, or run away. Yet we must be willing to investigate it, and sometimes this takes courage. Where does anger come from? How does it show up in your body? What is its impact on your sleep, moods, and relationships? What is it trying to tell you? Getting curious about your anger is a huge first step.

Anger is usually not just one thing; it often contains sadness, fear, helplessness, frustration, and panic. One year, at the end of summer, just a week before school started, I found out that I would no longer teach the elective course that I'd taught for years. Instead, I was assigned to teach a reading intervention course that followed a scripted curriculum. I was furious. How could this decision be made so late in the summer? Why didn't I have any say in it? Why were our administrators capitulating to the demands of the central office that didn't know our context or our students' needs? When my fury subsided, I also recognized that I felt hurt. I felt unappreciated. I felt as though the efforts I'd put into my elective class hadn't been acknowledged. I'd spent years refining it, and it hurt to hear that I would no longer teach it.

Under my anger there is often sadness, and sometimes sadness feels harder to deal with than anger. Anger gets me up and out the door; it provides a burst of energy. Sadness makes me feel scared and empty and tired. That's often why I don't want to explore anger. I'm too afraid of what I might find. It's taken a very long time, but now, when anger comes, I've learned not to be afraid of it. I also have more tools now to explore and respond to it.

Learning from and about anger may feel uncomfortable. Anger can breed fear and shame, because we fear being overwhelmed and losing control. We feel ashamed that such "negative" emotions are part of us, so we suppress our anger or act out. But you can learn how to productively engage with a strong emotion. Many of us suppress anger or act out of it as a way to avoid experiencing the full intensity of an emotion. We can experience an emotion and not act out of it in a way that causes pain, suffering, and problems. Anger can also hijack our rational mind, so we must slow things down so that we can think clearly and make wise decisions.

Use It and Let It Go

Anger might help us through a crisis moment, but it also stresses our bodies, causes us to lose sight of the big picture, clouds our judgment, and can manifest as aggression. It's easier to let go of anger if you think of it as energy that comes and goes, rather than as something you are. Americans often say, "I am angry" as if our fixed state of being is angry. In Romance languages, the grammatical construction to express this idea is "I have anger," and Tibetans say, "Anger is present." Our cultural mindset and the language that reflects it affect how we think about our emotions, but you are not your emotions.

People in positions of authority or privilege often tell others that they don't deserve to be angry, that they shouldn't get so worked up, or that whatever they're experiencing is their own fault, when, in fact, they have every reason in the world to be angry. This is true in unhealthy interpersonal relationships and in the context of social and political institutions. When we are confronted by unfair behavior, anger can help us say no, insist on better treatment, and energize our determination. But staying in anger can narrow the mind and shut down the heart, and often it leaves us confused, antagonistic, and resentful. We have a right to be angry, and we are responsible for how we manifest our anger. We can act in a way that doesn't perpetuate suffering and that doesn't have a negative impact on our own health and well-being. Repressing anger, holding on to it, and turning it into aggression deplete resilience.

The Power of Anger

In its purest form, when used skillfully, anger can bring good to the world. Feeling irritated, fed up, mad, or outraged can alert us to real threats and injuries in the world or in our personal lives that need correcting. Anger can energize and fuel us to do something about selfishness, exploitation, and injustice.

Anger is not required in order for you to speak from your heart or speak truth to power. You need agency, confidence, fierce compassion, and authenticity. Dr. Martin Luther King Jr. used the energy of anger, not aggression, to address injustice. South African archbishop Desmond Tutu; the Tibetan leader in exile, the Dalai Lama; the Indian leader for independence from Britain, Mahatma Gandhi; and others have shown that we can lead change without getting stuck in unproductive anger.

We must also learn how to be in the presence of other people's anger (not their aggression) and not freak out or shut down. In order to transform our schools and our society, we need to have conversations about our nation's history: About the genocide of Native people, about slavery, and about many other injustices that will surely elicit anger. If we are to heal the deep wounds that divide us, if we are to build equitable schools, we'll need skills and strategies to manage our own experiences of these feelings and those of others. That's why I hope that one day, educators might sit together and talk about anger. We could acknowledge anger, learn from it, listen to others express their experiences of anger, and one day release it. Such conversations would indicate that we are truly, finally, on a path toward healing and transformation.

I have yet to see such conversations taking place at a school site. But when I've offered the opportunity to discuss anger in workshops that I've facilitated, I've noticed several things: People lean into the conversation—apprehensively at first, but then with commitment; they share stories, and they listen to each other with curiosity; sometimes people cry; sometimes people look distressed. After the conversation, many people report feeling tired. They also express gratitude for the opportunity to share some stories that needed to be shared, and acknowledge their need to discuss anger. After I give people time to talk about anger, I always send them out on a walk. Physical movement helps tremendously. As they return and we settle back into the content of the workshop, I often hear people say things like, "I was so nervous about that activity, and I'm so glad we did it," and "That wasn't as hard as I thought it would be." Try it: Invite a colleague to have tea or take a walk after school, and say, "Tell me about the anger you notice and experience at school."

Disposition: Acceptance

"I'm a card player," Artie told me, "and it's like I'm looking at my hand, and right now, there's nothing I can do about what's there." Artie was a superintendent whom I'd been coaching, who was in a major battle with his board.

"What's there?" I asked, wanting to understand his analogy.

"I'm pissed off," he said. "I have been playing this game with them for a year, and trying to be calm and collected, but what I see now is that I'm angry." I nodded. I'd been nudging Artie toward recognizing his emotions for a few sessions, and he'd been reluctant to acknowledge the anger that was so apparent to me.

"So, is anger one of the cards? Or are the cards the situation?" I asked.

"Anger is one of the cards. Another is frustration. Another is irritation." He paused, shifted in his chair and looked away from me. The Core Emotions (Appendix C) lay on the table. "And sadness," he added. "I'm sad. Why are they doing this to me? I guess I also feel betrayed." I stayed quiet and let these statements sink in.

Artie turned back to me and leaned forward. "Maybe the emotions are the cards—for some reason it's helpful to see that I have anger and sadness—but the cards are also the situation. The board decided *this* last spring. They told me *that* at our last meeting. They want me to do *this*." With each statement, he made the motion of putting down an imaginary playing card. Then Artie laughed. "I've still got some aces up my sleeve!" he said. His mood shifted slightly.

"How are you feeling now?" I asked.

"Seeing my emotions as cards helped me also see the situation as a thing in front of me. Right now, it's just the hand I've got. This might change, but now I have to play with what's here. This makes me feel better. I've had far worse hands. I just need a little patience, clear thinking, and strategizing, and it'll be okay."

When our emotions are muddled, it's hard to have a clear picture of reality. We can't act with intention or clarity. Suffering is often a result of not accepting what is: We want things to be different; we don't want to be where we are; we don't want to be with the people we're with; we don't want to be who we are. We don't like and don't want the current reality and push it away, and that produces suffering. Resilient people are accepting. In an uncomfortable moment, they identify what they can change and accept what they can't.

Acceptance isn't resignation. Resilient people don't throw up their hands and say, "Oh well, I tried." Acceptance means recognizing that what is, *is* in that moment, even if we don't like it. That act allows us to feel calmer, gain clarity, and see the many paths forward. Acceptance can be a key to understanding and moving through emotions.

There were many uncomfortable moments I had to accept as a teacher, and when I accepted whatever happened as well as the emotions that came up for me, I found more energy within myself. I had to accept that I had no choice but to implement the new mandated curriculum—and accept the anger that came along with that. I had to accept that my partner teacher, Keiko, the best partner teacher ever, left teaching—and accept the accompanying sadness. I had to accept that I needed to leave the classroom and take on a different role in schools—and accept my mixed feelings of relief and grief. Initially in each of these moments, I didn't like what was happening. I wanted it to be different. I didn't want to experience the emotions that surfaced. But when I pushed against them, the emotions intensified or found other ways of expressing themselves. Acceptance helped me recognize those emotions and see that they'd wax and wane, and ultimately helped me find the possibility for growth.

Reclaim Your Right to Emotions

In further chapters, we'll explore how to intervene in emotion cycles, but we have to accept that emotions will happen. Understanding why we have emotions and how they serve us helps us accept them. Perhaps we'd appreciate emotions more if we understood that they've been crucial to our physical survival as a species. Our ancient ancestors on the African savannah survived, in spite of the many challenges, because they learned what to fear, how to bond, and how to build community and live in social groups for protection. Anger and jealousy have also played a role in helping our species survive—although it's easy to see how they've contributed to much harm. We've benefited from our so-called negative emotions.

Emotions motivate us to act, get organized, prioritize, and solve problems. Emotions also help us tune in to what others are feeling, and they help us build and maintain social bonds. Emotions help us identify and respond to opportunities. We can learn to hear the messages they bring us and heed their lessons. Understanding emotions is so foundational to cultivating resilience that in each chapter of this book, we take a deep dive into a specific emotion so that we can consider its purpose and impact, and acquire more language to describe the experience.

Resilience is the ability to encounter adversity and bounce back stronger than before, supporting us in fulfilling our purpose. Every day there are dozens or even thousands of decisions we make: How, or whether, to respond to a student's snide comment; how, or whether, to ask our principal to reconsider his decision about the field trip; how, or whether, to quit our job. Each decision can boost our resilience or deplete it. Understanding our emotional self allows us to discern our options and, ultimately, to accept what we can't change and put our energies toward what we can.

It may feel countercultural to talk about emotions with the dean of faculty or the PE teacher or our superintendent, because emotions have for too long been seen as having no place in a professional setting. They've been maligned for their unpredictability and messiness; they've been relegated to the terrain of women and children; they've been contained to the offices of psychotherapists. Emotions have been something that people have felt ashamed of or have been shamed for expressing. But we are biologically and socially wired to have emotions. To deny them is to cut off a part of who we are. For our schools to be places where big and little people thrive, we need to reclaim our right to experience emotions and talk to each other about them. In doing so, we will find a source of energy, strength, and connection that would allow us to fulfill our purpose as educators.

CHAPTER REFLECTION

- How does the content of this chapter shift your thoughts about discussing emotions at school?
- What information or which ideas in this chapter were new to you?
- What do you want to learn more about as it relates to emotions?

CHAPTER 3

Tell Empowering Stories

How you interpret and make sense of events is a juncture point where emotional resilience increases or depletes. You make the choice about what story to tell. When you tell empowering stories, your optimism may expand, and optimism is a key trait of resilient people.

August: Your thoughts are the keys to unlocking reserves of resilience. Start the year with this key habit.

❧ ❧ ❧

As a new teacher, I was overwhelmed. I worked constantly. I was exhausted. I didn't feel very effective, and small changes to a schedule or plans threw me for a loop. My classroom was always a mess, cluttered with stacks of papers, open paint bottles, abandoned science projects, and piles of lost and found items. I often thought, *I will never make it through this year, There's no way I can keep teaching, This is impossible,* and *I'm a total failure.*

Early in that first year, I sat down with a piece of chart paper and markers and drew the reality I wanted to experience. Using stick figures, comment bubbles, and scribbles that only I could decipher, I sketched out an image of myself in an organized, clean, calm classroom. On my desk, I drew a healthy lunch. My students were focused, engaged, and talking to each other about how much they were learning. Most important were the thought bubbles above my head, which read: "I love teaching!" "My kids are learning so much," "I got enough sleep last night, and even though my prep was cancelled, it's okay!" and "I can't believe how much better this year is!"

This was a turning point for me. I felt elated creating this poster, even though my mind tried to sabotage my efforts. It kept telling me, *This will never happen. Keep dreaming.* I told it to be quiet. Actually, I said, "Shut up," which I often do when the volume of my critical self-talk gets loud. Empathy comes later, but when it interrupts my work, I use colorful language to scare it away. When my poster was finished, it went up on my wall at home, reminding me every morning that a different reality was possible.

In the following weeks, when I noticed myself saying, "I'll never make it through this year," I'd talk back to myself and say, "You will. And next year will be different." When I looked at the mess in my room, I'd say, "What do you need to do to get this cleaned up? Let's get started." Little by little, it got easier. And the following year was remarkably better, and there were days—many of them, in fact—that mirrored the drawing on my wall.

The Promise and Pitfalls of Storytelling

Words shape how we understand ourselves and make sense of the world. When we weave the scattered facts and moments of our lives into narratives, we give the events of our life form, meaning, and longevity. Words bring the essence of things into being. Stories connect us with others past, present, and future; they hold our memories and pass on wisdom. Stories tell us who we are and what is possible for us. You can take the raw elements of your day as a new teacher and craft them into a variety of stories: You as a new teacher on a learning journey, or you as a new teacher who is terrible.

Stories can be dangerous. When a student rolls her eyes at us and we think, *She doesn't respect me,* we've woven a story that undermines our resilience. We also craft and propagate stories that dehumanize others, consciously and unconsciously, and that don't serve our greater mission. Because we author our stories, this is the precise spot where we can boost resilience.

This might be the hardest and most important habit to cultivate. It's the habit that gives you the power to decide what to think. When your principal passes you in the front office before school and doesn't say good morning, you can think, *What did I do? Why did she ignore me?* Or you can think, *She must have a lot on her mind.* That's the moment right there, in your interpretation, when your resilience for the day will go up a tiny bit or down, based on what you think—based on the story you tell. You can practice this habit hundreds of times every day and then select the elements to spin into the epic narrative of your life. This habit, Tell Empowering Stories, most directly fosters optimism, which is a core disposition of a resilient person.

In this chapter, we'll explore storytelling on the individual psychological level. We'll also consider storytelling on a larger scale—in our schools, districts, and society. We'll look at how to shift our thoughts and beliefs that don't serve us, and how to create new stories.

In order to tell empowering stories, it is useful to consider these six elements. Being aware of thoughts, recognizing and shifting distorted thoughts, uprooting the problematic core beliefs that lie below unproductive thoughts, crafting new stories, recognizing organizational stories around us, and sharing your stories. These are somewhat, but not entirely, sequential. You can craft a new story while you're learning to recognize distorted thoughts, but the new story may not be as powerful as it could be if you haven't deconstructed your distorted thoughts and exposed them as the erroneous creatures they are. Figure 3.1 illustrates the six elements of empowered storytelling.

Here's the bottom line: If you want to shift the way you feel, you must shift the way you think. Our stories are our thoughts, and we can craft thoughts that serve

Figure 3.1   Elements of Empowered Storytelling

us. Let's consider a starting point for creating stories—how we interpret what happens to us. With that understanding, we can narrate the events of our lives in ways that build our resilience.

Digging to the Roots of Interpretation

There's a famous Zen story of a man paddling his canoe slowly through the fog. It is a new boat, freshly painted, and he is very proud of its pristine condition. He sees another boat coming his way, and he yells a warning that is ignored, and in spite of his best efforts, he is unable to avoid the other boat. Although he is uninjured, his new boat has a nasty scrape. He is fuming, consumed with anger at the people in the other boat, until he looks more closely and sees that it's simply drifting, untethered and unmanned. His anger disappears instantly as his mental frame of the incident changes. The lesson is: You can manage your emotional responses by managing your mental frames. We'll start with first exploring storytelling on the individual level of the psyche.

Cultivating Awareness: Interpretation Is Everything

Remember, there are six steps in an emotion: the prompting event, your interpretation, a physical response, the urge to act, action, and the aftereffects. Things are going to happen—we can't do much about that. But we can intervene immediately *after* something happens and before our interpretation, which can open the way for a different experience.

Consider these simple scenarios that are common stressors for teachers, and interpretations of the events.

Event	Teacher X's Interpretation	Teacher Y's Interpretation
A parent emails asking to meet tomorrow.	What did I do now? I can't do anything right. He's just one more person criticizing me. I don't even remember interacting with his kid today. He's probably upset about something I did, and now I'm going to have to start my day dealing with an irate parent.	I wonder what's going on. I hope everything is okay with his kid. Maybe he wants to meet because he missed the last conference. It'll be good to connect.

Event	Teacher X's Interpretation	Teacher Y's Interpretation
The copy machine is broken again.	Nothing ever works here. Office staff are incompetent.	The copy machine is broken. It's old and hard to get replacement parts.
A student rolls his eyes when you ask him to do something.	He's disrespectful and rude. Nothing works to get him to behave.	I wonder what's going on with him. I need to develop a better relationship with him.
The principal doesn't greet you when you pass her in the hallway.	She doesn't like me. She doesn't even care if I teach here.	She's got a lot on her plate. Maybe she's having a hard day.

As you read the first column of interpretations, you might have thought, *That's jumping to conclusions,* and, yes, it is, but we do this without awareness *all the time.* We constantly interpret events in split seconds—we have to do this in order to survive in the world—but sometimes the stories we tell are problematic. Sometimes our thoughts are not our friends. Take a look at the second column for thoughts that foster resilience.

What you think is how you feel. Our interpretations can cause, exacerbate, or intensify emotional distress, or they can boost our optimism, help us connect with others, and enable us to care for ourselves and to engage in the many habits that boost resilience. It's your interpretation that produces an emotion; improve your interpretations and you may feel better.

Interrupting Interpretations

Okay, so what do you do? In order to work on your thoughts, you'll need to be calm. When you find yourself in the grip of a strong emotional experience, give yourself time to unwind. Deep breathing and progressive muscle relaxation help. (See exercises in the workbook for instructions.) Also, allow yourself a moment to actually feel whatever you're feeling. You don't have to lurch into problem solving and analysis; sometimes you need to just sit with a feeling and allow yourself to experience it.

Here's what to do: Sit down and let yourself feel sad or angry or rejected without needing to do anything about it. Keep breathing if your physical response feels strong. Say to yourself, *I'm really angry. I see my anger. I feel it in my jaw and shoulders. I see it.* This is what it sounds like to acknowledge your feelings, and it can help a lot.

Next you need to identify your thoughts, which is harder than it sounds. The following questions can help.

Identify Those Thoughts
- What was the first thing that went through your mind when the prompting event happened?
- What are you telling yourself about it now?
- What is so upsetting about it?
- What memories did the event stir up?
- What do you think this says about you? About your life?
- What do you think this makes others think about you?
- What does this tell you about another person or other people?
- What are you worried might happen now?

Identify Those Thoughts: An Example

Event: My principal walked right past me in the hallway this morning, the first morning after winter break, and didn't even make eye contact, smile at me, or say hello.

- First thing that went through my mind: I can't believe she did that. What a jerk.
- I'm telling myself that I can't work for someone who is so insensitive and rude.
- I'm upset because I feel like I'm not even seen here, my work is not appreciated, and all I get are critical notes and emails. She doesn't even care if I'm here.
- Memories are about working for other administrators who didn't respect me or care about me.
- I think this event says that I'm never going to feel appreciated or valued or even seen as a person at school.
- I'm not sure what this makes others think about me. Maybe that I don't need respect, or that I don't care if I'm disrespected. Maybe they think I'm just a servant who doesn't need recognition.

- What this tells me about my principal is that she's a jerk. I don't respect her either.
- Now I'm worried that maybe I did something and I'm in trouble and that's why she didn't acknowledge me. Or maybe she really doesn't care about me.

You might read the example of Identify Those Thoughts and again think, *That's an overreaction. She jumped to conclusions,* but many of us engage in what's called *distorted thinking,* which we'll talk about in the next section. A number of factors contribute to our interpretations, including our moods and earlier emotional experiences. If you are already in a negative place, you're more likely to interpret events negatively. But your thoughts can also help you avoid negative distress or curtail it when it happens. Remember, you *can* change your thoughts, which *will* change how you feel.

Implications for Leaders

In order for you to help your people grow and to lead systemic change, you must guide your staff to surface the narratives they tell about their practice, students, professional selves, teaching, and learning. Then support them to rewrite these narratives. Here are some things you can say to get this conversation started:

- It sounds as though you've drawn some conclusions about what happened. Can you name what those are? Can you tell me about how you arrived at them? Are there any other conclusions you could draw based on what happened?
- I hear that what happened was upsetting. What do you think that says about you? How do you think it makes other people think about you? Are there any other ways you could think about what happened?
- I hear that what happened made you feel _____, and that the conclusion you've drawn from that is _____. If that's the conclusion you've drawn, what is possible for you [for your relationship with another person, for your potential as a teacher, etc.]?

Distorted Thinking: How Stories Undermine Our Well-Being

The first step in changing our thoughts is recognizing what's unhelpful or inaccurate about them. What psychologists call distorted thinking comprises a set of patterns. These ways of thinking are hard to see because usually they're habitual; we engage in them with little awareness and have done so for many years. When we experience a strong, distressing emotion, many of us leap to one or more of these unhelpful patterns of interpretation. Some of us might use all of them at one time or another, or we might have our favorites. What follows in Table 3.1 are the most common patterns of distorted thinking.

As you read these, could you identify the ones you jump to most often? At times, we all engage in these distorted thinking habits, and they don't serve us. Remember: You can intervene in your thinking and interrupt an emotion cycle that's headed to an unproductive place. The workbook offers you exercises to help you become aware of and shift distorted thinking.

Table 3.1   Common Patterns of Distorted Thinking

Distorted Thought	Description and Example
Black-and-White Thinking	Maggie frequently uses words such as "always" or "every" or "never." Things are right or wrong, all-or-nothing, great or horrible. There are no shades of gray, no complexity in people or situations, no middle ground. When she planned a lesson that didn't go exactly as she'd hoped, she declared it a *total* failure. She says, "My principal *never* tells me anything I'm doing well!"
Jumping to Conclusions	Jason draws conclusions about a situation without knowing all the facts, or sometimes without *any* facts. Even without evidence, he makes negative assumptions. He feels supremely confident in assessing how someone else feels about him; he can infer others' motivations and feelings without hearing a word from them. He can often predict outcomes, which are almost always negative, about things that haven't happened. He says, "My principal stopped by to observe me today unannounced. I know she's going to write me up for something."
	He interprets other people's behaviors (including their facial expressions or nonverbal communication) with no other input than his own thoughts and without checking his assumptions. He thinks, *The coach doesn't like me because she never smiles at me.*

Distorted Thought	Description and Example
Unrealistic Expectations	Emily gets upset when someone else or life in general doesn't measure up to how she thinks things "should" be. She has uncompromising rules about how things should be. She blames herself and others for things that aren't controllable. She's relentlessly hard on others and on herself. She uses the word "should" a lot, and she says, "I'm not a perfectionist; I just have high standards."
Disqualifying the Positive	Reggie focuses on and magnifies the negative aspects of a person, situation, or experience. He ignores or explains away any positive fact or experience. If he has a day where kids are on task, he says, "Today was a fluke. Tomorrow they'll be out of control again." If someone appreciates him for doing something, he says, "It was nothing. Anyone could do that."
Overgeneralizing	Angie comes to speedy conclusions with only one piece of evidence. Early in the school year, her principal asks to see the unit she's teaching, and she thinks, *This guy doesn't trust me. I can't work with him.* The copy machine breaks and she thinks, *Nothing works in this school.* Conclusions are based on one selected fact, situation, or event.
Catastrophizing	Petra thinks that everything will go wrong. She's great at seeing worst-case scenarios and warning others about them. She tells herself that a situation is horrific and intolerable. She gets a new student a month into the school year and declares that now the precarious balance in her class will be thrown off and the year will be a wash. When her principal announces a new behavior management plan, she mumbles, "This will never work."
Emotional Reasoning	Max believes that his feelings reflect the way things actually are; his feelings are facts. He tells himself, *If I feel this way, then it must be true.* When he makes a simple mistake, he concludes that he must be stupid.
Personalization	For Anne, everything is about her, especially the bad things. She is sure that anything negative is directed at her or that she is responsible for it happening. She takes the blame for things that she could not control. If something goes wrong, she tells herself: *It must be my fault somehow.* If a meeting is rescheduled for a time that doesn't work for her, she thinks: *They did that just to annoy me or maybe because they hope I won't be there.*

Core Beliefs That Make Things Worse

When I began coaching Izzy, I was stumped by her responses to many of the typical things that happened in a sixth-grade classroom. Izzy had taught lower elementary grades for three years, so she wasn't new to teaching, but when her principal suggested she revise her introductory letter home to parents, or her students struggled with the first big project she assigned, or a colleague asked a question, she seemed to fall apart. She'd call me crying, saying things like, "I shouldn't be a teacher . . . I am such a fuck-up! . . . My department colleagues would never mess up like this . . . My kids would be better off with a long-term sub . . ." I would think, *That's an overreaction,* but I wasn't sure how to coach her out of that place.

I tried coaching around what felt like a boulder in the road. But it seemed as though every five steps, she'd crash into this solid wall of deeply held views about herself. Just under the surface of her thought process and interpretation, and fueling her emotional state, was a belief that she was inherently flawed or incompetent. When Izzy would talk about her challenges as a teacher, I would think, *The problem is your thoughts.* Every experience and event was filtered through these problematic thoughts, and she didn't seem to be aware of it.

One weekend, I was visiting a friend who is a social worker, and she began telling me about how her "core beliefs" about herself had shifted since we had first met some twenty years earlier. As we talked, I had an epiphany about what was going on with Izzy: Her core beliefs about herself were distorting her ability to grow and thrive as a teacher. I'd never heard of the phrase *core beliefs* before, and asked my friend to explain them. The following are the key ideas I gleaned:

- Core beliefs are stubborn, ingrained, and hard to change. They can feel like a part of us, inseparable from who we are. Sometimes they can be problematic.
- Worthlessness—a general sense that you're inherently flawed or incompetent—can be a core belief. Another example of a problematic core belief is feeling unlovable and assuming that others won't understand or accept you.
- Some core beliefs were formed in specific periods of our lives, maybe for good reasons, but we may no longer need them.
- Awareness of our core beliefs allows us to evaluate and change them.

As I researched core beliefs, I learned that problematic core beliefs tend to fall into common themes, including worthlessness, unlovability, lack of trust, helplessness, superiority, self-sacrificingness, perfectionism, and negativity. These are described in Appendix E, Common Problematic Core Beliefs. I suspected that Izzy was operating from a core belief of worthlessness.

The next time we met, I said, "I am really committed to supporting you in your development as a teacher, and I've been doing some learning that I want to share with you." I then described core beliefs and what I'd learned about worthlessness, and before I could ask her what she thought, she burst into tears. "What a relief to hear that," she finally said, which surprised me.

"What do you mean?" I asked.

"Yes, I often feel worthless," she replied, "but I've never recognized that, and probably would have been afraid to conclude that, but knowing that this is a thing, that other people deal with it too, makes me feel strangely better."

"What do you think it looks or sounds like when you're operating from that belief?" I asked. Izzy named a list of what she saw as indicators that the belief was just below her awareness. These included doubting everything she did, being super self-critical, and overreacting to criticism or feedback.

"If you operate from that belief, what's possible for you as a teacher and human being?" I asked.

"I'm going to continue to feel terrible and to suck at my job, and I won't help the kids I came here to help," she said.

"What could you tell yourself when that belief pops up? When you see it behind something you're feeling or saying or doing?" I asked.

Izzy paused. "I could tell it to go to hell," she said. I laughed. "And," she continued, "I could say, 'I know where that core belief came from, but it's not true. I don't have to let that belief affect me.'" I didn't probe about where Izzy's belief had come from; that's what a therapist does, not a coach. Uncovering the source of problematic core beliefs can be empowering because it enables us to distinguish their origins, the role they played when we adopted those beliefs, and their relevance now. Sometimes I suggest that someone I'm coaching work with a therapist to explore the origins of her core beliefs, especially really stubborn core beliefs.

Izzy called me a few days after we'd had this conversation. "I've been tracking how often I find myself running up against this belief that I'm unworthy," she said, "and so far this week it's happened 17 times."

"It's been so good to track them," she said. "Every time I recognize that I'm responding to one, I say, 'There's that problematic core belief,' and it makes it a little weaker. *I* don't suck—the *belief* sucks. I get to decide whether or not to listen to it."

Identifying Problematic Core Beliefs

Problematic core beliefs are those you hold to be true all of the time. They are global, not situational. One of the problems with such core beliefs is that because they filter your world for you, they also filter out the evidence against them. If you hold a core belief of "I don't fit in anywhere," you're unlikely to find a place where you feel you fit in, because your attention is drawn to evidence that upholds this core belief.

How do you know what your problematic core beliefs are? If you have a really hard time believing a more balanced interpretation of an event, then it's likely there's a core belief in the way. In the workbook, you'll find exercises to help you understand your problematic core beliefs and dislodge them from your mind.

᠅᠅

Do you see how the source of resilience lies in how you interpret events? How you might unlock the door to resilience by recognizing your thoughts, ridding yourself of those that don't serve you, and creating new thoughts? Can you glimpse the freedom behind empowering stories?

You have the power to select your thoughts, so what do you want to think? Which thoughts might help you live a happy and meaningful life? Which stories would allow you to fulfill your purpose at work?

Crafting New Stories

As your distorted thoughts and problematic core beliefs crumble, you need to identify empowering thoughts for your mind to latch on to. Creating these new story lines takes practice, and that practice solidifies empowering stories so that you can more easily find them next time there's an event to be interpreted. Then, next time your principal walks down the hall and ignores you, rather than clinging by default to a story line that emerges from a place of worthlessness and fear, your mind attaches itself to a stronger story that your principal is preoccupied and laser focused, and her behavior has nothing to do with you.

Throughout this book, I'm offering you new stories to live into. The workbook activities are also guides to crafting those stories. Let's look at three routines that are especially powerful for crafting new stories and that you can apply to the many habits we're exploring in this book: Visualizing what you want to be true, using affirmations, and setting intentions.

Visualization

One way to begin identifying new story lines is to visualize what you'd like to be true. You can literally close your eyes and create images in your mind's eye, or you can draw or write or talk to someone else about what you're envisioning. For example, if you want to be a part of a healthy professional community, visualize yourself there. Imagine the conversations you'd have with colleagues. Write down what you hear people saying to each other and to you, such as "We'd love to hear your thoughts on that situation" or "How did you respond when a student did that in your class? or "We're so glad you're on our team! We're so lucky." Visualize how your colleagues would smile when they see you arrive at the meeting; visualize how you'd feel when you leave school and head home.

If you intend to abandon narratives that don't serve you, you need to craft the new ones that you'd like to live in. Maybe you want to teach and be free of the story line that your students don't respect you. What would that look like? You need to get creative. If you can't see an alternate reality, it'll be hard to find it. This might feel hard: After all, how can you visualize something you don't know? If I told you to visualize a sharzetmsuao, you might have a hard time because you don't know what that is. (I made that word up—don't Google it.) Maybe you think, *I have no idea what it would feel like to teach and feel respected.* You can't even draw a picture in your mind. But other people know what that feels like. Ask them. It's like putting on a costume. Just because you aren't a fairy godmother doesn't mean you can't imagine what it feels like to be one. You need to start constructing a new mental model for yourself, a new story, if you want to inhabit it. And I think you actually might have some tiny little ideas about what it could feel like to be respected by your students, so don't engage in that black-and-white, *I have NO idea* thinking.

Here's another tip at this stage of the process: Embellish your stories; go wild with them. These are your thoughts. You can take them as far as you want. Script the words you want to say, what you want to hear, and what you want to think.

Affirmations

As you do this work of creating new narratives, try using affirmations. This practice may sound hokey or New Agey, but there's science behind it: Saying affirmations to yourself raises your levels of feel-good hormones and pushes your brain to form new clusters of "positive thought" neurons. This is basic rewiring for your mind. It's simple, easy, and powerful.

Tailor your affirmations so that the language resonates for you—because you're going to say them only to yourself. They need to be short and positive and to feel good when you say them. The most powerful affirmations will be those that you create, but these will get you started:

- I'll get through this.
- I am powerful.
- I'm valuable, and I belong.
- Everything is connected.
- I am enough. I do enough.
- Every day, I'm a better teacher.
- Difficult moments pass quickly.

Intention Setting

Intention setting is a practice that helps you form new stories. You can set an intention before you do anything—teach, go to a meeting, talk to a difficult student's parent, grade papers, and so on. It's a simple routine in which you make a statement to yourself about how you intend to experience something or be in a situation. Here are some examples of intentions:

- I'm going to be calm and patient with my fifth period today.
- I'm going to listen to understand in our grade-level team meeting.
- I'll be open to feedback in my evaluation conference.
- I'll enjoy the field trip.

An intention gives your mind a story to live into. It gives it direction. It also primes your mind to make the choices that will allow it to fulfill your intention. If you've told your mind that your intention is to enjoy the field trip, your mind might call out some validating piece of data when it sees evidence of your intention: *Hey, look at Katy's expression right now! She's enthralled!* And as you register the delightful expression on your student's face, you recognize how much you're enjoying the experience. If you've told yourself that you're going to listen to understand in a meeting, then when your mind starts down a route of thinking that whatever another teacher is saying is wrong, and it starts arguing with what he is saying, another part of your mind speaks up and says, *Hey, my intention is to listen today, so let me do that.*

Dr. Simon, a superintendent from Nebraska, attended a couple of my workshops. He was an older man who had lived his whole life in the Midwest and wore a suit every day. He told me this the second time we met:

"At your first workshop in Oakland, Elena, you talked about intention setting and I thought, *Now I know I'm in California,* but because I'm an eager learner, I decided to try it back home. A couple months ago, I had a school board meeting that I knew would be contentious and that would push me to my limits. I set an intention before the meeting, and I held myself to it—and that was the best school board meeting of my 12 years in this district. I was different. The board members were different. And I attribute this to my intention. I'm a convert now, and I've been spreading intention setting throughout my district. It might be a touchy-feely California thing, but it works, and I'm looking for things that work."

Setting an intention gives you an opportunity to declare how you want to be in a situation—and, ultimately, that's all you have true control over. How you show up. How you experience something. This is one of the most powerful routines you can integrate into your daily life. I can almost guarantee that if you try it every day for a month, you'll feel very different, perhaps even transformed. There's more direction on how to do this in the workbook.

> *We are our stories, stories that can be both prison and the crowbar to*
> *break open the door of that prison; we make stories to save ourselves*
> *or to trap ourselves or others, stories that lift us up or smash us against*
> *the stone wall of our own limits and fears. Liberation is always in part*
> *a storytelling process: breaking stories, breaking silences, making new*
> *stories. A free person tells her own story. A valued person lives in a*
> *society in which her story has a place.*
> REBECCA SOLNIT

Storytelling for Collective Empowerment

We all tell stories about the events that happen in our days and throughout our lives. We've explored how your interpretation can undermine or boost your resilience. The stories we tell ourselves become narratives that we share with the world—the stories we tell others. But once we reach the social level of storytelling, then power and privilege play a greater role, influencing which stories are told, who tells them, and how we hear those stories. Let's consider storytelling outside your individual psyche and in the broader context. Social storytelling can also be a path toward building the resilience of a school faculty, of staff across a district, and of a citizenry.

A Legacy of Destructive Dominant Narratives

Dehumanizing narratives of women, poor people, rural people, people with dark skin, people with disabilities, and people who aren't gender conforming or heterosexual are still pervasive in our world. Perpetuating them undermines our collective resilience. It is our responsibility to recognize when we tell them and when we hear them being told—and to unravel them.

Dehumanizing narratives have been used by dominant social, political, and economic powers as a way to objectify people and disempower them. As Europe began colonizing Africa, Asia, and the Americas, intellectuals crafted narratives about the cognitive inferiority of the inhabitants of those regions as a justification for their enslavement and exploitation. We still live with these narratives in our world; some have softened or shifted, some are disguised and insidious, and some are still overt.

One way that these destructive dominant narratives have operated is by silencing the stories of others. Too many people have been prevented from disseminating their stories to large audiences; access to the tools of speaking, writing, and reading has been restricted. Slave owners knew that if slaves could read and write, their stories would make the brutality of the system hard to justify. In other times and places, when the stories of the marginalized make it into the public domain, their stories are discredited, or sometimes just destroyed. One of the first steps taken by almost every authoritarian regime is to ban and burn books. Whenever people are silenced, and when the stories of some groups can't be told, collective social health, well-being, and resilience are undermined.

The healing of our world may lie in how we make space for stories to be told, how we listen to stories, and that we tell our stories. As Nigerian writer Chimamanda Ngozi Adichie said in her 2009 TED Talk, "Stories have been used to dispossess and to malign. But stories can also be used to empower and humanize. Stories can break the dignity of a people, but stories can also repair that dignity."

Storytelling is political. Telling your story can be an act of liberation. Listening to the stories of others can be an act of solidarity. Telling stories, and listening to stories, therefore are mechanisms to boost our collective resilience—whether at a school site, in a district, or in our country.

Speak Your Truth and Listen to the Truths of Others

While we work on a grand scale to shift access to power and privilege, there are things that you can do, today, to increase collective resilience. Invite someone you don't know too well to tell you her story. Pledge to do your very best to listen with an open heart and an open mind. If you disagree with someone else's opinion, set an intention to understand why he believes whatever he believes. You don't need to agree; you just need to listen to what he thinks, to be curious about where his beliefs come from, and to humanize him. Listen responsibly, holding the person's words in confidence, grateful to be a listener.

If someone invites you to tell your story, speak your truth. Hone your speaking skills and, as best you can, tell your story in a way that others can hear you. Be mindful. "Speak your truth" isn't permission to wield words as weapons. Nor is it an effective way to convince someone of your opinion or to make her hear you.

Within schools, there are many things we disagree on: What to teach, how to teach it, how to manage student behavior, and so on. We're not very good at having conversations about these disagreements, and conflict has undermined innumerable promising projects in schools. What would it take to listen to each other? And what might be possible if we did?

Listening to one another's stories might help us bridge our differences. Podcast host Krista Tippett writes, "I can disagree with your opinion, it turns out, but I can't disagree with your experience. And once I have a sense of your experience, you and I are in relationship, acknowledging the complexity in each other's position, listening less guardedly. The difference in our opinions will probably remain intact, but it no longer defines what is possible between us" (2016, p. 22).

Locate Opinion in Story

What are your opinions about how to manage student behavior? Is there a story from which your opinion emerges?

My opinion on student behavior is rooted in a story that begins with my little brother whose behavior, as a child, was perceived as being out of control. He was sent to the principal's office more times than we could count. If I was to tell you this story, I would tell you about his epilepsy and brain tumor, about the anxiety in our home after my father left our lives, and about the teachers who didn't know what to do with him. I'd tell you about how he never felt as though he belonged in school and how he dropped out on the day he turned 16.

Tell stories to help others understand your beliefs and opinions. Offer your stories, not in the hope that they will change anyone else, but because they are your stories to tell and they deserve to live outside you. And when you are a listener, allow the stories of others to change you.

Acknowledging Context: Organizational Narratives

Like individuals, organizations tell stories, and organizational narratives can bolster or undermine the individual stories we tell.

What You Tell Matters

In some schools, the same narrative has been told for decades: *What do you expect us to do given the circumstances we're working in?* Or *The district will always screw us over. Doesn't matter who the superintendent is.* These stories become embedded in the way things are done and are reflected in a myriad of behaviors. They work in much the same way as personal stories, beliefs, and thoughts: They help us feel empowered and resilient, or they contribute to stagnation and burnout.

General assumptions—positive and negative—about schools, leaders, and education can sound like any of these:

- All students can learn.
- Teachers want to help kids.
- School districts (and organizations) are characterized by complexity, ambiguity, and paradox.
- Leaders make decisions based on their personal political agendas.
- Schools are designed to protect the status quo.
- Schools are failing kids.
- Kids need to be controlled.

Which of these do you hold? Which do you hear echoed in the corridors of your school and central offices?

Destructive organizational narratives are tricky because there is usually some truth in what is said, but they are ultimately demoralizing, and they disconnect us from our power. Such stories are reflected in statements like, "This school has failed kids for too long" or "Until X, Y, and Z happen, we'll never be able to build the kind of school we want" or "Given what's going on in this community, there's not much more we can do." Identify the stories and listen for those people who agree with, feed, and uphold that narrative.

If you find yourself mired in disempowering organizational narratives, either interrupt these stories or get yourself out of there. If you're energized to take them on in your school or district, find allies so that you don't get worn down. And be conscious of the stories you're telling about the battle, the destructive organizational stories, and those who believe in them. Otherwise, you can inadvertently layer new destructive stories on top of the others.

That You Tell Your Story Matters, Too

At North Star School, there is no detention, no suspension, no uniform, no "walk in silent and straight lines." Students who have been historically underserved direct their own learning for the majority of the day, track their progress and design their courses of learning. From the outside, especially at the beginning, things looked a

---

Implications for Leaders

- What you think and believe have a tremendous impact on your organization. It is your responsibility to tell stories that cultivate resilience in your staff and ultimately serve children. If you find that you tell destructive or unhelpful stories, then it is your responsibility to shift them. You may have inherited a narrative at your school, so craft a new one in partnership with staff. Otherwise you may be responsible for propagating an unhelpful story.

- You don't necessarily need to do this alone. Seek out colleagues who are committed to telling empowering narratives, or find a leadership coach. Start this inquiry by paying attention to your own thoughts and listening for your stories, and by inviting staff to share the narratives they hear you telling.

- Your stories matter the most because they shape the stories that others tell. If you've found yourself blaming the district for all the woes at your school for many years, it may take time to shed that narrative. And remember: When you tell stories, your staff need to trust that you believe them, so tell the truest story you can.

little chaotic. In the school's early months, district leaders walked through the halls and expressed concern. Passing period was loud, kids wore hoodies, they walked arm in arm—and none of these things happened in the network's other schools. But the principal, a fierce, mighty, and optimistic woman, preempted central office anxiety and said, repeatedly, "We will tell the story of what we're doing here. We won't leave this story to be told by others, because they don't have the insights and understandings we have about our students." In a variety of creative ways that included video, parent panels, and student writing, North Star told its story and held outside concerns at bay while it developed a different way of doing school. It became the district's shining star, and its students have succeeded in ways they never had before.

When you're trying to do something new or different, whether in your classroom, department, school, or district, it's critical that *you* tell the story of what's happening. If you don't, other people will do it for you, and you might not like their narrative.

Regardless of where you are in your organization, be mindful of the stories you believe, those that you tell, and those that you create and put forward.

 ## *A Dive into Love*

Why reflect on love in a book about resilience in schools or in a chapter about telling empowering stories? Because love is the most powerful story we can tell; love is a story that deserves to be told, just as much as grief and pain. I hope the inclusion of this section surfaces our discomfort with discussing love in a school library during a Wednesday afternoon PD session, or our yearning to do so. What might happen if we had a conversation with colleagues about love?

When I want to talk about my love for my students, I come up against the limits of terminology. Here in the West, in this era, we have a dearth of words for love. The ancient Greeks had a more expansive vocabulary and offered us *eros,* romantic love; *filia,* the love of friendship; and *agape,* the expression of kindness that you extend to a stranger. What might be the word I could use to describe the dense, saturated emotion I felt for my students? For now, let's just use love—and let stories define it.

I didn't anticipate the expansive love that surged in me when 32 second graders burst in on that first September morning at Stonehurst Elementary School in deep East Oakland. It was unexpected, uncomfortable, and unwieldy. Planning lessons and developing grading systems were easy in comparison to managing the consuming care I felt for Oscar and Manuel, for Billy and Lizette and Vanessa—their names and faces come back without effort even though 22 years have passed. We always remember first love.

What if I asked you to tell me a story about a student you've loved?

I'd also want to know about the times your heart has been broken—perhaps at school, perhaps beyond the classroom walls.

I've found that love was what kept me going through years of challenging work in schools. There were many years, many students (I'm afraid there is no other phrase) *with whom I fell in love.* It was not all easy going. I found some students harder to connect with. Others triggered me. I don't pretend to be saintly, and I don't know if all my students felt loved by me. When we talk about love, we also have to talk about the moments when we missed the mark, when we didn't love, when heartbreak was self-inflicted. It would be a relief to include these topics in our conversations.

But let's start somewhere easy—with talking about love for students—so that we may see each other in an expansive realm and build that requisite trust. I've never met an educator who hasn't been able to tell me about one student she has loved. As she tells me about that young person, it's almost as if I can see the molecules of her being rapidly rearrange themselves into a renewed person: Eyes light up, posture straightens, facial muscles relax, tone and cadence become musical, and effortless smiles emerge. Storytelling is energizing, affirming, and anchoring, and some of the best ones remind us that we crave love and yearn to love others.

Eventually, we'll get to conversations about the kind of love that Dr. Martin Luther King Jr. insisted we embody, the kind of love that saints and Buddhas challenge us to demonstrate unflinchingly. What would it look like to practice this kind of love at school? What would it take for us to engage in our teaching, leadership, and coaching from a place of unconditional love? Think now of a colleague with whom you've had conflict, perhaps someone you don't like. What kind of love could bridge your many disagreements and divergent perspectives? What would be possible if we could do that?

In most schools, the list of nondiscussables is a mile long. It includes not only disagreements, conflict, and difference but also love. Let's start there and work our way through the list. Love deserves to be an agenda item on a Wednesday afternoon meeting in the library. Love deserves to be an explicit part of our storytelling.

Disposition: Optimism

A pessimist sees the difficulty in every opportunity;
an optimist sees the opportunity in every difficulty.
WINSTON CHURCHILL

When I first met Dee, the new principal of North Star School, I wondered if she was delusional: Although she seemed aware of the challenges she was walking into, her confidence in her ability to tackle them was astronomical. Dee was taking over a school that had struggled for decades, one with a predominantly new teaching staff; and at the time, the Common Core Standards were first making their way into curriculum, instructional practices, and assessment.

I asked her what she needed in order to have a successful launch of the year. "We've got everything we need already," she said. "These children are fantastic! They are kings and queens waiting for us to show them their thrones!" I commented that absenteeism rates for kids the previous year had been around 25%. "Well," she said, "we'll make this a place they can't stay away from. Within three years, we'll get that number down to 5%."

I expressed concern about the number of new initiatives that teachers would need to adopt, and the fact that she had so many new teachers on staff. "I'm grateful that I get to usher them into this profession," she responded, and she told me about how her first principal became her primary role model. "And yes, there are too many initiatives. That was a mistake on my part. I need to prioritize them and cut some out this year."

I'm not a pessimistic person, but I saw a lot of challenges at North Star. I was worried that Dee, who was only in her fourth year as a principal, would struggle and perhaps quit—as the previous three principals had done. Dee, interestingly, saw all of the challenges—but she also took a long view about the situation, and she was steadfastly confident. Regardless of the block in the road—be it pebble or boulder size—she had ideas about what to do and how to get around it.

One day, the school was broken into, and all the computers were stolen and the rooms were vandalized. Dee's response was, "Well, now we can use the insurance money to update our tech, and the rooms needed a paint job anyway."

"Have you always been this optimistic?" I asked.

Dee laughed. "You'd probably be surprised to know that when I started teaching, my principal jokingly called me Debbie Downer. I used to see the worst possible scenario whenever anything happened. It's been a journey for me to become optimistic."

As I watched Dee lead her school through a remarkable change that first year, I often thought about the role her optimistic disposition played in her own resilience, as well as in boosting her staff's. She was never naïve or unrealistic, she didn't downplay the truly difficult obstacles or the pain that anyone experienced, but she always maintained an attitude of optimism, which was infectious among kids and adults.

The Basics About Optimism

The experts affirm Dee's story: Optimism can be learned and strengthened, and it's a key trait of the resilient. It's not set at a fixed and permanent level, so if you currently tend toward pessimism, know that you can become more optimistic. This description of the two kinds of optimists helps us distinguish between a leader like Dee and a delusional Pollyanna:

- **Realistic optimists** like Dee seek to fully understand what is really going on, including any ways in which they might have played a role in causing the adversity. They believe they can make a difference in the future in spite of the challenges in the current reality. Realistic optimists have the ability to maintain a positive outlook in the face of adversity without denying the constraints posed by reality. Realistic optimists take the long view, because in the short term, even optimists can have negative thoughts. They believe that good things can happen, while still recognizing that a lot of work will be required.
- **Unrealistic optimists,** Pollyannas, are quick to make judgments about reality without taking time to understand what's happening. They underestimate the risks that adversity poses, and they firmly believe that they can make the best-case outcomes happen in the future.

An optimist is neither naïve nor idealistic, neither in denial nor blind to the realities of life. Optimists

- Look at the big picture and identify all possible options
- See opportunity in adversity
- Search for root causes of challenges and don't play the blame game
- Enjoy the journey—and see everything as part of the journey
- Understand that life contains ups and downs
- Accept that life can be unfair, difficult, and tough
- Recognize that struggles are outside them, are temporary, and are specific

- Look for solutions and don't complain
- Use positive self-talk
- Seek happiness within
- Appreciate little and big things
- Avoid negative people, because emotions are contagious
- Let go and forgive
- Smile

When I first read this list, I thought about Dee, checking off each action in the affirmative. I came to know Dee well. She certainly had days when her hope was damped, when she was tired, and when she was sad. But she forged on like few other leaders I've ever seen. She stayed at North Star for five years, during which very few teachers left her school, student absenteeism dropped to about 3% within a couple of years, and children rose to meet the opportunities with which they were presented.

In my research on resilience, the disposition that's discussed and referenced perhaps more than any other is optimism. The resilient are undeniably, unequivocally optimistic. Which doesn't mean they don't have days when they feel sad or worried. Over and over, I read about how we can increase our optimism, which for me was a good reminder, as I have tendencies toward being what the experts call a "realistic pessimist." I've definitely been intentional about cultivating my optimism for many years, the key to which is to be mindful of the stories I tell. This is the place of power—our interpretation, our story crafting—and it's the precise place where we can feed the seeds of our optimism.

Choose Your Stories with Care

We craft a short story every time we interpret an event—a kid ignoring us, a colleague being appointed to head a committee that we wanted to head, a short email from our boss. These interpretations boost or drain our resilience. These short stories also do something else: They strengthen the dominant narratives we tell about our lives. An overarching story line could be, "I'm not good enough" or "These kids don't respect me" or "I can make my life what I want it to be." Every short story fuels, shifts, or undermines those grand narratives. Choose your stories carefully.

Individual stories become collective tales. We craft institutional narratives that tell the stories of our schools or districts. And stories are also woven at a societal level: "Teachers are the hardest working and least appreciated group" and

"Those who can't, teach." What are those dominant narratives? Who tells them? Do they resonate for us? How can we dismantle those that ultimately don't serve us?

Storytellers have always held key positions in society; the stories we craft predict our futures, encapsulate our legacies, and impact our resilience. You have a choice, so tell powerful stories.

CHAPTER REFLECTION

- What insight did you gain about the stories you tell?
- Which feelings might shift if you told different stories?
- Which sections of this chapter helped you gain new understanding of yourself?

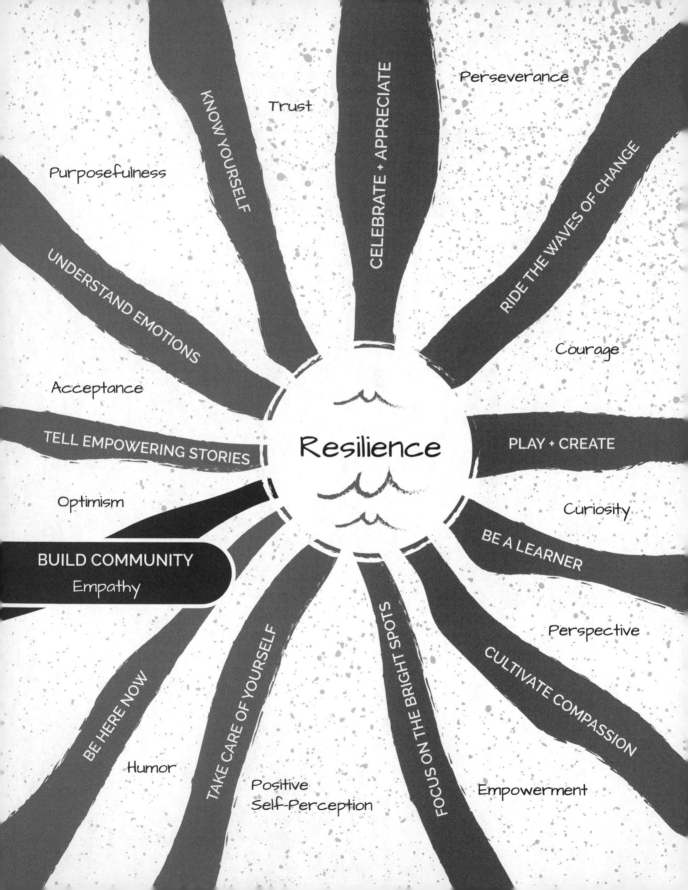

CHAPTER 4

Build Community

We are social beings, and we need each other to thrive. A strong, healthy community can bolster us through challenging moments and bring joy to our lives. When we build community, we can build empathy for each other; and building empathy for each other helps us build community.

September: During the month when we're surrounded by new people, building strong relationships must be our primary goal. The community we build is foundational for our resilience.

❧❧

In the first month of my first year teaching, I made my way to the staff lunchroom every day and plunked myself down at a table with colleagues. Not all teachers ate in the lunchroom—the newer teachers were noticeably absent—and I wondered about those who weren't there. Nevertheless, the lunchroom was filled with veteran teachers whom I assumed knew the community in which we worked. Wanting to glean from their wisdom, I stayed at the table and eagerly asked questions.

Instead, I found cynical, burned-out teachers who viciously complained about their students, disparaged their students' families, and bemoaned the lack of discipline. The former teacher of one of my second graders said, "Crack addicts, hos, and thugs—that's all that's around him, and you can tell by his behavior already. He'll be locked up by the time he's 15, you'll see." Another teacher offered this advice: "Treat them like they'll be treated in jail—order, routine, strict consequences, isolation—that's the kindest thing you can do for them so that they'll be prepared when they get there." When I asked questions about instruction, engagement strategies, and curriculum, I was handed worksheets. "The trick to surviving as a teacher is the copy machine," I was told. "Get there early because it'll be broken by 8:00 a.m. from overuse."

By October, I ate alone at my desk every day. I felt that I didn't belong in that lunchroom. But because I sought community, I sought out kindred spirits. In my second year teaching, I had lunch every day with Bettina, my school's speech therapist. Those 28 daily minutes of friendship, laughter, and camaraderie were a primary source of resilience.

Some years later, I developed a deeper understanding of my veteran colleagues. Many had taught in that neighborhood for decades; several teachers came from that community. Cumulatively, they had seen hundreds of former students end up in places that they never would have wished for them. These teachers may have felt powerless and resigned to the violence of systemic oppression. This didn't justify their ineffective instructional strategies or the way they spoke about children, but I saw how these teachers had also been chewed up by the system.

Throughout my journey as a teacher, I continued to seek out those who wanted to learn and whose hearts remained open to their students, and mentors who imparted wisdom and encouraged my convictions. I had students who became like family, whom 20 years after teaching them, I still talk to, addressing them as *mijo,* "son," or *mija,* "daughter." Forming community goes straight to the heart of what makes our work so rewarding: It is where connection and joy lay.

Why Focus on Community Building?

In the 1940s, the psychologist Abraham Maslow published a now-famous pyramid, the "Hierarchy of Needs" in humans, which sought to explain motivation. Maslow suggested that we work our way up the pyramid, starting at the bottom with physiological needs like sleep, food, and water. Safety needs, such as physical shelter and bodily health, come next. Whereas the bottom two levels are essential to our survival, the rest of the needs, Maslow argued, are nonessential. These are the need for love, a sense of belonging, and being esteemed. At the top of the pyramid is the need for self-actualization, for reaching one's full potential.

Humans Need Community

Matthew Lieberman, a social neuroscientist, has done research that's relevant to building community. He argues that Maslow had the order of this pyramid wrong. We all need food, shelter, and water, of course, but Lieberman points out that infants cannot get these needs met by themselves. They only survive if they have a caregiver who is committed to meeting their biological needs, which suggests that *social connection is our primary need* and should be at the base of the pyramid. Lieberman writes, "This restructuring of Maslow's pyramid tells us something critical about 'who we are.' Love and belonging might seem like a convenience we can live without, but our biology is built to thirst for connection because it is linked to our most basic survival needs" (2013, p. 43).

This theory is validated in Ben Rawlence's heartbreaking book, *City of Thorns* (2017), about the largest refugee camp in the world. In the desert of Northern Kenya some half a million East Africans eke out a meager living in this camp. Rawlence observes people endure a week of hunger in order to afford a phone and access to social media to connect to loved ones from whom they've been separated. They choose community over food because we need each other that badly.

In focusing on community building, we have an opportunity to sharpen our definition of a healthy community. This may mean different things for different people. For me, a community that fosters my resilience is one that is inclusive of different ways of being and one in which people listen well, individual and group accomplishments are celebrated, unhealthy conflict is addressed, and there's transparent decision making. My resilience has been undermined when I've been in a professional community that doesn't include these elements. What kind of community do you need to fuel your resilience?

The subject of what constitutes a healthy community is worthy of close investigation, and lies on the periphery of our conversation. My book *The Art of Coaching Teams: Cultivating Resilient Communities That Transform Schools,* is a deep consideration of this topic and could be a resource if you want to dive deeper into this subject.

Strong Communities Retain Educators

Here are the main reasons why we need to focus on community: Teachers don't leave strong communities, and children thrive in strong communities. The large urban district in which I worked for 19 years was rife with problems, and salaries were significantly lower than those in neighboring districts. I knew that if I drove an additional five minutes into another district, I could make an additional $10,000 per year. Yet I turned down a higher salary in favor of staying in a community where I belonged and felt loved.

What the Research Says

Here's a summary of research on the topic of resilience and community: *You cannot thrive unless you're in healthy relationships.* The resilient surround themselves with supportive friends and family and are in relationships characterized by mutual trust and empathy (Sarason, Sarason, Hacker, and Basham, 1985). A wide network helps us feel connected, whereas a lack of social support can engender feelings of social alienation, as well as depression, anxiety, and burnout. Researchers have spent time accumulating these findings, but I'm sure you know them to be true.

Ironically, in spite of the fact that teachers spend their days with dozens or hundreds of other people, teaching is one of the most isolating professions. That's because the kind of company needed to counter isolation is that of *peers*.

This research is relevant when we need to make decisions about how to spend time and resources. When you have 28 minutes for lunch each day, yes, you could sit at your desk and work or browse social media, or you could find a colleague to eat with—which might boost your resilience. If you are a team leader with only 55 minutes for the weekly meeting, 8 minutes for team building might boost the resilience of members. If you are a principal, taking your staff away on a two-day retreat before school starts in order to lay a foundation for trust and understanding can pay off in the bonds that are built between staff. Yes, it is expensive to do retreats, but teacher turnover is also expensive.

Relationships with Students and Parents

Peer relationships are essential, but so are the relationships teachers have with the young people with whom they spend the most time. Although I always worked to build healthy community with every group of students I taught, one experience transformed my notion of what might be possible. As a founding teacher of the Oakland public school ASCEND (we opened in 2001), I taught humanities to the same group of 45 students for their three years of middle school. Being together for that length of time and starting something new together helped us form close bonds. These were my most rewarding years of teaching, and the connections I built with these young people endure today. There is research indicating that knowing your students contributes to resilience, and as I reflect on the years when I felt the happiest and most effective as a teacher, those were the ones when I had the strongest relationships with my students (Beltman, Mansfield, and Price, 2011; Farber, 1991).

In those years at ASCEND, I also found community among my students' parents. When my son was born and I lacked older wise women in my life, the mothers of my students generously shared their wisdom. I often felt a sense of true partnership as we worked to raise our children, to guide them through challenging stages, and to problem-solve when they faced obstacles. These were also unique and nourishing relationships, characterized by mutual respect and appreciation. What kept me at ASCEND for many years were the relationships I had with colleagues, students, and their parents, and these relationships were critical when times were rough.

Implications for Leaders

Support from university staff, mentors, and coaches is vital to helping new teachers develop their academic, practical, and emotional competencies (Clements, 2013). There is also evidence showing how mutually supportive relationships with peers improve the "community of learning," which then enhances the ability of new teachers to cope with stress as well as develop their pedagogical skill set (Kevern and Webb, 2004). Peer support also helps new teachers develop a professional identity and enhances their commitment to teaching, which has the potential to improve retention (Clements, 2013). And there's an abundance of research concluding that social support is one of the most important mechanisms by which new and novice educators build their resilience (Collins, 2008; Jensen, Trollope, Waters, and Everson, 2008; Wilks and Spivey, 2010).

It is often assumed that people entering the helping professions already possess highly developed social skills, so neither teacher training programs nor new teacher PD focuses on expanding these competencies (Morrison, 2005). Research on resilience has implications for preservice programs, for new teacher support and development, and for the coaching that's offered to new teachers. This support should have as a central component the cultivation of emotional intelligence, social skills, and communication. You want your teachers to build healthy communities with each other.

We might wish that all new teachers arrived with these refined skills and knowledge sets, but they don't. We can either keep wishing or design PD that responds to reality. Yes, we can refine hiring techniques so that we're more likely to attract, hire, and retain those with stronger social and emotional intelligence (EQ), but, more than likely, we'll need to continue cultivating it—the stresses and pressures of teaching have their unique particularities, and even someone with strong EQ and resilience will be tested during her first years in the classroom.

Professional learning aiming to develop these skills can take place in small groups (perhaps in a new teacher professional learning community [PLC]), in one-on-one coaching sessions, and in whole-staff PD sessions. Here's the beginning of a list of topics that new teachers (and perhaps most teachers) need to explore:

- What to do when you disagree with a colleague
- How to respond to teachers in the lunchroom who are negative
- How to ask your principal for more support and help
- How to disagree with your principal
- How to develop a good relationship with your principal
- What to do with upset parents
- What to do when you feel as though a student dislikes you
- What to do when you dislike a student

I'm sure you could add dozens of topics to this list. Think about your own early experiences as an educator. Which skills might have helped you build healthy communities with colleagues, administrators, students, and their families? Leaders: If you want to stop the exodus of teachers from your school, create a nourishing, healthy community.

Trust: The Foundation of a Healthy Community

There's no way to avoid the fact that trust is a prerequisite for a healthy community. If you're trying to build community, whether that's among students in your classroom or with colleagues at your school, focus on building trust. Although positional leaders play key roles in establishing the conditions for trust among the members of a school community, you can't just sit back and wait until those conditions are optimal. You can actively seek out and build trust with colleagues.

Although we may all have intuitive feelings about what trust is, it has helped me to have an intellectual understanding of it. I have a strong sense of what it's like to trust someone, and when I think back to my years as a teacher, memories come to mind—for example, of the absolute trust I had in Bettina, my speech therapist colleague at my first school. Having a framework for trust has helped guide me to be more trustworthy and to recognize the behaviors in others that might lead me to trust them. It has also helped me reach out and cultivate trust with others.

What Is Trust?

Think about what trust has felt like in your personal and professional life. Call to mind someone you really trust. What led you to trust him? What do you think has led others to trust you?

Trust is an emotional state. It is the feeling of confidence we have in another's character and competence. Let's unpack this definition. *Character* is about integrity—how honest we are and how aligned our actions are with what we say, and whether our agenda is hidden or up front. *Competence* addresses skills and abilities: We trust people who have demonstrated that they have the skill and knowledge to do what they say they'll do. This element of trusting competence is very relevant in a professional setting. For example, I might *like* a colleague as a friend and believe that she'll have my back, but when it comes to her professional skill set, I may doubt whether she has the *competence* to teach my kids next year, which means I may not trust her. Distrust, therefore, is suspicion of integrity and capabilities, which is something I've witnessed in adult culture in many schools. Given that so much of the dysfunction in organizations can be traced back to a lack of trust, we need to spend time understanding this emotional state.

Relational Trust

Many years ago, learning about what's called *relational trust* helped me understand myself and the school at which I worked. It helped me recognize what I could do to change the experience I had working with colleagues; it also helped me recognize what I could not change. It helped me see how I could build stronger communities.

Relational trust, a concept put forth by researchers Bryk and Schneider (2002) refers to the trust that's a result of the interpersonal social exchanges that take place in a group setting. The following are three key findings from this research connecting to the role of community in resilience:

1. **Student learning is impacted by the amount of relational trust among adults.** Where there is high relational trust among staff and between staff and parents, students thrive. If you are in a school where there is low relational trust, the ramifications extend beyond the discomfort that's palpable any time staff come together. It means that students are being negatively impacted.

2. **For trust to exist, each group of adults who work in a school need to understand their own obligations, and they need clarity on what others do.** We depend on each other. Without each other, we can't achieve our goal of educating students. Role clarity is critical for trust to exist. It may be hard for me to trust my school's dean, for example, if I'm often wondering, *What does he do all day? He's either on the yard talking to kids or he's locked up in his office alone.*

3. **Trust is influenced by the conclusions we draw about our colleagues' intentions.** If I believe that my grade-level colleague is here to serve children, I trust her more. Many factors influence how we draw conclusions about our colleagues' intentions. These include our previous interactions with them, as well as assumptions about their race and ethnicity, gender, age, and educational background.

We draw conclusions about our colleagues' intentions based on our assessments in four areas: respect, personal regard, competence in core responsibilities, and personal integrity. When you feel that you can't trust someone, it's often because of your assessment of her in these areas. Think about a colleague whom you're not sure you really trust. Then ask yourself these questions:

Respect	• Do we genuinely talk and listen to one another?
	• Does she acknowledge my dignity and ideas?
	• Do we interact in a kind way?
Personal regard	• Do we care about each other both professionally and personally?
	• Is she willing to go the extra mile?
Competence in core responsibilities	• Do I believe in her ability and willingness to fulfill her responsibilities effectively?
Personal integrity	• Does she do what she says she'll do?
	• Do I trust her to put the interests of students first, especially when tough decisions need to be made?

When I reviewed these questions, thinking about a colleague I didn't really trust, I answered yes to the questions around respect and personal regard. But when I got to the question about competence in core responsibilities, I realized that I didn't think she was able to fulfill her responsibilities. That was why I had an unsettled feeling about trusting her. When I reviewed these questions again, thinking about a teacher whom I suspected didn't trust me, and I wondered why he didn't trust me, I stopped myself on the questions about personal regard. I realized that I wasn't sure whether I really cared about him personally or professionally. In theory, I did—because I care about human beings—but I didn't know him at all, and that felt like an obstacle to caring about him. When I put myself in his shoes, I could sense why he might distrust me: I didn't know him, and I didn't really care about him.

What does this mean concretely about building trust? For me it means that if I want others to trust me, I need to listen well, care about the other personally, believe in his competence, and do what I say I will do. These descriptors also help me understand why I may not trust someone who doesn't treat me kindly or who doesn't have the skill set she needs in order to fulfill the responsibilities of her role. Trust is complex and nuanced, and it lies at a nexus point of our past and present, our identities and purpose. An understanding of trust helps us make decisions that can foster our resilience and help us find healthy communities. In the workbook, there's an exercise to help you reflect on relational trust at your school.

Implications for Leaders

- Cultivating trust and creating the conditions for healthy communities are the primary charges of all leaders—whether you are a teacher building community in your classroom, a principal building trust among staff, or a superintendent building trust with the community you serve.
- To build trust, you must pay attention to listening and discourse, mission, vision and values, nonverbal communication, honoring commitments, and disagreement and conflict, as well as personal histories and differences. The community-building activities that most adults and kids engage in at the start of the year are not enough. A back-to-school BBQ does not build trust. Talking about what respectful communication sounds like does.
- Orchestrate neurobiology by creating situations that are low risk, in which people can learn about each other, engage in productive conversation, and have fun together. Aim to boost levels of oxytocin and dopamine by playing charades, building a Jenga tower, planting flowers, eating together—doing something outside the normal routines. Giving people 8 minutes at the start of a meeting to tell each other a story boosts oxytocin, according to research by Paul Zak (2014). Your job is to prime their minds to connect with each other and collaborate.

How to Build Community

Sometimes building community is described in a technical, superficial way. I've often read suggestions for how to build community that seem to skim the surface of social relationships and seem unlikely to create the kinds of truly resilient and healthy communities we all crave. For example, knowing your neighbors' names is certainly a part of building community, but their names are just the tip of the iceberg of things we need to know and of ways we need to communicate with our neighbors in order to actually create an inclusive community.

After considering many ways to build the communities in which we might all thrive, I landed on organizing my thoughts around four high-leverage strategies. I sought to group my ideas in ways that could be actionable, but that also honored the depth and challenges of building community. The four strategies are (1) refine your communication skills, (2) learn from body language, (3) increase cultural competence, and (4) address conflict. Figure 4.1, Building a Healthy Community, represents these four strategies.

In some ways, the overarching umbrella for building community should be cultural competence. This could be the lens through which we refine communication, learn from body language, and address conflict. However, I've teased these apart to look at each one in a more global way, and then focus on the cultural competence aspects of that strategy. This is not a comprehensive look; it's intended to provoke reflection and bring to the surface areas for further inquiry.

Refine Communication

How do you listen? Where does your mind go when you're listening? Sometimes, perhaps you're closely attending to what a speaker is saying, keeping your heart open and letting his words fill you. Other times, perhaps your mind wanders to a place of judgment or impatience, or perhaps you want to jump in and offer solutions and advice. It's time to take responsibility for how we've listened and for the questions we've asked. Listening lies at the center of healthy social relationships—it's time to attend to this skill set.

Constricted Listening

We have asked many questions that we disguised in armor, that marched out with the intent to provoke a fight. We have asked many questions that were proud of their brilliance and intellectual prowess, questions that sauntered forth with research tucked under their arms, assuming that erudite arrogance was acceptable

Figure 4.1 Building a Healthy Community

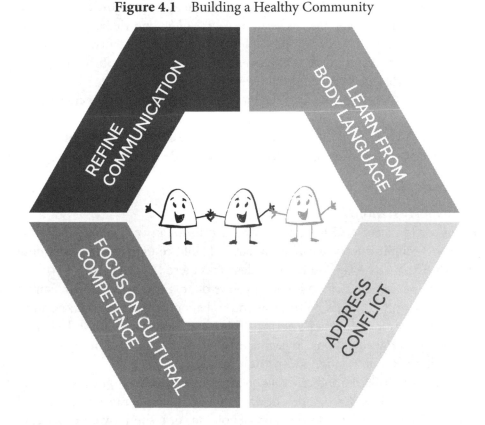

in the halls of learning institutions. We have asked questions that were feebly disguised manipulations.

Some of us discovered that our conversational militarism conflicted with our values, and we shifted tactics. We deluded ourselves into thinking we were listening by being silent while the other person spoke, and pausing for two seconds when she was done before making our point. This, however, is not listening. This is simply the technical skill of calculating seconds and monitoring utterances. We manipulated listening and responding to silence the other.

And then there is righteous indignation. This is the listening we do when there is only one heavily guarded mental gate through which all sounds pass into the fortress of Right. The sentries don't hesitate before beheading what looks like Wrong. No time for deeper understanding or to see the bigger picture or to hear the pain; no time for curiosity or compassion because that gate stands on Urgency. Justification has been amassed in volumes of injustices and statistics and THERE IS NO TIME.

There are other ways that we've listened: So that we can figure out how to Fix It and be the ones with all the answers, the source of all knowledge and solutions; the ones whom others need; the ones with the power. We've listened with pity, seeing another as small and weak. We've listened because we want affirmation, asking questions that disguise a need for validation.

Our constricted ways of listening may feel familiar, but we may crave more—real connection. We may have numbed ourselves to that desire, but occasionally it bursts forth. Constricted listening is suffocating. If we take responsibility for how we've listened, we can expand our listening and build stronger relationships with others.

Expansive Listening

In contrast to constricted listening is what I call *expansive listening*—a series of channels through which you can listen that will build connection and community. Table 4.1, Expansive Ways of Listening, describes these ways to listen.

Don't be ashamed of the listening you've done. Hold yourself with compassion and curiosity. You may be afraid as you embark on expansive listening and on asking new questions, and that's normal. This is unfamiliar terrain. And when you speak, ask generous questions. Invite honesty and dignity. Allow your questions to come from the kindest, most tender part of yourself.

Expansive listening and generous questioning take courage and practice. They take fierce commitment to a different way of being. They require a voyage into the unknown. You do not need to abandon all opinions or dishonor your experiences. You do need to be willing to be changed by what you hear. Our hearts and minds are designed with tremendous capacity for flexibility and expansion. This kind of listening is possible.

Asking Questions and Responding

What do generous questions that come from expansive listening sound like? I will not offer you the phrases because I trust you to find them. People will not care about the precision of your language. They will forgive your clumsy or rambling sentences if they sense your intention to listen expansively and offer questions from a place of humility. Think about it—that's all that you want too, right? To be listened to with love?

Here are some concrete tips to guide you on this exploration:

- Don't hurry your questions. Speak slowly.
- Take deep breaths while you listen.

Table 4.1   Expansive Ways of Listening

Listen . . .	Suggestions
For the big picture	Listen for the whole, the interconnectedness, the intersection of systems; see the person and situation embedded within the many moving pieces; see the forest and the trees.
With love	Listen with an open heart, with the knowledge that your heart will not break and that it can hold the pain and suffering of many; be present with and understand the humanity of the person who speaks.
For pain	Listen for pain, without trying to fix it; listen to hear the raw emotions under the story.
With humility	Listen with gratitude for the trust that's bestowed on you. Be humble in the face of emotion and experience.
With curiosity	Listen without an attachment to how you think things should be right now, without conjuring up the past or clinging to notions of the future. Be willing to be surprised. Let go of assumptions.
With compassion	Suspend judgment of yourself and others, appreciating and accepting that everyone makes choices based on her knowledge and skills and what makes sense given her history and worldview.
With confidence	Listen with confidence in yourself, in your abilities to listen expansively and respond from that expansion; be confident in the other person's abilities to solve his own problems.
For relationships	Listen to build healthy relationships with others who might be resources; listen for untapped sources of strength and nourishment.
For possibility	Listen with the conviction that there are other ways that things can be, with belief that the other person can discover those ways; listen for unseen potentials.
With hope	Listen while remaining unattached to outcomes, but with deep conviction that transformational possibilities exist that you may not perceive.

- When the other person finishes talking, say, "Thank you. Tell me more."
- Don't talk too much.
- Say, "I need a moment to think," before you respond. During your moment to think, look out a window and let your mind wander. Don't worry about what the other person is thinking. Taking time to think is honorable.
- Soften the space between your eyebrows, relax your arms, let your jaw drop, and smile slightly.
- Think mostly about the place from which you are listening and make a choice to do so from a place of love.

Here's what you have to gain: Relationships that redefine what it means to be with another; intimacy; and partnerships with colleagues, bosses, students, and families in which you feel accepted, grounded, hopeful, and effective. In the workbook, you'll find more guidance on this kind of listening.

Learn from Body Language

Recall, as if you were watching a video, the last team meeting you went to. See yourself sitting at the table. What do you notice about your body language? What message do you think you were communicating through your body language?

Recall the body language of a colleague or of the team leader at that meeting. What do you remember? How did you interpret his or her body language? How did your interpretation of the person's body language impact how comfortable or safe you felt in the meeting?

When I recall a recent meeting that I didn't want to attend, I suspect my body language communicated that. I sat with my arms crossed, leaning back. I recall that the team leader didn't make eye contact with me, which made me feel that I couldn't trust him. He spoke at a hurried pace, his tone somewhat flat, his volume louder than it needed to be in the small room we were in. I refrained from asking questions, sharing my opinions, or offering suggestions. This was not a new experience for me in this group: This is not a community in which I feel safe; it's not one that fuels my resilience.

Nonverbal communication may say more than the words that emerge from our mouths; our words may communicate only a part of the message that we wish to convey. As we go about building community, we need to peel back the layers of communication to examine our own nonverbal expressions and consider how we interpret those of others. This reflection will take us into places that we otherwise wouldn't explore, but where the potential for true community can be born.

For the majority of us, the messages that we seek to communicate are delivered in our pitch, tone, volume, pace, and body language. Experts suggest that some 65% of communication is delivered and received nonverbally—in our posture, gestures, facial expressions, and eye movements (Pease and Pease, 2004). These typically subconscious behaviors clue us in to someone's attitude or state of mind, so we constantly scan the nonverbals of others and attach meanings to them.

Body language plays a role in building community in these ways:

- When we talk with someone and perceive a mismatch between his selection of words and his body's nonverbals, our trust in the other person diminishes.
- When our own body language doesn't match what we're saying, others won't trust us as much.
- If we can't read a person's nonverbals, we feel uncomfortable around her.
- When we misinterpret someone else's body language, we can miss an opportunity for connection or can even take actions that have a negative impact on the other.

In this section, we'll jump back and forth between how you express yourself through nonverbals and the impact that might have on the relationships you form with others, and how you interpret the nonverbals of others and how those interpretations might influence your relationships with others.

Body Language Is Both Universal and Cultural

Body language is both universal and culturally specific. Researchers have found that many physical expressions of emotions—fear, pride, anger, joy, shame, and grief—look the same worldwide. Shame, for example, is expressed by curling our bodies up, folding in on ourselves, and making our bodies small. The same physical expression of this emotion has been seen all over the world. The fact that many expressions of emotion are shared cross-culturally allows us to more accurately interpret the cues of others, to express our own, and to have some assurance that regardless of language or culture, we can communicate.

However, all cultures also have specific meanings around different aspects of body language and physical interactions. This is where communication gets complicated in our increasingly diverse society. Let's look at a few examples. In some cultures, it is disrespectful for children to make eye contact with authority figures, whereas in others, it is disrespectful for children *not* to make eye contact with authority figures. In some cultures, when a teacher meets a student's parent, it is respectful to extend a hand and shake, whereas in other cultures, it is inappropriate for a female teacher to greet a male guardian in this way. Some cultures speak with their hands as a way of animating their words, whereas for others, excessive gesticulating is seen as rude.

As a teacher, I encountered all of these dynamics in my classroom. I was confused and unsettled by kids who wouldn't look me in the eye. I didn't know how to greet a Yemeni father, awkwardly dropping my arm to my side when he looked at my extended hand with shock. Furthermore, there were parents whose nonverbals (pitch, pace, and volume) baffled me. *What were they so angry about?* I wondered, as I registered their loud and intense communication. When I taught middle school students, their psychosocial developmental stage added another layer to this confusing mess of communication: They certainly used a great deal of theatrics to get their message across.

These differences in communication style impacted my ability to develop community in a few ways. First, there were times when I erroneously interpreted messages. This prevented me from truly connecting with a parent, for example. There were other times when my response to certain nonverbals (students not making eye contact, for example) led me to take actions that created unnecessary distance between myself and my student. There were times when my ways of communication were misinterpreted, which meant that I missed out on relationships that could have been nourishing.

Can you think of a time when your nonverbal communication might have been misinterpreted? Can you recall a moment when you interpreted someone else's nonverbals in a way that may have been erroneous, and that, as a result, may have created distance between you?

Implications for Action: Hit the Brakes and Think

So, what do we do with this knowledge and awareness? In Chapter 2, I discussed how you can cultivate awareness of the emotions you express through your body. We'll return to this topic again later in this chapter, but let's turn our attention to how we *interpret* the nonverbals of students, parents, and colleagues.

Here's the first implication: Put the brakes on your interpretations of others. Refrain from drawing quick conclusions about someone else's message or emotions. Create space between your observation and your assumptions. That's a critical place to start.

Implications for Action: Explore the Role of Unconscious Bias

This is where things get even more complex, because when we pause, we can explore culturally ingrained expectations and assumptions of which we're often unaware.

Let's start with gender roles and the widespread cultural expectation that women be nurturing, kind, and polite, which is reflected in body language that includes a great deal of smiling. A woman who doesn't smile can make some people feel uncomfortable. We may even think she has "resting bitch face" if she's unsmiling. This is a term for which there is no equivalent for men. When men don't smile, they are perceived as being thoughtful, serious, or stoic; men are not asked to "smile more." If these are your unconscious cultural assumptions about gender roles, then if your new principal is a woman and she doesn't smile much, you may not trust her or give her a chance in the way that you would a male principal. Your interpretation might impede the development of a nurturing relationship that could boost your resilience.

Although your interpretation is part of the problem, systemic oppression is at the root. This deeply impacts our perceptions of others and manifests as implicit bias. Implicit biases are the unconscious attitudes and stereotypes that affect our responses to certain groups of people, especially around race and ethnicity, class, gender, and language. Implicit (or unconscious) bias often operates without our awareness. We've been absorbing biases since we were born, so we all have them. It takes work to become aware of them and to make sure we're not operating from them.

Let's take a moment to explore how implicit bias affects our interpretations of nonverbal cues and our actions. Social scientists have done a great deal of research linking our unconscious bias and our behavior. An oft-cited example is that of a white woman walking down the street who faces a black man walking toward her. She clutches her purse and crosses the road to walk on the other side. This is implicit bias in action, and it's a reflection of centuries of racism and the perception that dark-skinned men are dangerous.

How does this play out in schools? How does implicit bias affect your ability to build healthy communities that can boost your resilience? Researchers at Stanford (Okonofua and Eberhardt, 2015) conducted studies on the question of whether an African American student would receive the same punishment, for the same behavior, as one of his white counterparts. Here's how one experiment was conducted: Teachers were shown behavior records of middle school students and told to imagine that they were their students. The records were those of boys who had misbehaved twice; they'd been off task and defiant. The researchers gave some of the students stereotypically black names, such as DeShawn or Darnell, and they gave other students stereotypically white names, such as Greg or Jake.

The teachers reviewed these behavior records and responded to a series of questions, which included the following:

- How irritated by the student do you feel?
- How severely do you think he should be disciplined?
- Would you call the student a troublemaker?

The only difference on these records was the name of the student; their misbehaviors were exactly the same. The researchers found that teachers were much more likely to increase punishment for Darnell or DeShawn than they were for Greg or Jake. They were much more likely to want to suspend Darnell or DeShawn. Furthermore, there wasn't a difference in how African American teachers responded— implicit bias was just as strong in black teachers.

African American students are three times more likely to be suspended or expelled than their white counterparts, according to a 2014 report from the US Department of Education. One of the top reasons why African American girls in this country are sent to the office is that they rolled their eyes at a teacher. This is a direct result of how body language is interpreted and distorted through the filters of implicit bias, and interpretations of these kinds contribute to the school-to-prison pipeline.

The research hasn't been done, but here's how I imagine that implicit bias might further affect the ability of colleagues to form relationships with each other. Imagine this: A young, new teacher from a small town joins a staff in an urban area. On the first day at his new site, he enters the cafeteria where the back-to-school staff meeting is held, and surveys the room for a place to sit. He sees older women who don't come from his cultural group speaking loudly with each other, and because of the quick and unconscious assumptions he makes about their body language, he chooses to sit at a table alone. Perhaps later he is joined by someone else, but perhaps at that table with the loud older women there was a teacher who could have been a mentor, who might have helped him navigate the cultural differences that he soon finds himself swamped by, and who could have been a friend.

Our interpretations of the nonverbal communication of others, interpretations that may be distorted by implicit bias, can prevent us from building community with colleagues or supervisors, and can lead us to undermine our primary purpose for doing what it is we became educators to do—to serve children.

Take a moment to pause and reflect on these ideas. Can you think of a time when you may have interpreted someone else's body language in a way that created distance between you? Can you think of opportunities for connection that you missed because of how you perceived someone else? Can you think of times when someone else may have misinterpreted your body language? What comes up for you when you recall these incidents?

> *Beloved community is formed not by the eradication of difference but by its affirmation, by each of us claiming the identities and cultural legacies that shape who we are and how we live in the world.*
> BELL HOOKS

Focus on Cultural Competence

Cultural competence is the ability to understand, appreciate, and interact with people from cultures or belief systems different from one's own; it is the ability to navigate cross-cultural differences in order to do something—be that teach students, collaborate with colleagues, or socialize with friends. These differences can be generational, racial, gendered, and so on. To build strong communities that can support you to be resilient, you'll need to develop your own cultural competence.

In order to be culturally competent, you must be able to do the following:

1. Be aware of your own cultural identity, beliefs about difference, and unconscious biases.
2. Have knowledge about the general role that culture plays (in communication, emotions, enforcing norms, and relationships) as well as knowledge about specific other cultures.
3. Effectively navigate difference. Self-awareness and knowledge don't automatically translate into the ability to act.

Regardless of our race or ethnicity, gender, and socioeconomic background, we all need to cultivate cultural competence; this learning is necessary for all of us if we truly want to create healthy communities. Let's consider an example of how a leader worked to build his own cultural competence and that of his staff.

Richard, an African American man from the East Coast, is a principal I coached for many years. His way of talking—with me—was loud and animated. He used his hands a great deal, and displayed a range of emotions. However, I noticed that when he interacted with his staff, which was predominantly white, he was toned down.

Richard's work with me focused on understanding the racial dynamics at his school, and himself as a leader within that context. As part of this inquiry, he interviewed staff members about how they experienced him. I sat in on many of those interviews, including one in which a young, white female teacher said this: "I feel nervous when I'm in a room alone with you because sometimes you just seem so angry, and I'm not sure what you'll do." In the moment, Richard seemed calm and collected as he received this feedback, although I noticed his hands trembling.

Later, when we debriefed this exchange, Richard spoke about leading a predominantly white staff. "It's a dehumanizing experience," he said. "They're afraid of my blackness, and then I'm expected to take care of *their* emotions, to make *them* feel okay. I mean, she's 'afraid' of me? She doesn't know what I'll do? I barely talk above a whisper when I'm with them!"

Richard is not the only leader of color I've coached whose body language and way of talking made others uncomfortable. I've worked with numerous African American women leaders who were told they were too loud or too angry and that they "intimidated" their staffs. These situations present an opportunity for social critique, self-reflection, and building cultural competence in ourselves and in others.

Scrutinize Culture

The culture we live in is dominated by white/European, middle-class, patriarchal values. When those from nondominant groups don't conform to these cultural rules, they are admonished: *There's something wrong with you. You're not doing it right. Quiet down; be nice and smile; say things in this tone of voice and in that syntax.* Culture is an insidious and forceful mechanism for oppression; it reinforces the values of a system, and those individuals who don't fall in line are accused of violating cultural norms. This context is what led Richard to receive feedback that his way of communicating was scary.

Here are some questions we need to ask: Within a nondominant group, if a form of communication is acceptable, then should members of that group be expected to abandon those ways and demonstrate the dominant culture's norms when they are in mixed company? Is it fair for dominant culture to demand conformity from those it oppresses? And should those of us from nondominant cultures acquiesce, assimilate, and adopt the language and expressions of the dominant culture for our own safety and acceptance?

When we debriefed, Richard was angry about what he'd heard from the teacher, and he was sad. After he shared his feelings, I paraphrased what I'd heard, and added, "You have a right, as a human being, to be yourself at school, to be here as a black man and not have to conform to society's distorted notions of black men." This is one part of the truth.

Look Inward

Here's another truth: We all have a responsibility to look at ourselves in a metaphorical mirror. All of us. We will never be able to put down the mirror, because change is constant and the journey of self-awareness is infinite.

When Richard looked in the mirror, he recognized his role in creating the situations he was in. Richard discovered that when he interacted with his youngest white female teachers, he was so afraid that they'd be afraid of him that he toned himself "down to the lowest setting," as he described. "I feel intense anxiety when I'm talking to them," he explained, "and I can actually see how that could be unsettling. They read me wrong: They are afraid of me, when actually I'm afraid of them, or afraid of doing something that would make them uncomfortable. But I guess they're having a hard time making sense of my emotional landscape, and then you layer on distorted notions of black men, and they perceive me as angry. I'm not angry, but I'm definitely not comfortable or authentic."

In Chapter 2, I described Sonia, another principal who reflected on her body language and video-recorded herself frequently. When Sonia looked at herself (literally because she videoed herself on many occasions), she recognized that, unconsciously, she was demonstrating nonverbal cues that reflected frustration, impatience, or even disdain and contempt. Both Richard and Sonia came to the same conclusion: Others perceived them in a distorted way, *and* they themselves needed to take responsibility for their emotional states and shift some aspects of their communication. They hadn't created the conditions of their oppression, but they needed to take responsibility for elements of their communication, while also working with their staff to interrupt and transform dominant culture.

Learn and Change

It was Richard's job, as a leader, to hold a mirror up for his staff and to create (in partnership with others) a learning space for them to examine their sociopolitical identities. His young, white female teachers needed to reflect on their privilege, recognize the implications of dominant culture, and understand the different ways that social groups communicate. At Richard's school, the implications of this need extended beyond the relationship that teachers had with their principal and directly impacted students. Richard knew that if teachers perceived his behaviors as threatening, then they were likely to perceive those of the African American male students the same way. The consequences of those perceptions were seen in the disproportionately high numbers of African American male students who were sent to the office for "defiance." In response to his observations and reflections, Richard developed a multiyear plan to build his staff's cultural competence.

This story and these lessons are relevant to educators regardless of position or role. We all have a responsibility to boost our cultural competence for the sake of our relationships with each other and with kids and their families, and to serve children's academic and social-emotional needs. Without cultural competence, we won't be able to build healthy, beloved communities and fulfill our purpose of educating young people.

Address Conflict

What comes up for you when you think about conflict? For most people, it's a host of nervous, fearful feelings. That's the hardest thing about dealing with conflict—the emotions evoked by it. Conflict doesn't have to be that difficult. In fact, given a little learning about conflict and practicing the skills for addressing it, you will feel differently. Furthermore, you'll learn that *healthy* conflict can build resilient communities. In fact, it's a vital aspect of a thriving community. We have few models for dealing effectively with unhealthy conflict or for fostering healthy conflict, so we'll need to be creative and seek out resources. Conflict is inevitable and can either strengthen or undermine a community, so the only option we have is to learn how to deal with it.

Unhealthy Conflict

There is a tremendous variety of unhealthy interpersonal conflict in our organizations, and, unfortunately, I probably don't need to offer you examples of what it looks like. But think about the impact of unhealthy conflict—on other adults, on kids, on the broader community. I've worked in many schools where interpersonal conflict coats everything like an oily residue. You sense it in every interaction between teachers, you hear it between administrators and staff, and you see kids acting out in ways that reflect how the grown-ups around them behave with each other. There's often a lot of staffing changes at these schools, but sometimes the most toxic people are the ones who stay year after year. I think most of us know that unhealthy conflict has to be addressed, but we don't know how.

The first thing to do in order to address conflict is to activate your *why*, your purpose for addressing the conflict. Otherwise, you'll avoid it. Think of a conflict you might want to address. How could dealing with it strengthen your community? What might it feel like to be in a staff meeting and be paired with someone with whom you've resolved a conflict? Dealing with conflict is scary, so activate your internal motivation to do so.

Preparation is key when dealing with conflict. In order to be successful and build your confidence, think about what you want to say, and practice saying it. Depending on the complexity of the conflict, you may need to invite a mediator or facilitator, or someone to help you prepare. You can learn to address conflict. It's just another skill. Prepare, practice, and reflect afterwards. It'll get easier each time. In the workbook, you'll find some guidance in addressing conflict.

Gossip and Toxic Cultures

Interpersonal conflict manifests in many ways, and when it's not dealt with, it tends to grow and spread. Gossip can be a barometer for the overall interpersonal health of a community. It also seems to be a behavior that can quickly spread if not addressed. Mike Robbins (2007) writes, "Gossip to an organization is like cancer to the body; it slowly eats away at the fabric of the team until the team itself dies" (p. 29). I suspect that many of us have witnessed the destructive impact of gossip in our workplaces.

Robbins advocates for creating gossip-free zones in which people commit to speaking positively about others. If you have an issue or complaint about someone, you take it directly to that person, get some coaching or feedback about how to resolve the issue, or let it go. In a gossip-free zone, if someone slips up, you kindly remind him of the agreement.

Left unmanaged, rampant gossip fuels toxic cultures, which are further characterized by individuals working independently all the time, warring camps, divisions across racial or ethnic lines, perpetual negativity, hostile faculty meetings, and misdirected values focused on enforcing rules, teaching basic skills, and serving a small group of elite students (Deal and Peterson, 2009). Toxic cultures are contagious. New teachers can become acculturated in only weeks because of the strong negative personalities of the informal leaders in a faculty. Positive staff members tend to leave or are driven out.

In the workbook, you'll find a tool to help you reflect on your organization's culture. As you build your resilience, if you find yourself in an unhealthy school culture, you might dedicate energy to changing your school's culture, or you might draw lines around the behaviors you're willing to tolerate. You may also recognize that you need to be in a healthier culture. Resilient people are not martyrs, nor do they put themselves in a place where their skills and aptitudes can't be maximized. There's a difference between conflict and toxicity: Even the most resilient person cannot thrive in a toxic culture.

Healthy Conflict

There are also communities in which people may seem to get along, but this is just a veneer of artificial harmony. In such places, people don't raise hard or important questions. These fragile communities are thrown into chaos by a small upset because they don't build collective resilience; they have not shared difficult conversations or hard times together.

Healthy conflict leads to growth and connection in a social group. There may be moments that feel uncomfortable, or even rough, but as we navigate those, we feel closer to each other. Healthy conflict is marked by an exchange of ideas, a sincere asking of questions, and a genuine willingness on everyone's part to listen and learn. This takes a relatively high level of trust and vulnerability, and sometimes a courageous soul to initiate and engage in this kind of healthy conflict.

Sparking healthy conflict is subtle. It can sound like incorporating any of the following sentence stems into a conversation:

- I have some concerns about that suggestion. Could you explain it more?
- I want to push back on that idea. I've noticed . . ., and I would suggest . . .
- I disagree with you about that, but I want to hear your thoughts.
- I disagree with you about that, but I'm willing to change my mind.
- It would help me get behind that idea if I could hear more about . . .

You'll find a whole chapter on dealing with conflict in *The Art of Coaching Teams* (Aguilar, 2016). Understanding conflict is worth your time because there is a connection between dealing with conflict and cultivating resilience. Social confidence, assertiveness, and well-developed communication and conflict resolution

---

Implications for Leaders

- You are responsible for shaping the culture of your school or organization. As Peter Drucker says, "Culture eats strategy for breakfast." If there's a toxic culture at your school, it will take only a few weeks for a new staff member to become infected.
- If you are aware of conflict between two staff members, don't ignore it. Encourage them to address their issues, and perhaps offer them mediation.
- You may need more support than the sentence stems in this chapter to deal with conflict—it's a big task. Consider enlisting the guidance of a leadership coach.

know-how are essential skills and dispositions for helping professionals build emotional resilience.

A Dive into Fear

During a difficult period when I was a child, I had recurring nightmares that everyone in my family was killed and I was left alone. It's been 40 years since that time, and I still vividly remember the end of those nightmares: I floated in a dark, outer space–like void of infinite aloneness. This was an extreme subconscious representation of my fear of being alone, but I know that I'm not the only one who fears abandonment, isolation, or being ostracized from a community. This fear, deeply human, connects us all. We need each other; we crave belonging.

The fear of being alone is what holds me back from saying to a colleague, "The way you talk about our kids with such a deficit mindset makes me uncomfortable." This fear of not being liked is what gets in the way when I'm in a team meeting and we're off topic and we're not getting our work done and I'm frustrated, but I don't want to say anything because I don't want my colleagues to feel as though they don't want me on the team.

How does your fear show up? What are you afraid of? How does it interfere with getting what you truly want?

My fear has held me back from being vulnerable, from sharing my stories, and from speaking my truths with compassion. My fear has held me back from advocating for children. It has stood in the way between the community I want and where I am, which is ironic—that my fear of being alone prevents me from building community. It is the fear that if people saw who I truly was, they wouldn't want me. Now, as I approach my late 40s, I recognize that that fear belongs to the child I once was—not the person I am now. I no longer need that fear.

Fear is pervasive in our schools. We're afraid that if our students don't score high enough on tests, we'll lose our jobs. We're afraid that our names will be published in a paper because our students' test scores were low. We're afraid we aren't doing a good job; we're afraid of being criticized; we're afraid that others will see that we don't know what we're doing sometimes or that we can't do a critical task or that we're not doing it as well as so-and-so does. We're afraid that our work and contributions won't be acknowledged, that our experience and perspective won't be welcomed.

In some schools, I've seen teachers who are afraid of their students; students who are afraid of their teachers; teachers who are afraid of their principal; principals who are afraid of the parents; and parents who are afraid of teachers.

Fear might be the biggest problem we face in schools. Fear erodes community. It stops teachers from observing each other, prevents kids from confiding in the adults around them, and holds parents back from asking teachers for help. Fear of being judged, fear of being rejected, fear of being ostracized. Fear may hold us back from advocating for the real systemic changes that need to be made in order to truly transform our schools, changes that include the obsessive focus on test scores in some places.

Before we condemn fear, let's take a moment to acknowledge and honor it. Fear has helped our species survive. It drove our ancient ancestors to live in social groups for protection, and it hardwired the urge to go into battle or run from anything that threatened our safety. However, we are no longer hunted by saber-toothed tigers. If we do something that seriously offends our community, we are likely to find another one in which we will be accepted. We will not be banished to the barren plains for professing an idea that conflicts with that of the masses, or for loving someone whom our community says we shouldn't love.

What might be possible if we had less fear? What kinds of communities could we build? How might we more effectively serve children if we were less fearful?

Without as much fear, I suspect we could

- Admit to making mistakes, ask for forgiveness, and have a chance to make things right with our community
- Ask for help
- Share stories about love and sadness and pain and fear
- Address injustices more immediately and directly
- Invite a colleague to have tea
- Hold team meetings that are meaningful and productive, and that impact student learning
- Give our leaders feedback and challenge their authority
- Interrupt the status quo
- Challenge ineffective structures and dysfunctional systems
- Name and discuss the elephants in the room
- Appreciate others, ask for appreciations, and celebrate together

Fear is part of what it means to be a human being. But when it's left unchecked, running rampant and directing the show, it blocks our ability to connect with others, achieve our purpose, know ourselves well, and experience joy.

What are you afraid of? What might be possible if your fear was uncovered?

Disposition: Empathy

The golden orb-weaver is a spider that spins the largest and strongest web in the world. Its silk is five times stronger than steel and more flexible than nylon; the webs are waterproof and enormous (over 20 feet tall), and can last for years. The golden orb-weaver's silk is used to make artificial ligament scaffolding, bulletproof vests, and much more, which is why people are spending lots of money and time trying to mass-produce it. This harmless spider lives in many places in the world, and, in spite of my aversion to insects, I've often admired it in the Costa Rican rainforest. Be warned: The fine silk is easy to walk into if you're not paying attention.

In a community, empathy could be the equivalent of the golden orb-weaver's silk—it could hold us together with super strength. Empathy is the sense that someone feels our pain, and it could fill the places where there are gaps, misunderstandings, and divisions among us. Call to mind a time when you were struggling and someone empathized with you. What did that feel like? How did you intuit the empathy? How did that affect your relationship with that person?

As I contemplate these questions, the memories surface—of exchanges with colleagues, mentors, and supervisors when I experienced empathy, recollections of moments when I felt low but, through someone else's empathy, found myself feeling deeply connected, and that connection helped me feel better. Often these were passing moments—a question that a colleague asked in the hallway that expressed her concern for how I was doing, words of encouragement on a difficult day—but those moments of empathy built bonds that withstood the numerous trials and tribulations of working in schools. Those moments became connections that, like a web, held us through disagreements, exhaustion, and tumultuous change.

The memories keep bubbling up. I recall my budding empathy for a second-grade student, Mateo, and how it helped me respond to his challenging behavior on rainy Friday afternoons. I recall the empathy I discovered for a student's mother, and how it clarified the decisions she made and her occasional meltdowns at my classroom door. I recall the empathy I gained for a struggling principal, and how that allowed me to find inroads to a productive partnership. I can think of hundreds of times when, in my work as a coach, my empathy opened paths through resistance and into a meaningful coaching relationship. The empathy I have felt has carried me through innumerable rough patches, made me more resilient, and helped me do what I am most committed to doing: serving children.

Empathy is an emotional state essential to forming healthy relationships and communities. When community members have high levels of empathy for one another, there is less hurt, people regulate their own behavior, and there is more forgiveness, acceptance, and kindness. Perhaps it would be hard to measure with standardized assessments, but imagine what might be possible if we spent a year prioritizing, strategizing, and striving to build empathy in our schools—empathy among teachers and students, among students and their peers, among teachers and administrators, and among staff, parents, guardians, and the community at large. I suspect we'd meet all kinds of goals, because the lack of empathy in our schools and society might be one of the root causes of a great deal of dysfunction.

Love and compassion blend and blur into this conversation. Compassion is the action taken in response to a feeling of empathy. Often we perceive empathy from people's actions—giving us a hug, asking a thoughtful question, extending a word of kindness. Technically, that's compassion, but the emotion that fuels it is empathy. Love is perhaps the greatest aspiration. Although we often act with compassion when we want to relieve someone's suffering, when we act with love, it's an act of creation, an attempt to bring someone else happiness, joy, or well-being. In a sense, compassion is reactive (we act to end suffering), and love is proactive (we act to cultivate happiness). But I don't know that we need to get caught in definitions—love, compassion, and empathy are all valuable and worthy, and any amount of any of them will be good for our communities.

Toward a Beloved Community

Imagine what would be possible if you felt connected to others whom you trusted, who listened to you, and who believed in you and encouraged you, as well as to those from whom you could learn and with whom you could do great things. Imagine if you experienced this inside school halls and on your street. Can you see how significant this would be when things get tough?

Community can be built every day, in every interaction with another person, when you listen, bridge differences, and embrace healthy conflict. Know what kind of community you want to be a part of and to create, and then move to build it.

Dr. Martin Luther King Jr. spoke of building a "Beloved Community," one that strives for a society based on justice, equal opportunity, and love of one's fellow human beings. The King Center (www.thekingcenter.org) explains: "Dr. King's Beloved Community is a global vision, in which all people can share in the wealth of the earth. In the Beloved Community, poverty, hunger and homelessness will not be tolerated because international standards of human decency will not allow it. Racism and all forms of discrimination, bigotry and prejudice will be replaced by an all-inclusive spirit of sisterhood and brotherhood." This vision of community guides this book.

To construct a Beloved Community, we must reckon with our past and dismantle the structures of racial, gender, and economic oppression. In this community, all people will be welcomed. The path to this community must be forged with compassion and curiosity. Let us aspire to create a Beloved Community wherever we find ourselves, but especially in our work as educators, in our schools and classrooms and playgrounds.

CHAPTER REFLECTION

- What was a big takeaway from this chapter about how to build community?
- What role do you think implicit bias might play in how you build relationships or cultivate trust?
- What do you feel motivated to do in order to strengthen your community?
- What did you learn about yourself in this chapter?

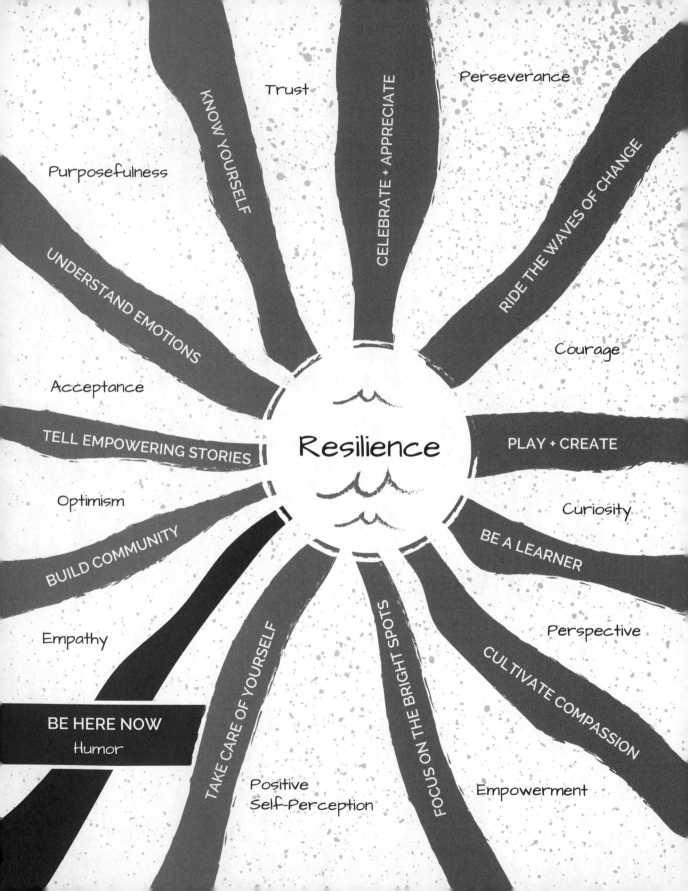

CHAPTER 5

Be Here Now

Learning to be in the present moment, without judging it, boosts our resilience. It can allow us to feel accepting and clearheaded about our options for response. When we're fully present, we're more likely to find appropriate levity to moments of challenge and to relieve stress by finding humor in a situation.

❧❧

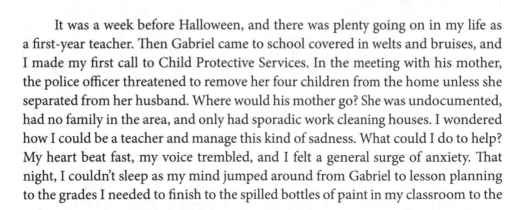

October: As we move into the fall, our energy wanes, and we're triggered more easily. Learning to be in the present moment enables us to cultivate awareness of our emotions and make choices that foster our resilience.

It was a week before Halloween, and there was plenty going on in my life as a first-year teacher. Then Gabriel came to school covered in welts and bruises, and I made my first call to Child Protective Services. In the meeting with his mother, the police officer threatened to remove her four children from the home unless she separated from her husband. Where would his mother go? She was undocumented, had no family in the area, and only had sporadic work cleaning houses. I wondered how I could be a teacher and manage this kind of sadness. What could I do to help? My heart beat fast, my voice trembled, and I felt a general surge of anxiety. That night, I couldn't sleep as my mind jumped around from Gabriel to lesson planning to the grades I needed to finish to the spilled bottles of paint in my classroom to the stack of unpaid bills I couldn't find time for, and back to Gabriel. *How do teachers do this?* I wondered.

By around 5:00 a.m., after managing to get only a few minutes of sleep, I got up, grabbed a pillow off my couch, and sat down on the floor. I'd dabbled in meditation for a few years by then, but it always felt so hard to sit still. I got bored quickly. I didn't see "the point." Somehow, after a night of insomnia and anxiety, I went into autopilot mode—and whoever was in the driver's seat directed me to meditate.

Meditation is not magic. I still got bored. But in that first year of teaching, the days I meditated before school were notably easier than those when I skipped my 20 minutes on the pillow. In the spring of that first year, I had to make another call to Child Protective Services for Gabriel. As I sat with his mother and the police officer that second time, I was much calmer. I still felt incredibly sad, but I didn't feel frantic and unsettled. I wasn't wondering how I'd "do this." I undertook one task at a time—the phone call, the meeting, the cleanup, the drive home. My mind was more often present than fluttering anxiously through the past and future.

In this chapter, I'm going to do everything I can to convince you to sit down for a few minutes a day (ideally for around twenty), close your eyes, and observe your breath. Yes. I'm going to ask you to meditate. I'll offer scientific reasoning and persuasion, emotional pleas, and inspiring anecdotes. I've spent decades sorting through the vast resources on managing the endless stresses of life, and, as a result, I've got zero doubt that meditation is key. It's also portable, easily available, cheap, and quick.

Mindfulness: What, How, and Why

Mindfulness is the nonjudgmental cultivation of moment-to-moment awareness. It's a mental state in which you are focused and without judgment. You can drink tea or eat mindfully. You can listen mindfully to someone else talk. You can wash dishes, play with Legos, or walk mindfully. Mindfulness helps us *be here now* so that we can make clearheaded decisions in the moment. We cultivate mindfulness through meditation, and mindfulness meditation is a portal into the deepest underground springs of our resilience.

Two Paths: Habit and Mindfulness

Let's return to the moment between stimulus and response—the moment after your principal sticks his head in the door and says, "I'm sorry, but you'll need to cover so-and-so's class today because the sub didn't show" and before you blurt out a response. For me, that was a moment that happened too many times and to which I responded in a way that I later regretted. Take a second to recall a triggering incident and a response that you regretted.

A triggering incident like the one you've called to mind creates a fork in our path. One route is the trail we habitually take when we're distressed—whatever we've done for years. We make a quick assessment of the event (*My principal disrespects me* or *This school is a shitshow*), which launches an emotion cycle. Here's what I did after my principal told me I had to cover a class: I'd emit an exaggerated sigh and say something like, "Okay, fine. I had a meeting scheduled with Quizalde's mom, but I guess I'll cancel it. Are there even sub plans, or do I have to create something on the spot?" I felt resentful, and spun a narrative of the principal's incompetence.

The path was familiar, so it was easy for me to charge down it, but this feeling also eroded my resilience. Sometimes there was damage to a relationship that I then had to repair—for example, there were a few times that I snapped at my principal. And often, the aftereffects of this emotion cycle were not positive for the kids I had to teach. I'd head off to the class where I had to substitute feeling irritated and disempowered, which had a negative domino effect on the students in the class. There was more than just my own resilience at stake.

The second path is a route of mindfulness. On this path, we notice our feelings, have awareness of their origins, accept whatever is happening in the moment, and are intentional about what we say or do next. Mindfulness allows us to take a timeout from the drama of the moment to view the situation without judgment and, perhaps, even with compassion. This route allows us to make more clear-headed decisions.

On the path of mindfulness, when my principal tells me I need to cover a class during my prep, I acknowledge my feelings of annoyance, my disappointment over the lost time, my concern about the missed meeting with Quizalde's mom, and my frustration at the ineffective systems in the school. I recognize also that my principal is working as hard and as well as he can, that these things happen, that in 10 years I won't remember this missed prep, and that right now, there are children for whom I need to be calm and present. When I respond to my principal, I can do so without heaps of judgment, enabling me to preserve our relationship and keep my blood pressure from surging. When I head off to the classroom, I can teach from the part of me that got into this field because I wanted to serve children.

The Pause Button

Practicing mindfulness is like hitting an internal pause button on the drama of life. When a student refuses to follow your instructions, or a colleague sends you a nasty email and cc's the whole school, or you're called to an emergency staff meeting at 3:15 p.m. on Friday, you swiftly hit *pause* before you snap back, hit "Reply all," or storm out of school. You keep your finger on pause for as long as you need, and when you remove it, you feel confident in your response, aligned to your core values, and calmer. When I recall the moment in my first year teaching when I broke down in tears in front of my principal (I shared this story in the opening of Chapter 1), I imagine what might have happened with a dose of mindfulness. Perhaps I could have hit the pause button, quickly registered my feelings of anxiety and frustration, and then responded in a more productive way.

We think we *are* our thoughts. Mindfulness teaches us to notice that our thoughts have their own existence: They come and go. When we practice mindfulness, we learn to watch those thoughts come and go, to see how our emotions cycle. We learn that we are not our thoughts or our emotions. We see that emotions and thoughts are born out of conditions; they are not inherent to our being. Many of us have stories about ourselves, etched in stone, about who we are and who we will always be. Mindfulness shatters those stories.

Mindfulness connects us more directly to the present moment. Our perceptions are often distorted by bias, habits, fears, or wishful thinking. Mindfulness helps us cut through our distorted perceptions, and, without those distractions, we can engage with whatever stimulus is occurring and be discerning about our choices. Mindfulness is what holds you back from sending that 10th-grade girl to the office because she rolls her eyes at you every time you ask her to put her phone away. It's what allows you to calmly state the rules and enforce the consequences rather than lurch into a cycle of irritation that just leaves you exhausted.

Can you think of some moments recently when you would have liked to hit a pause button? When having some time to reflect on what was going on would have helped you make clearer decisions?

Interested? Let's jump in to how to build mindfulness muscles.

Sit Down and Focus on Your Breath

If you want to cultivate mindfulness, you must sit for at least a few minutes every day. Our minds are like monkeys, jumping from past to present, from worry to regret, from one thing to the next. Often our minds are so quick we're not even aware of their unruly and wild activities—and, because we're so accustomed to them, we don't even notice they're wreaking havoc. When we're triggered by something, our monkey-mind jumps in first and responds. The first step in mindfulness is to cultivate awareness of what our minds are doing.

The best way to do this is to sit down, close your eyes, and focus on your breath. This can be challenging. Here's what happens. You sit down, get your body comfortable, close your eyes, and then inhale. Then you exhale. Then you inhale. Then your mind goes sort of crazy. It tells you that your back aches and your nose itches, and it asks you why you're doing this. You probably look ridiculous, and if people walked in and saw you, they'd just laugh. You remember you really need to send an overdue email and restock your vitamins and earthquake supplies and— what's that smell? When was the last time you changed the litter box? Are your cats overdue for their annual checkups? Your foot has fallen asleep and your nose is still itchy, and where is that distant beeping sound coming from? Maybe just going for a run or organizing your classroom would be better because just watching your breath is a stupid waste of time.

If you've never tried meditating, I hope this description won't dissuade you. It is an honest account of what our minds tend to do when we sit still. But you can learn to refocus on your breath, without judging yourself for having a flighty mind, without telling yourself you are a bad meditator. You just gently return to observing your breath. And you feel your chest slowly rise and fall. You sense the cool air on your nostrils and upper lip. You might say to yourself, *breathing in, breathing out,* or you might softly count your breaths to 10 and then start again.

That's it. That's essentially how to do sitting mediation. (You'll find more detailed instructions in the workbook.) What you'll notice, as you practice returning to your breath, is that it gets easier. You find yourself staying with your breath for longer and longer stretches. When your mind jumps away, you notice more quickly. You redirect it with less drama. The monkey jumps less often. And then, occasionally, you notice something else: Quietness. Stillness. A centeredness. It feels as though you're floating in a calm pool of water, effortlessly, peacefully.

One way to help yourself get motivated to meditate, and to keep up a practice, is to reflect on why you're meditating and what it might do for you as well as for others in your life. When you sit down to meditate, begin by setting an intention. This could sound like, *My meditation today will help me respond kindly to my students and will help me find joy in teaching today.* Or *My intention in sitting today is so I may be aware of my emotions.*

If you're tempted to close this book right now and sit for five minutes, I endorse that idea.

A Mindfulness Practice

Meditation can be part of a robust mindfulness practice. I think about it in the same way I think about exercising: I go to Pilates classes for concentrated attention to strengthening my core and aligning my posture. Then, throughout the day, I bring awareness to how I'm sitting, standing, lifting, and walking. A class keeps me on my game, but the continuous, ongoing implementation of that practice makes the biggest overall difference.

Yard duty was one of the things I liked least when I started teaching elementary school. I resented the fact that I couldn't have that 10-minute break to go to the bathroom, prepare for the next lesson, or just have a quiet moment. And then there was a gorgeous October day when, standing on the cement yard, I closed my eyes for a second and tilted my face to the sun and registered the sounds of happy children playing. I found a moment of peace in the soft breeze, the warmth on my skin, the gleeful chatter of people I cared about, and the cries of a passing seagull. Yard duty became an opportunity to practice mindfulness, a recess for my mind. There are ways to integrate mindfulness into your day.

There are also other forms of meditation that perhaps you've heard of—for example, focusing attention on an object such as a candle flame. Transcendental Meditation (TM) is centered on the repetition of a phrase. Relaxation exercises and guided imagery are close cousins of meditation, as they help us calm our bodies and deal with anxiety. Try different forms of meditation and see what you like.

A Nod to the Origins of Mindfulness

A great deal of mindfulness is drawn from Eastern traditions, specifically Buddhism. In general, many Eastern traditions hold a holistic view of communities, the individual, and health. Sitting in silence is considered to be a great gift to yourself and your community. An appreciation is owed to a handful of Americans who in the 1960s and 1970s traveled to India and Southeast Asia to learn from meditation masters. They made what they learned accessible and practical for those of us in the West. In the last 40 years, many in the fields of psychology, health, and neuroscience have been directly and indirectly influenced by what this group of American truth-seekers and meditators brought us.

One of the pioneers of this movement was a Harvard psychiatrist who, after his years spent in India, became known as Ram Dass. His 1971 book, *Be Here Now*, is a classic on the subject of meditation and Eastern spirituality. It was this book that (in the early 1990s) set me on a path of learning that helped me strengthen a set of resilience muscles that I then drew on during my first year of teaching. That first year had its rough spots, that's for sure, and I still remember those vividly (even though over 20 years have passed). But I also had many joyful moments during which I knew I was exactly where I wanted and needed to be. Teaching made me feel more like myself than I'd ever felt in my life. There were countless days when I left school feeling elated. I attribute this experience in great part to what I learned and to who I became after I opened that tattered copy of *Be Here Now* I'd found in a used bookstore for 50 cents.

Meditation Changes Your Brain, Body, and Classroom

You may have never heard of Matthieu Ricard, but he has a very famous brain—at least in some circles. Ricard, the son of a famous French philosopher, is a scientist and a Buddhist monk. Neuroscientists hooked him up to machines to study his brain and were stunned to find that, while he was meditating, Ricard's brain looked as it would if he were under anesthesia (Davidson and Harrington, 2001; Davidson and Lutz, 2008). What this means is that just by sitting down and breathing, you can change your brain, block out pain, and completely alter your physical experience.

In the last decade or two, neuroscientists have joined forces with saffron-robed Tibetan monks and the Dalai Lama to form a fascinating partnership between science and ancient contemplative practices. The scientists are helping bring meditation practices into the mainstream as they show us how we can use meditation for our physical health as well as to shift our minds and emotional experiences.

Here are the highlights of what neuroscientists have found about how meditation changes our brains:

- The **amygdala** is the ancient part of your brain that responds to danger and activates when you experience fear. When it's aroused, it pulls the emergency alarms in your brain, which then send your neural and hormonal systems into panic. A great deal of the time, your amygdala overreacts. Following mindfulness training, this part of the brain is less active (Lutz, Slagter, Dunne, and Davidson, 2008; Hölzel et al., 2010).
- The **hippocampus** is critical to learning and memory, and it helps regulate the amygdala. With a meditation practice, this part of the brain is more active (Goldin and Gross, 2010; Hölzel et al., 2011).
- The **prefrontal cortex** is the part of your brain that regulates emotions and behaviors and makes wise decisions. Regular meditation activates this part of the brain (Chiesa and Serretti, 2010).

Taming your amygdala is essential if you have a high-stress job. Part of what happens when a kid is disrespectful on a rainy Friday afternoon is that our exhausted bodies and minds overreact: The amygdala perceives danger in that obnoxious seventh grader and screams, "Danger!!! Fight! Or flee! *DO SOMETHING!*" Meditation helps settle the amygdala.

By contrast, our hippocampus and prefrontal cortex need tuning up. Those parts of our brain help us think clearly, learn, and reflect on our teaching. They help us see our part in the challenges we face and rationally identify solutions to these problems. With a high-functioning hippocampus and prefrontal cortex, we can pivot to the obnoxious seventh grader and calmly say, "Within the next five minutes, please pick up that paper you threw and drop it in the recycling box, okay?" Crisis averted. Greater density of gray matter in our hippocampus and prefrontal cortex is good—it's the sign of high functioning—and there are very few ways to increase that density aside from meditation. Meditation inoculates us against stress and anxiety unlike almost anything else we can do.

There's more good news from neuroscientists. They found that our brains can not only change but change *quickly*. After eight weeks of meditating for 25–30 minutes per day, people who had never meditated before showed measurable changes in the amygdala, limbic region, and prefrontal cortex (Zolli and Healy, 2012).

Furthermore, until recently, psychologists believed that someone's temperament is relatively fixed after adolescence. Now neuroscientists know that because our brains can change, our whole experience of emotions can change. We can train our minds to focus on emotions such as empathy, optimism, and acceptance.

Mindful Schools is a fantastic resource for educators. This nonprofit, founded in 2007 in Oakland, California, serves educators and children in all 50 US states and in over 100 countries. Check out its website for resources and to learn more about its online and in-person courses (www.mindfulschools.org).

Meditation Is Good for Teachers and Kids

Are you distressed by the mess in your classroom? Are the counters covered in crusty tempera paint bottles, moldy science experiments, and dusty stacks of papers? Try mindfulness and see what happens!

Here are some highlights from the research on mindfulness in education. Teachers who practice mindfulness

- Experience lower levels of stress and burnout (Flook, Goldberg, Pinger, Bonus, and Davidson, 2013)
- Report greater efficacy in their jobs (Jennings, Frank, Snowberg, Coccia, and Greenberg, 2013)
- Have more emotionally supportive classrooms (Jennings et al., 2015)
- Have more organized classrooms (Flook et al., 2013)

Our emotions are contagious. This is science—not just metaphor. We have brain cells called mirror neurons that respond to the actions and emotions of others. If you see someone yell and throw a book across the room, your brain will fire signals of anger. If you're with a child who is in great distress, you'll also feel upset. If you are in a terrible mood, even if you try to put on a happy face, your students will pick up on it and may get cranky. If you are calm, focused, and self-aware, there's a much greater likelihood that your students will also be calm, focused, and self-aware. As Mindful Schools says on its website, "Children reflect the nervous systems of adults around them."

Let me try to entice you with how mindfulness can help address other problems, in case you're not yet sold on trying it. Mindfulness helps improve attention, memory, and self-control. It is a powerful aid in recovery from addiction. It boosts your immune response. It helps with insomnia, and it's invaluable in trauma recovery and in managing depression and chronic pain. And, again, remember: There are no strange side effects, it doesn't cost anything, and you can do it anywhere.

In Chapter 3, we considered how the stories we tell frame our experiences and form a script for our lives. We can change the story we tell and create one that is more empowering and—*or*—we can just notice our story. With mindfulness, you don't even need to change your story! You just notice it—acknowledge the underlying emotions that are triggered and the impact the event and story have on your body. You might see the fuller context for the story. You accept that your mind is making that story and then you go back to focusing on your breath.

Meditation Relieves Confusion

For two years, I worked in a supremely dysfunctional school, but I had a hard time accepting my need to leave. I thought, *Every place has problems* and *Someone needs to be here to try to make things better for these kids.* I couldn't see my options clearly.

I'd been in a nonmeditating phase (I'm a terribly inconsistent meditator, although on a steadily improving trajectory), and when I returned to these practices that grounded me, I started setting boundaries and getting clarity. Meditation helped me extricate myself from the drama and gain insight into the situation. I also saw how leaving the school and following other paths might bring me more peace, move me closer to my long-term goals, and help me feel more aligned to my core values. When I made the decision to leave, I didn't feel as though I was escaping. I felt that I was moving onward toward my purpose and reason for being alive, toward my joy and satisfaction, and toward healthy community and well-being.

I find confusion and lack of clarity to be among the most excruciatingly difficult emotions. I hate that feeling of being all muddled and going over and over choices and decisions and options. Meditation helps me sort through all that. The moments of clarity come faster and sharper when I'm in a meditating season.

ě♭ě

I hope you are convinced of the potential for mindfulness in general and the practice of meditation in particular to improve your health and well-being. Mindfulness is a resource not only for changing our inner world and experience but also for helping us change some of our most entrenched habits of thinking about other people. Mindfulness might just be the key resource for creating equitable schools.

Mindfulness as a Tool for Cultural Competence

In this book, I focus on what's within your sphere of influence to improve your life and that of others. That's why I'm focusing on your consciousness. You can sit down today and hone your awareness of your thoughts. One pattern of thought we'd all benefit from exploring is how our thoughts about other people have actually been socially, culturally, and politically conditioned.

We all have unconscious bias—automatic thoughts and feelings that arise when we look at an image of someone of another race or ethnicity. (We also have unconscious bias about any identity marker, but here I'll focus on racial unconscious bias.) Although these often operate below our level of consciousness, they shape our views and affect our behaviors. But there's good news. Researchers say that our prejudices are not inevitable and are in fact quite malleable. Rewiring our minds to override our impulses toward those who seem different from us will require that we challenge stereotypes and cultivate empathy and perspective taking. We also need increased opportunities for contact between different groups of people. Mindfulness can be a tool that enables us to notice the unconscious bias that we all have and to begin to interrupt it.

When Unconscious Bias Surfaces

I was coaching Ms. K, an experienced teacher who was reviewing five years of her office referral data. She was sobbing. "I don't understand what I'm seeing here," she cried. "Clearly I've disproportionately sent more black boys to the office than any other group, and I'm horrified by this."

I offered her the box of tissues, and acknowledged the courage it took to look at this data. She had asked me to gather it, although I knew she didn't expect to see these trends.

"When I think about my kids," Ms. K said, "I'd never say one group was more trouble than another. It's me, isn't it? Something about how I work with my black boys? Am I prejudiced?"

What we're dealing with, I explained, is socially conditioned, neurologically rooted, and often automatic; it's unconscious or "implicit" bias. I won't tell you what Ms. K's race or ethnicity is because she could have been white, black, Latina, or Asian. We are all subject to implicit bias, and it's an insidious contributor to the inequities that are rife in our schools. We all have a responsibility to understand our own biases, recognize our distorted ways of thinking, and uproot those biases. Mindfulness can be a key tool in this process.

Most Americans publicly hold a position of racial equality and don't profess explicitly racist views. However, racial inequality persists. Racial prejudice also manifests in the classroom in the kinds of data that Ms. K was confronted with, as well as in data around who succeeds in school, who graduates, and who is imprisoned. Berkeley professor john a. powell (2015) explains that the unconscious plays a significant role in creating the discrepancy between our aspirations and our reality. He writes, "The unconscious mind is partially the source of today's *new* order of racial discrimination and bias."

This research can feel challenging to accept. Ms. K (who thought of herself as a champion of equity) didn't want to hear it, but social-neuroscience researchers have demonstrated that prejudice works automatically and unconsciously. Within milliseconds, we identify another person's apparent race, gender, and age, which activates a complex network of stereotypes, prejudices, and behavioral impulses. Our snap judgments are informed or perhaps even formed through our culture's influence in shaping prejudice. Years of explicit and implicit cultural messages—transferred to us from family, the media, our experiences, and countless other sources—link particular physical characteristics with a host of traits. In some cases, these messages (such as the superiority of Caucasians) originated centuries ago with colonialism, modern capitalism, and the enslavement of African and other non-European people. These messages of superiority and inferiority have become internalized in our consciousness and entrenched in our institutions. These messages are all around us. You could think of racism as a virus like a cold—it's easy to catch, so it's hard to blame someone for it, but that doesn't release us from the responsibility of containing it, not passing it on to others, and cleaning up any messes we might have unintentionally created.

Life-and-Death Implications

The problem isn't just our erroneous thoughts. It's not just that some people might think others aren't as smart. Unconscious bias has life-and-death implications. University of Chicago psychologist Joshua Correll and his colleagues have shown that police officers, community members, and students playing a video game are faster to "shoot" an armed black man than an armed white man. Cultural stereotypes and implicit bias can register in our brain in *a fifth of a second* (Correll, Park, Judd, and Wittenbrink, 2007).

Implicit bias contributes to the deaths of innocent people, as evidenced by the hundreds of unarmed black men and women who have been killed by police. Killing unarmed people of color is not a recent phenomenon, although now these incidents are occasionally captured on camera, leading to more focused and organized public outcry and inquiries into these crimes. According to an independent investigation, in 2015, a young black man was *nine times* more likely to be killed by a law enforcement officer than any other American (*The Guardian,* 2015).

I acknowledge that some people do not hold egalitarian values, and, in fact, they believe in the superiority of their own group and the inferiority of others. How we respond to overt racists is a topic that we won't get into here. If you are in a place where this is happening, you'll need to find allies in all corners of your organization and community with whom to partner. You'll need to strategize together, practice conversations, and plan to address the systems and structures in which this behavior is occurring. If you are a leader in a school where there are overt racists, it is even more incumbent on you to do what it takes—the learning, strategizing, courage boosting, and practice—to address this behavior.

Addressing the problem of racial bias only at the individual level is not enough. Bias, racism, and oppression live within the walls and foundations of institutions. There cannot be equity or justice until these structures are thoroughly overhauled or, in some cases, dismantled. Our education, housing, criminal justice, health care, and employment systems are set up in ways that privilege some and underserve others. To learn more, see the recommended resources for this chapter in Appendix F.

What Can Mindfulness Do?

Mindfulness helps us pay attention to what's happening right now. It helps us see and speak clearly and act with intentionality. Mindfulness is the antithesis of operating on autopilot, which is inherently flawed and even deeply biased. Finally, it guides us to align our actions with our aspirations and core beliefs, thus perhaps preventing us from acting on unchecked unconscious bias.

Here's a commonly studied example of unconscious bias that I noted in Chapter 4: A white woman walks down a street and sees a black man walking toward her. She clutches her purse and may cross the street to avoid him. She may not consciously feel afraid of him; she just automatically reacts.

With a practice of mindfulness, this same woman might see a black man walking toward her and say to herself, *The fear I'm experiencing now is not real or founded. It's the result of internalizing false messages about the danger of black men. My fear is dehumanizing to the man, and it cuts me off from making meaningful connections with others. Right here, right now, I have no reason to be afraid.*

Perhaps this woman would walk past the man, make eye contact, and even smile, just as she would if she was passing another white woman or another man. After many such moments of mindfulness, as well as after learning about bias, her impulse to clutch her purse might subside or disappear. Mindfulness is *one* tool that can help interrupt previously established associations (Lueke and Gibson 2014), but for us to uproot implicit bias, mindfulness needs to be complemented by additional learning, and we need to truly and deeply commit to that learning in order for us to grow.

At the very least, mindfulness and compassion practices help create the general conditions that minimize bias: They help us become aware of our emotions, take multiple perspectives, regulate our responses, reduce anxiety, and increase empathy. In order to uproot bias, we'll need to cultivate all of these mental and emotional states. The unconscious mind has internalized so much and is so efficient that the conscious mind alone doesn't stand a chance. If we aspire to create equitable schools, we need to find ways to align our unconscious with our conscious values. Addressing racism only at the conscious level won't be enough.

Mindfulness is also an invaluable resource to help you feel better equipped to respond when you experience others making decisions based on unconscious bias. Whether you've long been aware of implicit bias or you're becoming aware of it now, you'll likely notice that your awareness triggers strong emotions. Any time we are caught by strong emotions, if we can be mindful of our thoughts and feelings, we'll be more likely to find a way for those emotions to serve our greater purpose. Mindfulness can help your heart stop racing when you perceive implicit bias, help you think about what to say next, and help your heart stay open to others—which is essential as we address bias.

Back to Ms. K

Here's what happened with Ms. K. First, I said: "It seems like you have unconscious bias. We all do. You do send more black boys to the office than any other group. And you're right, they aren't more trouble than other kids."

Ms. K was demonstrating strong emotions at this point. "What are you feeling?" I asked. Through her tears, Ms. K said: "Guilt. Shame. I'm horrified at what I contributed to—undermining their self-esteem, contributing to the school-to-prison pipeline. I can't believe I was a part of this."

I took a deep breath. I held back from saying anything, wanting just to allow her feelings to come up rather than to try to understand or fix them. I also recognized in that moment that I was experiencing my own set of feelings that deserved a moment of recognition. Ms. K cried a bit more and then took a deep breath. "I'm grateful for this learning," she said, "and it's going to take me some time to absorb all of this."

In our following coaching session, we created a plan that included what Ms. K might do in the moment when students were off task or broke a rule, how she could track data more effectively to see trends and patterns, and how she could explore her biases and uncover their roots. She also agreed to a daily mindfulness practice before school. "I'll try anything to be a better teacher and serve all my kiddos," she said. "I feel such guilt over what I unconsciously did, and I'm committed to changing my behavior."

Shortly after this conversation, the school year ended, my job changed, and I stopped coaching Ms. K. About a year later, I ran into her on a Friday evening in a local grocery store. I felt drained after a challenging workweek, but she looked positively energized. "Guess what?" she said proudly. "I haven't sent a single kid out of my room all year!" She beamed. "And that's not because I keep them in my room in a timeout corner, and it's not because I don't have any challenging kids. I do." She grinned and continued, "It's because I'm staying in the bleeping moment. It's because I don't get triggered like I used to. I can redirect kids calmly and quickly because I'm not reactive to whatever they say or do." She paused and took a deep breath. "It's because," she continued, "I now see that my responses to the black boys had been more charged. As I started practicing mindfulness, I realized, to my horror, that I *was* sort of afraid of them. That I *was* harder on them. That awareness alone helped me change a lot because that's not who I want to be as a teacher or human being."

I congratulated Ms. K and thanked her for sharing her story. She continued: "I thought it was going to be so hard when you first told me about implicit bias. And I'm certainly not rid of it, but my actions are changing. I'm getting closer to who I want to be. And sometimes I think, it's only taken 20 minutes a day of sitting quietly. Couldn't we all do this?"

It will take more than mindfulness meditation to create equitable schools, yet I don't think we can do it without mindfulness. It certainly would be an easy place to start.

Implications for Leaders

- Understanding the role that implicit bias plays in your school could make it easier to address inequities. It might remove some of the blame and emotional charge, but not the responsibility to do something.
- A challenge for you in doing this work is that you need to do some of your own work first—your own reflection, understanding, learning, and processing—but this could take a long time, and the learning and reflection must begin in your organization. We can't keep asking kids to wait to get what they deserve while we prepare. Slow down, sit down, learn to calm and watch your own mind, and then get up and transform your school.
- Start now, today. Add time for mindfulness to your calendar this week.
- Consider opening a staff meeting with mindfulness activities. At the end of the meeting, reflect on the impact the opening had on the meeting.
- Identify teacher leaders who are interested in teaching these practices to students, and provide them with the training to do so.

The ability to be present in each moment is nothing more and nothing less than the ability to accept the vulnerability, discomfort, and anxiety of everyday life.

THE DALAI LAMA, DESMOND TUTU, AND DOUGLAS ABRAMS

A Dive into Joy

This book is ultimately about joy—about how we can find more joy in this life, in one another, and in our work as teachers and leaders, and how we can create the conditions in which others experience joy. This book is about *thriving*, not just surviving. Thriving implies joy. You deserve to feel joy. Although emotions are often entirely ignored, when we do talk about them or explore them, we often focus on the challenging emotions—sadness, anger, fear. We less frequently consider or talk about the emotional states that we're hoping to cultivate. We need to do this if we are going to thrive.

What does joy mean for you? For some, joy might be quiet, subtle, and soft, whereas for others, it's exuberant, bubbly, and noisy.

Pause right now: What comes to mind when you think about moments in your life that have been full of joy? Were they moments of connection or intimacy? Playfulness or silliness? Integrity and appreciation? What images come to mind when you think about joy? How do you express joy?

What about at school? Can you call to mind moments that have felt joyful? Maybe you first thought of grand moments of joy. When I think about my joyful moments as a teacher, I recall the winter I took my third graders on an overnight field trip to Yosemite National Park. Many had never seen snow, and their delight and the sense of community we shared were exceptionally joyful.

Then, as I continue recalling moments of joy, a patchwork of memories comes together: A literature circle in which a group of sixth graders who previously struggled to connect with each other engaged in a lively text-based discussion. That was joy for me. Or telling my class that silent reading was over and hearing their pleas for "just a few more minutes!" Or the pride on a kid's face as he shared his final project with his mother. The afternoon when I sat during recess with a distraught student and comforted her. The look of curiosity on the faces of students when I introduced a new unit. The gratitude from a grandmother after I spent time explaining the process of testing a child for learning difficulties. The satisfaction of locking my classroom door in late June and wrapping up another year. There were so many moments of joy—of satisfaction, contentment, connection, presence, appreciation, and fulfillment.

What if we experienced joy more often at school? What might be possible? Might it be possible to have little moments of joy every day?

Let's back up. Do you believe that joy is a birthright? That you deserve to feel joy just because you are alive? If your response wasn't an adamant "Yes!" you might benefit from exploring those assumptions. Know also that research says that experiencing joy will help you be better at your job. In *Your Brain at Work,* David Rock (2009) explains that stress decreases our cognitive resources and that happy people have more new ideas. Check out his book if you need utilitarian justification for bringing more joy into your life.

Try This Right Now

Recall a time when you felt real joy. Imagine the experience, vividly, in detail, bringing your senses into the recollection. What were the colors, sounds, and scents of the experience? What did your body feel like in that moment? How does it feel to remember that moment?

You most likely have many micro-moments of joy every day, tiny fleeting moments of connection, satisfaction, fulfillment, and contentment at school, but you probably don't notice many of them. And so they're missed. Because the brain has a negativity bias (we notice and recall the hard moments very well), we're simply missing the joyful moments. At least this is what happened to me—the moments of contentment were there, but my awareness skipped over them.

Here's a powerful practice for collecting joy, which is based on one taught by Rick Hanson (2013):

1. Instruct your mind to notice moments of joy, contentment, or happiness—whatever you want to call it. Say, *Hey, mind! If one of these emotional states passes through me during the day, could you please let me know? Thanks.* Maybe tell yourself this in the morning, or when you're walking into school. (This is connected to setting intentions, which we looked at in Chapter 3 and is described in the workbook.)
2. When your mind calls out, *"It's here! One of those (joy) moments!"* then pause and savor the moment. Use your senses to take in the experience. Notice how your body feels. Notice the chatter running through your mind. Imagine highlighting the most important elements: What exactly do you hear? What's the scene? How do you feel physically and emotionally?
3. Let your awareness of the moment sink in. Perhaps imagine a treasure chest in your heart in which you store these memories. Or imagine them being absorbed

into your body and mind. Say to yourself, *I'm saving this moment of well-being.* And thank your mind for bringing it to your attention.

You have a right to feel content and joyful every day. Accept this notion and hone your ability to recognize those moments. They do exist. And your resilience, I promise, will skyrocket.

Implications for Leaders

- Happy people do better work, and "appropriate challenge" makes us happy. In his book *Stumbling on Happiness,* Harvard psychologist Dan Gilbert (2005) describes how people are happiest when they're appropriately challenged to achieve difficult but attainable goals. Remember that it's your job to create the conditions that are conducive to a positive and productive learning and work environment.
- Given this direct relationship between personal challenge and job satisfaction, your job as a leader is to figure out how to provide your staff with just the right amount of personal challenge. You'll need to consider what is "appropriate" challenge, because if the challenge feels like a threat, people will do only as much as they have to do.
- When you draft a school-wide "appropriate challenge," use a broader spectrum of data that could include office referrals disaggregated in multiple ways, student and teacher attendance, number of positive home contacts, and so on.

South African archbishop Desmond Tutu, and Tibetan spiritual and political leader the Dalai Lama, personify resilience. Both endured decades of oppression and exile. And they are also, undoubtedly, two of the most joyful people on earth. Find a video of either man talking (easily available online); their smiles and laughter are infectious. In each other's company, they're described as "a comedy duo" (Dalai Lama, Tutu, and Abrams, 2016, p. 215).

In 2015, Tutu and the Dalai Lama came together to reflect on their lives and discuss an essential question: How do we find joy in the face of life's inevitable suffering? These conversations were captured in *The Book of Joy,* an uplifting, captivating, and mesmerizing read.

Disposition: Humor

A person without a sense of humor is like a wagon without springs.
It's jolted by every pebble on the road.
HENRY WARD BEECHER

I was raised amid some funny people. They used humor to lighten grim or uncertain moments, to poke fun at our human foibles, and to create perspective when there were challenges. Humor was a way to say things you weren't supposed to say and to bring people closer together as only peals of laughter can do. My grandparents specialized in self-deprecating humor, which seemed to be a way to forgive themselves for predictable blunders. With refined finesse, they wielded satire as an outlet for anger. Morbid humor let us indirectly explore really scary things like the Holocaust and torture. My grandfather's deadpan humor made it hard to know when he was serious—which made it easy to assume he was joking all the time. Humor was dished out as though it were an essential food group. When hard things happen now, I often imagine how these people who raised me, who are no longer living, might react. Just imagining their commentary brings levity to any situation.

Humor helps you be here now. It yanks you out of the drama of an experience, away from ruminating over the past or worrying about the future, and plunks you in the present. On a Thursday afternoon at the end of my first month teaching, I found myself trying to manage 34 second graders rotating through learning stations when the following events unfolded within just a few minutes: A dozen open bottles of tempera paint fell over and spilled into a colorful pool on the carpet; a bird flew into the classroom and, frantic to find a way out, started hurling its body against the window; and Marlena had "an accident" and bolted from the room sobbing. It was right then, on that afternoon, that my principal, who had never been to my classroom, decided to pop in to congratulate me on reaching the end of September. Her usually composed face dissolved into an expression of concern, and when Oscar, who was trying to corral the bird out, slipped in the paint, his pressed white shirt looking as if it had been tie-dyed, all I could do was laugh. "Everything is fine, Mrs. Cooke," I said. "I'm doing great!" And, in that moment, I really did feel fine.

Laughter is grounding. In fact, the origins of the word *humor* come from the same place as the words *humility* and *humanity*: from the word *humus*, "earth, fertile soil." When we laugh at ourselves, we don't take ourselves as seriously. When we laugh with others, humor breaks down barriers, brings us onto common ground, and builds our resilience (Larsen, 2015; Pande, 2014). As Victor Borge wrote, "Laughter is the shortest distance between two people."

There is scientific justification for laughter. In 1964, Norman Cousins, who had a stressful job as editor of a magazine, was diagnosed with a rare disease and given a few months to live. His doctor told him that he had a 1 in 500 chance of surviving and was advised to "get his affairs in order." Cousins ignored his doctor, took a sabbatical from his job, and checked into a hotel, where he watched funny movies and laughed to the point where his stomach ached. About six months later, he returned for a check-up, and the doctors pronounced that he had been miraculously cured. Since then, much research has shown that laughter strengthens the immune system.

Remember that, like all dispositions, humor can be cultivated. Desmond Tutu advises, "If you start looking for the humor in life, you will find it. You will stop asking, 'Why me?' and start recognizing that life happens to all of us. It makes everything easier, including your ability to accept others and accept all that life will bring" (Dalai Lama, Tutu, and Abrams, 2016, p. 222).

> *Like a welcome summer rain, humor may suddenly cleanse*
> *and cool the earth, the air and you.*
> LANGSTON HUGHES

Those 65,000 Daily Thoughts

You have around 65,000 thoughts a day (Blackburn and Epel, 2017). How would you like to have greater say over which thoughts take up residence in your mind? Thoughts and emotions are visitors who knock on the door of our house. With meditation, we can learn to greet them, acknowledge them, exercise choice about how to relate to them, and then watch them go. Those thoughts that make you anxious, insecure, irritated, or ashamed don't need to stay with you. And these thoughts are *not you*.

Without mindfulness, we invite unwanted emotions into our minds, offering them free rein. We identify with those emotions—we no longer notice them squatting in the dusty corners of our mind. When things are challenging, we assume that our current state will always be—that it's *just how we are*. This makes a difficult situation unbearable as we lose the sense that we can make choices and that things can change. This is how negative mindsets start feeling permanent. Life doesn't have to be this way.

Emotional resilience relies on openness, on broad mental awareness that enables us to see what is happening in our lives. We can learn to weather the storms in our life, teaching our mind to be like the sky, allowing everything to be there. The storms will roll in—that's inevitable—and mindfulness allows us to watch them pass and not get sucked into their thrall.

You don't have to fiddle with beads or recite foreign words; just pay full attention to whatever is going on right now, right here, and don't make judgments about it. Essentially, that's all mindfulness is. Practiced daily, with a bit more formality and precision, mindfulness helps you strengthen deep resilience muscles that you never knew you had.

CHAPTER REFLECTION

- How might being more fully in the present moment help you manage stress and build resilience?
- How might mindfulness help you boost your cultural competence?
- How might mindfulness help you fulfill your purpose?
- What are you inclined to do or learn more about after reading this chapter?

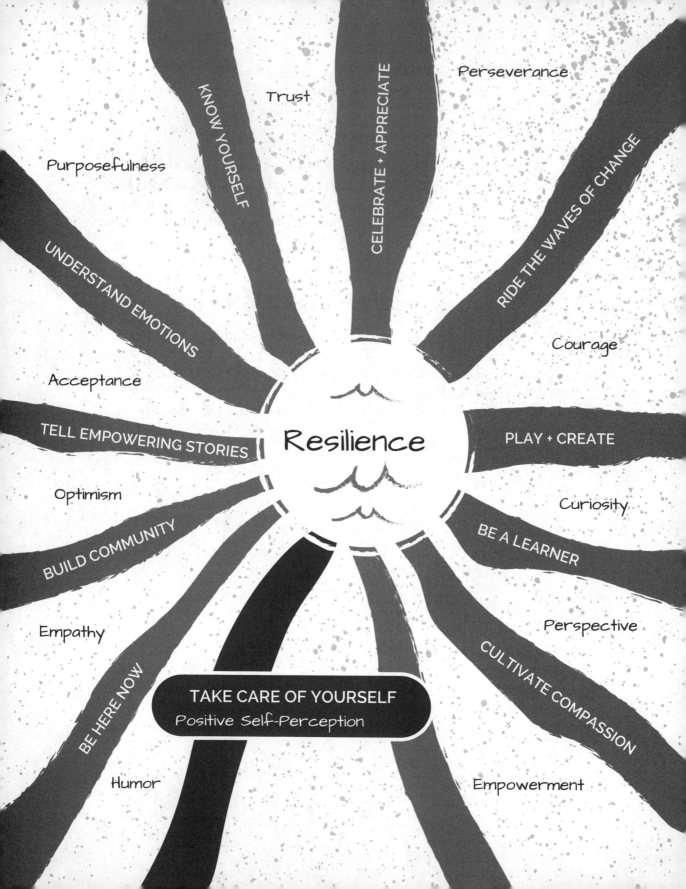

CHAPTER 6

Take Care of Yourself

Physical self-care and well-being are foundational for many other habits. When your body is cared for, you're better able to deal with emotions. Resilient people have a healthy self-perception, are committed to taking care of themselves, and accept themselves more or less as they are.

November: Self-care is the root of resilience when you're dragging yourself toward winter break and your emotions are raw.

❧ ❧

In my third year teaching, I wrote myself a letter that contained the following section:

> You will not save the world by working yourself to the bone. You can't be patient and attentive with kids, and deliver carefully crafted, differentiated lessons, and keenly capture formative assessment observations if you're congested, hungry, achy, weepy, phlegmy, jittery and have burning eyes from sleep deprivation. You won't be an amazing teacher if you work until you can't stand up.

Maybe you know this already. It took me a long time to learn. I suspect you know that you're not your best when your definition of self-care is that you brushed your teeth and changed clothes. You know that you get sick when you're run down and depleted, and that after a good night's sleep everything feels easier in your classroom. I'm sure you know that self-care is important.

So why don't we take better care of ourselves? What would it take to make us do so?

Our bodies and emotions are inextricably intertwined—our physical state creates emotional states; our emotions are affected by our physical state. This whole book is about emotional self-care, but in this chapter, we'll explore what it'll take to get us to sleep more, eat well, exercise, and take care of our bodies. If our bodies are strong, rested, nourished, and enjoyed, tending to our emotional selves will be exponentially easier.

Pause and Reflect

- What's your history of self-care? Are you on a trajectory of improvement, or has it been deteriorating?
- Why do you think you don't take better care of yourself?
- What might better self-care look like for you?

When Disillusionment Sets In

For new teachers, the stretch between mid-October and Thanksgiving is the most emotionally challenging phase of the school year. The New Teacher Center (NTC) calls this phase the "disillusionment period," when the excitement, hope, and adrenaline of the new school year have worn off and winter break seems impossibly distant. Ellen Moir (1990) of the NTC writes, "After six to eight weeks of nonstop work and stress, new teachers enter the disillusionment phase . . . The extensive time commitment, the realization that things are probably not going as smoothly as they want, and low morale contribute to this period of disenchantment. New teachers begin questioning both their commitment and their competence. Many new teachers get sick during this phase." This phase, as well as the others in a new teacher's year, is depicted in Figure 6.1.

Furthermore, by November, kids haven't yet demonstrated their learning in a way that matches our output of energy and effort. We can't yet see the results of all

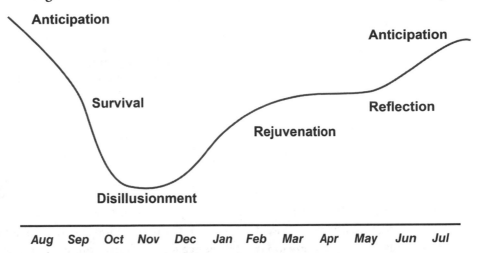

Figure 6.1 Phases of a First-Year Teacher's Attitude Toward Teaching

Anticipation

Anticipation

Survival

Reflection

Rejuvenation

Disillusionment

Aug Sep Oct Nov Dec Jan Feb Mar Apr May Jun Jul

that hard work. This is what makes us say to ourselves, *Is it really worth it to work this hard?*

November can be a low point for experienced educators as well. Whether I was working as a teacher, coach, or administrator, late October was a hard time for me. I'd been exerting tremendous energy for several months to get the year launched, to build relationships, and to be my best self, and my own self-care had fallen low on my list of priorities.

As we roll into the month of November, what would happen if we devoted time and energy to tending to our physical and emotional needs? What if during this time, teachers supported each other to take walks, eat nutritious lunches, and sleep? Isn't it worth focusing on our self-care for a month if there's a chance we could prevent illness, feel happier, and serve children more effectively?

Over the last 20 years, I've been on a steadily improving trajectory, but I'm not yet where I want to be in my self-care goals. Perhaps this is why I've been obsessed with getting people to take care of themselves. Our schools are bursting with educators who rarely put themselves first. Whether as a teacher in conversation with colleagues, as a coach working with clients, or as an administrator managing direct reports, I was faced with this issue again and again. I've probably thought about this question—*What would it take to get so-and-so to sleep eight hours a night?*—more than any when it comes to behavior change. Far too many times, a lack of self-care has surfaced as the root cause for lack of growth for a teacher or leader.

Four Reasons Why We Don't Take Care of Ourselves

Here's why I think we don't take care of ourselves:

1. We're missing information. Let's call this a **knowledge gap**. Sometimes we hear new information (or even something we've heard before) about exercise or sleep or kale, and it catapults us into behavior change.
2. We don't know how. We want to eat better, but where do we start? What exactly do we do? We all have **skill gaps** of different sizes. Self-care is learned.
3. We don't really think we need to take care of ourselves. We get by on minimal sleep, we can teach with a cold, and we figure we can rest later. This is a **will gap**.
4. We don't feel we deserve to take care of ourselves. We feel that our value is tied to our output and that if we don't work hard, people won't respect us, like us, love us, or want us. We don't say no to anyone; we take on too much work and overcommit. This is an **emotional intelligence gap**. Valuing yourself and feeling that you are worth self-care are core to emotional intelligence.

Gaps tend to coexist, so if you don't believe you are worthy of experiencing physical well-being (your emotional intelligence gap), you'll be unlikely to listen to a podcast on how sugar destroys your body. It's hard to know which gap came first—did an emotional intelligence gap spur a will gap? Or did the will gap come first? It can be useful to reflect on the root gap, but at the same time, it doesn't really matter which gap came first. What matters is that you start addressing the gaps—and sometimes it's easiest to start closing whichever one feels easiest.

You are reading this book because you want to be emotionally resilient, right? A healthy, well-rested body is foundational for emotional resilience. In this chapter, I'll focus on addressing will and emotional intelligence gaps around self-care, whereas the workbook offers some support in closing knowledge and skill gaps.

Outside Permission Can Be Motivating

I coached an assistant superintendent whose sleep deprivation wreaked personal and professional havoc on him, and, because he was such a physical and emotional mess, my leadership coaching was going nowhere. After observing his disastrous facilitation of a team meeting, I got tough. I said, "That's it! I'm going to quit being your coach unless you sleep! You can't get your team to make thoughtful decisions that impact thousands of kids if you don't get some sleep, eat breakfast, and drag your clammy face into the sun for 15 minutes a day. Either you sleep or I quit."

This administrator trusted me. He knew that I had his best interests at heart. He also wanted me to coach him. His response was, "I respect your opinion and I want to be a better leader, so if you say I should sleep, I'll sleep." We wrote a self-care plan, which included SMART (specific, measurable, attainable, relevant, and timely) self-care goals, and these moved to the top of his strategic planning documents.

As we created these plans, this leader also talked about his beliefs around hard work. "Growing up, all around me, there were messages around the value of work, warnings about laziness, about the role of men to work hard and provide. Those are in me," he said. I acknowledged that many of us have wholeheartedly adopted cultural mindsets and values around work and rest. I added that women are often told to care for everyone else before caring for themselves. These messages around sacrifice, hard work, and service have great value in our world—but they also need to be balanced with caring for ourselves. We don't have to abandon these values; they may just need to be tempered and updated with what we now know about our bodies, minds, emotions, and spirits.

Self-care is not the end of the conversation—it's the beginning. This assistant superintendent had three other goal areas that directly impacted children in his 25,000-student district, and, that year, he met them all. At the end of June, when I asked him in our final reflection, "To what do you attribute your success this year?" he said, "I slept eight hours a night, ate breakfast, and sat my clammy face in the sun."

"What convinced you to do that?" I asked. He'd been sleep deprived in this role for several years.

"I needed someone to make it a mandate or maybe give me permission," he said. "I haven't yet been able to do this for myself—that's the next step—so you telling me I had to do it got me started."

The moral of this story is this: If the Protestant work ethic has you trapped, or if another dominant mindset about who should care for themselves is choking you, get help. Tell a few people whom you trust and respect that they can yell at you. This kind of permission—granted or received—is a scaffold. It'll help us along this journey of self-discovery and true self-care. Don't turn down scaffolds; they exist for a reason.

Maybe you'd listen to your doctor telling you that you have to quit smoking or do something about your weight. Maybe you'd listen to your partner tell you to take the day off and get a massage. Maybe you'd listen to your mom or best friend or coach or boss or sister or kid or neighbor or pastor or Oprah tell you to treat your body well. If there's someone you'd listen to, let that person know. Most likely, people who care about you have tried before, but you've turned away. Let them know they can try again. Request help in getting started on this project.

When You Are in Self-Care Crisis

Are you reading this chapter now because you're falling apart and you can't figure out how to return to the classroom (or office) tomorrow? In Chapter 6 of the workbook, you'll find an intervention plan that has pulled many educators back from the edge. (It's called "When You Are in Self-Care Crisis.") Note that you'll need to do the things described there every day for a week in order to feel better.

> If you know that you really struggle with self-care, it might be worth turning to a mental health professional. This can be an area where deep-rooted issues lie, their origins often from childhood and, sometimes, trauma. You deserve this kind of care.

Implications for Leaders

- In the late fall, lighten up on the requests for evening or weekend duties. Help new teachers prioritize their time. Feed them. Give them refillable water bottles. Hold a staff meeting outside in the sun or even cancel a staff meeting and tell everyone to go home early. Don't let new teachers go into school on the weekend or launch an after-school program in the fall. You may need to set boundaries for new teachers so that, as they learn the rhythms of the school year, they can focus on their top priorities.
- Your own calendar cycle of energy and emotions might be different than that of a teacher's. Many principals find April-May to be the most punishing season of the year. During this time, they simultaneously finish one school year (including all the testing and celebrations of the season) and launch the next year (and do hiring, budgeting, master schedules, PD plans, and so on). This is also the time of year when, especially in secondary schools, kids tend to unravel. Plus, you're exhausted. Prepare for May as you would prepare to climb a mountain and, while climbing, prioritize your own rest.
- If a staff member is in crisis, use the plan in Chapter 6 of the workbook called "When You Are in Self-Care Crisis." Gently and kindly hold her

---

accountable for taking action: Ask her to call her doctor then and there to make an appointment, or to text her partner and say she needs help.

- You may also, at times, insist that a staff member take a sick or personal day. New teachers and perfectionists can have a really hard time giving themselves permission to take a day off. With your experience and perspective, you may recognize when it's in the best interest of the students that the teacher steps out for a bit. Relieve the teacher from having to make the decision.
- Make sure all teachers have an Emergency Substitute Folder prepared by week 1 that contains a couple of lesson plans, a seating chart, daily schedules, and the student roster so that on the occasion when he needs to step out and take care of himself, he doesn't have to go through this logistical process.

To Hell with Martyrdom

Some of us ignore our own health because of a nebulous and sinister force that we unconsciously create. Read these statements and note how many you've said or perhaps heard from a colleague:

- "No one appreciates how hard I work! I'm the first one here and the last to leave every day."
- "I don't even see my own kids because I'm so busy taking care of other people's."
- "Do you see that stack of notebooks on my trolley? That's what I take home every night. Who else is going to read 120 journal entries? How else will their writing improve?"
- "I can't take a day off! My classroom would crumble without me."

These are the kinds of statements that martyrs make, and, in most schools, there's at least one person bearing the scars of a savior and pleading for recognition. Many of us have tendencies toward martyrdom—as a new teacher, I did too—but our schools don't need martyrs. Let's consider what the martyr complex looks and sounds like, where it comes from, and why it's destructive.

Examining the Complex

Many educators, at different times in their career, have found themselves on a martyrdom continuum, which contains a range of behaviors and attitudes. It's useful to know the indicators of a martyr complex so that you can recognize it in yourself and understand it better in others.

At their most intense, martyrs are righteous and self-sacrificing. They don't set personal boundaries or say no to anything, and they can emotionally manipulate others into doing what they want. Work comes before everything, and everyone else's needs are put above their own. Martyrs also have an obsessive need to be right. They evade guilt and taking responsibility, and blame others for their misfortunes, disappointments, and turmoil.

Martyrs frequently talk about how hard things are, find lots of problems to complain about, and want others to know how underappreciated they are. Martyrs exaggerate suffering, hardship, and mistreatment; they expect admiration and heaps of sympathy. Publicly, martyrs actively seek appreciation, recognition, and attention for their efforts, sometimes creating drama in an effort to generate them; privately, martyrs take some pleasure in the suffering. It affirms some aspect of their self.

This is a depressing depiction, isn't it? It hurts to think that you would ever be among such a despicable bunch—but, perhaps, sometimes you play the martyr card. I've played it when I've been blind to my fears, frustrations, or insecurities, or when I've simply been too exhausted to think clearly. I've also played it when I was angry at others, as a way to make myself look better and indirectly to put them down. Ultimately, acting this way didn't get me what I wanted; it didn't compel others to work hard or help me, or to appreciate my contributions. It made people distance themselves from me.

You need to get real with yourself and determine where you are on the continuum. If you only dabble in martyrdom, work to shift those behaviors. Seek to understand the underlying emotions of fear, anger, and sadness. Ask someone you trust to call you on it when they see you playing the martyr. If you have fully donned the martyr's cape and have the scars to prove it, then you probably need outside help. Committed martyrdom probably has its roots in your childhood and has to do with your sense of self-worth. It can also be tangled up with perfectionism, which we'll explore later in this chapter. Seek help from a mental health professional to explore the origins of this tendency.

Recognizing the Dangers

Implicit in a martyr complex can be a deficit mindset about students and their communities—that the children and parents can't and haven't helped themselves, so they need an outside savior. I've encountered this mindset in school reform or transformation efforts in which teachers, thinking they are revolutionary, enter a community with big goals and inspiring slogans intent on saving kids (who are often black or brown and from low-income communities) from the ravages of inequities. Be careful—martyrdom can converge with racism and classism.

Martyrs can also undermine the health of a staff community. A martyr, by definition, thinks that he or she is in some divine way superior to others. Martyrs make this known to colleagues by detailing their sacrifices and suffering, and holding their own actions as exemplars.

Martyrdom is also problematic because it kills you, and usually pretty fast. You may have internalized some messages about suffering (there are institutions and mindsets that promote such ideology), but it's usually optional. Teachers can do amazing work and transform the lives of kids and also have their own families and hobbies and eight hours of sleep every night.

> *If we're not supposed to dance,*
> *Why all this music?*
> GREGORY ORR

Acknowledging Origins

Martyrdom is complicated. The reality is that it's unproductive and often ugly, but it can also feel seductive, particularly to new teachers. There are good reasons why some of us are tempted to compete for a spot among famous educator saviors—they are heralded, and movies are made about them. Who didn't choke up watching *Stand and Deliver, Dead Poets Society, Freedom Writers,* or *Dangerous Minds?* What new teacher doesn't think, *I want to be like Jaime Escalante or Ellen Gruwell and enlighten my "at-risk" kids and save them from gangs?* But these movies contribute to the problem of the martyr complex by deifying educators who see their students as victims to be saved and who get sick and burned out trying to save them.

For those of us who have found ourselves fantasizing about being Jaime Escalante, I acknowledge that educators have few praiseworthy role models (and if you're a person of color, even fewer). When you're a new teacher, it's hard to figure out whom to emulate, especially if you've got a fire in your belly to make the world better. Furthermore, teachers are seriously underappreciated in all ways, including financial compensation. The lack of acknowledgment and even empathy for the work that teachers do exacerbates this whole martyr thing. There's nothing wrong with wanting recognition; but needing to be recognized and making a martyr out of yourself are two different things, and martyrdom is deadly.

Even though we can find a martyr or two in most schools, we can also find their antitheses—healthy, effective, humble teachers—working in classrooms. They are grading papers at school so they don't have to take them home, getting help from students to organize the classroom, taking a moment of quiet during lunch, and facilitating productive and often (but not always!) exciting classes. The best role models might not be the most charismatic or the busiest or the ones who stay at school the longest. But they do exist. Seek them out—those who live balanced lives and do great work with kids.

> *If you have come here to help me you are wasting your time.*
> *But if you have come here because your liberation is bound up*
> *with mine, then let us work together.*
> LILLA WATSON, INDIGENOUS AUSTRALIAN ARTIST,
> ACTIVIST, AND ACADEMIC

Seeking Antidotes

We need to shift our mental models of what it takes to transform schools, and redefine what it means to be an educator. Our kids need teachers who sleep eight hours a night and walk every day and eat dinner with their families—and they need teachers who are highly skilled at their craft and who make good on the promise of education for all. And principals: Teachers need leaders who do the same.

If you have tendencies toward martyrdom, try these tactics for change:

- Find role models in your schools and communities. Talk to veteran teachers and ask, "Whom do you know who does great work with kids in our school/district and who lives a balanced life?"
- Look at things through a strengths-based lens: What works in this community?
- Cultivate a vision for your life that's holistic—one that includes self-care, personal growth, adventure, and celebration.
- Consider working with a therapist to explore the underlying emotions.

New teachers, I know you got into this work because you want to contribute to the lives of young people. It might take a while to see evidence of your contribution. Be patient. Yes, you should see growth in student learning within a couple of months or even days, if you know how to look. Doing daily formative assessment will help you see how your kids are progressing. But transformational change takes longer to show its face.

In my journey as an educator, some of the most meaningful evidence of student learning took 10 or 15 years to materialize and showed up as a Facebook message from a former student. Dear new teacher, you may not believe me now—especially if you're in the midst of a grueling first year—but I will tell you, there has been *nothing* in my professional life that's been as rewarding as those messages that retroactively obliterated the exhaustion of teaching. If when I was a novice in the classroom I had known that this affirmation would one day come, I may have worked differently, less anxiously. I may not have lamented the lack of appreciation from my principal or society at large. I would not have wondered, *Is this really worth it?*

Work hard. Learn your craft. Connect with kids. But don't ask for, seek, or demand appreciation. Ask for feedback and stay committed to your learning, and you will learn and grow and have meaningful impact on kids.

Implications for Leaders

- Martyrs can undermine the health of a staff community. If you have self-righteous teachers among your ranks, do what you can to address their behavior and minimize their impact.
- Leaders can contribute to the martyrdom syndrome if they pick the "hardest-working" teacher to lead the new initiative and don't ask for more from the teacher who clocks out when the last bell rings. Don't perpetuate martyrdom by rewarding it with attention and accolades.
- Recognize and acknowledge the teachers who live a balanced life and do good work. Highlight self-care. Commend teachers for doing strong, solid work and for meeting their personal and familial commitments.
- Make sure you model balance and self-care.

What Your Body Desperately Needs

We all have knowledge gaps. And we all forget. Let's review what the body we live in needs from us. I'll try to make it fast and fun.

Sleep: The Magic Resilience Booster

Sleep deprivation is a torture technique because it erodes your mental and emotional stability. If you're feeling really off balance in the self-care domain, if you're in crisis, if you're wondering where to start—begin with prioritizing sleep. Here's what happens to your brain and body when you sleep:

- Your brain creates and consolidates memories and organizes thoughts. If you sleep well the night before a conference, your brain prepares to form memories. If you sleep well after, your brain cements in the new information.
- Your brain makes creative connections, remote associations, and unusual connections, which can lead to a major *aha!* moment upon waking. There's science and truth in the old adage, "Sleep on it."
- Your brain processes information, prepares for action, and makes decisions.
- Your brain is cleaned up. Toxic molecules flush out of your body systems, including out of your brain. Researchers connect lack of sleep with the plaque that builds up in the brains of people with Alzheimer's.
- Your brain remembers how to perform physical tasks. Short-term memories, stored in the motor cortex, move into the temporal lobe, where they become long-term memories.
- Your hunger hormones regulate themselves.
- Your body rests and recuperates because normal physiological processes slow way down. Your intestines rest. Your liver detoxifies more efficiently. Your muscles grow.

In study after study, the findings are the same: Sleep is correlated to improved psychological health. "Sleep is the most underrated health habit," says Dr. Michael Roizen (Huffington, 2014, p. 74). Sleep more, and your resilience will almost magically be boosted—and most of us actually enjoy it (unlike feelings about exercising). The workbook offers specific pointers on improving your sleep.

If you're not convinced that you need more sleep, or it feels too hard to get the full amount right now, see what happens if you get to bed just 30 minutes earlier for one week. How does that extra sleep make you feel during the day? What's the impact on your teaching?

There's one caveat to my insistence on sleep, which is that sleeping a lot can also be a symptom of depression. If you sleep a lot but don't feel the way you want, see the section "When to Call the Doctor" in Chapter 2 or use the self-assessment tool in Appendix D.

Nutrition: You Are What You Eat

I'm going to keep this short, because I suspect you know this and will tune me out if I get on my soapbox and deliver a long rant about healthy eating, so here's what I want to remind you of: What you eat affects your health and mood. There is a pile of research that would stretch from here to the moon on the connection between diet and our physical and mental health. The average Western diet mainly comprises processed foods that are devoid of the nutrients needed for a healthy body and brain. Our bodies need a whole-foods diet that contains the full range of vitamins, minerals, essential fatty acids, amino acids, enzymes, and good bacteria. If you find yourself tired and draggy every afternoon, and you get depressed and think you want to quit teaching, and you're impatient and snappy with kids—look at what you eat for lunch. There might be a connection.

If you weren't raised by a health food nut in the 1970s or you've been dealing with back pain for a decade or you'd like to reduce or get off antidepressants, please see Appendix F and do more learning. The workbook also offers some more tips and information on healthy eating. If you're feeding your body crap or not giving it what it needs, you're going to find it almost impossible to figure out which aspect of your emotional distress comes from how you fuel your body, and which is from circumstances and thoughts. Resilient people have resilient bodies, bodies that are fed every day with nutritious food.

Exercise: Put on Your Shoes and Take a Walk

Solvitur ambulando—It is solved by walking.
DIOGENES, FOURTH CENTURY BCE GREEK PHILOSOPHER

To become more resilient, we need to build new neural pathways. We need to integrate new ways of thinking about and responding to events in our brains; we need to change behaviors and dislodge mindsets that don't serve us. To create new neural pathways so as to change your mind, you need to move: Physical movement brings blood to your brain; blood provides glucose for energy, and oxygen to soak up the toxic electrons; and blood stimulates the protein that helps neurons connect (Medina, 2008).

The human brain developed during an evolutionary period when our ancient ancestors walked about 12 miles a day. According to paleoanthropologists, our unique cognitive skills developed under the conditions where motion was a constant presence (Medina, 2008). Few of us now walk 12 miles a day. Yet it is clear that we still need to exercise to be our most resilient selves.

I probably don't need to tell you that exercise is good for your heart and bones and lungs and just about every single cell in the organism that you are. I probably don't need to tell you that it'll boost your mood and energy. I just want to remind you, because we forget, don't we? The following movement-related facts often get me out of my chair, so perhaps they'll be useful reminders for you, too:

- Whether or not you move is one of the greatest predictors of how well you will age. What's your vision of yourself at age 78?
- Exercise improves long-term memory, reasoning, attention, and problem solving. This is why kids need recess a couple times a day.
- The risk of Alzheimer's, heart disease, and cancer is slashed in people who exercise for 30 minutes a few times a week.
- Exercise regulates the neurotransmitters that govern our mental health. Almost every doctor or psychiatrist will prescribe exercise for depression.
- Cognitive performance can be measurably boosted through cardiovascular exercise in as little as four weeks.
- It doesn't take a lot of exercise to reap the physical and mental benefits. Walking a few times a week is very beneficial, and if you can get aerobic exercise two or three times a week, you're doing great.

Movement: Your brain needs it, your physical body needs it, and your emotions need it too. Find something you like to do, enlist a friend to join you, change things up so that you don't get bored, and just do it. Dance, box, climb rocks, do yoga or Pilates, hike, swim, bike, go to Jazzercise, do Zumba, or just walk. Now go! Put on your shoes and take a 20-minute walk, and you will be more likely to remember what you're reading! Go!

Sex, Forest Bathing, and Other Fun Stuff

Folks I'm telling you,
Birthing is hard and dying is mean—
So get yourself a little
Loving in between
LANGSTON HUGHES

Aside from attending to our body's basic functions, there are so many ways that we can enjoy this body we're in as well as take care of it. Let's consider some of these.

Get It On

Human beings are social creatures, and we need interaction with people our own age—not just with the 130 high school sophomores with whom we spend our days. But sometimes we forget this, don't we? So let me remind you: You need friends, confidants, relatives, and lovers. You need emotional and physical intimacy. I've worked with many brilliant educators who put cultivating relationships low on their list of things for which to carve out time.

Would a smattering of science convince you to tumble in the hay? Entertain your intellect with a few facts about the physiological benefits of a healthy sex life. Sex can

- Lower your blood pressure
- Help balance your estrogen and testosterone levels, which can help prevent osteoporosis and heart disease
- Boost your immune system (see research done at Wilkes University in Pennsylvania if you're really interested)
- Induce relaxation and improve sleep
- Increase your heart rate, engage muscles that you don't use in the classroom, and burn more calories than watching TV
- Stimulate bonding between people (oxytocin, the "love hormone," is released during sex)

That's enough science—just know that sex is good for you (with or without a partner). And, by the way, you have permission to enjoy your body. You have a right to pleasure. You deserve it.

One last thing: Although sex has unique physical and emotional health benefits, hugs and touch can also be therapeutic and healing. In *The How of Happiness*, professor Sonja Lyubomirsky (2007) cites a study in which people assigned to give or receive hugs five times a day ended up much happier than their nonhugging counterparts in the study. But you know this is true, right? I doubt you need the studies about which neurotransmitter does what when someone you care about grabs you in a bear hug or even just holds your hand. So do it!

Let's consider some additional fun and easy ways to take care of your body that also have physiological benefits.

Spend Time in Trees

> *Thousands of tired, nerve-shaken, over-civilized people are*
> *beginning to find out that going to the mountains is going home.*
> *Wilderness is a necessity.*
>
> JOHN MUIR

In Japan, there is a practice called *Shinrin-yoku,* which translates as "forest bathing" and is considered a form of preventive health care and healing. We all most likely know and agree that being in nature makes us feel good, and Japanese researchers have produced a robust body of literature on the physical and mental health benefits of soaking up the sights, smells, and sounds of the natural world. In Japan, forest bathing is considered a medical practice and is even covered by insurance.

Here's what scientific studies have found about the benefits of forest bathing:

- Many trees give off organic compounds that support natural killer cells that boost our immune system and help fight cancer.
- Many plants also give off substances called phytoncides, which are antimicrobial organic compounds. Breathing these substances promotes relaxation.
- Being in the forest lowers blood pressure and the stress hormone cortisol.
- Forest bathing improves mood, energy, sleep, and the ability to focus.

Forest bathing differs from hiking because it centers on the therapeutic aspects of being in nature. The goal is not exercise or reaching a destination. To practice *Shinrin-yoku,* go to a forest. Walk slowly. Breathe. Open all your senses. That's it.

Sit near Water

Sit by a stream, splash in a lake, gaze at the ocean, or dive into an underground spring—there's science behind the therapeutic benefits of being in and near water. An entertaining read on this subject is *Blue Mind: The Surprising Science That Shows How Being Near, in, on, or Under Water Can Make You Happier, Healthier, More Connected, and Better at What You Do,* by marine biologist Wallace J. Nichols (2014). According to Nichols, water gives the brain a rest from overstimulation, induces a meditative state, evokes feelings of connection to something beyond ourselves, and spurs creativity—just think about how many great ideas you've had in the shower.

The ocean (and waterfalls and thunderstorms) also emit high levels of negative ions—and we need those! The atmosphere we breathe is full of positive and negative ions, but most of us spend our time indoors. Air conditioning and poor ventilation remove negative ions, which can make us feel low energy, sleepy, and even depressed. You feel more energized at the beach because of the negative ions. When you can't be near naturally running water, just open the windows, go outside whenever you can, and even consider an air purifier (which emits negative ions).

Immerse Yourself in a Flotation Tank

For a unique mind and body therapeutic experience, float in a sensory deprivation tank. By diminishing nearly all sights, sounds, smells, and touch, your mind can settle, sparking creativity, relaxation, and even emotional breakthroughs. Floaters not only claim relief from insomnia, pain, and anxiety but also use this therapy as a way to hone their mental concentration. Golden State Warrior's MVP Steph Curry is an avid floater and credits it with his ability to be calm and focused on the court. If you're really curious, there's even scientific research on the therapeutic impact (just Google it). Obviously, floating is not for the claustrophobic, but don't let the weirdness of it deter you from trying it—it's surprisingly fun.

Get Your 15 Minutes of Sun

Our bodies need direct sunlight several times a week in order to get vitamin D, and many of us are vitamin D deficient. Numerous studies have shown that optimizing your vitamin D level may help prevent different types of cancer. The best way to get more vitamin D is through sunscreen-free exposure to the sun. Aim for 15–30 minutes a few times a week, and try to get midday sun.

In the winter, it's even more important to get sunlight. Our bodies are governed by circadian rhythms, our body's natural clock that regulates important functions, including sleep/wake cycles and mood. Shorter days and less sunshine affect these rhythms. An estimated 20% of Americans experience seasonal affective disorder (SAD) each winter (*Psychology Today*, 2017). When you're in the sun, your body releases serotonin, which helps elevate your mood and energy. Knowing this information about sunlight might help alleviate the annoyance of doing yard duty. Perhaps you could eat lunch outside once or twice a week, take a walk before school, or greet kids as they arrive at school in the morning.

Put Your Feet on the Earth

Have you noticed that you feel better when walking barefoot on the earth? Recent research explains that our immune system functions optimally when our body has an adequate supply of electrons, which we get through barefoot contact with the earth (Mercola, 2012).

You can reap these same benefits from other forms of direct contact with the ground: Walking on the beach, sitting in a park, or lying in the grass, as long as there isn't anything between your body and the earth. There's growing evidence that this kind of connective contact is beneficial for our health, and, in any case, it's a nice way to be outside. You meet your sunlight requirements, and, if you do it surrounded by trees, you can soak in that goodness too. So try it! Spend 10 minutes a few times a week sitting on the earth; tell yourself, *This is a boost to my physical and mental well-being,* and see if you don't feel better.

Learn to Say No

Saying no is liberating. *No, I can't attend the social hour. No, I can't join that committee. No, I can't take the kids to the park tomorrow.* What would you like to say no to right now? Saying no means saying yes to something else. If you say, *No, I can't join that committee,* you might be able to say yes to an hour of walking in the sun twice a month during the time when the committee meets. What do you wish you could say yes to right now?

If you have a hard time saying no to people, you most likely have a problem with overcommitting. And then what happens? As the event or obligation approaches, you berate yourself for having made the commitment, you fantasize about ways to back out of it, or make up excuses and cancel; or you show up with an aura of resentment and unhappiness about you, or force a smile and push yourself through it, all the while feeling tired and aware that you're denying yourself whatever it was that you really wanted to be doing. You tell yourself, *I never should have said yes to this—I knew I would be too tired,* or *I knew I didn't really want to do it.*

So why did you say yes? Why do you overcommit? The answers to these questions most likely lie in your sense of self-worth. You say yes because you want people to like you. You say yes because you want people to think you are good or smart or skilled or capable. You say yes because you want to be wanted. You say yes because you're afraid that if you say no, they won't ask again. They won't be your friend. They won't want you in their school. They won't love you. You say yes because you're afraid.

But here's what you may or may not know. First, when you say yes to something you don't really want to do and then you show up, other people sense that—consciously or unconsciously, they can know that you don't want to be there. That's not really fair to them, either. Do things, give of your time and energy, because you want to and because you can—not because you feel obligated.

When you say yes to something because you're afraid, the fear won't go away. It'll bubble noxiously under the surface, and you'll still be obligated to fulfill your commitment, because it's really not fair to agree to something and then back out. Take responsibility for the choices you've made, learn from them, and make different choices in the future.

When you say no, you're likely to let some people down. You may disappoint them. Learn how to say no kindly and thoughtfully. Maybe they'll say, "I'm hurt that you won't be there," and you can hear that, acknowledge it, and live with it. You may feel sad, but you can also recognize that you need to take care of yourself; and in that moment, that's the cost of doing so. Let others deal with their emotional response.

When you say no, some people might get angry. Don't get freaked out by anger, and don't be the recipient of people's aggression. Get away from them if they get angry. There's a difference between disappointment and hurt, and anger. You don't deserve it.

When you start saying no, when you draw boundaries around what you will give and do for others, you're likely to gain insight into whom you should have in your life. Toxic relationships will come into focus. You'll gain clarity on whom you need to compassionately remove from your life so that you'll have more space for yourself, for your well-being, for your happiness. Your resilience will always be undermined if you have energy vampires clinging to your neck.

You are not a victim in this scenario; you can detach those vampires and set them free by saying no. As you clear away people who want things from you but may not truly care for you, you'll find you have more space in your life for the people who can appreciate you for who you are, who accept you as you are, who will say no to you when they need to, and who take care of themselves.

At its root, your struggle to say no has to do with your sense of self-worth. The resilient have a herculean sense of self-worth, self-esteem, and self-regard. There's no getting around this on the path to becoming resilient, which is why there are so many points in this book where I suggest working with a therapist. The origins of our lack of resilience are often deep in our childhoods. Reading this book, engaging in the workbook exercises, talking about this with colleagues, and working with a coach are all significant steps toward well-being, but they may not be enough to live the kind of life that deep down you know you want to live.

Here's the most powerful way to figure out how to respond to a request. Ask yourself, *What do I want to do?* Keep asking yourself this question over and over as you contemplate the rest of the mental chatter that rattles through your mind. Sort through feelings of obligation, fear of not being wanted, fear of disappointing others, fear of someone else's anger, and keep asking yourself, *What do I want to do?* It may take time, and at first your response might be a barely audible whisper, but keep asking the question and listen carefully. Then act on what you hear.

A Dive into Perfectionism

At the heart of perfectionism is a belief that, in order to be loved and accepted, we must strive to act and be the best all the time. Our very worth as a human being is tied to our perfection. The pursuit of perfection consumes a great deal of time and energy because every time we feel shame, blame, or criticism, our response is, *I wasn't perfect enough. So let me be more perfect next time.* And this goal, remember, is not possible.

Perfectionists

- Get upset when someone else or life in general doesn't measure up to how they think things "should" be
- Have uncompromising rules about how things should or must be
- Blame themselves and others for things that aren't under their control or the control of others
- Think in black-and-white terms
- Quickly discount positives
- Are relentlessly hard on others and on themselves and hold rigidly high and unrealistic standards
- Use the word *should* a lot
- Claim they're "not a perfectionist"—they just have high standards

Perfectionism may not actually be an emotion but, rather, a dysfunctional emotional tendency. It is one of the most challenging emotional tendencies to confront, but, left unchecked, it can be corrosive. If you are a new teacher and you know you're a perfectionist, or you sense the potential to become one, it's worth it to dig out the emotional roots of this trait now rather than live under its rule for years. Perfectionism has been associated with increased stress, physical health problems, mental health issues, and a high risk of burnout. It will eat through your resilience the way a colony of termites can churn through wood.

Here is why perfectionism is so dangerous: There is no such thing as perfect, at least among humans. It is inherent to our condition that we make mistakes, and without mistakes, we would have little chance to learn or grow or adapt to new situations. Perfection would obstruct evolution. So perfectionists are always striving for the impossible, and when they inevitably fail, they experience a surge of difficult emotions—shame, inadequacy, fear, anger. These hurt the perfectionists as well as those around them.

Perfectionism shouldn't be confused with a commitment to excellence and a strong work ethic. You can have tremendous energy, conscientiousness, and persistence and not be a perfectionist. Perfectionism is about seeking external validation, whereas healthy striving is all about internal drive. A healthy striver has high expectations and commits to a task while also making mistakes and knowing that those mistakes don't indicate a personal flaw. A perfectionist's sense of self-worth is overly tied to external praise and accomplishments.

Brené Brown is one of the world's experts on perfectionism. She says that shame gives birth to perfectionism. Perfectionism isn't healthy striving, says Brown; it's not *Let me be my best self.* It is a thought process that says, *If I look perfect, live perfectly, work perfectly, and do it all perfectly, I can avoid or minimize shame, blame, judgment, and criticism.* Perfectionism is not a protective shield; rather, it stops someone from being seen. Brown's TED Talk, books, and speeches are powerful resources if you want to better understand this characteristic in yourself and others.

> *The core of authenticity is the courage to be imperfect,*
> *vulnerable, and to set boundaries.*
> BRENÉ BROWN

What Can I Do If I Suspect I'm a Perfectionist?

First, get real with yourself. Write a list of problems that perfectionism causes in your life. How does it consume your time and energy? How does it get in the way of forming healthy relationships? What's the impact on your physical health and well-being? How does it hold you back from doing things you want to do? Find someone you trust. Ask, "Do you think I'm a perfectionist? How do you think this has affected me?"

Then make a list of what might be possible if you curtailed your perfectionist tendencies. What could you do in your life? How might you feel? What would your job be like if you cast out these termites?

Commit to exploring and uprooting the origins of your perfectionism; otherwise, like unwanted weeds, they will regrow. Depending on how pervasive your perfectionism is and how deep the roots go, you may need to get help from a mental health professional. Perfectionism is about self-worth, and many perfectionists had childhood experiences that led them to doubt their self-worth.

While you're exploring your perfectionist roots, begin making behavioral changes. Set time limits for yourself for tasks like writing emails or grading papers, and, when the timer goes off, obey it. Set a time for leaving school and don't deviate. Notice your self-talk, and substitute unhelpful self-talk with new language. Say to yourself:

- This is good enough, and good enough is great.
- I am enough. I do enough.

And, finally, if you think you might be a perfectionist or you want to rid yourself of any perfectionist tendencies, just do everything I'm telling you to do in this book! Get to know yourself, understand your emotions, tell empowering stories, build community, practice mindfulness, sleep and walk, cultivate compassion, and so on.

Implications for Leaders

- Perfectionism can complicate martyrdom further and make it even more problematic. Because perfectionists are very effective at what they do, the martyrdom-perfectionism combination depletes resilience and results in burnout. But martyrdom can also be a shield from accountability and expectations that the martyr improve his or her teaching practice. In these cases, martyrdom and mediocrity can go hand in hand, and sometimes to get to the hard conversation around the need to improve, you have to slash through layers of martyrdom.

Disposition: Positive Self-Perception

If you want to bounce back quickly after setbacks, if you want to be resilient, you must place high value on the bouncy object: *Your self.* When you value your mind, heart, body, and spirit, you'll make choices that foster your resilience; you'll do whatever it takes to bounce back. The self-care habits in this chapter can help you cultivate healthy self-esteem, which starts at the most fundamental level of your physical existence. You must value your body to value your emotional self and your mind. This, say the researchers, is a key trait of the resilient: We value our self. We want this self to rebound quickly after adversity.

Resilient people aren't overly critical of themselves, don't strive for perfection, and set boundaries: This is what it means to have high self-esteem. Self-acceptance and self-love must be aspirations if you want strong resilience muscles. With positive self-perception, we take responsibility for choices, actions, and mistakes. We accept ourselves as we are and forgive ourselves for mistakes.

Positive self-perception is a tricky one because the foundation of self-esteem is laid down in our earliest years of life. If the first people responsible for caring for you did not love you exactly as you were, if they did not think that you were the most perfect, precious creature on the planet, if they wanted you to be anything other than the person you showed up as, then this disposition is more challenging to cultivate. If that is the case, I encourage you to work with a therapist and tackle this beast at its place of origin. If you don't, those old feelings of inadequacy will unexpectedly pop up with devilish ferocity and cruelty when you least expect them.

Although I hope you might explore the roots of your fragile self-esteem, doing so can take time. It is the route toward transformation and true resilience, but there's another path you can explore simultaneously: Fake it until you make it. This approach is underused, and there's growing neuroscience research explaining that our mind will change in response to our behaviors. Take care of yourself (and fake the concern if you must) until you believe that you're worthy of self-care. See what happens to your emotional landscape if you just take care of your physical self. My bet is that you'll not only feel better but also start valuing yourself more, and your self-esteem will surge. Now, put on your walking shoes and get outside.

Strive for Balance

Maybe this doesn't need to be said, but this chapter is not a free pass to call in sick day after day when you're just not feeling like going to school, or to leave school with the kids at 3:00 p.m. I doubt that most educators read this chapter seeking such permission—but, in case you did, you probably need to do some soul searching about what you're doing and where you really want to be.

Everyone else: Make balance your goal. It might be hard (or unrealistic) to do every day all of the self-care things you know are good for you; time is truly limited, and maybe you have a family to care for and a long commute and night classes. But ultimately, the time you put into taking care of yourself will reward you with productivity, efficiency, and emotional well-being. Without attending to the underlying physical causes of stress, you'll find it harder to bounce back from rough moments.

Prioritize self-care. You may need only one extra hour a day for sleep, exercise, preparing a healthy salad, and even some meditation. No need to completely eliminate sugar or alcohol or caffeine—just reduce it. Reduce TV time and replace it with a walk. And as you reduce the things that deplete your energy and increase the self-care, pay close attention to how doing so impacts your emotions, your patience with kids, your tolerance for an annoying coworker, and your ability to plan lessons and assess papers. Manage your vices, find the middle way, and strive for balance.

> *Caring for myself is not self-indulgence, it is an act of self-preservation,*
> *and that is an act of political warfare.*
> AUDRE LORDE

I believe I am alive to heal and repair the world, and I appreciate receiving permission from others who have walked this path. Audre Lorde does this for me. Have you read Audre Lorde? Her poetry and essays hurl me through emotional landscapes of anger, hope, and love and land me firmly in the conviction that the pen is mightier than the sword. Audre Lorde died at age 58 after a long battle with cancer. She penned many volumes of poetry and prose, founded a publishing press for women of color, and fiercely advocated for women, black women, and queer women. She was also a mother, partner, and traveler. If she tells me to rest, I will do so. Thank you, Audre Lorde.

CHAPTER REFLECTION

- What are a couple of learnings you're taking away from this chapter?
- What needs to happen so that you take better care of yourself?
- What's one thing you could do immediately to improve your self-care?

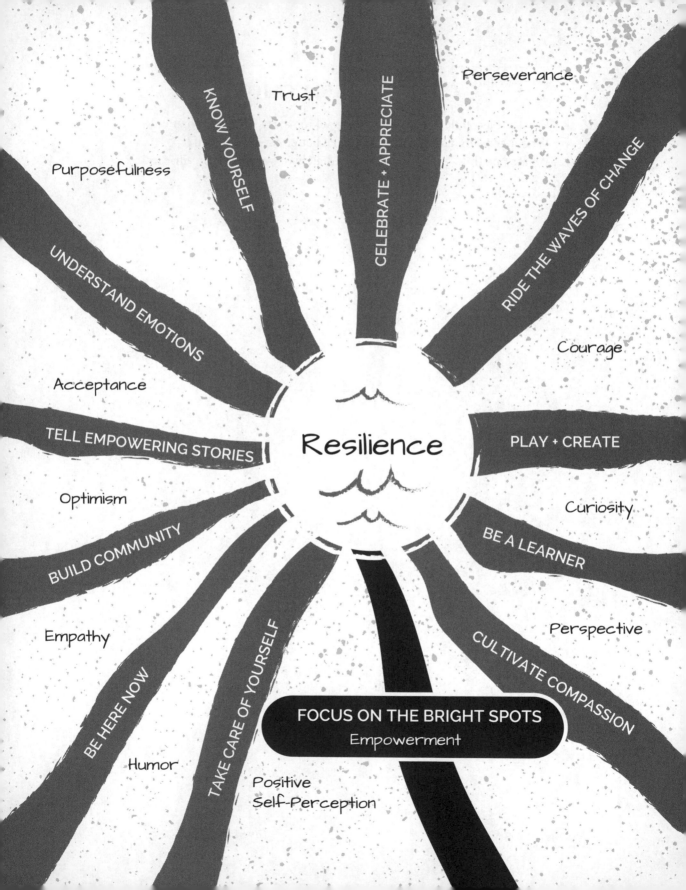

CHAPTER 7

Focus on the Bright Spots

We can hone our attention to focus on our strengths, assets, and skills. This helps us generally feel better and enables us to respond to challenges more effectively. Focusing on strengths also boosts our levels of self-efficacy, and we feel more empowered to influence our surroundings.

December: When the days are short and you haven't recovered from the exhaustion of late fall, look for the light.

❧❧

   Although it seemed as if my second graders returned from Thanksgiving more settled and focused, it might have been that I was more adjusted and comfortable in the classroom in the early winter of my first year. At the start of December, I was hopeful, energetic, and increasingly confident about the learning routines I'd established in my class. Yet cliques had formed among some of the girls, and, too often, kids were not nice to each other. A teacher I'd met in the summer had given me a book called *Tribes: A Process for Social Development and Cooperative Learning* (Gibbs, 1987) which was a guide to building a learning community in the classroom. Because my administrators did not offer me or my teacher colleagues an approach to building classroom culture, I'd wholeheartedly adopted *Tribes*.

   Committed to addressing student dynamics, I found an activity to try in *Tribes*. At the beginning of the day, in our morning circle, each student pulled the name of another and became that person's "secret admirer" for the day. The rules included that you couldn't tell anyone whom you had, and you had to observe the person all day and find *behaviors* to appreciate. At the end of the day, we squeezed back into our tight circle on the rug, and students revealed the person they'd been watching, and shared appreciations: "Oscar gave Manuel his soccer ball during recess," "Lizette walked quietly to lunch," "Billy helped Tomas with math."

As students offered and received appreciations, their expression shifted and revealed pride, joy, and connection. I was surprised at how astutely these seven-year-old children had observed each other, identifying specific, admirable behaviors in a classmate who may or may not have been their friend. As we debriefed and wrapped up the activity, Tomas asked if we could repeat the activity the next day, to which the whole class echoed their approval. "Sure," I said, "why not?"

At the end of the second day of Secret Admirers, I got the same request: "Why can't we do this every day?" asked Elizabeth. So we did. Day after day, the kids pulled names from the hat. Sometimes we had "challenge days" where everyone drew two or three names. Other days were "Me too!" days, and students also had to identify their own behaviors for which they wanted recognition. We created and posted lists of the student behaviors that kids were most proud of or most liked observing—those reflecting kindness, cooperation, personal responsibility, courage, and so on.

The day before winter break started, we reflected on the school year so far. "Over break," I said, "I'll be planning for the rest of the year. What would you like more of? Or less of? What suggestions do you have for our class?" Without contention, Secret Admirers was unanimously endorsed. "All year!" they chanted. Oscar, who had to exert a great deal of energy to regulate his behavior, said, "I love coming to school now, and every day I think, 'I can't wait to get caught doing good things!'" "Okay," I said, "we'll keep doing it," and their cheers attracted the attention of my colleague next door.

As I observed their excitement, I noticed that my behavior chart on the wall hadn't been used in weeks—not since before we'd started this routine. I'd always had mixed feelings about this classroom management device; every time I asked a student to turn his or her card to orange or red, it only seemed to exacerbate his or her behavior, and the element of public shaming made me uncomfortable. When I walked into my classroom on the first day after winter break, I took it down.

In January, my students settled back into school routines, and I held my breath in the hopes that all would be smooth. And it was. Secret Admirers continued throughout the year. The kids never tired of it, and the behavior chart never went back up. *Could it really have been that easy?* I thought to myself, over and over. It was as if a switch had been flicked in my classroom and 90% of the unpleasant interpersonal behavior between students was eliminated. Our community felt good. I didn't know why this activity worked so well, but I was thrilled to be avoiding many of the classroom management challenges that my new-teacher colleagues were dealing with.

Many years later, I gained an understanding of why this approach worked, as well as words to describe it: I was focusing on strengths, assets, or "bright spots." This is an extensively researched approach in psychology, organizational change management, and neuroscience—and researchers in all these fields agree that focusing on the positive not only feels good but also *works* when you're trying to change or you want others to change. This approach is another key habit in building resilience.

Implications for Leaders
- Secret Admirers works for kids and grown-ups too. I've used this activity at the start of a staff retreat or sporadically throughout the year in team meetings, and adults love it.

A Trifecta of Mental Habits

A strengths-based approach to change is a habit that blends two dispositions. First, focusing on bright spots is closely related to appreciation, which we'll explore in Chapter 12. The connection is probably obvious: When you see what's working, you're likely to feel grateful. Second, focusing on bright spots is tied to cultivating a habit of learning. This habit is addressed in Chapter 9, but already you may recognize that focusing on strengths can make you feel open, curious, and receptive to new information. Tying these three mental inclinations together—focusing on the bright spots, curiosity, and appreciation—is an inoculation against many of the daily stresses of teaching and leading.

A Strengths-Based Approach

Think about an aspect of your life that you'd like to change. Perhaps you yearn for work-life balance, or you feel physically unhealthy and want to make exercise and dietary changes. As you contemplate making these changes, what thoughts come to mind? What are the first ideas you have about how to make these changes?

If you're like most people, you might have started thinking about things you don't want to do anymore. Maybe you thought, *I have to leave work by 5:30 p.m. every night, I need to get to the gym five days a week, I've got to stop eating bags of potato chips for dinner.* And so on. Your mind most likely identified many behaviors that are getting in the way of your hopes and goals. This is what most of us do when we're embarking on a change endeavor, and it has some limitations and drawbacks.

Most simply said, here's what it comes down to when we want to make change: We can focus on what isn't working and do less of it, or we can focus on what is working and do more of that. Ideally, we'll do a bit of both, but if we start with what *is* working, we can galvanize energy to make change.

When we focus on the bright spots—on what we want to see more of—it doesn't mean that we deny challenges. If you want to be healthier, you'll need to stop eating bags of potato chips for dinner, but you'll have more emotional energy to exert the willpower to do that if you are also focusing on the behaviors that are leading you on a path of physical health. A strengths-based approach to change works because when we look at our strengths and at what's going well, we gain confidence in ourselves, we can harness our positive feelings, and we can direct that energy to areas where we're struggling.

There's More Good Going On Than We Think

I discovered strengths-based coaching when I was assigned to coach a midcareer teacher who was unenthusiastic about receiving coaching. Misha was reluctant to let me in her classroom. "I'm so tired of hearing about all the things I'm not doing well," Misha said. "I just don't need anyone else to point out all the areas that I already know I'm struggling in."

"How about this," I proposed. "I'll just look for what's going well. I'll only offer you positive feedback about what I see." Misha looked curious, but also doubtful.

"So you'll just suppress your criticism and tell me that my bulletin boards look nice and you like my hair?" she asked.

I made a joke and persisted. "Let me try just once. For 10 minutes. I want to challenge myself."

Misha pushed back again. "I like you," she said, "and I don't want you to see how badly I suck as a teacher." I validated her feelings and acknowledged how vulnerable we feel when someone else observes us, and, again, I persisted.

"Just once," I said, "Let me try. This is a test of me as a coach: Can I find authentically positive things in the classroom of a teacher who sucks?" I said in a light tone of voice. She relented.

When I walked into her classroom the next day, I was nervous that I wouldn't see good things. But then my thoughts changed quickly to *Oh, today must be a uniquely good day because things seem to be going so well in here!* It felt like that moment in the movie *The Wizard of Oz* where Dorothy wakes up in Oz and everything is in Technicolor. Two kids were distributing materials in a systematic and organized way; a Do Now had students working in pairs, against a timer, to solve math problems; Misha was talking to the aide of a student with an IEP and sharing her suggestions for how to modify the lesson; and Javier, who was sitting front and center in the room, screamed, "I love math the best forever!" And this all happened within the first three minutes. I frantically scribbled notes. I watched Misha open the lesson and then left per our agreement.

When Misha and I met to debrief, I refrained from pouring out effusive amazement at all that I'd seen going well. Instead, I asked, "How did you feel like those 10 minutes were?" I expected she'd say that it had been a rare "great day" and that I hadn't seen the real thing. "Oh, you thought I sucked," she replied, her shoulders rounding over. "I couldn't manage Javier, I was unprepared, kids were off task, and it was chaotic."

I couldn't hold back. "I don't know what you are talking about, Misha. Seriously. That class was great! I have a list of 28 things I noticed that were going well. And it would be 29 if I counted your bulletin board—which was beautiful." As I went through what I'd observed, Misha dropped her head into her hands. "I guess that's all happening," she said when I was done, "but it's like I can't even see it anymore. I just see Javier jumping out of his seat and shouting. I don't even hear what he's saying. I'm thrilled that he loves math! He's been retained and usually complains of hating school."

At the end of our debrief, Misha asked if I could come back the next day. "I need your eyes," she said. For two weeks, I stopped in for 10 minutes every day to share what I saw that was going well. Within a few days, Misha had started echoing my observations with comments such as, "Yeah, I saw that too!" or "And then after you left, Javier was the Materials Collector, and he took the job so seriously and maturely." I'd run into Misha in the halls, and she'd make comments like, "You're not going to believe what just happened! The whole class finished the math challenge in half the time I'd planned—and they solved the problem!" It felt as though Misha's orientation to her students and herself had shifted radically, right before my eyes.

About a month later, at a grade-level team meeting, Misha shared how these 10-minute observations were changing her. "I can't believe how much good was happening that I never noticed," she said, "and I feel that by recognizing all of that, I'm so much stronger and able to look at the things that aren't going well. My confidence is back, I feel energized, and I'm enjoying teaching so much more." As her colleagues commented on how she'd changed, they started asking if I could observe them.

Then I had an idea—I decided to challenge this team who had worked together for several years. I said, "How about if you start observing each other for 10 minutes a couple times a week—perhaps during your prep periods? I can also occasionally stop in, but imagine what you'd be able to learn about each other and your students if you tried this?" Misha was the first to endorse the idea, and, with some reluctance, the rest of her team agreed. We made a schedule. We discussed a protocol and how and when a debrief would happen, and within a few days, this team began observing each other for bright spots.

Several months later, I attended another team meeting. "We're talking about how to get our female English language learners to talk more," Misha explained. "One day we noticed that these girls were talking up a storm in Alex's class, and we've all started trying the strategies he uses, and so many girls are now talking."

What had started from a place of acknowledging strengths had moved seamlessly into looking at how to improve practice. The teachers asked open and vulnerable questions, talked about what they were proud of, and shared their visions and goals. Unlike the discussions during many of the team or PLC meetings I'd observed on a Wednesday afternoon, theirs was lively and energized. And Misha—who had never been seen as a leader—steered this effort.

Why It's Hard to Focus on the Bright Spots

If you find it hard to focus on the positive, you're not alone. There are real reasons, anchored in our neurology, culture, and emotions, for why it is hard to see bright spots.

Our Brains Have a Negativity Bias

Blame your brain if you struggle to see the positive. That mass of mush in your head is very useful, but it also has a built-in negativity bias. This means that if on the first day of school, 34 students walk into your fourth-period class, and one of them has an angry expression on his face, you will immediately notice and perseverate over him. *Why did he come in with that attitude? Will he be difficult to manage? Is he the student that other teachers warned me about?* That evening, you'll keep thinking about the one kid; the other 33 will be fleeting thoughts.

The brain perceives negative stimuli faster and more intensely than positive stimuli. Within a tenth of a second, we can store negative stimuli in our memories. Big portions of our brain and neural system activate in response to what we perceive as a threat—such as a grumpy high school junior, a curt email from a parent, or a critical comment in a staff meeting that we're leading. In comparison, positive experiences are harder for us to spot and must be focused on for 12 seconds before we can retain them in our memories. Pause for a second and take that in: Danger lodges itself in your brain within *a tenth of a second,* whereas a positive experience requires *at least 12 seconds* to be absorbed. That's a significant difference!

Although this bias is frustrating, it explains how our ancient ancestors survived for hundreds of thousands of years as they wandered the African savannah, risking becoming a meal for a predator, stepping onto a hot lava field, or eating a poisonous berry. Humans evolved because we overestimated threats. Our ancestors were adept at spotting danger, and our brains are still wired to perceive danger. Our task now is to retrain our neural pathways—and this is what happens when we focus on the bright spots.

When I notice that my brain has latched on to something it perceives as a threat (a rustling in the bushes; a frustrated kid; a cranky colleague), I tell myself, *With all due respect to my ancestors, there are no more saber-toothed tigers,* and then I say, *Right now everything is okay,* and I direct my attention to something that's neutral or positive—the passing of a cloud, the student who has already pulled out his notebook, the welcoming look on a colleague's face. Managing my brain's negativity bias is a daily practice, but one that has grown easier through the strategies I'm sharing with you (in this chapter and in the workbook), as well as through meditation, which calms the mind so that it's not hijacked by someone's grumpy expression.

The brain's negativity bias is exacerbated by fatigue and poor self-care, so the start of December is an optimal time of the year to focus on the bright spots as we are often dragging ourselves toward winter break.

Focusing on the Positive Is Countercultural

Focusing on bright spots challenges entrenched social and cultural mores. In countless seminars and meetings that I've attended, the person who is seen as the smartest is the one who tears apart an idea or plan and points out all of its flaws. In many organizations and institutions, a high value is placed on being critical, rational, and analytical. In these contexts, if you focus on the positive, if you point out all the strengths and contributions of a plan, you're seen as naïve, and your intellect is questioned. In order to focus on bright spots, we'll need to address this dynamic that is present in many organizations, and challenge unstated values.

Furthermore, in many work environments, complaining is culturally accepted. It is socially customary for people to get together and commiserate about problems, issues, and complaints. Certain spaces in a school seem as though they are dedicated to complaining; the staff lunchroom, for example, can feel like a vortex of misery.

Venting rarely makes us feel good, and often leads to cynicism. In some organizations, cynics are placed on a pedestal. They are seen as wise, sophisticated, and knowing; they have seen initiatives and people come and go. They warn others: Don't be fooled by this or that shiny thing. They shame the hopeful, dismissing them as unrealistic, naïve dreamers, and scoff at those who incline toward the positive.

As I mentioned in Chapter 2, a friend once told me that behind every cynic is someone whose heart has been broken. I can see that. Yet cynicism is corrosive to a community; it not only hurts the cynics and those around them but also kills possibility and collaboration. We have to find other ways to deal with our broken hearts.

Emotions Are Real

The third reason why it's so hard for us to focus on bright spots is that we don't recognize, or know what to do with, our expansive, complex feelings. Our anger, resentment, frustration, and sadness get in the way of being able to see the bright spots, and, without strategies to address those emotional states, we become blind to the big picture. At the heart of this book is the notion that we need to know our emotions and learn to deal with them. Once we have a skill set that's deep and wide, we can look at the whole picture, which includes challenges, areas for growth, and bright spots.

When we're focusing on our deficiencies and areas of struggle, we reinforce unproductive neural pathways in our brain—the pathways that produce self-defeating statements like, *I'm such a failure; this won't work . . . I know I'm not good at X, and I've been trying to get better for many years . . . What's wrong with me? Why am I so bad at this?* The majority of us know our weaknesses intimately. Casting more light on them only creates distress and decreases our ability to take action.

When we focus on our strengths, we can access the positive emotions that open us to learning. Whether we're looking at our own behavior or that of our colleagues, students, or bosses, what we focus on *grows*. Highlighting the positive doesn't deny challenges, but it eliminates a day-after-day scrutiny of someone's faults that builds a wall of alienation. Finding one good thing about someone broadens our view of that person. We may feel a different quality of connection to the person, illuminating a few entry points that might allow us to promote change.

Focusing on the bright spots isn't about gritting your teeth and ignoring the student who is placing thumbtacks on her neighbor's seat, or denying the fact that you're disorganized. It's about expanding your perspective and beginning an exploration of areas for growth from a place of power. This strategy allows you to more fully embrace your complicated emotions—your sadness, anger, envy, and frustration.

Implications for Leaders

- If you're in a culture that prizes being critical and analytical, begin to shift that culture through appreciative inquiry (see the next section in this chapter). You may also need to directly address this communication dynamic and collaboratively explore some alternatives. (My book *The Art of Coaching Teams* is a resource for strategies to deal with conflict and establish healthy communication.)

- As you begin pointing out bright spots and encouraging others to do so, remember that it can be difficult to receive positive acknowledgments. Praise or appreciation can feel uncomfortable for many of us; perhaps we were taught that it is a sign of arrogance to claim our strengths, or we value humility.

- Recognize that people like to receive appreciation and praise in differing formats; not everyone wants his accolades to be made public in front of the full staff. A staff survey at the beginning of the year could be helpful here.

- Give people explicit instruction on how to receive acknowledgment: Suggest that they don't dismiss or downplay the appreciation, but just say "Thank you" and soak in the appreciation.

Training the Brain

Let's get concrete about how to direct your mind and emotions to focus on the bright spots. The five practices that facilitate this are setting intentions, taking an inquiry stance, engaging in appreciative inquiry, dealing with emotions, and practicing reflection. Let's explore how to systematize a strengths-based focus and train your brain.

Set Intentions to Direct Your Mind

In Chapter 3, I described how intention setting can help you craft powerful stories. Intention setting can do more than that because it is a simple practice that primes your mind to look for whatever information you tell it to look for. It's not goal setting—an intention is softer and more personal than a goal—it's a statement about how you want to be or show up in a situation. It's about how you want to orient your mind and heart, and what you want to pay attention to.

Here's how I use it: Before a meeting, perhaps one in which I'm sharing a proposal for a new initiative, I might set an intention to be open to new ideas. I then identify what it might look or sound like when I'm holding my intention—and "sound like" can be internal self-talk. So, if I'm holding my intention to be open to new ideas, then I will ask nonjudgmental questions, seek to understand others' perspectives, mentally acknowledge suggestions, and be willing to change my mind and accept a different outcome. At the top of my notebook, I write my intention. If sharing our intention is part of our team's opening routines, then I'll also share it with a colleague—which makes me more accountable to it. Throughout the meeting, I might stray from my intention, but with some practice, my mind can quickly move back to it.

Your mind wants instruction. It wants to serve you well and make you happy. It needs clear and explicit directions. This is what intention setting does, in a kind and compassionate way. There's a lot of instruction on how to do this in the workbook.

Take an Inquiry Stance and Open Your Mind

Orienting your mind to take an inquiry stance allows you to observe with open expansiveness, an appreciation for strengths, and a willingness to be surprised. It means asking questions for which you don't have answers. You can take an inquiry stance in your classroom, about a specific child with whom you are struggling; in a PD session when you're wondering how the session might best help you tomorrow; or when you're frustrated with a colleague who seems never to follow through with what she says she'll do. When you broaden your vision and questioning to see a bigger picture, you'll be able to see bright spots.

If you take an inquiry stance, you'll also be more likely to ask questions of unexpected people. For example, if you're trying to figure out how to get kids to arrive at school on time, you might ask them for their thoughts on this matter, or the school custodian for his thoughts, or the grandmother of a student for hers. When you truly embrace an inquiry stance, you'll be surprised by what you hear. And you'll see new possibilities open up.

Reflection Prompts (and an Example)

- What's a problem you'd like to address in your school or classroom?
  - My kids don't turn in homework.
- Generate three open questions about this problem.
  - Why don't my kids turn in homework?
  - What do I need to do differently in order for them to turn in homework?
  - What purpose does homework serve, or what purpose should it serve?
- Identify three people whom you could ask for their perspective.
  - Another 10th-grade teacher on my team
  - Our school's learning specialist
  - A student's parent
- Can you identify a place where this problem isn't apparent? What do you suspect might be the reason? How might you learn about how that problem has been dealt with in that context?
  - I think that kids turn in their homework more often in English. It might be because they don't get that much English homework, or maybe because they're more interested in it. I can talk to the English teacher, and I can ask kids why they turn in English homework but not homework for my class.

Engage in Appreciative Inquiry

Think about an aspect of your school that you'd like to change. Maybe staff turnover is high, or too many kids arrive late in the morning, or math proficiency scores are low. How might you go about making changes? Traditionally, when we approach organizational change, we analyze, assess, and solve problems. We ask, "What needs to be fixed here?" We focus on deficits, shortcomings, and failures, and then we quickly move to action. This doesn't always work.

Einstein once said that if he had an hour to save the world, he'd spend 55 minutes defining the problem and 5 minutes finding the solution. How we think about "the problem" and how long we think about "the problem" matters.

Appreciative inquiry (AI) is an approach to organizational change that focuses on strengths. It is based on the idea that the questions we ask focus our attention in a particular direction, and that organizations evolve in the direction of the most persistent and passionate questions asked. AI pushes us to see the whole of a system and to explore that system's strengths, possibilities, and successes. It proposes that the moment we ask a question, we begin to create change. If we choose positive questions, we lead ourselves to positive change. What are the questions that your school has been asking?

AI suggests five steps to making change—change to one individual's teaching, to leadership practice, or to a whole system. Here are the five steps:

1. Define: What is the topic of inquiry? What is the project's purpose, or what needs to be achieved?
2. Discover: What works already? What are our successes and strengths?
3. Dream: What could be? What are our hopes, wishes, and aspirations for the future?
4. Design: What should be? What might happen if we combine what is already working with what could be? What's the ideal?
5. Deliver: How can we create our ideal? What do we need to do?

AI trains us to see and act differently because it pushes us to hold a wider assessment of a situation and to seek depth. Like most things, our inquiry skills will need practice and time to refine, but for teams and schools that have used AI, I've witnessed ripple effects throughout staff and student culture that are notably more positive, hopeful, and productive.

Appreciative Inquiry Feedback Survey

The AI-based 360-degree feedback tool described here can be transformational in a leader's practice. In this process, people are invited to respond openly (not anonymously) to the following questions about their leader. This tool is modified from one developed by the organization Leadership that Works (http://www.leadershipthatworks.com).

Process
The prompts and questions can be provided in an online survey or in an interview format conducted by a neutral person, such as a coach.

Part A: Discover
- Describe a time when you really enjoyed working with your supervisor.
- How has this person contributed to your success? How has this person enabled you to do your best work?
- Describe a time when this person positively impacted our school and students.
- Describe something innovative that this person did. What challenges did the person face in this effort? What impact did he or she have?

Part B: Discover and Dream
Share a story about a time when this person demonstrated his or her strengths in each of the following areas, and then offer the person one wish to help further develop this competency.

- Making decisions
- Leading toward a vision
- Fostering creativity
- Developing teams
- Building relationships
- Communicating powerfully
- Developing self and others
- Modeling integrity and honesty

Part C: Dream
- What's the biggest positive change you've seen in this person this year?
- When you think of this person overall, what strengths stand out? How could this person better utilize those strengths to serve our school?
- What are three things you wish for that would make this person even more effective?
- What requests would you like to make of this person?

Deal with Emotions

You're only going to be able to focus on bright spots if you have the ability to deal with challenges, whether that is with a student's behavior, your own professional growth, or a supervisor who pushes your buttons. Without skills to respond to your feelings of frustration, anger, sadness, or fear, you'll feel uncomfortable focusing solely on bright spots.

There are many ways to deal with strong emotions, some of which I've incorporated in other parts of this book. Here is a powerful strategy for dealing with difficult emotions, one that's taught by many mindfulness teachers. The acronym for the four-step practice is RAIN, which stands for **r**ecognize, **a**ccept, **i**nvestigate, and **n**onidentification.

Recognize that you are experiencing something—annoyance that the same student always forgets her homework or that your principal's emails make you nervous. Step back into observation rather than reaction. Bring awareness to your thoughts, emotions, and sensations. Name the emotions that are present—annoyance, anxiety, sadness.

Accept whatever is. Acknowledge that your experience is what it is—that you get annoyed by a student forgetting her homework—even if you wish you wouldn't. Exercise self-compassion rather than self-criticism.

Investigate. Kindly ask yourself, *What's going on inside me? Where is this coming from? What does this feeling want from me?* Get curious. Maybe you wonder if your feelings about your student forgetting her homework are connected to concerns you have about her organizational abilities. Maybe you suspect that your response to your principal's emails has something to do with your insecurity as a new member of the staff. You don't need to psychoanalyze yourself; just bring an attitude of curiosity to whatever you're experiencing.

Nonidentification asks you to remind yourself that you are not your emotions or the stories you spin. You *have* the thought or feeling; you *are not* the thought or feeling. Feelings are transient, and when you recognize this, you'll feel more at peace and able to deal with whatever is happening. You can see that your feelings of annoyance at your student will pass, and that anxiety is not who you are.

Reflect and Gain Clarity

Reflection involves pausing to think about our experiences and considering our future choices of action, emotion, and interpretation. It's an underused tool for understanding our emotions, building resilience, and increasing the joy in our lives.

How do you reflect? Thinking about something that happened could be reflection—but it could also be perseveration or unhealthy rumination. Productive reflection leads you to deeper insight into yourself and others. It clarifies further actions and your own behaviors, and helps with decision making. Mulling things over is a component of a productive reflective practice, but you can maximize this practice by taking two further steps: Reflecting aloud with someone else (talking) and writing. Writing is the ultimate reflective power strategy. It forces you to put your experiences into words and commit them to paper, enables you to keep a record of your experiences to recognize patterns and trends over time, and helps solidify the neural pathways that you want to strengthen.

I wrote the accompanying workbook in part because I know how powerful it is to write down your reflections, and I know that this builds resilience. I know this from extensive research and from my own 20-plus years of being a writer. Here are two cheers for the positive impact of reflection:

- Reflecting on personal strengths and limitations can foster many of the competencies associated with resilience, particularly improvements in self-awareness and in coping and problem-solving skills. Grant and Kinman (2013) found that adults who reflected on their practice, considered their personal motivations, and explored the nature and impact of their interactions with those they served reported higher levels of psychological well-being and were more resilient.
- Well-developed reflective abilities have been found to underpin emotional literacy and accurate empathy in helping professionals, as well as facilitating supportive interpersonal relationships that can buffer workplace stress (Grant and Kinman, 2013; Ruch, 2007). Developing reflective ability, therefore, has strong potential to enhance emotional resilience and foster competence.

Acknowledging Context:
Leadership Development Matters

Dear principals: In every section of this book where I've added "Implications for Leaders," I've thought about you. I've hoped that you have your own coach and weekly PD and maybe even a high-functioning PLC to support you in implementing these ideas. I've thought about you as a learner, and, unfortunately, in most of the schools and districts that I've worked in, I've seen very little quality PD for site (or central office) leaders.

I've also thought about your resilience. Whereas we have data on teacher burnout and turnover, we have less on principals. In the large urban district where I worked for many years, turnover for principals was just as high as it was for teachers, which created instability and the inability to advance change.

If we're going to truly transform schools, big changes need to happen in the area of principal PD. There are ever-growing volumes of research that delineate the critical impact that a principal has on student learning (see Louis, Leithwood, Wahlstrom, and Anderson, 2010; Wallace Foundation, 2011). Among all school-related factors that contribute to what students learn at school, leadership is second only to classroom instruction (Louis et al., 2010). Your job is to attract and retain those amazing classroom teachers, create the conditions in which they will flourish, shape student and staff culture, lead effective teams, hold a compelling vision, model emotionally resilient leadership, and so much more—you need a massive skill set. Principal PD (both before and after assuming the position) lags far behind teacher development.

This book is my theory of how change will happen in schools. We can't wait for those at the top to fund PD for leaders, who will then create the schools our students need. Change will happen if each of us takes responsibility for what we can do within our sphere of influence. And if we push on that sphere a bit, it will grow and influence more than we usually imagine. Change can come from all directions, from the bottom and the top, the sides, the inside and the outside.

Principals: You can make more decisions than you think. Do what you can to get the professional learning you need and deserve. Do what you can to carve out the space and community in which you can take up the content of this book to develop your own resilience, as well as to think about cultivating the resilience of those you lead. Budget for your own coach, demand the time for a PLC, and ask your supervisors for meaningful PD sessions. Your leadership, and the development of your leadership, matter tremendously.

 ## *A Dive into Sadness*

I've procrastinated on writing this section. I avoided it, drafted analytical musings on this topic, and even considered cutting it, because I don't want to deal with this emotion. Are you tempted to skip it? Perhaps we don't need to "dive" into this emotion, but rather just get our toes in the water. That would be progress for many of us—especially if we're in a professional setting with colleagues where intense emotions rarely show their faces.

As I dip my toes into the topic of sadness, what I notice immediately is that my *fear* of sadness surges. It is fear of being out of control. Fear of the unknown. Fear of being alone. Fear that a riptide of sadness will sweep me into the middle of the ocean. I also fear the unpredictability of this emotion.

The strong part of me says this: *Today we are just looking. Yes, you have been in the depths of bleak sadness that threatened to obliterate your being, but you did not stay there.*

And then my husband's words cut through my memory like a lightning bolt: "You will not always feel this way." He repeated this statement so many times, mornings when he'd find me crumpled on the floor wracked by grief. His words challenged my assumption, my belief that my emotional state was permanent—how could it not be when I had watched my beloved mother die of cancer? His words offered perhaps the only source of hope during a season of sadness. Then and now, it is fear that stands like a menacing sentry at the gates to sadness, and prevents me from understanding and exploring it. Fear of intensity, fear of my own ability to look, fear of permanence.

There was a different time when an injustice was wrought upon innocent people and, in one turn, anger, sadness, and fear swept me up. I turned to my wise husband, crying, "I don't know what to do!" I pleaded for direction. My hands shook. My breathing was rapid. (In reflection, I see that I was asking for help, which is a lesson for us all: *Ask for help.* You don't have to do this alone.)

His response was, "Just sit with the sadness. Be with it."

"What does that mean?" I demanded, with a hint of anger. I wanted solutions. I wanted him to take the feelings away.

"Sit down. Close your eyes. Feel the emotions. Let them course through your mind and body. Watch their journeys. Cry. Just experience them."

I was doubtful. Suspicious. And a little annoyed. I had no other ideas, however, and I have learned to trust my husband, so I "sat" with that sadness, and not just once. What I discovered (much to my surprise) was that it ran its course. After it made my chest feel achy, and after it morphed into and out of other emotions, and after it illuminated fears unknown to me, it faded.

Some sadness doesn't go away. And that's okay. I do not want to entirely lose my sadness over my mother's death. It is not as intense as it once was—it does not sweep me off my feet—it has become a part of who I am, a part that exists because of the intense love I had for her. Although I would gladly trade my mother back for the lessons I've gleaned from losing her, I am also aware that her illness and death, and my journey of grief, have made me a kinder and more compassionate person. That is also a part of me now.

Another lesson I unwillingly acquired was that I can survive a tsunami of sadness—and even thrive in its aftermath. It's not a journey I chose, and I would not want to repeat it, but I made my way through it. My experience with grief strengthened my conviction that we can become more resilient through adversity.

That is what I remember as I look at sadness: The intensity is not permanent. One must ask for help. We can become more resilient. Emotional residue remains, but it is okay.

Sometimes, the aftereffect of sadness can be action. Following my husband's instruction to sit with my sadness, and after I'd explored my sadness and anger and the intensity faded, I stood up and began to act in response to the injustice.

When anger is present, look carefully, because sadness often lurks below. Sometimes we stay on the level of anger because it has energy: Anger can be galvanizing and mobilizing, propelling us onto our feet and into alliances with others; it makes our heart beat and our legs move, and sometimes our speech is smarter when we're angry. But we all know there is danger in spending too long in anger. And there can be a power and freedom in uncovering sadness.

Sadness can push us under the covers, make us curl up in a ball and become immobile. Sadness can suck all the life force out. Perhaps that's another reason why it's scary to explore sadness: Because depression is real and can result in death for those who can't find the help they need. I've feared that just experiencing an afternoon, a week, or a season of sadness might lead to untreatable depression. And I've seen what that has done to people.

What is it like, I wonder, to have a healthy relationship to sadness? I believe this is possible. I think it would entail sharing our sadness with others, accepting its existence and shedding the shame of it. Sometimes we are sad when we feel hurt, left out, or treated unfairly; we can wonder, *Did I deserve that? Am I unworthy of love?* Those fears feed shame, and distance us from the sadness. We get quiet. We don't share those updates on our social media platforms. Yet, in our quest for happier lives, we can't block out sadness.

What would it be like to talk about sadness at school? When I think back to times as a teacher and coach when I felt angry or frustrated, I now see sadness. Times when my work wasn't appreciated, when colleagues didn't listen, when students didn't do what I wanted them to do, when test scores weren't what I wished they'd be, when new curricular adoptions came and went, when teammates left, when leaders left, when I had to do things I didn't want to do—I see sadness that was cut from the same cloth as the sadness I experienced when my mom died. There are different degrees and intensities of sadness, but at its base, sadness is sadness. How might I have felt more supported, stronger, and better had I been able to talk about sadness with my teaching partner, principal, and grade-level team?

Here's what I wish could happen in schools: Occasionally, we'd come together voluntarily, and we'd promise to listen well to each other with an open heart and no intention to fix each other's problems. We'd speak with integrity (honestly, kindly, without blame or shame). One person would lightly facilitate and maintain a safe space, offering an open prompt like, "Talk about sadness," and those who want to speak would do so. And, if there were tears, we wouldn't be afraid of them, and, after the speaker shared, we'd say, "Thank you." Then maybe there'd be a quiet moment and then someone else would share. We'd leave our time together feeling more connected to each other, less alone in our fears and sadness, more understanding of each other, and more convinced that we could talk about intense emotions in a way that builds resilience.

We cannot see the bright spots if we cannot also see the bleak moments.

Disposition: Empowerment

I had an epiphany when Latrice threw up her hands and said, "The only way I can deal with Michael is if the special ed aide is in class with him every day." We'd spent a lot of time talking about this squirrely third grader with an IEP and a tendency to bolt from class when he got overwhelmed. I'd provided a lot of technical coaching around management, structures, and systems. But it was not helping Latrice.

"Latrice," I said, "the problem is not Michael. It's that you don't feel that you have the power to respond to this teaching challenge." Latrice, a first-year teacher, had tried a lot of strategies to work with Michael, but it was also only December, and her disposition was one of exasperation and resignation.

"I just can't," she said definitively. "He needs a full-time aide."

"You're going to have a Michael every year," I said, "and our school doesn't have full-time aides. You have a choice: Either learn how to support Michael or quit in June."

"I've tried!" she responded.

"Yes, you have, but do you feel like there's *anything* else that you can do to support Michael? Anything?" She shrugged.

"Listen," I said, "you will always face challenges as a teacher. That's a given. It's what makes this profession interesting; there's always something else to figure out. After a while, you'll appreciate the challenges. But you must shift your attitude. You can't give up on yourself, and by saying that you need a full-time aide, you've surrendered your power."

That day my coaching approach with Latrice shifted. Our goal became to expand her sense of power. Latrice stumbled and fell that year, but rather than swoop in to pick her up as I'd done in the fall, I stood at a distance while guiding her through recovery and next steps. As Latrice tried different approaches with Michael, she constantly reminded herself that she was on a learning journey, that she struggled because she didn't *yet* have the skills she needed, but that she could figure it out.

In June, when we reflected on her growth that first year, she said, "One thing I learned this year is that I don't *need* you. In December, I felt like I couldn't make it through a week without meeting with you. Now, while I love coaching and I want to continue, it's different. I don't feel like I'll die without it."

Latrice taught in this school for 10 years. When Michael graduated from high school, he sent her an invitation that said, "You never gave up on me. You made me realize that I could do anything if I didn't give up on myself. I wouldn't have graduated without you." I treasure the photo she sent me of the two of them from his graduation, tears streaming down their smiling faces. It's a reminder that new teachers need more than technical coaching: They need to be coached on their way of being—their disposition and attitude. And it's a reminder that when we find the resources to deal with challenges, we learn to believe in ourselves.

≈≈

In order to build resilience, you must feel that the ability to respond to challenges lies within you. To manage the endless stream of challenges that you'll confront, you need to cultivate a disposition of self-efficacy and empowerment. Personal experience has taught me this, but educational research on resilient educators validates my belief (Larrivee, 2012).

When we feel empowered, we believe we can influence our surroundings and the outcome of events, which contributes to a sense of competence and confidence. We empower ourselves when we take risks, make mistakes (or even fail), and discover our own ability to get up and move on.

Here's how to cultivate your own sense of power:

1. Identify an aspect of your professional (or personal) life that you want to improve. Perhaps you want a more organized classroom, or you want to revise a unit you've taught several times to make it more engaging. Perhaps you have a student, like Michael, whom you need to support.
2. Sketch out an action plan and carry it forth. Be sure that with whatever you do, there's some risk. Find the edge of your comfort zone and step slightly beyond it. If you don't feel a little nervous, you're not taking a big enough risk.
3. Reflect (ideally in writing) on what happens as you implement your plan. Notice your range of feelings. Identify the moments of struggle and self-doubt.

4. When you encounter a challenge, or when you stumble and fall, ask yourself, *Is it within my influence or control to do something about this challenge?* If you answer yes, then you'll cultivate your own power.

5. When you struggle, tell yourself: *I'm having a hard time because I don't yet have the skills or knowledge I need in order to do this well.*
   Then ask yourself, *What else can I do to deal with this challenge?*

6. As you implement your plan and see the changes you are striving for, document them. Recognize your accomplishments. Take credit for them—even if someone else provided advice, suggestions, or help along the way. You must see your own role in your growth, or you won't cultivate empowerment.

7. Ask yourself, *What went well today, and what was my role in making things go well?* Recognize the bright spots every day in your teaching practice where your actions help you accomplish little and big goals.

Resilience is internal. Sometimes it might feel as though the waters of your inner well are low, and then the task is to feed those waters and fill that pool. But the source of your resilience is always inside you.

Implications for Leaders

- A typical characteristic of people who feel burned out is powerlessness, making the concept of self-efficacy particularly relevant (Maslach, 1982). Self-efficacy is your own judgment of how capable you are of coping effectively and realistically with a specific task in the future (Bandura, 1997).

- When working with new teachers, be intentional about cultivating their self-efficacy. It's tempting and easy to be too instructive and directive with new teachers. Use the concept of the gradual release of responsibility to guide them; they do need direct instruction, but they also need to be weaned from the support of an administrator, coach, or mentor.

- Guide your teachers, especially new teachers, to see their growth for themselves. They need to recognize this journey and the struggles they surmounted. If you (or someone else) points out their strengths and accomplishments too much, it denies new teachers the power to see their own resourcefulness and ability.

- Consider ways to incorporate these practices into the required practices of teacher goal setting and evaluation. Think how much better it would be if those postobservation conversations over the course of the year were the product of using this lens.

Look for the Light

In the Northern Hemisphere, we have ancient traditions of celebrating light in the short days of winter. We gather around candles and fireplaces, display stars as symbols of promise, and decorate our homes with colorful bulbs. People from many different traditions celebrate miracles, hope, renewal, and resilience as our planet approaches the winter solstice.

In December, as the first half of the school year comes to a close and our planet cycles into winter, perhaps our school communities could gather to identify and celebrate bright spots. In partnership with parents and students, we could celebrate children and highlight their learning and development. We could name our own growth and surface the connections between our own learning and the growth of others. I might say, "I'm proud of myself for . . .," and a colleague would add, "I also saw you grow when you . . ." We'd look for the light—in ourselves and in others—being reminded that when the nights are long and the sun hangs low on the horizon, we just need to pay closer attention. The light is always there.

CHAPTER REFLECTION

- How do the ideas in this chapter affect your perception of your current reality?
- How might your days be different if you saw more bright spots?
- Of the ideas shared in this chapter, which would you like to explore further?

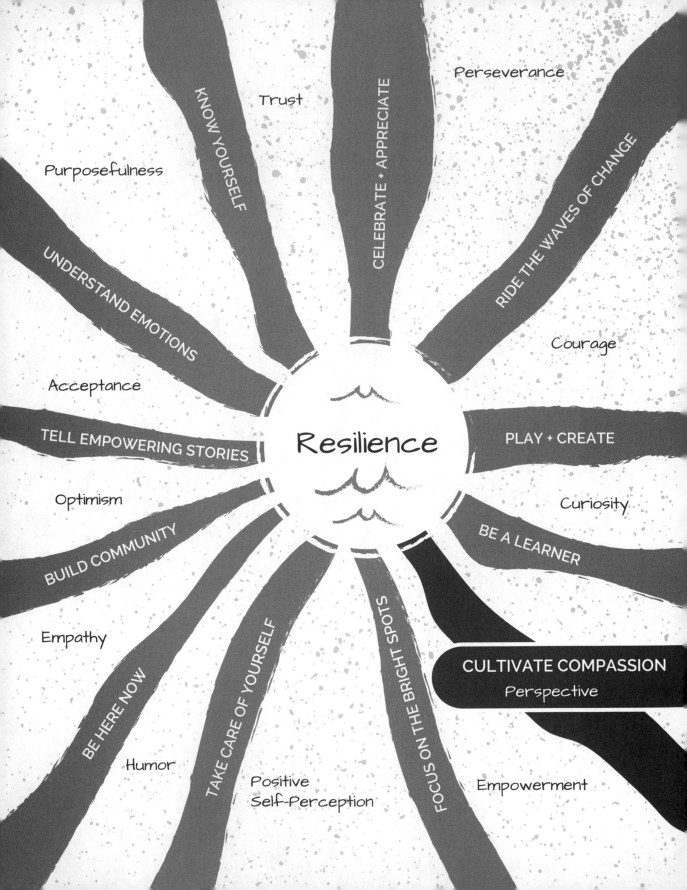

CHAPTER 8

Cultivate Compassion

Compassion for ourselves, as well as for others, helps us deal with the interpersonal challenges we face on a daily basis. Perspective allows us to recognize the complexity of a situation. Perspective allows us to empathize with others, see the long view, extricate ourselves from the drama of a moment, and identify a wider range of responses to an event.

January: Start the new year by strengthening your compassion for yourself and others, and unlock another resource for resilience.

❧ ❧

During the first week after winter break, I was walking through the hallway in a school where I coached several leaders, when Sandra, the English Department head, approached me. "Do you have a minute?" she asked. Before I responded, she proceeded to describe the many ways that her school's administrators were failing—what they weren't doing, what she thought they should be doing. She lamented how much of a mess they were making. Her speech was rapid; her mannerisms made her exasperation obvious. "I felt so rested after break. In just a few days, their incompetence has unraveled the benefits of two weeks off," she concluded.

I considered my options for responding to Sandra's rant: Part of me wanted to give her a hug—I cared about her tremendously. I thought about helping her process her emotions or deconstruct the story she was telling. I'd often been concerned about Sandra's resilience; she worked so hard and was deeply committed to her students, but she was sick a lot and seemed emotionally fragile. I decided to respond with what I think of as an "arrow of compassion."

"Do you want to shift your perspective on your administrators?" I asked. She nodded.

"Then consider that everyone is doing the best they can. Based on their knowledge, skills, and experiences, they are making the best choices available to them."

Sandra looked away. "But it's *not* good enough," she said, her voice calmer and her speech slowing. "Our kids need us to do more."

"Yes, and *everyone is doing the best they can* with what they have—you included," I said. "Yes, we need to acquire more skills and knowledge, but you can't get mad at people for their areas for growth. Try this way of thinking and see what happens."

Sandra paused. "Why does that make me feel a little better?" she asked, her voice barely above a whisper.

"Well, how does that thought make you feel about your admin?" I asked.

"Better, I guess. I don't want to feel like I'm at war with them," she said.

"We crave connection with others," I said. "And you know that people can change. That thought probably makes you feel better because it's anchored in compassion, which is our natural state of being."

Our exchange ended there, but we returned to this conversation in many subsequent coaching sessions because compassion for others (as well as compassion for herself) was what Sandra needed to boost her own resilience.

For whom would you like to cultivate more compassion? A student? A colleague? A supervisor? Take a moment to identify one person in your professional life whom you'd like to keep in mind as you read this chapter, for whom you'd like to develop more compassion. How might your life be different if you had more compassion for this individual?

Definitions of Terms

- **Pity:** When you feel pity, you recognize someone's suffering from an emotional distance; it can be condescending and dehumanizing.
- **Sympathy:** When you feel sympathy, you care for someone who is suffering, but maintain some emotional distance.

- **Empathy:** When you feel empathy, you place yourself in someone else's shoes and feel their pain. When you feel empathy, there's no distance between you and the other person as you sense her emotions and imagine what she is thinking and feeling.
- **Compassion:** When you feel compassion, you are moved to take action to relieve someone else's suffering. You may have experienced this suffering through your empathy. Action is what distinguishes compassion from empathy.

What Compassion Offers

Think of compassion as a muscle that we all have, that we are born with and need to strengthen. When you have weak muscles in your body—say, your core muscles are weak—other muscles, such as your hamstrings and lower back muscles, work harder to compensate to make sure your body can do what it needs to do. But then the imbalance causes pain—your hamstrings pull at your back muscles, and your back aches. At the root of the problem are weak oblique and abdominal muscles. Our bodies hurt when they're unbalanced. Likewise, our emotional body experiences pain when one skill set has been neglected.

I regularly practice Pilates so that my back doesn't hurt. In the same way, I have to be intentional about building compassion—otherwise, I just forget to attend to it. I don't know about you, but I don't have a 5:00 p.m. Building Your Compassion class. That's why I find myself relating to others from a frustrated place of judgment—and my annoyance, disappointment, resentment, and other yucky feelings ultimately wear me down. When we exercise compassion for others, our heart softens, we strengthen relationships, our perspective broadens, and we see possibility. Just as we practice an instrument or hone a disposition such as optimism, we must cultivate and refine compassion.

Compassion is empathy in action. When you hear your student's mother talking about her fears that her son might have a learning disability, you might empathize with her. If you respond by saying, "I hear how worried you are, and I want you to know that as his teacher, as someone who cares about your son, I'm going to be your partner in this process," you are being compassionate.

When you notice that two of your high school girls, whom you know are friends, seem to be ignoring each other, and you ask one of them if everything is okay and she bursts into tears and tells you that her friend doesn't want to be her friend anymore, you might empathize. If you invite them in at lunch to talk about what's going on, you are being compassionate.

When your principal sends out a snippy email asking teachers to turn in attendance reports on time, you might recognize how stressed he is and remember that he's usually thoughtful. If you pass him later in the hallway and ask him how he's doing, or let him know that you appreciate his efforts, you are being compassionate.

Compassion and love overlap. Love might just be a deeper intensity of compassion, but they are so close to each other that I often use the terms synonymously.

A Simple Compassion Practice

Sit quietly and bring to mind someone you care about who is going through a hard time. Feel the connection you have for that person and the love you feel for him. Then silently direct these phrases toward him: *I care about your suffering. May you be free from suffering.* Now do the same for a student who seems to be really struggling.

As an extension, direct those phrases to yourself, and perhaps then to someone you have difficulty with, and perhaps even to people you may never know (such as refugees in distant countries and so on). As you do this practice, pay attention to what happens in your body and mind.

You can do this practice at any point throughout your day—as your students enter your classroom, during a staff meeting, or as you walk through the halls. It's portable, quick, and invisible to others! And it's likely to make you feel good.

How Compassion Makes Us More Resilient

After more than two decades of work in schools, I believe that one of the primary challenges we face is a shortage of empathy and compassion—for each other, for students, for their families and communities, for our bosses, and for ourselves. Even though many of us feel that we are compassionate people, something happens once we enter those dusty corridors of our institutions. Cultivating compassion is like taking a really good multivitamin: It addresses many needs, prevents problems, repairs systemic imbalances, and makes you stronger.

Building compassion ought to be a primary goal for schools, districts, and organizations. It needs to find its way into staff meetings and PD sessions. I'd love to see an agenda with a section called Compassion Practice, perhaps before analyzing benchmark assessments. And, yes, compassion building should extend into the curriculum for kids; they deserve support to build those muscles too. Compassion is good for our physical health, may allow us to collaborate more effectively, helps us deal with difficult people, and, ultimately, strengthens our communities. Can you imagine how different our schools might be with these benefits?

Compassion Makes Us Healthier and Happier

First of all, compassion is simply good for your body. When we are compassionate, our heart rate slows, our stress hormones decrease, and our immune response strengthens. Compassion can reduce the risk of heart disease and possibly other diseases. It is literally preventive medicine. Furthermore, compassion activates the pleasure circuits in our brain. Neurologists find that when thoughts are directed toward others in compassionate ways, people's minds wander less to what has gone wrong in their lives or what might go wrong in the future (Mongrain, Chin, and Shapira, 2011). As a result, they're happier.

Compassion Primes Our Minds for Collaboration

Imagine a group of English teachers sitting down together after school on a Wednesday in November, preparing to look at their students' recent writing assessment. In August, they'd created the assessment and rubric, identified the learning targets that would lead to mastery, and spent months delivering lessons. Now, as the teachers pull out the stacks of student papers, they start thinking, *What will my teammates think about my kids' work? Are their kids' essays better? Are they better teachers?* Their stress hormones skyrocket.

In order for this to be a productive conversation in which teachers can be honest, vulnerable, and open, and also one in which teachers can productively challenge each other, something needs to be done about those hormones. The neurochemical answer is oxytocin, which reduces cortisol and flips our on-off switch for trust. Oxytocin affects how willing we are to take social risks in interpersonal exchanges, and it promotes long-term bonds and commitments. Ultimately, oxytocin is responsible for, and entwined with, many behaviors that lie at the heart of compassion for ourselves and others. Although cynics may dismiss compassion as touchy-feely or irrational, scientists have started to map the biological basis of compassion, revealing its deep evolutionary purpose (Keltner, Marsh, and Smith, 2010). This research has shown that when we feel compassion, the regions of the brain linked to empathy, caregiving, and feelings of pleasure light up. Before a team meeting in which we'll be called to be vulnerable, we need to get the oxytocin flowing.

Here are some ways to incorporate compassion building into PD sessions or team meetings:

- Tell stories to each other and listen to one another's stories. Suggested prompts:
  ○ A positive experience I had as a student in school was . . .
  ○ A teacher who positively impacted me was . . .
  ○ A student whom I've been thinking about is . . .
  ○ Three things I'd like to know about are . . .
  ○ The story of my name is . . .
- Invite parents and students into staff meetings to describe their experience at your school. A panel discussion format or fishbowl discussion can create space for them to share their thoughts and feelings. This helps teachers and staff cultivate empathy for students and parents.
- As a team-building activity, hold space for staff to talk about emotions. Use passages and prompts from this book and the workbook.
- Eat chocolate during meetings. It boosts oxytocin.

If we could begin team meetings and PD sessions with a sense of empathy for students and for colleagues, I imagine our work would be far more meaningful and impactful, and I think we'd enjoy our time together more.

Compassion Makes Difficult Relationships (a Tiny Bit) Easier

Let's say the mother of one of your students is a challenging person. She yells at you. She sends you long, mean emails, and gets angry when you don't respond within two hours. If all you think about is how impossible this mother is, you build a solid wall of alienation between the two of you. Compassion offers a way to see her with more complexity and figure out how to work with her.

A first step to increasing your compassion is to find one good thing about that difficult person, which broadens your perception of her. You'll still see problems and challenges, but you might also feel a different quality of connection to the other person.

When I activate compassion for a parent who yells at me, I recognize her fear and anxiety, see her suffering and pain, and recall moments when I've had those same emotions, and it makes it a tiny bit easier to ask her to sit down with me (and maybe my principal) and talk about her concerns. Sometimes, it's that tiny bit that makes a huge difference—that prevents me from yelling back or shutting my classroom door or taking my anger out on her child.

Sometimes when I'm dealing with a difficult person, I feel foggy—as though I can't see a path through the obstacles. Yet when I activate my compassion, it's as if the fog lifts; I can see some rickety bridges of connection. Compassion helps us remember that people are capable of a range of possible behaviors, which helps us recalibrate how we see them, and listen to them more openly. Having compassion isn't about negating challenging behaviors; it's about widening our understanding of another person to include her complexity and potential.

Compassion Strengthens Communities

Think about a way in which you are suffering right now. Maybe you're having a hard time feeling motivated to go to school, or you're stressed about how much prep you have for an upcoming unit, or you have a cold. Now think about all the other people who might be going through a similar situation. The word *compassion* literally means "suffering with." When we remind ourselves that our suffering is not separate from the suffering of others, we lessen our individual pain and remind ourselves that we are not alone.

Since the age of Darwin, scientists have debated a key question: If living things evolved through competition for resources, what is the role of cooperation? An increasing number of scientists believe that compassion may be vital to the survival of our species. Although we don't often think of Darwin as a leading advocate for compassion, almost 150 years ago he argued in *The Descent of Man* that sympathy is our strongest instinct, sometimes stronger than self-interest. He theorized that it would spread through natural selection, for "the most sympathetic members would flourish best, and rear the greatest number of offspring."

Recent studies of compassion argue persuasively for a take on human nature that rejects the preeminence of self-interest and suggests that, at our core, we are wired for compassion—including across lines of difference. These studies support a view of emotions as rational, functional, and adaptive. In social communities that experience extreme challenges, those with high levels of trust and cooperation fare better (Zolli, 2012). When challenges hit these communities, people quickly move into cooperation with each other. If our schools and districts established a strong foundation of cooperation and trust, and fostered compassionate communities, change could be much easier when budget cuts strike or when a beloved leader leaves. And when we aren't in a crisis, I think you can imagine how much nicer it might be to belong to a community in which compassion is a living, breathing entity.

Self-Compassion

You wanna fly, you got to give up the shit that weighs you down.
TONI MORRISON

Maria was a high school principal with 10 years of experience in a charter school network. In our first coaching meeting, she shared that she had a difficult relationship with her boss. "This year, my intention is to understand him better," she said. "If I'm more compassionate, maybe I can build a better relationship with him. I know he's under a lot of pressure, so maybe if I put myself in his shoes, that would help." I encouraged her to see where this inquiry led.

For the first half of the year, we focused on other areas, and then in early February, Maria wanted to prepare for a conversation with her boss. We talked through her goals, hopes, and intentions for the conversation; she scripted some of the things she wanted to say; and then I suggested that we role-play the conversation. "Can you be me?" Maria asked me. "I really want to see how you'd respond to what he says."

I'd never met her boss; I only knew that he was a man about her age who had been in their organization for many years. Getting into my persona as Maria, I opened the conversation by thanking the boss for meeting. I shared my hopes for the conversation—that we could understand each other better. Maria (getting into character as the boss) crossed her arms over her chest, furrowed her brow, and interrupted me. In a harsh tone of voice, she said, "Get to the point already. I don't have all day to hear about your feelings."

I was taken aback, but I continued, explaining that I needed more support around a specific challenge, and I suggested two actions. Maria slammed her palm down on the table and said, "Listen. If you can't handle these things, you shouldn't be a principal. Go back to the classroom or take a secretary job. If after 10 years you can't deal with the basics, you don't belong."

We were only role playing, but I felt as though I'd been slapped. Her tone and body language were cruel and contemptuous. I wanted to get up and walk away. I said, "Let's pause on this role play. Is *this* what he's like?"

"Oh, he's so much worse!" Maria said. "It's hard for me to impersonate him."

As I asked for more examples of his management and communication style, I became concerned. It seemed like a hostile work environment. "He's like this with a lot of people," Maria said, "although he seems to really dislike me. I just keep trying to understand his perspective and have compassion for him."

"If you saw your best friend in this situation," I asked, "what would you say to her?"

"I'd tell her to file a complaint or quit. No one should treat her like that!" Maria said. I sat quietly in the hopes that this would sink in. I also wondered, just a little, if she was exaggerating or taking his communication style too personally.

"I know what you're saying," Maria responded. "Why do I take this if I would be appalled if my best friend worked for this guy? I can't quit, and he's not going to be fired. Maybe I'm taking it too personally. I don't know what I can do. I've just been trying to get on his good side and understand him."

The following week, Maria had a network meeting, and I accompanied her. During the meeting, her boss made at least a dozen curt, snide comments to Maria, but one stood out. The boss was reviewing a data report about compliance paperwork submission, and although several schools hadn't submitted their documentation on time, the boss singled out Maria in front of some twenty-five of her colleagues, and said, among other things, "You aren't fit to be a principal," "I expect more from you," and "Your own children probably don't listen to you." I was just about to leap up and hurl my binder at him when an older male principal, in a jocular tone, said, "Damn, that's harsh! Too much coffee this morning?"

A few minutes later, when we left the room, I lost my coach-cool-calm-and-collectedness and used some colorful language. "I guess I haven't been overreacting," Maria said. I asked a couple questions and then said, "I want to share a few thoughts. First, you're not overreacting. He's being mean and nasty. Second, you're not going to thrive as a principal under him. You can't trust him or turn to him for help because you don't believe he has your best interests at heart. His actions are creating a toxic work environment. Third, I think you should file a complaint. It's not okay for him to treat you this way. And, finally, my intuition tells me you've had some experience with bullies or an authority figure who made you feel powerless and afraid. You don't need to tell me about that, but I suspect you need to do some exploration, because I have a hunch that history has played a role in how you've related to your boss."

We talked for a couple minutes, but Maria had to return to school. The next day, she texted me and said, "I filed a complaint, and yes, my father was abusive. Maybe it's time for me to finally go to therapy." My response was brief: "Congratulations on taking that huge step, and, yes, maybe."

In our next coaching session, I asked Maria to tell me about her core values. She had them posted on the wall in large colorful marker script: "Compassion, courage, and community."

"What does compassion mean to you?" I asked.

"It means that I think about everyone with an open heart, that I treat them with love, respect, and positive regard even when I don't like them. It means that I seek to understand them, see their humanity, and love them as I do my own children," Maria responded.

This was a full and moving description of compassion, and I told her so. Then I asked, "When you think about compassion, are you anywhere in the picture? Self-compassion or self-love?"

Maria looked at me with wide eyes. "No," she said, shaking her head. "No, I'm not." And so I shared the following information about self-compassion.

What Is Self-Compassion?

Here's a sure way to undermine your resilience: Be ruthlessly self-critical and unforgiving when you make mistakes, constantly berate yourself for your shortcomings and flaws, and establish no boundaries about how others treat you. The antidote to these self-defeating behaviors? Self-compassion. *Compassion for others must begin with self-compassion.* You cannot have true compassion for others if you do not have it for yourself.

Compassion is how you respond in the face of someone's suffering. You cannot proclaim love and care for others without extending that to yourself. If you don't feel that you deserve to be free from suffering, how can you believe that your compassion for others is true? Is their suffering justified at times? If you aspire to hold compassion for all, you must include yourself among the "all."

Compassion includes setting boundaries around someone else's behavior. If someone is causing you suffering, you might be able to separate him from his actions, and you might understand what causes his behavior, and in turn, feel empathy for him. *However, you also factor importantly in this picture.* You must acknowledge the impact that someone else has on you and then draw boundaries. This is self-compassion.

Self-compassion does not let you off the hook from looking at your own actions, growing and changing, or taking responsibility for your part in a problem. Self-compassion is simply about extending kindness to yourself so that you can have the strength and energy to examine yourself and make changes. It's about refraining from judging yourself harshly and berating yourself.

How Do We Practice Self-Compassion?

The first step to practicing self-compassion is to recognize and name the painful emotions that arise due to difficult circumstances and our own inner critic. For example, let's say your principal observes a lesson that does not go very well, and leaves you feedback that stings. You're embarrassed and also a little angry toward the student who was off task and distracting others. Then you feel ashamed of blaming a student for what might have been a poorly designed lesson. Now you get mad at yourself for not spending more time prepping the lesson or for not moving that student to a different seat. If you were to step onto a path of self-compassion, rather than going further down this road of beating yourself up, you'd recognize these emotions, name them without judgment, and allow them to settle in for a moment. Doing this would enable you to then have the energy to look at the lesson and the feedback and learn from it, rather than to shut down to potential growth.

The second component of self-compassion is to recognize that you're not alone. Being human means being imperfect. We *all* make mistakes. At times, we *all* feel frightened, vulnerable, embarrassed, sad, angry, and ashamed. You can boost your resilience by not getting lost in the fears that arise or by making yourself feel as though you're the only one who has ever made such mistakes.

The third step in self-compassion is to extend kindness to yourself when you make mistakes, fail, or suffer. Talk to yourself as you would to a close friend—gently turn down the volume on the hypercritical self-talk. Say, *Hey, that wasn't your best lesson, but that's okay. It also wasn't terrible. Everyone has lessons that aren't great, and your principal knows that. What can you learn, and what can you do differently next time?* Be curious about what you're feeling and gently accept it. Stay out of the realm of rejection, self-criticism, and judgment.

With some healthy distance from your initial emotional reactions to a tough situation, you can choose how to respond, and you can choose to let go. You can identify with the mistake by saying things to yourself like, *I should have . . .* or *Why do I always . . .* Or you can open your heart to yourself and say, *I thought the lesson would go well. I didn't anticipate the need for procedures around passing out and using the materials, and I forgot to check for procedural understanding. Next time I'll make sure to clarify materials procedures and . . .* Self-compassion opens a door to learning and growth.

Talk to yourself as you would talk to a friend.

Shame and fear make us feel alone. They make us wonder, *What's wrong with me?* In those moments, practice self-compassion and recognize that everyone makes mistakes and everyone suffers. With compassion, you can accept what you are not satisfied with and work to change that; compassion also prevents you from berating yourself as you make those changes.

How to Deal with Critical Feedback

If your principal gives you critical feedback, self-compassion isn't permission to dismiss it, crawl under the covers and hide, or write your principal a defensive email. Self-compassion allows you to acknowledge your emotions and stay open to your flaws, shortcomings, and areas for growth. When you accept that you are human and make mistakes, when you can refrain from judging yourself, you can use the feedback to improve your teaching. But your personal sense of well-being cannot depend on universal acceptance and praise. When you base your happiness on other people's opinions, you will be subject to far too many ups and downs. The key is to care, but not to care too much.

Here are a few more tips for practicing self-compassion:

- Your self-love won't be reliable if it's dependent on what others think, because external judgment, criticism, praise, and appreciation come and go. Don't get too attached to praise, and don't crumble from criticism.
- Don't refrain from speaking your mind because you're attached to people liking you. On the flip side: Know that self-compassion isn't permission to lash out at others in the name of loving or defending yourself.
- As you practice self-acceptance and compassion, be open to hearing criticism that's useful and true; don't automatically reject it. Listen to criticism with an open mind in order to learn.
- Practice humility—it's liberating. You will never be perfect. When you don't expect perfection of yourself, you'll be less reactive to blame and judgment from others.

How to Deal with Difficult People

While you're working on building your compassion muscles, both for yourself and for others (and while everyone else is working on becoming a kinder person), you may still have to deal with some people who can be difficult. Maybe these people aren't really difficult—you just perceive them as being difficult. Or maybe they really are difficult. Maria's boss was a difficult person.

Here are 10 tips for dealing with difficult people:

1. Listen to their complaints, but without comment. Be very careful that you're not feeding their negativity.
2. Don't get hooked into their story lines or worked up about their attitude. Imagine you're watching stormy weather.
3. Get curious about what's going on for them. Your curiosity can stay in your mind, or you can ask a truly curious question or two.
4. Don't take other people's behavior personally. It is never about you.

5. Cultivate awareness of common ground. It's there, somewhere. You might have to search, but find connections.
6. Remind yourself that people can change. Make sure you're not holding on to a fixed mindset about their ability to grow.
7. Say this to yourself: *Just like me, this person has suffered in her life. Just like me, this person wants to belong. Just like me, this person wants to be happy.*
8. Stay clear about your own values. You can let go of anger (if you want), be compassionate, *and* stay true to values.
9. Give yourself permission to step away. Draw boundaries.
10. Ask for help. Turn to a colleague, a coach, or your supervisor, share what's going on, and ask for help in dealing with the person.

Implications for Leaders

If you supervise a difficult person, then you have a responsibility to set boundaries for how that person affects the community. You can follow tips 1–8 in the previous list, but you don't get to walk away. Because your job is to help others grow and change, you may need to establish firm and clear lines about how those difficult people act in your school or organization. Remember, if you've got a difficult person in your organization, you need to act with compassion for all of the other people who are affected by this person—the students, staff, and community.

Compassion Fatigue

From the day I stepped into a classroom as a teacher, I was acutely aware of the kids who I suspected didn't feel seen, loved, supported, or accepted, and who weren't thriving. I often felt as though I soaked up their pain, which made me empathic, but was also problematic.

Empathy is a powerful building block for compassion, but when our distress over what we witness takes center stage, the emotional experience becomes known as *empathic distress*. Empathic distress erodes our happiness; causes us to feel overwhelmed, exhausted, and depleted; and can lead to burnout. Empathic distress is made worse when we don't acknowledge our painful feelings and when we believe that expressing emotions at work is not acceptable.

Empathic distress can lead to what's called *compassion fatigue*, the feeling of being less motivated and less able to alleviate suffering. In response, we may put up a wall between ourselves and others' suffering. Many educators and people who work in the helping professions are very compassionate, but we can become swamped by the pain we see. There were times when I was definitely overwhelmed by the distress my students experienced, which was deeply corrosive of my resilience.

When scientists look at the brain scans of the average person watching videos of other people suffering, the area of the brain that is activated is the area associated with feelings of sadness and pain. We literally feel someone else's pain. This is what makes us feel worn down by someone else's suffering. By contrast, scientists have also studied the brains of Buddhist monks who have engaged in tens of thousands of hours of compassion meditation. When these monks were shown videos of people suffering, their brain scans showed heightened activity in other regions—in those associated with care, nurturing, and positive social attachment. The areas of their brains that feel pain and suffering were not activated as they were in the brains of nonmeditators (Salzberg, 2013). This is good news for those who work with people who are suffering—for teachers and social workers and those in the medical profession and many more. It means that we have the capacity to observe suffering and experience empathy without intensifying our own sadness, without becoming fatigued.

The key to preventing empathic fatigue is to cultivate a particular kind of detachment. In this state, we acknowledge the pain we witness and the distress it causes us, but we have some distance from it. This is *not* about being emotionally detached. At its most simplistic, it's about training our brain not to activate the regions of pain and suffering when we witness other people suffering. This can be done through compassion meditation, as the Buddhist monks have done, and also through cultivating a mindset of equanimity—the ability to see and accept things as they are.

Buddhist teachings offer direction on how to open your heart and accept the limits of what one person can do. This involves finding a balance between compassion and equanimity—which is not indifference or apathy; it's wisdom. It's the ability to be determined, resolved, and committed to making positive change and serving kids in the best way possible. It's also the ability to say to yourself, *In the end, it's not entirely up to me and my will.* Wishing things were different drains our energy and diminishes our response. When we accept the way things are, we can think *Now, what can be done?*

I wish I had known how to prevent empathic distress as a new teacher. There were times when I felt consumed by the suffering that some of my students experienced—the violence they lived with at home or the challenges their parents confronted to make ends meet. When I reflect on the episodes of my teacher burn-out, they were often tied to feeling emotionally overwhelmed and helpless in the face of suffering.

As I learned to manage my empathic fatigue and cultivated my equanimity, I also found new ways of seeing the suffering my students experienced. My attention could be more equally balanced between the hardships they endured and their strength and resilience. There were times when I thought, *I can learn a lot from these kids,* and could recognize both their struggles and their tremendous efforts at managing those struggles. This also helped me see more clearly what I could and couldn't do. I could do a great deal to create an environment in the classroom where children were treated with kindness and respect, where their intellectual needs were attended to, and where they could acquire the academic and social emotional skills to thrive. I couldn't do a lot to change immigration laws and find jobs for their parents or get the city to pick up the garbage that was dumped on their streets—at least, that wasn't where I was choosing to put my energy. Making these distinctions allowed me to cultivate my equanimity.

Resilient people do hard work for a long time. They remain open to suffering, and they can be a witness to it, but they do not soak it up; they practice a form of letting go. Letting go allows us to hold an expansive picture of life and our existence. While holding this picture, we can do work to alleviate suffering every day. This is equanimity. And true equanimity infuses compassion with courage.

Forgiving Yourself and Others

If you've ever felt wronged, you know that forgiving someone can be hard. Take a moment to think about a few people who have hurt you—perhaps just in professional circles. Maybe you've felt unappreciated as a teacher or leader, maybe you felt that a supervisor's feedback was unfair, or maybe a colleague betrayed your trust. See if you can call up some moments at work when you felt insulted, offended, or wronged. If you want, you can extend this reflection into your personal life.

Now think about how you responded, or wanted to respond, to being wronged. Many of us are inclined to reciprocate with equal harm, to seek revenge, or to avoid the person. But, as we know, acts of revenge or attempts to avoid rarely end well. They can make us unhappy and can damage or destroy relationships. There are, of course, productive ways that we can deal with conflict (see Chapter 4), but there is usually also a place for forgiveness. This is where compassion comes in as an unrivaled resource.

First, let me be clear about one thing: Forgiveness is not reconciliation; it does not necessarily mean the reestablishment of a relationship with a person you feel did you wrong. Forgiveness doesn't mean excusing or denying the harm. Forgiving definitely doesn't mean forgetting or not seeking justice. In fact, in order to forgive someone, you will need to contemplate the hurt that the person inflicted.

The Dalai Lama speaks of his forgiveness for the Chinese hardliners who perpetuate the oppression of the Tibetan people, and he says he won't stop speaking out against the Chinese occupation until there is freedom and dignity for his people. This seeming contradiction makes sense when we draw a distinction between forgiveness of wrongdoing and acceptance or approval of wrongdoing. The Dalai Lama describes this as the difference between the actor and the action, or between the person and what he or she has done. You need to stop wrong action, explains the Dalai Lama, but toward the person, you choose not to develop anger or hatred. The power of forgiveness lies in the ability to see the person's humanity while responding to the wrong with clarity and firmness.

Forgiving is something you do for yourself—not for the person who has wronged you. The Buddha said, "Holding on to anger is like grasping a hot coal with the intent of throwing it at someone else; you are the one getting burned." Research confirms that people who forgive are less likely to be depressed or anxious and more likely to be happier, healthier, calmer, and more empathic. (Lyubomirsky, 2007). Forgiveness is about taking care of yourself.

> *Forgiveness is the only way to heal ourselves and to be free of the past.*
> *Without forgiveness, we remain tethered to the person who harmed us.*
> *We are bound to the chains of bitterness, tied together, trapped. Until*
> *we can forgive the person who harmed us, that person will hold the*
> *keys to our happiness, that person will be our jailor. When we forgive,*
> *we take back control of our own fate and our feelings. We become*
> *our own liberator.*
> ARCHBISHOP DESMOND TUTU AND MPHO

How do you know when you've forgiven someone? Think of one of the people you brought to mind a few moments ago and consider how much you agree with these statements:

- I'll make him/her pay.
- I want to see him/her miserable.

- I live as if he/she doesn't exist.
- I keep as much distance as possible between us.

The more you agree with any of these statements, the more work you still have to do to forgive. If you harbor any feelings of revenge or avoidance, you haven't yet forgiven this person. Right now, think of someone you're angry with. Perhaps it is a student who was disruptive when an important visitor came, an unresponsive parent, or a colleague who never follows through on agreements for team meetings. Or you're angry at your principal, who just told you that next year you'll be teaching a different grade, moving rooms, and collaborating with the most difficult person in the building. Many of us harbor low-level anger or resentments all the time. This might be a good time to take a break and dip into the workbook, where you'll find more activities to help you forgive others.

> *For me, forgiveness and compassion are always linked: how do we hold people accountable for wrongdoing and yet at the same time remain in touch with their humanity enough to believe in their capacity to be transformed?*
> BELL HOOKS

Forgiveness is tied to letting go of our expectations for people. We often want people to be somewhere that they aren't, and when they act from that imperfect place of development, we feel angry at them. But why focus on the negative? It just creates more negativity. If we expect people to let us down, they will. Take a moment to think: *Whom do I need to forgive for being human? For being imperfect?* Forgive that kid for being a kid. Forgive the parent for being wherever it is he or she is. Forgive your principal. Try this thought on: *We're all doing the best we can.* Then notice how you feel. If there's even a fleeting moment of relief or lightness, take it. Forgiveness is a step toward acceptance.

And remember: You can forgive someone and still not want to be around him, or still file a grievance about his behavior if it's abusive and demeaning.

A note on forgiving yourself: Forgiving *yourself* is about bolstering self-worth. It's about accepting your own imperfections,

When Nelson Mandela was asked how he was able to forgive his jailers, he said, "When I walked out of the gate, I knew that if I continued to hate these people, I was still in prison."

accepting where you are in your journey, and having the courage to look at your own actions and learn from them.

A note on apologies: Apologies produce empathy. When you have hurt someone and you apologize, you are showing a side of you that is vulnerable and imperfect. To show your perspective, you might offer an explanation of what you were thinking when you hurt the person. This can make forgiveness easier. But if you've hurt someone, offer the apology without attachment to the person's response (that is, without hoping he or she will forgive you); otherwise it's not a true apology.

 ## *A Dive into Envy*

Recall a time you felt envy. It's a particular kind of stinging pain, isn't it? How might your life be different if you could tame your green-eyed monster? I offer good news: You can use the compassion that you're cultivating for yourself and others as an antidote to envy.

Quick definitions: Envy is pain over something you don't have; jealousy is fear of losing something you already have. They blur, so we'll explore both emotions here. Envy and jealousy can make us compare what we have to what others have, try to control others, get into other people's business, obsess over what we don't have, criticize someone else, accuse someone else of not being loyal, act clingy or needy, or do something to get even. Envy can trigger fear, embarrassment, or shame, which can make us want to hide or disguise our envy with claims of unfairness. We know it's something to avoid—there's nothing glamorous or remotely righteous about it—and it makes us feel awful. If left unchecked, it can corrode our well-being and relationships with others. Buddhists think of envy as poison, which seems pretty spot-on to me.

There are two ways to use compassion as a response to envy. First, when you notice envy arising in yourself, pay attention to what it's trying to tell you. What's behind it? What's missing from your life? Which other emotions are connected to your envy? Is there sadness? A yearning for love and appreciation? Be kind to yourself. Your envy is trying to tell you something about a part of you that is hurting. If you only get angry with it, you won't learn. Use the self-compassion muscles you're building to courageously turn to your envy and be with it.

Second, you might find relief from your envy if you practice compassion for the other person. When someone gets something or has some success, if you can be genuinely happy for this person, you can temper your envy. Remind yourself that nobody has it all. Everyone experiences pain; everyone has troubles. Recognize your interdependence, shared humanity, and interconnectedness. We are all connected, so the good fortune of another can bring a positive benefit to you, too.

Here are a few more things you can do when you experience envy or jealousy:

- Practice gratitude: Make a list of what you're grateful for. This can help you gain perspective.
- Use envy as motivation to improve your situation. Do something about an area of your life that dissatisfies you. What is it that you want?
- Stop spying on people. Stop trolling around on Facebook, or just get off of it altogether. For some, this just feeds the green-eyed monster, so cut off its source of fuel.

Life is not a zero-sum game. We are not competing with each other for scarce resources. If someone else finds love, takes a vacation, or publishes a best seller, that doesn't mean that there's less available for us. Envy arises from feeling that there's a limit to the amount of joy that's available for human beings—and the feeling that someone else got something that now we can't have. It comes from feeling that we're in a constant struggle with others, that if someone else accomplishes something, we're somehow less successful, less lovable, and less accomplished—and this just isn't true. Joy, love, friendships, community, and abundance are limitless. If you find yourself feeling envious, try saying this to yourself: *There is enough for everyone.*

Envy happens. It is deeply corrosive to our well-being and resilience and relationships. When envy surges through your system, examine it, understand it, and face it head-on, using compassion as a tool.

Disposition: Perspective

When my son was four years old, Google Earth fascinated him. We'd put in a location that he knew—our house or the park—and he'd name everything he saw. As we zoomed out, his eyes widened with excitement as he took in the objects that had entered the frame. And then, as we zoomed out farther and farther, he'd marvel at the expanse of our country, hemisphere, and planet. "That's where we live?" he'd ask incredulously as we looked down on Earth. "We can see important things from here—like the ocean—that we can't see when we're in our house in Oakland." His favorite perspective was one that took in a great expanse of land. "Zoom out! Zoom out!" he'd cry. "I want to see everything!"

Late one afternoon, I was at work in a coaching meeting with a few teacher leaders and the principal of the school. The meeting was tense. I was attached to my ideas and opinions about our reading intervention program. We had a decision to make, and we weren't getting anywhere after an hour and a half. For some reason, my son's enthusiasm for Google Earth popped into my mind, and I imagined his little voice demanding, "Zoom out!" I visualized the office we were in at our school, and I imagined zooming out, above the building. *What might I see from here?* I thought. I imagined zooming out again, and again, and again, and each time, I asked myself *Now what can I see?*

This thought experiment profoundly affected me. First, I felt momentarily extricated from my own frustration, fatigue, and annoyance—and I recognized that my colleagues were similarly feeling challenged. Ironically, I felt less alone and more connected to them—we were all tired and irritated. From my new perspective, I also felt more curious about the other "objects" in view—my colleagues—and I wondered why they were advocating for the ideas they proposed. As I continued imagining that I was zooming out, I became even more curious about my colleagues, the situation, and the broader terrain of our conversation. I saw features that I couldn't see from ground level.

When I "landed" back in my chair in the office, I felt clearer and better equipped to contribute productively to the conversation. I offered some strategies to move us out of our stuck place and toward a decision. I felt calmer and more open. I also felt humbled by that broader view of the situation and its challenges.

Since then, "zooming out" has been a strategy that I prompt myself to use when I want or need perspective. It helps me feel differently. It helps me see differently. It helps me take different actions than I could have taken with a ground-level focus.

We are self-involved creatures, most often seeing and acting from within our own tiny sphere of experience and based on our own needs, wants, and fears. When you open yourself to a wider perspective, you escape self-referential thoughts and ruminations. A wider perspective leads to equanimity, helps you empathize with and connect to others, and enables you to access strength and creativity to respond to a problem. Perspective can help you recognize what is in your sphere of influence and what is outside your control. This cultivates a greater sense of humility, acceptance, and even humor.

Whereas transforming emotions is hard, changing your perspective can be easier because perspective is in your mind—and you can influence your mind. To gain perspective, look at a situation from many angles, including from others' point of view. When something bad happens, can you see any good emerging from it?

Can you see any joy in the struggle? When we have perspective, we can see the good in the bad, we can see things from others' point of view, and we can see things within a bigger context. All of these ways of having perspective cultivate our resilience. Perspective doesn't diminish suffering or even a tragedy—it just expands our vision. It allows us to see the long view, which sometimes helps us gain insight. Perspective moves us out of our own limited point of view and limiting self-interest.

Perspective not only helps us improve situations but also improves our health. Dr. Larry Scherwitz (n.d.) found that people who more frequently said *I, me,* or *mine* had a higher risk of having a heart attack—the constant use of personal pronouns (reflecting higher self-involvement) was a better predictor of death than smoking, high cholesterol levels, or high blood pressure. In contrast to this scary research, psychologist Sonja Lyubomirsky (2007) found that one of the greatest influences on our happiness is our perspective toward life and our ability to reframe our situation more positively.

The way we see the world is the way we experience the world. When you're feeling stuck, when you are disappointed or frustrated, zoom out and see what else comes into your frame of reference. Changing the way you see changes the way you feel and act.

Love Is the Only Way

Reggie was one of the most compassionate teachers I ever worked with. Perhaps because he was an algebra and biology teacher, and wore a jacket and tie every day, I assumed he'd be more rational and less emotional than other teachers. However, when speaking about his students, he spoke with tremendous empathy, his voice catching sometimes, his eyes occasionally welling with tears. He was quick to act if there was something he could do to help someone else, and seemed to want no recognition for his kind acts.

One afternoon, just before a staff meeting in the library, I noticed Reggie emptying the library's trash cans into the large receptor in the hallway. "Did you get another job?" I asked. He shook his head. "Claudia's limping today," he said, referring to our janitor. "I just thought I'd help out a little. She got here before I did this morning, and she'll be here even later."

"How did you get to be such a good person?" I asked. Reggie looked away and seemed uncomfortable.

"I'm just going with what my faith tells me to do," he said.

"What's your faith?" I blurted out of curiosity.

"Doesn't matter," he said. "At the heart of every religious tradition is a message of love and compassion. Some of us lose our way at times, but it's in there, in every tradition, and in each of us." I nodded, feeling a little awkward to be talking about religion. Reggie seemed to notice this, and he smiled.

"It's not just religion," he said. "It's science too. All of the research is pointing in the same direction: Basic human nature is compassionate. We are hardwired to connect and care for each other. Our brains get the same pleasure from helping someone else as we do from gratifying personal desires. Religion and science are just different mechanisms to find the same thing: Love is the only way. Helping people makes me feel good—that's all there is to it."

I don't remember what the staff meeting was about that day. I remember Reggie emptying trash cans, and I remember wondering where I might be able to extend more love and compassion. It shouldn't be a surprise that among students, Reggie was unequivocally their favorite teacher.

CHAPTER REFLECTION

- What connections did you make to the ideas raised in this chapter?
- How might your life be different if you increased compassion for yourself and others?
- Of the ideas presented in this chapter, which do you want to further explore?

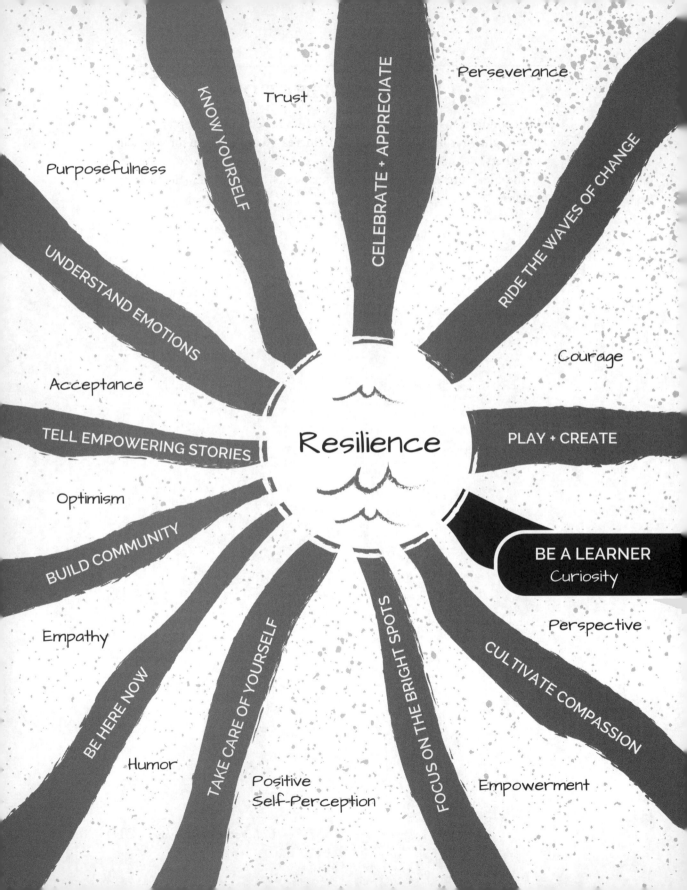

CHAPTER 9

Be a Learner

If we see challenges as opportunities for learning, if we engage our curiosity whenever we're presented with an obstacle, we're more likely to find solutions. This habit and disposition help us not just survive adversity but thrive in the aftermath.

> *February: Around midyear, you may have the bandwidth to reflect on how you learn and to return to your beginner's mind, because learning is a path to growth and resilience.*

ﻉ‌ﻉ

My first year teaching wasn't the hardest—it was my sixth, when I helped start a school, and taught a new grade and content area. I felt competent in the fundamentals of teaching, but it was as if I was standing on a clear plateau, having ascended a foggy mountain, and the steep terrain of what I didn't yet know as a teacher lay ahead of me. Seeing that gap between the knowledge set I possessed and what I aspired to do for my students demoralized me.

I was only ever tempted to quit teaching when I felt that I wasn't serving children well. By my sixth year, I had reached the limits of my ability to figure out how to improve as a teacher, and I started contemplating other careers. Then I met Liz Simons, a coach who worked for a nonprofit that supported new schools, reminded me of my Jewish grandmother, and saved me as a teacher.

Liz supported me in three ways that no one else ever had in my teaching career. First, Liz demonstrated unabashed, unwavering curiosity—about me, about what I was doing in the classroom, and about my students. She'd sit at the table in my classroom, listening and taking copious notes, and, in response to my often long reflections, would say something like, "That's *so* interesting." She'd pause and think and then ask another question like, "Why do you suspect they're doing that?" her curiosity permeating each word. Her questions unlocked insights, connections, and possibilities for action in my mind.

Liz also demonstrated unabashed, unwavering belief in me. She held up a mirror and helped me see myself in new ways, giving me language to appreciate my skills, strengths, disposition, and orientation as a teacher. Her constant encouragement and affirmation unlocked my self-confidence.

The final way Liz helped keep me in the field of education was introducing me to action research, or what some people term *classroom inquiry*. Discovering inquiry was like tumbling down a rabbit hole. Yet, unlike Alice, I found that everything made more sense to me, and I felt better than ever as a teacher. I found energy, empowerment, and a deep understanding of my students; I uncovered solutions to perplexing problems. Everything—my kids, my future, even my condemned portable classroom—looked different after I discovered the inquiry process.

What happens in this magical land of inquiry, you're wondering? To start, I incessantly asked questions like, "I wonder why this might be happening? I wonder what could happen if I tried . . ." There was no judgment here in this land—not toward myself or the kids or the outcomes. Regardless of what transpired every day, my response became, *Oh, that's* so *interesting!* And then I'd peel back layers, on a mission of understanding.

In the inquiry world, I discovered that the answers to vexing problems were often right in front of me—within the little bodies in my room, within my own mind, and within accessible resources. I understood that I was on a quest for answers, but also that once I found an answer, more questions would be uncovered, because the quest is eternal. The answer to one question unlocked another question. But the joy of learning, the delight of growth, the unending pursuit of questions propelled me forward. I lost myself in the questions and in the data that surfaced; every day, I found myself wondering, *What might happen if tomorrow I . . .* and then I'd jot down my ideas, observations, and especially the insights—because those piled up—and I'd think, *Finally! I'm figuring some stuff out! I am getting better as a teacher!*

Then I started seeing the data. First it made a subtle appearance as a shift in my students' attitudes, engagement, and effort (which I documented religiously on sticky notes: *Luis begged for another five minutes of reading time today; Sandra said she loves books with strong female characters*). Then, in June, I did a reading assessment and thought, *Wow. They made a lot of growth this year.* And in August I got the mother of all data sets. I'd administered the standardized test that previous spring and had said to my kids, "I wish you didn't have to take this, but it is important in some ways. Just try your very best." And that data showed that my kids had made several years of reading growth in one year. The numbers attracted attention from around the district: "How did she do that?" people asked. "Inquiry," I said.

The numbers were validating and useful, but what mattered most was that in August as I returned to start my seventh year teaching, I felt *good*. I knew how to continue learning to be a better teacher, I felt confident that I could serve my kids, and I was excited about the next year (which turned out to be my best year ever).

That was where Liz took me in the year that I had seriously contemplated leaving education. She guided me to a place where I could be a learner again and find answers to the questions that kept me up at night.

⁊⁊

This chapter explores these questions: How do we learn? How do we change? How do we improve? How do we create the conditions in which we can learn? To answer these questions, we'll consider how we use time and manage our energy—essential resources for learning. And, of course, we'll explore the emotional experiences that run parallel to these questions. Learning, and its correlating disposition of curiosity, open a path for resilience that's sometimes overlooked.

By the time you're roughly halfway through the school year, an interesting thing can happen. You may feel more energized. You may see evidence of all your hard work—your kids appear to be learning. You also may feel a boost of confidence because you are making it through the year! You might feel increasing clarity about what you're doing and why, which might help you feel more committed to teaching. By midyear, you might feel enthusiastic about the rest of the year and even start having thoughts about next year—what you'll repeat or do differently.

Midyear is an optimal time to reflect on yourself as a learner, but if this isn't what's happening for you in the middle of the year—if you don't feel energized or hopeful or clear—fear not. It might happen later in the year, or during the following year. Although some patterns are predictable, we are also all on our own schedule and timeline. This chapter will still be applicable and useful.

Learn About Learning So That You Can Learn

Learning about learning is an empowering starting point. With a deeper understanding of your learning development, you'll grow more effectively. In order to better understand this process, let's look at two useful frameworks: The Conscious Competence Ladder and Mind the Gap.

The Conscious Competence Ladder: Understanding the Learning Journey

Think about something you really wanted to learn in your life, maybe something fun, such as a sport or a hobby. Choose something that you have tackled and in which you've gained some competence. What happened as you started learning it? What was the journey like?

Once I wanted to learn to make pottery, so I signed up for a class. I had assumed there was skill involved, but I had no idea how hard it was to throw a pot. Week after week, I hunched over a wobbly blob of wet clay, trying to wrangle it into a shape, watching it slide off the wheel or split across the middle, while my self-talk incessantly muttered, *This is SO hard. I am so bad at this. Everyone else seems to get this faster than me. I suck.* That inner dialogue reminded me how scary and exhausting it is to learn something new, which made me kinder and more patient with my students that semester. And, because I am persistent, I finished the pottery class with two short, thick bowls that I still treasure 15 years later.

Emotions accompany our learning experiences. Initially, when we set out to learn something, we may not appreciate how much we need to learn. When we begin to see the breadth and depth of this new subject or skill, we can become disheartened or even give up. If we have a sense of the emotions we're likely to feel as we move through the learning process, we'll be better equipped to manage them along the journey.

The Conscious Competence Ladder (see Figure 9.1) is a framework that helps us understand four stages of learning (the theory was developed at Gordon Training International by Noel Burch in the 1970s). The model highlights the factors that affect our thinking as we learn a new skill: Consciousness (awareness) and skill level (competence). It identifies four levels that we move through as we build competence in a new skill:

- **Unconscious incompetence.** At this stage, we don't know that we don't have a skill or that we need to learn it. We are blissfully ignorant, and our confidence exceeds our abilities. Our task on this rung is to figure out what skills we need to learn.
- **Conscious incompetence.** At this stage, we know we don't have the skills we're trying to acquire. We realize that others are much more competent and that they can easily do things that make us struggle. We can lose confidence at this stage or give up on our learning. This is when we most need to manage discomfort, fear, and anxiety, and to boost our confidence.

Figure 9.1 The Conscious Competence Ladder

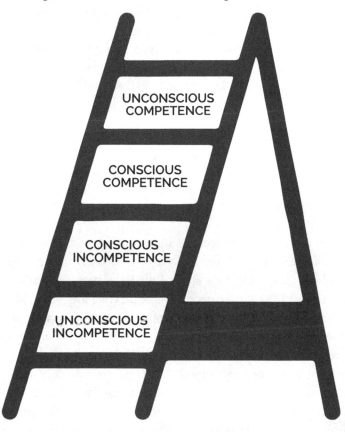

- **Conscious competence.** On this rung, we know that we have the skills we have worked to attain. As we put our knowledge and skill set into regular practice, we gain even more confidence. We still may need to concentrate when we perform these skills, but, as we get more practice and experience, these activities become increasingly automatic. We need to use these skills as often as possible in order to move into the next stage.

- **Unconscious competence.** At this level, we don't know that we have the skills. We use our new skills effortlessly and perform tasks without conscious effort. We are confident of success. In order to keep growing, we need to teach these newly acquired skills to others. This deepens our understanding of the material and keeps our skills finely tuned; teaching the skills also can be rewarding. Be warned: We can go backwards down the ladder if we don't regularly use our skills.

The Conscious Competence Ladder explicitly names core emotions in the learning process. The normalization and predictability of this experience can help us stay motivated and manage our expectations. When you're on the consciously incompetent rung, reassure yourself that, even though learning a skill is difficult and frustrating, it will feel easier one day. And when you're unconsciously competent, remember to value the skills that you've gained and be patient with those who are still learning them.

Implications for Leaders—and Coaches

Use the Conscious Competence Ladder when guiding people through the learning process. Here are some additional tips for each rung of the ladder:

- At the beginning of the process, people may not know how unskilled they are. You'll need to make them aware of how much there is to learn and explain how they'll use these skills. Rubrics, exemplars, and artifacts that show the level of skill they need are useful. Give lots of positive feedback at this stage, help people see their strengths, and make sure to show clear and concrete models of high competence. Most important: Normalize the experience of emotion at this stage.
- During the conscious incompetence stage, provide encouragement and support, and share the Conscious Competence Ladder. This helps learners understand feelings of discouragement and see that it's a phase they can move through. Use strategies to cultivate a growth mindset (see Exhibit 9.1) and keep reminding learners that they can't do whatever they're trying to do *yet*. *Yet* is the key word.
- At the conscious competence level, keep people focused on the skills they've learned and give them plenty of opportunities to practice those skills.
- When people become unconsciously competent, watch for complacency, offer opportunities to stay up-to-date with their skills, and invite them to teach their skills to others.

Fixed versus Growth Mindset

Another concept to understand is that of mindset. Carol Dweck's 2006 book *Mindset* has become a core text in education for good reasons. When we hold a "fixed" mindset, we assume that intelligence and talent are fixed at birth. We believe that we are either good at something or bad at it, that our character, intelligence, and creative abilities are static and unchangeable. Success is the affirmation of that inherent intelligence. This pushes us to strive for success and avoid failure at all costs as a way to maintain a sense of being smart or skilled. With a fixed mindset, we're unable to take criticism, we avoid challenge, and we give up early.

With a "growth" mindset, we assume that intelligence and talent can go up or down. A growth mindset thrives on challenges and sees failure not as evidence of a lack of intelligence but as motivation to grow and stretch abilities. Holding a growth mindset creates a passion for learning rather than a hunger for approval; failure becomes an opportunity to learn.

A growth mindset is the mindset of resilience. As Dweck (2006) explains: "Why hide deficiencies instead of overcoming them? . . . The passion for stretching yourself and sticking to it, especially when it's not going well, is the hallmark of the growth mindset. This is the mindset that allows people to thrive during some of the most challenging times in their lives" (p. 7).

These mindsets offer profoundly different ways to approach what we can't do. With a growth mindset, we curiously explore discrepancies between what we want to do and what we are able to do. This search reveals paths for improvement. Understanding the concept of mindset and becoming aware of your own is another tool on this journey to resilience.

Mind the Gap: Identifying Learning Needs

My first attempt at making sushi didn't go so well. It was barely edible: The rice was too gummy, the seaweed was burned, the proportions of fish and fillings were unbalanced, and the rolls disintegrated. I knew I had failed, and the expression on my husband's face confirmed it. But, instead of feeling ashamed, I wondered: *Why did I fail? What would I need to do differently next time? What do I need to learn to be able to make sushi?*

The fact that I was even willing to envision a "next time" comes from a concept I'd been exposed to years earlier. I've expanded on this concept and named it Mind the Gap. The title is a reminder to "mind" or pay attention to the space between a desired ability (such as to make sushi) and current ability (which results in a heap of mushy rice and mangled fish). This framework proposes that we can parse into six groups the things interfering with our ability to do something. This helps us get clear on what we need to learn and offers insight into entry points to start

Figure 9.2 Mind the Gap

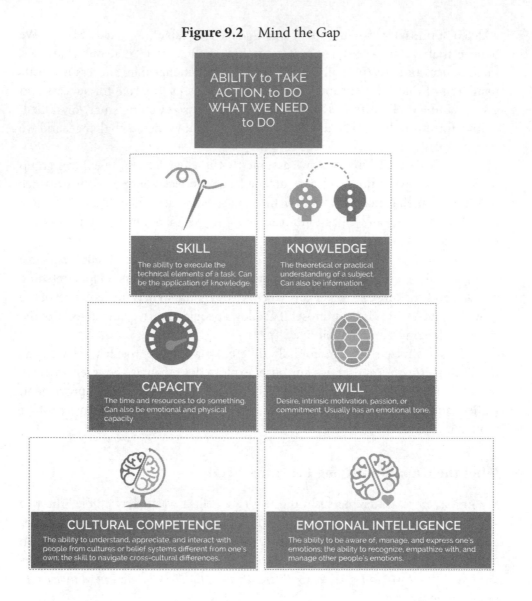

ABILITY to TAKE ACTION, to DO WHAT WE NEED to DO

SKILL
The ability to execute the technical elements of a task. Can be the application of knowledge.

KNOWLEDGE
The theoretical or practical understanding of a subject. Can also be information.

CAPACITY
The time and resources to do something. Can also be emotional and physical capacity.

WILL
Desire, intrinsic motivation, passion, or commitment. Usually has an emotional tone.

CULTURAL COMPETENCE
The ability to understand, appreciate, and interact with people from cultures or belief systems different from one's own; the skill to navigate cross-cultural differences.

EMOTIONAL INTELLIGENCE
The ability to be aware of, manage, and express one's emotions; the ability to recognize, empathize with, and manage other people's emotions.

that learning. Figure 9.2, Mind the Gap, depicts this concept, and Exhibit 9.1, The Gaps Defined, offers a description of each gap and an example in a school context.

When I apply this framework to my sushi disaster, I see that I have a number of gaps in different areas. I didn't have a good knife, which is why the fish and rolls shredded when I tried to slice them; my oven was broken and got too hot, which is why the seaweed burned; I was pressed for time and simultaneously tried to do laundry; and I felt impatient and frustrated because the whole thing took so long.

Exhibit 9.1 The Gaps Defined

Gap	Description	Examples
Skill	The ability to execute the technical elements of a task. Can be the application of knowledge.	• Frontloading vocabulary • Using discussion structures • Getting the whole class quiet • Breaking down the steps to solving complex equations • Identifying a doable learning target for a lesson
Knowledge	The theoretical or practical understanding of a subject. Can also be information.	• Understanding polynomials • Knowing discussion strategies • Knowing students' names • Knowing how to redirect behavior • Knowing grade-level standards
Capacity	The time and resources to do something. Can also be emotional and physical capacity.	• Having time to call students' parents (may know how, may want to call, may have the skills to call, but may not have the time) • Having books to differentiate learning (may understand the need to differentiate, may know how, may want to, but may not have the material resources) • Having the emotional wherewithal to manage an irate parent • Having the physical energy to attend evening and weekend school functions
Will	Desire, intrinsic motivation, passion, or commitment. Usually has an emotional tone.	• Loving the work • Wanting to serve a community • Feeling a calling to interrupt educational inequities • Holding a commitment to helping kids learn

Gap	Description	Examples
Cultural Competence	The ability to understand, appreciate, and interact with people from cultures or belief systems different from one's own; the skill to navigate cross-cultural differences.	• Recognizing assets in students who come from different cultural backgrounds • Understanding that eye contact has different meanings in different cultures • Validating students' background through selection of curriculum • Appreciating the contributions of students from different cultures
Emotional Intelligence	The ability to be aware of, manage, and express one's emotions; the ability to recognize, empathize with, and manage other people's emotions.	• Awareness of feeling anxious when an administrator enters the class • Ability to draw boundaries around requests for help from colleagues • Ability to manage one's irritation with a perpetually difficult student • Ability to connect with a difficult student • Ability to calm a distraught student

I also didn't know what kind of rice to use. A capacity gap might have been at the root of my inability to produce a plate of delectable rolls, but a gap in one area can also produce a larger gap in another. Because gaps are often interconnected, it can be hard to identify the original gap.

When Gaps Show Up in Teaching

Now let's consider this framework in a school context. As I do a quick survey of my gaps as a novice teacher, I conclude the following:

• My inability to teach vocabulary effectively was due to a knowledge gap about best practices.

- My inability to execute smooth routines and procedures was due to a knowledge gap about which routines I needed, and I lacked the skills of organization.
- My inability to have an organized classroom (and to be able to locate the supplies I needed for lessons) was due to a capacity gap. (I didn't have the time.)
- My inability to work with a grade-level partner teacher was due to an emotional intelligence gap. (I didn't know how to manage my impatience with him.)

Here's another example of applying Mind the Gap in a school context. Deana was a new teacher I coached who stepped in as a long-term sub when the eighth-grade English teacher resigned three months into the year. When I observed Deana in her first weeks, I was concerned about what I saw: She had poor classroom management, kids were off task for more time than they were engaged in learning, and she seemed frazzled and nervous. I began intensively coaching her on management, routines, and procedures. However, when I observed her implementing the strategies we'd discussed, she struggled to execute them. I assumed she needed more modeling, so I demonstrated the strategy in her first-period class and then observed her trying to copy what I'd done in her second-period class. This didn't work either.

When we met after school, I asked Deana what she thought was going on. "I just can't talk with as much confidence as you," she said. "I know you told me to speak loudly, but it's more than that—I can talk loud, but not with confidence."

Aha! I thought. *Confidence is an emotion.* I had been coaching Deana on her skills, and although she did have skill gaps, other gaps exacerbated that skill gap. Deana had shown commitment to this class; I was fairly certain she didn't have a will gap. I was also sure that she had capacity; she only taught four periods, which gave her three periods for planning, coaching, and observing other teachers. She had all the materials she needed. I knew that Deana had knowledge gaps; she was a brand-new teacher, so it was inevitable. But I hadn't thought about her emotions.

"Tell me about what you feel when you're teaching," I said.

Deana sighed. "Well, I guess this is normal, but most of the time I'm nervous that I'm not doing a good job, that our principal will regret hiring me, that I'm not really meant for teaching. This is all I've wanted to do since I was in first grade, and I'm scared that I'll fail."

"Yes, those are normal feelings," I affirmed. "Think about the moment when you open your classroom door and you're getting kids settled into the warm-up activity. How are you feeling then?"

"Nervous," Deana said. "I'm afraid they won't stop talking and I'll lose control and that they'll stage a rebellion." She chuckled self-consciously.

"I appreciate your honesty," I said. "So, would you say that you experience some fear?"

Deana groaned. "That's so embarrassing. I guess so. That's wrong, isn't it? I shouldn't be afraid of my students."

"It's honest," I said. "What do you think it is about them that makes you afraid?"

"First, they're all taller than me. And I don't understand them sometimes," she said. "They're so much louder than the kids I went to school with; they dress so different; they talk different. I wanted to teach in Oakland, but I didn't realize that I'd feel so out of place."

The wheels clicked in my mind: Deana was dealing with *a cultural competency gap.* Although she was a person of color, as were all of her students, Deana didn't share the cultural background of her kids, and she'd been raised in an upper-middle-class community by two university professors. She didn't know how to interpret her students' verbal or nonverbal cues, which fueled an emotional intelligence gap.

I shifted my coaching approach to simultaneously address her cultural competence and give her new skills. While we worked on things like how to give clear instructions and how to interpret eye contact (or the lack of it), Deana's confidence grew. One day, as we talked directly about this, she said, "So it's not that I'm a bad teacher, I just have a cultural competency gap? And it's possible that one day I'll feel comfortable and at ease with my kids?"

"Yes" I nodded.

"That's good news then," she said. And, after a while, Deana did feel comfortable with her kids, and one step at a time, over the course of some years, she developed the competencies necessary to be an effective teacher.

The Hierarchy and Interconnectedness of Gaps

As I mentioned earlier, gaps are interconnected. When we're struggling to do something, we need to understand the gap size in each domain and then consider whether there's a root-cause gap. Sometimes, however, the gaps are interconnected in a way that's not linear; there could be several simultaneous root-cause gaps. This framework isn't a science; it's a tool to provoke insight.

In presenting this concept as a pyramid (as in Figure 9.2), I'm suggesting a hierarchy. Emotional intelligence (EI) and cultural competence are the foundations for all other areas: a skill gap can create an EI gap, but if our EI isn't solid, then we can't truly close gaps in other areas. It's true that a will gap can blur with an EI gap. In a way, will is an emotion—but I've kept it separate because I think that too often, we ascribe a will gap to someone (a child or an adult) when what the person is experiencing is an emotion such as fear or shame. If that person lacks strategies to deal with those feelings, the inability to do something appears as a will gap—but it really isn't. If we can shift from thinking about something as a will gap to thinking about it as an EI gap, there are more options for action.

In schools, whether with adults or kids, in class or in PD sessions, we focus on the uppermost buckets—skill and knowledge. Sometimes we address will, trying to cultivate a sense of urgency or stoking the flames of mission and purpose. Capacity is also sometimes attended to, but often overlooked, as is evident any time district leaders roll out seven new initiatives in one year and then get frustrated that programs aren't implemented with fidelity when there just isn't the time to do so. The foundational domains, EI and cultural competence, are those most neglected. When was the last time you attended a PD session on how to calm your nerves when a high school senior in her last semester of school cusses you out? Or how to deal with the first grader who can't stop crying every morning when her mom drops her off? Or how to shift the discomfort you experience when your little group of English language learners speak to each other in Spanish and you don't understand what they are saying? Or how to deal with the low-intensity conflict in your department that makes every single meeting you attend excruciating? If we attended to these foundational competencies, we'd make more growth, and quicker growth, in developing our skills and knowledge.

How to Use This Framework

Use this framework as a resource to push you into the stance of a learner, into a place of curiosity devoid of judgment, and into a growth mindset. We all have gaps; we'll have gaps for as long as we live, because there's no person alive who has the ability to do everything. Gaps are indicators that we can still learn and grow. We can learn to delight in our gaps, to see them with joy and clarity. This framework is not about deficit thinking, not about finding weaknesses; it's about recognizing our true potential and examining what lies in the way of fulfilling it. It's not a tool for self-judgment or criticism. If you find yourself struggling to use this tool in a way that feels useful, explore your feelings about this framework.

This framework is also intended to lay a road map for action. As you gain clarity on your gaps, you gain insight into the actions you can take to close those gaps. You may need to do some more investigation about what you suspect are your gaps: *Do I really have a knowledge gap about polynomials, or do I not know how to explain them to my kids in a way that they understand?* Let this framework help you anchor yourself in the place of a learner.

Sad Sundays and How to Stop Having Them

There may have been a number of moments in this book when you've thought, *I'd like to do that, but I don't have the time.* In order to be a learner, to do inquiry or read or write or meet with colleagues and talk about what you're reading, you'll need to come to terms with how you spend your time. I'm including this section for two reasons: First, managing your time better will allow you more opportunities to learn. And second: Most of us have a knowledge and skill gap when it comes to how we manage our time. Let's address that knowledge gap.

For many years, I dreaded Sunday. I barely enjoyed Saturday, because I knew that a day of drudgery followed: Laundry. Groceries. Grading. Lesson planning. Week after week, I'd leave school on Friday hauling away bags full of student journals, curriculum guides, young adult (YA) novels, and a professional text or two that I was sure I'd start on Saturday morning, maybe as I drank my coffee or while sitting in a park. Yet how many times did these canvas sacks spend the weekend sitting inside the front door, untouched? How many Mondays did I pick up those bags and pledge that next weekend I would read all the YA novels for the upcoming round of literature circles?

I didn't even spend Sundays doing fun, relaxing, or other productive things. Often I lay on the couch with my green lesson planner on the coffee table next to me, and I moaned and groaned a lot. And dozed. Then I'd find some urgent thing to take care of, such as trimming my cat's nails. (This was in the old days before we had the endless distractions of digital devices.) I usually did laundry and planned a lesson or two. But on Monday morning, I'd wake up to feelings of dread, and I'd head off to school feeling unprepared and disappointed in myself.

Yet a series of moments over the course of a year or two shifted my weekend (and weekday) routines. I grew deeply tired of my procrastination, and relieved it slightly with small tweaks here and there—and after a while, those tweaks added up to a major time makeover. By my seventh year as a teacher, I had a solid routine every day after school that included reviewing the formative assessments I'd done that day and tweaking my plans for the next day. On Friday afternoons, as soon as the kids were out the door, I spent two to three hours planning for the following week. I was tired, but extremely focused during those hours. By 6:00 p.m. at the latest, I left school, carrying maybe one book, and met my husband at our favorite sushi restaurant for our regular Friday night dinner. On Sundays, sometimes I did more prep—fine-tuning lessons, gathering another resource, or refining a long-term unit plan. By 5:00 p.m. on Sunday, all work ended, and I spent the evening reading fiction, watching movies, seeing friends, or preparing a good meal. I'd wake up on Monday feeling rejuvenated and prepared for the week.

You don't have to hate Sundays or dread Mondays or perpetually go to school unprepared. You can do what you need to do, have more energy, and live with 24 hours in a day. Let's talk about habits and behaviors that will help you manage your time and energy so that you open your weekends up for rejuvenation.

Keep a Time Log

One year, at my principal's urging, I kept a time log. I'd been working 70 hours a week, and although I knew I was using time ineffectively, I couldn't see why, or what to change. I diligently kept my log for a week and was shocked by what I saw. Here is how I spent my time and the conclusions I drew:

1. I wasn't doing the most important things when I had the most energy. I'd arrive at school 90 minutes before the kids, and I spent most of that time doing mindless busywork.
2. I did a number of tasks that I could ask parent volunteers and school staff to do. They could make copies, fold packets, organize books, and so on. I just needed to get organized and ask.
3. I underestimated how long I needed for some tasks. After school, I'd intend to get through five tasks, but the first took almost the entire time, so I never felt satisfied with what I accomplished.
4. I didn't prioritize my work and therefore didn't make thoughtful decisions about how to tackle my workload. I gravitated toward doing less meaningful tasks (such as cutting out images for a bulletin board) because I avoided doing things that I didn't know how to do (scoring writing assessments).
5. I was distracted easily because I felt so overwhelmed.

Completing this time log was sobering. I felt embarrassed as I talked to my principal about what I'd learned, but I got some clarity on how to change my behaviors.

If you feel as though you don't have enough time to do what you want to do, the first question you need to ask is, *Where is my time actually going?* Not where you *think* it's going but where it's *actually* going. To figure this out, you'll need to document how you spend your hours. Write down what you do for every hour of the day for a week. If you don't do this, you won't know which of the following time and energy management suggestions (summarized in Exhibit 9.2 and discussed in the next sections) to implement.

> ### Exhibit 9.2 A Summary of Time and Energy Management Strategies
>
> - Confront the planning fallacy
> - Chunk it
> - Make to-do lists
> - Obey the calendar
> - Use focusing mechanisms
> - Stop multitasking
> - Pause and renew
> - Get the hardest stuff done first
> - Enlist company
> - Celebrate small wins

Manage Your Time

As a new and novice teacher, I wish I'd had the summary in Exhibit 9.2 and an understanding of those habits. I often thought I was just a procrastinator or disorganized or slow to get things done. I spun all kinds of stories about my relationship to time. What I see now, however, is that all I needed were some basic, technical tips on managing my time.

What follows are the time management strategies I've found most useful and relevant for educators.

Confront the planning fallacy. We have a tendency to underestimate the time it takes to complete a task, and to overestimate how much time we have left to finish a task. Let's say it's December 1, and grades are due on December 14. You have weeks left, you tell yourself. Grading won't take that long this year. But you are not accounting for the final projects that you need to assess before you can get to the grades, or for the hours you'll spend trying to locate that one student's final project, or the time it'll take to input the grades and deal with the inevitable technical challenges of the grading program. So on the weekend before they're due, you have to spend 26 hours getting them done.

A time log helps you figure out how long things actually take, as opposed to your optimistic underestimates, so that you can make realistic plans. Because I fall into this fallacy often, I double the amount of time I think something will take me. If I finish earlier, I feel successful and accomplished! Think you'll need 10 minutes this evening to call a couple of parents and share good news about their kid? Allocate 20 minutes.

Chunk it. Break large projects into small, easier-to-complete steps so that your mind can focus on one thing at a time. If you struggle with procrastination, this is especially helpful. List each component of writing report cards, and each time you finish an item, check it off and soak in the satisfaction of accomplishment.

Make to-do lists. Make a to-do list, prioritize the items on it, and determine the length of time for each task. Be realistic—remember the planning fallacy. Allocate time in your calendar for each item.

Obey the calendar. Don't wait for the mood to strike to print out rubrics; just enter it on your calendar: Thursday, 3:30–4:00, print rubrics. Commit to your calendar. Also schedule time on your calendar for breaks, lunch, and open time to address things that need taking care of. Things always pop up: Anticipate that you'll need that time each week and those things won't throw you off your plans.

Use focusing mechanisms. When you have a task that requires concentration, identify things that help you stay focused. For example, leave your phone in another room or put it on Do Not Disturb, disconnect the Internet, turn notifications off on your computer, and/or only respond to email during two predetermined times during the day. When I sit down to do cognitively challenging or tedious work, I put my phone on Do Not Disturb and set a timer for 45 minutes. During that time, I forbid myself from moving or doing anything else. When the timer goes off, I take a 5–10 minute break and then I set it again. This routine took getting used to, but now my mind is well trained and well behaved. After around three hours of work, I take a longer break and then return for a few more hours. All of my books have been written in 45-minute increments.

Stop multitasking. Multitasking severely undermines productivity. A temporary shift in attention from one task to another—stopping to answer an email or take a phone call—increases the amount of time necessary to finish the primary task by as much as 25%. Furthermore, when we respond to an email, check Facebook, or get distracted by other minutiae, we feel an instant hit of gratification; our brain actually releases dopamine. This may be why for some, compulsively checking social media or email can feel addictive.

Manage Your Energy

There's a subtle difference between managing time and managing *energy*. Some productivity experts suggest that our focus should be entirely on managing energy, and the two are inextricably connected (Schwartz and McCarthy, 2007). I've found the time management strategies that I just shared to be very useful. Here are some further strategies that appear to be for time management but will help you manage your energy.

Pause and renew. Every 90–120 minutes, our bodies need a short period of recovery. When you start yawning, feeling restless, or having difficulty concentrating, take a break for a few minutes and disconnect completely. Talk to a colleague about something other than work, listen to a song you love, walk around the yard a couple of times or up and down a set of stairs. Meditation and deep breathing are also renewal strategies. The length of time is less important than the quality of the activity you engage in, and doing this every 90–120 minutes will help you sustain your energy all day.

Get the hardest stuff done first. When you have the option, do the most important and most cognitively demanding work first thing in the morning. Your brain is sharpest and most disciplined in the two to four hours after you wake up.

Teachers: I know you don't have a lot of say over your school schedule, but see what happens if you set a goal to get weekend planning and prep done on a Saturday or Sunday morning. It might just get done much faster than if you save it for Sunday afternoon. Principals: Given that you have more flexibility with your schedule, save your emailing, busywork, calls, and meetings for the afternoon, and do mentally taxing work in the morning.

Enlist company. Just having friends physically nearby can push you toward productivity. Distractible people get more done when there is someone else there, even if that person isn't coaching or assisting them. So when you're facing a task that is dull or difficult, such as organizing your classroom, grading heaps of essays, or inputting data, ask a friend or colleague to keep you company.

Celebrate small wins. Acknowledge yourself for the smallest successes. Progress is incredibly motivating. As you read through those stacks of student journals, keep the piles of finished journals in front of you as evidence of your success. Every time you finish one, take 10 seconds, close your eyes, and tell yourself what a good job you're doing and how focused you are. This recharges your emotional batteries and makes the next journal easier to pick up.

❧ ❧

When you acquire time and energy management habits, you'll be amazed at how much better you feel—physically and emotionally—every day. You'll find yourself with more energy to dedicate to the activities I've suggested in this book—self-care, reflection and introspection, involvement with community, and learning. You'll find that weekends become opportunities for rejuvenation and for building immunity to the stressors of the workweek. To cultivate resilience, you need to internalize dozens of behaviors, and sometimes the gap between knowing about these things and doing them is simply one of technical knowledge and skill.

Implications for Leaders

- Adults and kids need duty-free breaks every 90–120 minutes. When you're creating the master schedule, consider how you can build in opportunities for true renewal for teachers during the day.
- Consider a late start for kids (rather than an early release day) so that PD and PLCs can take place in the morning when everyone is more alert and can engage in rigorous cognitive processes together.

Acknowledging Context: On the Conditions for Learning

Throughout this chapter, I've encouraged you to take charge of your learning—to close the gaps between what you aspire to do and your current abilities. However, because we don't exist in a vacuum, it's critical to acknowledge the optimal *conditions* in which we learn.

On the Time Needed for Learning

It will take you about 10,000 hours of deliberate practice to become a master at something as complex as teaching. If you're wondering how many years this is, it's between five to seven school years. But just grinding away at the hours alone won't make you a masterful teacher, because practice alone doesn't make perfect. Practice with feedback, correction, and refinement helps you get *better*—there's no such thing as perfect.

Educators need instructional and leadership coaches because we require these 10,000 hours of practice and feedback. Coaches facilitate practice, create opportunities for feedback, cultivate self-reflection, and provide guidance so that we don't keep repeating the same ineffective actions year after year. Although effective instructional coaching is not the only way to do this, it's a well-researched and proven mechanism for teacher improvement. Even beyond the 10,000 hours: Coaching is a way for professionals to continue refining their skills; after all, even professional athletes at the top of their game have coaches.

Implications for Leaders

- According to one study, teachers need some 50 hours of PD in a given area to improve their skills and their students' learning (Darling-Hammond, Wei, Andree, Richardson, and Orphanos, 2009). These 50 hours can include coaching, because instructional coaching is a form of PD.
- When you're creating your annual PD plan, keep this number at the forefront of your mind. If you want teachers to get really good at one skill, you need to limit the number of programs, goals, and initiatives you roll out. Count the hours and make sure you devote 50 hours to boosting skill in one area.
- Right now might be an optimal time to pull out this year's PD plan for teachers and reconsider it with these facts in mind.

Learn from the mistakes of others. You can't live long enough to make them all yourself.
ELEANOR ROOSEVELT

What Your Brain Needs

There are some basic biological requirements in order for human brains to maximize learning. Let this note serve as a reminder that your brain needs oxygen (so go take a walk around the block) and glucose (and eat a handful of almonds and dried fruit) to function optimally and let the learning sink in. Brains also need nutrients (what you eat matters), including amino acids. In all that I've learned about nutrition and optimal brain functioning, the role of and need for amino acids has been the most enlightening. Talk to a nutritionist, do some online research, or chat with a worker at your local health food store about supplements such as 5-HTP, DLPA, and SAMe. Taking an amino acid supplement can do wonders for your mental concentration, sleep, mood, and more. Of course, I am not a nutritionist and everyone is different, so do your own research. Your brain might thank you.

The Need for a Learning Organization

A *learning organization* is essentially what it sounds like: an organization in which everyone is learning—the teachers, the principal, the counselors, the kids, and so on. Individual teachers reach high levels of functioning when they work in extraordinary learning organizations. Schools thrive when they are run as learning organizations.

Rate your agreement with the following statements on a 1–5 scale (5 being full agreement) as they apply to your work environment, then total your ratings:

- I can disagree with colleagues or supervisors; I can ask any kind of question.
- I am encouraged to take risks and try new things, and I do so.
- I can express a divergent opinion with colleagues and supervisors.
- I'm provided with time to pause, thoughtfully reflect on my processes, and learn from my experiences.
- I get feedback on my work from multiple sources (including from colleagues and supervisors).
- I share what I learn with others and outside my group and organization.
- Leaders make their learning visible and model the practices of a learner.

If your total is between 28 and 35, you work in a strong learning organization. If your total is between 20 and 27, you work in an emerging learning organization. Anything lower than 20 means that your organization is a weak learning organization.

In my book *The Art of Coaching Teams* and in the *Onward Workbook,* you'll find a more extensive list of indicators of a learning organization.

A Dive into Shame

Shame shuts down the learning circuitry in our brain. It makes us feel like hiding or disappearing, recoiling from taking risks or asking questions. Shame may be the most malignant of all emotions, with nothing beneficial to offer. I'm hoping that this brief discussion of shame might provoke reflection on its presence in your life. If you suspect that shame plays a role in your happiness and well-being, I hope you'll find support to dissipate it. High levels of shame will profoundly undermine your ability to learn and to cultivate resilience.

Shame is a feeling that you are somehow wrong, defective, inadequate, and not good enough. You can experience it to different degrees, with embarrassment on one end (a mild form that results from trivial social transgressions like tripping or burping) of the continuum and chronic shame at the other, when you feel that the very core of you is bad.

Guilt and shame are not the same. We feel guilt when we recognize that we may have negatively affected someone else; it's a feeling of remorse about our behavior, as opposed to a feeling about ourselves. Guilt can produce a sense of responsibility and can motivate us to change our behaviors, making it a more useful emotion than shame.

If you feel (or see in someone else) a lot of anger or blame, shame may be hiding below those feelings. Projecting anger or blame onto someone else is an ineffective way to rid ourselves of shame. In comparison, anger is a more comfortable emotion than shame. Blaming others might help us feel as though we've regained some control, but there is a high cost to ourselves and our relationships when we dwell in anger and blame. Shame-prone individuals are also vulnerable to drug and alcohol abuse, which helps mask feelings of shame.

As a teacher and coach, I've seen shame in far too many little and big people. I've coached educators who work themselves to the bone, who are viciously critical of themselves, and whose expectations for perfection (from themselves and others) erode relationships, health, and joy. There was little space for learning when there was so much fear and shame. Even using very refined coaching strategies, I had limited impact because the shame ran so deep. Intensive, pervasive shame usually has its origins in childhood. If you experience a great deal of shame, please seek the professional help you deserve.

Disposition: Curiosity

My grandmother was insatiably curious; she epitomizes the disposition for me, and she was a remarkably resilient person. In the last decades of her life, she traveled around the world—to Ecuador, Zimbabwe, China, and Romania, often on music and dance tours. When she was 85 and in very good health, she exclaimed, "There are just too many good books still to read. I can't die yet!" She lived for 89 years, reading voraciously until the end.

Curiosity is almost the opposite of shame. It's a disposition that makes us want to investigate, listen, ask questions, and take risks. It can make us question our assumptions about people and look beyond stereotypes. Curious people are attracted to new people and ideas. Curiosity might even be an elixir for longevity because it produces such a yearning and quest for knowledge about our inner experience and the world around us.

Everyone possesses curiosity—it's an innate disposition—but people differ according to the strength and breadth of their curiosity and their willingness to act on it. You can turn up the dial of your curiosity by asking open-ended questions: *I wonder how bricks are made? I wonder why Johnny can't read? I wonder why I get so irritated when kids forget their supplies? I wonder how many questions I can ask today?*

Learners embrace their naturally curious disposition and view obstacles and challenges as opportunities for growth. Any time we ask ourselves, *What can I learn from this moment? From this challenge?* our perception of the experience changes. When you are curious, you are open to ideas and you pursue solutions, trying almost anything and asking for help along the way. That's what resilient people do, and often it's curiosity that is compelling these actions.

Curiosity has many benefits. It helps us see with fresh eyes and access more of our brain for problem solving; it naturally reduces our fear and can help us break out of old, unhealthy behaviors; it can make us literally feel good—triggering our brain to release dopamine. Dopamine, a natural opiate, also plays a role in enhancing the connections between cells that are involved in learning. As a result, curiosity helps us learn better and retain information. (This is why the most engaging lessons we teach kids are the ones they remember best.) There is an upward-spiraling relationship between curiosity, knowledge, and resilience. The more we learn, the more we want to learn, and the better we are at managing challenges, the more curious we become, and so on.

A Beginner's Mind

Imagine yourself standing in your classroom right now, taking a learner's stance: Maybe you're on the edge of the room, looking out at your students. Maybe your head is tilted slightly and resting on your fist, and maybe your expression is open and quizzical. You're not confused—you're in a learner stance. When you take this stance, you transform into a superhero, and your power is in the questions you generate.

When Gabriel crumples up his paper and throws it across the room, you think, *He hasn't done that in a month. I wonder what's going on with him today?* When Eli is absent for the fifth time in two weeks, but hasn't seemed ill, you wonder what might be going on. When you get tired of grading journals, you wonder whether students are tired of writing them.

Curiosity and taking a learner's stance lead us to asking bigger, wiser questions and to solving problems. When the superintendent makes a surprise visit to your classroom, and it's during a moment that's not your best as a teacher, you wonder how you can help him get a more robust look at what happens in your class. When your principal tells you that Susie's mom has requested a meeting between the three of you after school that day, you think, *Could this be an opportunity to talk about how Susie's behavior has been changing?* There's a subtle distinction between curiosity and problem solving, one that's worth honoring, but also not necessary to always notice.

Remember—resilience is cultivated in the space between stimulus and response. In that space, we can ask questions and reconnect with our beginner's mind, for that is where possibility, opportunity, and hope reside.

I trust that you know a lot about learning. After all, you're an educator. Give yourself permission to keep learning, every day, in every moment.

CHAPTER REFLECTION

- Which feelings came up for you when reading this chapter?
- What was a new idea in this chapter?
- What's an action you might take as a follow-up to reading this chapter?
- What did this chapter make you more curious about?

CHAPTER 10

Play and Create

Creativity and play unlock inner resources for dealing with stress, solving problems, and enjoying life. When we are creative, we are resourceful, and we problem-solve in new and original ways, which fuels our courage. Our thinking expands, and our connections with ourselves and others deepen.

March: Spring break brings an opportunity to explore play and creativity so that you can integrate these activities into daily life. Resilience arises from creation.

৯৪ ৯৪

Whenever I designed instructional units, I'd lose myself in research and planning. One year, creating a sixth-grade humanities unit, I contemplated the art of our ancient ancestors. Deep in the caves of southern France and Spain, where the greatest concentration of prehistoric paintings are found, the walls are covered with running horses, rolling cows, swimming stags, and fighting bison. Early human art had always captivated me, and I now had the chance to read up on the latest findings from paleoanthropologists.

My husband, Stacey, is an artist, and, at one point, I asked him why he thought the artists of Lascaux painted animals. "Whoever painted them loved line and movement," he said. "When I was a kid, I sketched horses for those reasons—I wanted to capture their movement."

Scientists who study cave paintings also seek to explain the purpose behind the art. They tell us that ancient humans wanted to understand how herds moved and how animals behaved so that they could figure out how to hunt them. Or they theorize that people painted themselves killing animals as a way to represent past or future hunting successes. Overwhelmingly, these interpretations relate to humans understanding and dominating nature, and there is always functionality ascribed to the purpose of the paintings.

As we looked at the art and I wondered more about why ancient humans painted, Stacey said, "Maybe they were just trying to capture the essence of the animals, and maybe the painters just loved painting. That's why I paint," he said. "Why does there need to be a purpose beyond the love of the movement of the animals, the materials, and the process?"

Maybe the reason the ancient artists painted was because they loved to paint.

Of course, we don't know whose theory of the cave artists' purpose is correct, but that idea unsettled me. I'm purpose driven, I always have been, and I consider it a personal strength. I yearn for my daily actions to have meaning and a reason. But there's a downside to ascribing purpose to every action: Being so results oriented reduces the potential for pure play and, perhaps, creativity.

Artists and philosophers have long debated whether art needs to have a purpose, or what purpose art should play. Related are the differences between creating and appreciating art. In some ways, these serve the same role in our lives—both help us access creative, abstract, wider ways of thinking. But our experiences interacting with the creative world exist on a continuum: at one end, we consume or *appreciate* art; perhaps around the middle, we *play;* and at the other end, we *create* art. At each point on the continuum, we activate different parts of our minds, hearts, and spirits; it's likely that the greatest opportunity for cultivating resilience lies in the most active point—in creating art.

In the exploration of play, creativity, and art, questions arise: Is play a precursor to creativity? Are all creative expressions art? Is "playful work" an oxymoron? As I've contemplated these questions, I've found myself falling into a logical trap—wanting to find a correlation between play, creativity, and art; considering whether a cyclical or symbiotic relationship is more apropos. I want to nail down these distinctions, contain them to a linear graphic in order to honor the essence of the activity—be it play, creation, or art. These questions feel both philosophical and practical, and I don't have answers. I invite you into this exploration: Perhaps you can find answers by playing around with the questions.

I'm hoping that if you're reading this chapter in the spring, you'll have a chance to incorporate this habit into your spring break. Regardless of when you're reading this, I would bet that you're overdue for a creative break—maybe it's time for a mini creativity boot camp. Strive to incorporate creativity and play into staff meetings, weekends, and even into your instruction, and you'll become more resilient. Refine your ability to appreciate and generate art of all kinds, and you'll most likely enjoy life more.

Why We Need to Play Every Day

I was working at home one day when my son, then five, hovered next to me and said, "I'm lonely. Play with me!" I was only a quarter of the way through reading 120 student book logs, but I was tired of telling him that I had to work. I took off my glasses, put down my pen, and agreed. "Let's have a water fight!" he said as he ran outside to gather supplies. It was a hot spring afternoon. *I can do this*, I thought. *I can be fun.* It takes me a little effort sometimes.

An hour later, I begged for a break. It hadn't been that hard to pick up the water toys and chase each other around the yard with no other goal than to squirt his little body. As we lay in the sun in the driveway, soaking and out of breath, I felt proud of myself. *It wasn't that hard,* I acknowledged. *And it was fun.* When I returned to the stack of book logs, I noticed that I felt more energized. *All the running and laughing must have oxygenated my brain,* I thought. But I also felt happier, my mind felt clearer, and it felt easier to focus.

Some years later, when I read Stuart Brown's book, *Play: How It Shapes the Brain, Opens the Imagination, and Invigorates the Soul,* I recalled this afternoon of water fighting and recognized it as embodying the very definition of play.

What Is Play?

What did you love to do when you were a child? What could you lose yourself in for hours? Maybe it was reading fiction, building Lego cities, climbing trees, dressing up and staging elaborate tea parties, or drawing horses. Can you remember that feeling? How would you describe it? When was the last time you did something that was enjoyable and all-consuming? Play, by definition, is something we do because it's fun and not because it helps us reach a goal. Experts say that the key to getting the most out of play is to incorporate it into our lives and not just relegate it to vacations. I've taken the research on this topic very seriously, as I'm committed to boosting my own resilience—and yours as well, of course.

A large cadre of scientists who study play, including neuroscientists, developmental biologists, psychologists, and social scientists, have concluded that play serves a critical role in the development of animal species (Brown, 2009). These researchers have written volumes, explaining how play shapes brains, makes animals smarter and more adaptable, fosters empathy, and makes possible complex social groups. And for humans, play lies at the core of creativity and innovation.

But play serves even greater purposes. Recall a time when you felt most alive. Take a moment to close your eyes and remember that time, to let yourself be back in that memory.

Most of you will have remembered a time when you were engaged in some form of play—something that was deeply pleasurable, energizing, revitalizing, and enlivening. Yet when was the last time you engaged in an activity just for the pleasure of it? Children are experts at play. It's natural and instinctive to them, and, in some ways, it's their work. They can commit hours to building a Lego structure or to playing make-believe with stuffed animals. They are playing, very seriously. When we get older, however, we're told that playing is a waste of time; we focus on being productive, and the busyness of our lives takes over.

Stuart Brown has made it his life's mission to bring more play back into the lives of adults. In addition to authoring *Play*, he's the founder of the Institute for Play. His core message is that just a little bit of "nonproductive play" will make us more productive, invigorated, and resilient. Stuart reminds us that without play, the world would be pretty grim, as play is often the basis of art, games, books, sports, movies, fashion, humor, and music. In fact, Brown (2009, p. 12) argues, play is "the basis of what we think of as civilization. Play is the vital essence of life."

According to Brown, play has the following attributes:

- Apparent purposelessness: It's done for its own sake and not for any practical reason.
- Voluntary: It's not obligatory or required by duty.
- Inherent attraction: It's fun and makes you feel good.
- Freedom from time: You lose a sense of the passage of time.
- Diminished consciousness of self: You stop worrying about whether you look good or stupid. In imaginative play, you might even be a different self. You are fully in the zone.
- Improvisational potential: You are open to doing things in a variety of ways. You get new ideas.
- Continuation desire: You want to keep doing it.

Now think of something you love to do that might be play. How does it measure up to these criteria? It's okay if you find that there are things you love to do but that don't meet every criterion. For example, maybe you love to hike, but one of the reasons you do it is that it's good exercise and helps you stay healthy. Keep on hiking, but also challenge yourself to occasionally do something that's purely play. Similarly, true play is also non- or low-competitive play. Many times when people "play" golf or basketball or some other sport, the element of competition overshadows the pure fun.

Also, binging on Netflix isn't considered play. Being too passive in an activity diminishes its play value. Perhaps watching a movie can be justified as play, but, as you make your way through an entire series, the benefits of play are undermined. Here's another way to think about it: As I noted previously in this chapter, there's a continuum of play activities with appreciation and absorption on one end and creation on the other end. You might *appreciate* and *enjoy* listening to music, and this can produce some of the relaxation and pleasure indicative of play, but if you *create* music (belt out a song or tinker around on the piano), you reap the full benefits of play.

What Are the Benefits of Play?

Whenever I play, I remember how good it feels. It doesn't take much for me to get absorbed in blowing soap bubbles in a park or searching for sea glass on a beach. But then I forget. Of course, early childhood educators and kindergarten teachers know how important play is (and in recent decades have advocated for it to remain a central part of the experience in school for young children). But if you're like me and many others, reminders help us see the benefits for big and little people. Let's review what the experts have concluded are the benefits of play.

- **Play relieves stress.** It triggers the release of endorphins, the body's natural feel-good chemicals. (Even just remembering an intensely playful experience can do this—try it right now!)
- **Play improves relationships.** Sharing laughter and fun can foster empathy, compassion, trust, and intimacy with others. Play doesn't have to be a specific activity; it can also be a state of mind. Developing a playful nature can help you loosen up in stressful situations, break the ice with strangers, and make new friends.
- **Play improves brain function.** Playing chess, completing puzzles, or pursuing other fun activities that challenge the brain can help prevent memory problems.

The social interaction involved in playing many of these games is an added benefit.

- **Play stimulates the mind and boosts creativity.** Young children often learn best when they are playing—and that principle applies to adults as well. You'll learn a new task better when it's fun and you're in a relaxed and playful mood. Play can also stimulate your imagination, helping you adapt and problem-solve.
- **Play keeps us feeling young and energetic.** In the words of George Bernard Shaw, "We don't stop playing because we grow old; we grow old because we stop playing." Playing can boost our energy and vitality and even improve our resistance to disease. In fact, it might just help us live longer. A group of scientists spent 15 years studying Alaskan grizzlies and concluded that the bears who played the most survived the longest (Brown, 2009). I hope those scientists had fun studying the bears.

Some years ago, when I first read Stuart Brown's book, I described the benefits of play to an acquaintance who was a high school French teacher in her mid-50s. She listened to me as I recited statistics and made my case, and then she interrupted me. "I don't need convincing," she said. "I made a commitment to play about 15 years ago after I got divorced. Play isn't just a thing I do; it's an attitude I take toward life. Yes—I love to dance, I wear sparkly nail polish, I make mobiles out of found objects, I cook with spices, but more than all of that—I just don't take life too seriously."

Small, Regular Doses of Play Are Powerful

With all of these benefits, play is like an essential multivitamin that we should be taking daily. When we're playing, we're creating new imaginative cognitive combinations. Our brain gets to try out new things without threatening our physical or emotional well-being. When the risks are small and fun is present, we more readily learn new skills.

What might be possible if we incorporated more play into our work—if we could find spaces here and there where we could weave in play and make teaching or leading or coaching easier and more enjoyable?

Although it would be fantastic if you could frequently raft down rivers or engage in whatever large-scale play meets your fancy, regular play will contribute the most to your emotional well-being. If you can play every day, you'll probably be among the happiest and most resilient people in the world, but start with a goal to play every week. It's never too late to develop your playful, humorous side. Set aside regular playtime, and play in public or in private. The more you play, joke, and laugh, the easier it becomes.

Let the Good Times Roll

Okay, so you're ready to play. Where to start? What to do? Begin by brainstorming play activities of different sizes: For some play, you'll want a day, whereas other play might need only five minutes. For me, dangling a string in front of my kitty is a quick way for me to dip into play. I also find preparing an elaborate dinner lots of fun, but it may take an entire day. Perhaps among my all-time favorite activities is anything I can do in a warm ocean—float, snorkel, and dive under little waves. But that doesn't happen very often. So as you build up a bank of activities for playtime, include some that you can engage in easily.

Another way to build a bank of play activities is to ask others about how they play and create. Ask your colleagues this question; ask your supervisors. (It's also a way to get to know them better.) Recently, I asked some educators how they play, and the answers I heard included dressing up in a wild costume, dancing through a field of flowers, plinking away on a piano, making a sumptuous meal, racing a dog on a beach, making pyramids of play-dough balls, and experimenting with hair dyes.

Role Playing: Another Form of Play

José was a teacher leader at a school with a new principal. This principal was attempting to implement a long list of new initiatives, and the staff was not having it. José's department had pleaded with him to push back against the changes on their behalf, but José was nervous. "I have no idea how to have that conversation," he told me, groaning and regretting his decision to be the department head. "Where would I even start?"

An enthusiastic proponent of role play, I suggested we do that. As José struggled through the conversation, he found the words he wanted to use, the tone of voice that reflected his feelings, and the body language that could best help him communicate. At the end of our session, he was grinning. "That was a lot of fun," he said.

"That's why it's called role *playing*," I said.

In this case, the purpose of playing was to help José identify how to have the conversation with his principal. Role playing helped José try out his communication skills in a low-risk environment, and it helped him feel lighter, calmer, and more confident. Teachers: If you're working on improving classroom management or developing relationships with students and parents, or even on having hard conversations with colleagues or supervisors—role-play the conversation. You'll get more than just practice; you'll also benefit from the fun elements of play.

Implications for Leaders

What would it look like if you played more often with your staff? Here are a few of the ways I bring noncompetitive, low-risk play into meetings:

- Have teachers share the ways they like to play. Consider ways to incorporate those into meetings; you will have already identified activity leaders.
- Provide clay, play dough, or putty in supply boxes. I love Crazy Aaron's Thinking Putty because it doesn't dry out and feels really good to play with. When our hands can fidget or explore something while we're learning or talking, our ideas are better.
- Include a game from improvisational theater as a community builder or grounding activity at the start of a meeting. One of my favorites is Zip Zap Zop (look it up). It always gets people laughing.
- Provide basic percussive instruments and make simple rhythms. I also love Boomwhackers (look them up) because they're *really* fun and you can easily make decent sounds together.
- Play games with tennis balls—just toss them to each other in increasingly complex patterns.
- Offer check-in or discussion prompts that are fun, such as: If you could live another life in a parallel universe and be anything, what would you be? Or: If you could have dinner with anyone—living or dead—who would that be and why?

Finally, consider how you can incorporate play into activities that have a purpose. If you are leading a PD session on standards-based assessments, could you incorporate a random pairing game (such as Barnyard Babble) to create new partners? Could you design a way to meet the session's goals while engaging participants in activities that provoke laughter and creativity? In my coaching workshops, I offer multiple opportunities for educators to engage in role playing as a way to explore coaching strategies and interpersonal challenges. Inevitably, as people take on different characters, there is laughter in the room. Laughter connects us and helps us feel more invested in what we're doing, and we have better memories of the experience.

You'll find videos of these and other play activities that you can do with a team—and also with students—at www.onwardthebook.com.

Art: Where Play Can Take Us

In this conversation about play and creativity, we must acknowledge art (visual art, music, theater, film, performance, and so on) and its role in resilience. When you think about art, what thoughts come to mind? Which feelings surface? When I asked educators these two questions, here were the responses I commonly heard:

- I'm not good at art, so I feel anxious.
- Art is boring. I think about being bored in museums.
- I wish I had more opportunities to do art; I loved art classes as a kid.
- Sometimes it's nice to look at, but what's the point?

In order to embrace play, it helps to have an appreciation for art and the time to explore it.

Human Beings Make Art

According to the archaeological record, our ancient *Homo sapiens* ancestors made art before they waged war or built cities or farmed crops. They sought to represent and think about their world pictorially and symbolically, and they created music (and most likely dance) long before they picked up swords and planted seeds. The oldest known instruments are 43,000-year-old bone and ivory flutes. On cave walls in Australia, southern Africa, Europe, and Indonesia, paintings of animals, human figures, and hands date back 35,000 years. Around 30,000 years ago, sculptors in the area of southern Germany carved ivory figurines of animals and women. Although we certainly don't know why our ancestors created this art, *they did*. The call to create, and to create things of beauty, is primal.

Alain de Botton and John Armstrong have written a magnificent book called *Art as Therapy*. They poetically and visually present the premise that art (in which they include design, architecture, and craft) "is a therapeutic medium that can help guide, exhort and console its viewers, enabling them to become better versions of themselves (2013, p. 5)." De Botton and Armstrong propose seven functions for creating and consuming art that are useful to consider:

- We create art to remember (think about writing and photography).
- We create and/or appreciate art because it gives us hope and optimism. Art teaches us "how to suffer more successfully" (p. 24).
- Art helps us rebalance emotionally and understand ourselves—whether by creating it or experiencing it.
- A work of art (think poetry or song lyrics) can illuminate a mood or give an experience a clear expression.
- Artistic creations can challenge our thoughts and values, pushing us to grow.
- Art helps us appreciate what is always around us, the values of ordinary daily life, and what we might take for granted.

This little book—a work of art in itself—is worth having on your shelves.

Art, Resistance, and Resilience

A novel, poem, movie, or play can shatter our misconceptions of each other and break down the walls that separate us. Can you call to mind a piece of art that's helped you see and feel the experience of someone you perceived as different? Most recently, the film *Moonlight* did this for me. It's a gorgeous piece of moviemaking that might wrench your heart open yet leave it more whole than it was before. Art is a vehicle for connection and empathy; it combats loneliness, alienation, and dehumanization; and it helps us understand ourselves better. Creating art that does this is an act of political resistance against those who seek to divide us.

Art has long been an essential tool for social justice. It has proven itself as such for centuries in various forms, from satirical plays, protest anthems, and street theater to posters, puppets, cartoons, murals, and more. When artists creatively express political messages, a unique form emerges that inspires emotions, including humor, hope, grief, and commitment. Consider, for example, the underwater sculpture in the Caribbean Sea that evokes the Africans who were thrown off the slave ships during the Middle Passage. The sculpture, created by James deCaires Taylor, is a life-size circle of people holding hands and facing outward. It's eerie and devastating. Google it. See how it makes you feel. After that, take a look at Picasso's *Guernica* again.

This is how art boosts my resilience: A painting, poem, sculpture, song, or novel that conveys an injustice unlocks my empathy, moves me to sadness or anger. Yet, perhaps because the message is conveyed artistically, I also experience optimism. I'm reminded that human beings have the capacity to commit acts of both tremendous violence and stunning beauty. The memorialization and permanence of the artwork also makes me feel hopeful; because of this artist's work, the experience of the suffering will not be forgotten.

During the course of writing this book, I visited Berlin, a city that was once the epicenter of the most horrific violence of the twentieth century. You can't visit Berlin without being reminded of the consequences of fascism, due in part to the art throughout the city. All around Berlin, laid into the sidewalks, are "stumble stones," cobblestones that commemorate Holocaust victims. In 1992, German artist Gunter Demnig began laying these brass plaques in front of the last place of residency for a victim of Nazi persecution. The stones typically contain the name of the person, his or her date of birth, the date the person was deported, and, if it's known, the date of death and the name of the concentration camp where he or she died. As of early 2017, Demnig had laid over 56,000 stumble stones, in 22 European countries. You might be standing outside a German café, enjoying a delicious streusel and admiring the architecture, and look down to see a stumble stone, and you are made to remember.

The great majority of educators I've met aspire to positively impact the lives of children. Embedded in our teaching is the social justice mission to leave the world better than we found it. Because of the daily wear and tear on the vision we aspire to build, we need regular doses of inspiration and kindling for our spirits. Art can provide that infusion of hope and optimism that keeps us moving onward and that reminds us of our innate capacity to create beauty.

When times get hard, and batter and bruise our spirits, it's more important than ever to pick up our pens and paintbrushes. Writer Toni Morrison (2015) speaks to those with creative inclinations who feel demoralized in this stunning passage: "This is *precisely* the time when artists go to work. There is no time for despair, no place for self-pity, no need for silence, no room for fear. We speak, we write, we do language. That is how civilizations heal."

Resilience is what enables you to bounce back after a storm; it's the internal reserves of strength that fuel your ability to live your life and do what you were born to do. As I will touch on more in Chapter 12, art emerges from the realm of the transcendent, of the sacred and spiritual. When we connect with that energy source in the world and refuel our inner reserves, we become immeasurably stronger.

Take a few minutes now to contemplate the forms of art that connect you to your deepest wells of resilience. Perhaps take a break from reading to dip your toe into those waters. Resilience is cultivated a little bit at a time.

Then why have we kept up the singing for so long?
Because that's the sort of determined creatures we are.
GALWAY KINNELL

Creativity as a Habit and Disposition

Recall the last time you wore a costume. Maybe it was Halloween, and you went to a party or trick-or-treated or entertained your students with your alter ego. What did it feel like to be someone or something else? What did that allow you to do? How did it shift your sense of yourself? When I ask educators these questions, they smile un-self-consciously, their eyes twinkle, and they share amusing anecdotes.

Dressing up (even just putting on a mask) is a low-risk, easy way to access our creativity while bypassing our mind's anxious self. It's a shortcut to the parts of ourselves that crave expansive expression. It allows us to try things we otherwise wouldn't try, to say different things, to feel differently. Imagine what could happen in the classroom if you came from a place of otherworldly power. How might teaching or leading be different if every day you wore a Wonder Woman costume?

Creativity is a habit and a disposition. It's hard to say when it shifts from being a habit into a disposition, or whether it can be a disposition without being acted on through habits. Just about every research study on the resilient identifies creativity as a key trait, behavior, or disposition. Most of this research is not worth reading; ironically, it's boring, but the conclusion is worth considering: Creativity is essential. It's simply the ability to dream things up and make them happen, to live driven by curiosity and not by fear, as the writer Elizabeth Gilbert names it in the title of her book *Big Magic: Creative Living Beyond Fear*. Let's dig a little deeper into the whys of creativity and then into how you can cultivate it.

Why We Need Creativity (In Case You Need Convincing)

Rational, analytical minds often need convincing as to why they should try something creative. At least mine still does. In spite of my deep appreciation for the role that creativity has played in my life, I still find myself wanting research that explains why it's good to be creative and why making art is a valid use of time.

Creative processes enable us to see the root of a problem or see a situation in a different light; we can make connections between seemingly unrelated phenomena and gain new perspectives. Creativity and its cousins—imagination and innovation—are the missing ingredients in many school reform efforts. School transformation almost always relies on deeply creative thinking.

Let's consider a common complaint that teachers have: Their students' behavior. In fact, in research on middle school teachers, student behavior is the top reason cited for burnout. In many schools I've worked with, administrators respond to student misbehavior by creating procedures and consequences, posting rules all over the school, increasing staff presence in the hallways, and printing out behavior contracts for students who repeatedly break the rules. These technical solutions sometimes work to control student behavior, for the short term, but relying on a culture of policing leaves teachers less than satisfied. These schools are sometimes quiet and calm, as students walk through the hallways in neat rows, silently, with their hands at their sides, looking straight ahead, but to me they also feel sad and a little scary. I wouldn't want to be a teacher in one of these schools; I wouldn't want my child to be a student in one. To have healthy learning communities, kids need to adhere to high behavioral expectations, but we can change *how* we get kids to engage in those behaviors. This is where creativity comes in.

Here's another argument for indulging in creativity: It's good for your brain. It gets your alpha waves going. Alpha waves are signals in the brain that closely correlate with states of relaxation. Scientists have found that when people are relaxed, they're much more likely to have big *aha!* moments, those moments when impossible problems seem to solve themselves. This is why when you're going around and around a problem, the best thing to do is take a walk, play table tennis, or take a long shower. These activities produce alpha waves in your brain.

Would you indulge in creativity or play in a staff meeting if I told you that it's good for your emotional health? It is. Numerous studies show that activities such as drawing, knitting, and creative writing raise serotonin levels and decrease anxiety. Used therapeutically, creativity allows us to explore our emotions and perhaps heal wounds in ways that talking about experiences can't. Creative expression can also boost empathy and understanding for each other. And, because failures and mistakes are inevitable when creating, engaging in creative expression provides opportunities for strengthening resilience because setbacks and mini breakdowns offer us opportunities to get up and try again.

Let me make one final plea: Indulge in creativity because it is your birthright. Creative expression is a part of who we are. You won't find a single culture in the world in which people don't create expressions of beauty. In the same way that I hope you tend to your body and care for your emotional self, I urge you to nourish your creative spirit. You deserve it.

How to Boost Your Creativity

Creativity is both a state of mind and a thing you do. When you're in a creative state of mind, you'll find yourself asking open-ended, truly curious questions. You'll gaze out a window and daydream. You'll look at two foods that are usually not combined and think, *What might happen if I eat them together?* You'll think about how Billy always gets in trouble during afternoon recess, and you'll wonder what might happen if you tried this or that or even *that*.

Creativity is born from curiosity, but we can be curious without being creative. Once you are asking questions, you need to take action. Then you breathe life into your curiosity and it becomes creativity, an entity all its own. As you start creating, don't be surprised if you experience fear and find yourself at a juncture: You might see your creative idea wanting to take flight and materialize, or wanting to hide. Try using some of the strategies I've suggested in this book for responding to strong emotions. And you have another option: Just do it. Just act on your creative idea and see what happens. Combine those two foods. Invite Billy to be your recess helper. Paint your bathroom royal blue. Taking creative risks gets easier with time.

If you're itching to explore your creativity and you're not sure how to start, do something with your hands. Get a tub of play dough; make long snakes and then coil them into a bowl and then smash them into a ball. Do finger painting. Bake bread. Plant flowers. Draw circles and stars with fat crayons. Getting your hands dirty helps settle an anxious mind.

Reclaiming Your Right to Artistic Expression

Art has been relegated to second- or third-class status in the United States for far too long. It's been constrained to a 40-minute period once a week or an elective class in high school, or it's been relegated to the sterile and institutional walls of museums in our major cities. In some schools, art has been invited in as long as it agrees to "integrate," to serve a higher master: Arts integration has served to help students understand scientific concepts, remember literature, or demonstrate their analysis of a historical event—but it must be in service to a core subject. Art has been useful in these moments, and it deserves recognition. But it rarely gets to be its own thing, to be experienced just for what it is.

There are contextual reasons why we're afraid of art, disconnected from our artistic sides, and perhaps even afraid of artists. (They've been stereotyped as messy, mentally unsound, perpetually unemployed eccentrics.) Appreciating art, letting it sink into our weary bones, will boost our resilience, but to maximize its potential, we'll need to get our hands dirty and make it.

If you have a fear of art, if your immediate response is, "I'm not an artist" or "I'm bad at art," there is help for you. First you might reframe your definition of art and what it means to create it: Remember, you are not aspiring to create objects to display in a museum. You must rein in your perfectionist tendencies, your insecurities about what others will think, and your fear of failure. Then, perhaps alone, or with support and guidance, you'll want to dabble in many forms and play with a range of expressions to find what feels best to you. There is a vehicle out there through which to channel your creativity: It might be a clarinet, a calligraphy pen, a bottle of spray paint, a pair of knitting needles, a Nikon, a set of colored pencils, or a pair of tap dancing shoes, but it's out there. You just need to look and play and see what feels good. I've met many people who were afraid of making art, but after exploration, they liberated their creative souls and found a means of expression. You likely have a yearning for creative expression, and you have a right to it.

 ## *A Dive into Flow*

The most glorious, exquisite, sublime state of being I've experienced is called *flow*. It's a state in which I'm doing something creative, and I lose track of time and feel as though I'm in a trance; the words (for it's often when I'm writing) tumble out of my mind and heart and perhaps from somewhere else as well, somewhere beyond me, and effortlessly pour onto the page, leaving me energized and alive. There's no feeling I'd rather have, no other state I yearn for more than flow.

Have you experienced this? What were you doing? How did you feel afterwards?

Flow is a mental state in which you are in "the zone," sharply focused and absorbed by an activity that you enjoy. You lose track of time, space, and even your own physical needs. Named "flow" by the Hungarian psychologist Mihaly Csikszentmihályi, this state is most likely to be experienced when you're doing something for its intrinsic value, and the challenge is high but you also have the skill set required to do it. In this state of supreme concentration, you may also feel a dissolution of the boundaries between self and object; for some, it's a near-mystical experience. Although flow has most often been noted while someone is in the midst of a creative or artistic process, people also experience it while engaging in sports, martial arts, and video games.

Although I've mostly found myself in flow while writing, I've also experienced it in teaching and coaching. In those moments, the people with me also found themselves in flow; it was contagious. There was a winter day once when I taught seventh grade when my students and I were so deeply engaged in our classroom activities that none of us noticed that our two-hour block had ended and lunch was halfway over. (Perhaps there are benefits to not having working clocks or bells in a school.) During what I consider my best year of teaching, I regularly lost track of time and found myself pleasurably immersed in teaching. I worked long hours that year, and I experienced devastating personal losses, but it was the first year that I thought, *I could be a teacher for a long time.* The work felt sustainable because the emotional rewards of satisfaction, fulfillment, and flow outweighed the daily fatigue and strain.

Flow plays a role in boosting the resilience of educators. The most effective teachers, leaders, and coaches I've seen have used creativity to respond to challenges and make their work enjoyable. Their creativity was a portal for innovative problem solving and resource gathering, as well as for making connections. Flow fed their creativity, and creativity opened them up to flow.

Do what you can to find flow. It can emerge in experiences of play or creating art or moving your body; it can emerge while teaching a lesson or facilitating a PD session or talking to a parent after school. Look for it with light determination, because the harder you look, the harder it will be to feel. Pursue it gently, knowing it is rare, and, when you find yourself experiencing flow, bask in it. Take in the unique sensation and indescribable pleasure and give thanks.

Disposition: Courage

The resilient are courageous. When we are called to be creative, we must access reserves of courage, for creativity without risk reaps shallow rewards. All of the dispositions of the resilient are strengthened by courage. Purposefulness, acceptance, optimism, curiosity—to take any of these stances implies risk.

Think of a recent challenging moment at work. Recall your actions. How much courage would you say you had in that moment? What might have happened had you had more courage? What would you have said or done?

When I encounter obstacles and find myself down in the dust, hands shaky and raw with scrapes, when I wonder how I'll rebound and get through yet another setback, courage floods my muscles and makes me stand. Courage allowed me to leave a job at a toxic school where I wasn't fulfilling my purpose as an educator.

Courage opened my eyes to my ineffective behaviors as a coach and enabled me to change those. Courage propels me onto stages where I share personal stories about challenges as an educator.

What has your courage helped you do in your life? In which parts of your life could you use more courage? What might more courage allow you to do?

Given the prevalence of fear in our lives and in our world, we'd surely benefit from deep and sustained explorations of courage. We'd benefit from telling and consuming stories of courage and from choreographing interpretive dances to courage and from building monuments to the kind of courage that will strengthen our resilience and allow us to transform the world.

The burning question is this: Where does courage come from, and how do we activate it in ourselves?

Courage may not have a definitive origin, because when you trace back your courage, you are likely to see seeds in your own behaviors and in the actions of those around you. The seeds of our courage lie scattered throughout our individual, family, and social histories. Each one of us at some point in our life said or did something that was courageous, most likely as recently as yesterday. Recognize those little acts of courage—they count.

Within our family histories, many of us have people who took big or little courageous steps: The aunt who never married and lived out her dream of traveling the world collecting fabric; the great-great-grandparents who left their family to go west where the weather was warmer and they could farm; the single mother who raised three kids while battling depression; the brother-in-law who came out to his homophobic mother. You have courage in your DNA; I'm absolutely sure of it. Find these stories and then share them with others. When you share your stories with others, you strengthen your courage.

Then discover and channel the courage of others—your commonality as a human being permits you to do this. Pay them homage and let the strength of those who have gone before you, or who are fighting honorable battles now, fuel your own courage. Draw inspiration from the courage of Malala Yousafzai, the Pakistani advocate for female education; imagine the particles of her courage—which are infinite and abundant—infusing your reserves of courage. Draw inspiration from those who escaped from slavery or fought fascists or went door-to-door registering voters or toiled in the strawberry fields demanding fair labor practices. History overflows with stories of courage—we just need to find them.

I have long been on a quest to seek out the courageous—in my family, in my community, in history. I want to hear those stories, to understand what enabled these people to get up another day and do what they needed to do. I have found these stories in the slums of Nairobi, among the *santeros* in Havana, in historical fiction and memoir, in elementary classrooms in Oakland, and in the lives of my ancestors.

In my inquiries into my own family history, there are survivors with unimaginable courage: My Jewish great-grandmother who literally carried my grandfather out of Europe, where, had he stayed, he would have been killed. I find courage on my father's side, in another family of Jews who some five hundred years ago converted to Christianity to survive the Spanish Inquisition. But I also find stories of oppression and violence—the Spanish colonialist who raped my indigenous ancestor. Her courage I keep; his violence I release.

This is not to say that we do not have to reckon with the ugly parts of our history or acknowledge the privileges that we live with because of the actions of our ancestors. But when selecting narratives to fuel our courage, we can be discerning. And through the act of looking at those ancestors whose actions may have been reprehensible, we build courage. Select and keep the stories that make you strong. Use that courage to make right the injustices of the past and present.

Now, go and excavate your courage. Identify those DNA strands. Absorb the courage of others. The resilient are courageous.

The Healing Salves

The anthropologist Angeles Arrien (quoted in Roth, 1998) explains that in many traditional cultures, when an ill person goes to the healer, he or she is asked four questions:

- When did you stop singing?
- When did you stop dancing?
- When did you stop telling your story?
- When did you stop sitting in silence?

Arrien calls these—singing, dancing, telling your story, and sitting in silence—the "healing salves." I find this an evocative way to think about illness and healing. If I imagine my life without creative expression, without people who listen to me, without moments for inner reflection and contemplation, I know I'd feel unwell.

When I apply these criteria to the health of the physical entities of a school or district, I gain new insight. I have worked in schools and organizations in which the interpersonal staff toxicity was so high it was dripping down the walls like an oily sludge and saturating the carpets. In those toxic establishments, children and staff were frequently out sick, and there was no creative expression, no sharing of stories or listening to each other, and no reflection. Conversely, in the schools in which I've seen the greatest organizational health, where teacher retention is the highest and children are thriving, there is student art on the walls, and adults listen to young people; I've even seen periods of the day when the whole school goes silent for "quiet time."

I'm not just speaking abstractly. You would see this kind of organizational health if you visited Cal Prep, a 6–12 public school in Richmond, California. As you walk through the door, the staff warmly welcomes you, and art covers the walls. In classrooms, young people are engaged in critical and creative conversation. They dive deep into content and make connections between subjects that give them deeper insight than most college classes ever offer. Teachers facilitate learning from the sidelines and undertake inquiry projects through which they refine their practice. Staff turnover is extremely low, and well-being and joy permeate the school.

How did this school come to be this way? It's due to the transformative leadership of its humble and fierce principal, Javier Cabra Walteros. Javier has developed high-functioning, collaborative teams by allocating time and resources to staff learning and growth. He also honors the creative needs of students and staff and provides time to share stories and to sit in contemplative silence—and he attends to his own well-being in these areas as well. For the last several years, Cal Prep has anchored my conviction that we can transform schools and that creativity plays a central role.

Play, art, and creativity are not supplemental extras, hobbies, or filler activities for when we've already done this and that. They might be what help us patch up our torn spirits after we've fallen hard, what open our perception to the beauty and grandeur of the world, and what help us unlock the doors to transforming our schools. Go now and let them find a place in your life.

CHAPTER REFLECTION

- What's the first thing you feel like doing after finishing this chapter?
- How might you boost your own courage?
- How could you explore and expand your creative self?

CHAPTER 11

Ride the Waves of Change

Change is one thing we can count on, and when we encounter it, we can harness our physical, emotional, mental, and spiritual energies, and direct them where they will make the biggest difference. Perseverance, patience, and courage help us manage change.

April: Although change is constant, spring brings especially high levels of change to schools. Learn to ride those waves of change with focus, patience, persistence, and courage.

❧❧

My first year teaching, I worked in a building with no walls. Imagine a narrow, low-ceilinged, carpeted room the length of six classrooms, and then visualize six groups of 32 elementary students clustered within. Rolling cabinets created a division of spaces, but didn't block sound. If this physical design seems crazy and not conducive to learning, you're right—it was.

However, on the first day of school, I discovered what a gift it was not to have a wall between me and the teacher next door. Jen Clary was experienced, calm, and organized, and I could watch everything she did. I could listen to her explain an activity, and then I'd pivot and repeat those same instructions to my kids. I'd watch her distribute materials, lead her class to lunch, deal with an angry parent or a child having a meltdown, and then I'd recalibrate my own approach. Because I chose a nontraditional path to the classroom, with no student teacher training, my proximity to Jen provided invaluable opportunities to observe a master teacher and immediately put what I learned into practice.

In the spring of that year, when Jen told me that she was leaving our school, I panicked. Once my fear subsided, I realized I might be able to loop up with my students the following year (Jen would have been their teacher) and move into her coveted end-of-the-hall class space. I did both. Jen's departure also allowed me to join a science leadership team at our school, which opened up a number of opportunities. I missed Jen the following year, but I also realized quickly that what I had assumed would be a terrible change offered me many advantages.

In the two decades that I worked in schools, there wasn't a year when unexpected waves of change didn't come crashing down in the spring. Colleagues left, beloved leaders were fired, schools were closed, departments were "reorganized," programs were ended, new initiatives were announced, federal mandates were imposed, money dried up, class sizes shrank, class sizes grew, and so on. And, in the majority of those cases, after some time, I viewed the change more expansively—I saw the benefits.

In addition, there were times when I wanted to make a change—to teach at a new school, teach a new grade level, or take on a leadership role—and those proved unexpectedly hard. As I struggled to adapt to those new circumstances, I paid close attention to how I managed the adjustments, finding that those same strategies worked when I was responding to unwanted change. As I discovered more strategies to manage change, I also found myself initiating the changes I wanted to see in schools.

The range of experiences we have with change can be seen as a continuum that extends from defensiveness on one end to leadership on the other. When we are defensive about change, we are focused on mitigating its disturbance in our lives; when we are leading change, we are inviting the turbulence. Whether trying to manage unwanted change or leading it, we know that the key to resilience is learning how to get back to the surface when a ferocious wave knocks us over, how to ride those waves, and, perhaps, even how to find joy when surfing the waves.

Change Is Here to Stay

You might want to pause now to refer to Exhibit 11.1 and reflect on your feelings about change. For many of us, our first response when talking about change reflects our fears and dislike of it: "Change is hard," "Change is uncomfortable." We want things to stay the same—until we don't. When we want something else or we don't like what we have or we want to teach a different grade level, move across the country, find a spouse, have a kid—then we're seeking change. Many of us may also want to see more change in our schools and feel that change is too slow. There's a difference between unwanted change and the kind we pursue.

Exhibit 11.1 Reflect on Your Feelings About Change

- Finish this sentence in a few different ways: Change is . . .
- What are some ways that you deal with change? Which strategies have been really helpful in dealing with change, and which have been unproductive?
- How have you seen others deal well with change? Which of their behaviors would you like to emulate?
- Recall a change that you initially resisted, but the benefits of which you saw later. What do you wish you had known when you first encountered the change?
- How would you like to feel about change?

We wouldn't need resilience if things never changed. Resilience is how we deal with obstacles, challenges, and setbacks—and these wouldn't exist if we were in a static universe. Change is a constant in our universe. It's the only thing we can count on. It's also true that, for educators, the rate of change is faster than in many other professions. The rhythms of the school year, even the rhythms of the day, build in the opportunity and necessity for change.

Change often feels unexpected, unwanted, too fast, or too rough. It happens *to* us. Or at least it feels that way, like something forced on us by those with more power. Change challenges our mental models of how things should be or how we want them to be, which can trigger an emotion cycle. Human beings like control, yet at the core of change—whether it is a change we want or one we don't want—is a grand shift in our relationship to control. If we examine how we interpret change, we can expand our emotional response and options for action.

The Potential: Danger and Opportunity

The Chinese word for *change* is made up of two symbols—one for *danger* and another for *opportunity*. Resilience comes from how you perceive and adapt to change—and thinking of change as holding the potential for both danger and opportunity is crucial.

Resilient people accept that change is the norm and believe they can exert great influence over the events in their lives. They also accept that all they can *control* is their response to things that happen. Resilient people aren't resigned; in fact, they have an astute sense of their agency (their capacity to act) in any situation, and they gently push to expand their agency. This blurs the line between unwanted and sought-after change. We'll travel along this continuum of the change experience and consider interpretations and options for responding to change.

The Spheres of Influence

Make a quick list of all the things you've complained about (or wanted to complain about) in the last week. The big stuff and the little stuff. Here's a portion of mine: The weather is too cold, I don't want to live in the city, my desk is disorganized, my house is noisy, a friend is driving me crazy, I have a ton of work to do, and I didn't sleep well.

Now, for each item, determine whether it falls within your control or your influence. If it falls within neither sphere, then it's outside your control. Figure 11.1, The Spheres of Influence, is a visual representation of this concept.

What did you notice as you classified your complaints?

As I went through my list, I had to conclude that I could influence many, if not all, of my complaints. The weather is cold: I can't change the weather, but I can turn up the heat, put on warmer clothes, and so on. I can definitely influence the mess on my desk—if I want. I could also do something about living in the city and my noisy house if I made it my goal. I feel more empowered when I recognize this, although I also see that certain items require some decision making if I choose to deal with them.

The Key to Energy

The idea of the spheres of control and influence is simple: Classifying our complaints into those we can control, those we can influence, and those we can't control is a step toward using our energy wisely. The clarity that can emerge from this sorting activity frees up a lot of emotional energy and helps us see that we have more agency than we think.

I clearly remember my top complaints from one year when I taught third grade: I hated the mandated, scripted literacy curriculum; my principal lacked vision; teachers were dismally underpaid; two second graders were added in the first month, which made my class a combo; I taught next to a teacher who screamed at his kids so loudly that the bookshelf on my wall rattled; and my classroom was

Figure 11.1   The Spheres of Influence

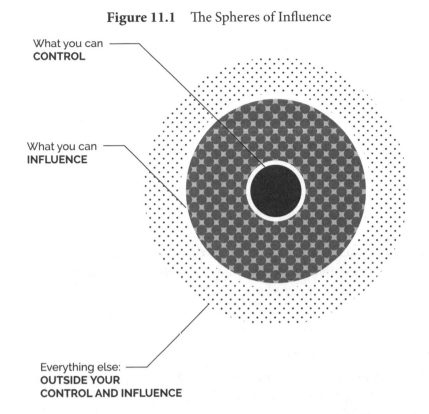

What you can
CONTROL

What you can
INFLUENCE

Everything else:
**OUTSIDE YOUR
CONTROL AND INFLUENCE**

always disorganized. The question is: Which of these complaints were within my spheres of control and influence?

Let's take my principal. She lacked vision (and other leadership skills), and there was nothing I could do about that. I had a choice available in the future: I could choose to teach at a school that was led by an effective leader, but, in the moment, there was nothing I could do about my current principal's skill set. So I could place this item in the "out of my control" sphere. Similarly, I could do little about the mandated curriculum or teacher salaries. However, as I considered my list of complaints, a theme emerged: I could influence *how I felt* in these situations. My state of almost constant, low-level frustration and dissatisfaction was within my control.

As I acknowledged and accepted my emotions, I began to reframe my situation, which galvanized my energy to do something about it. In the spring, I found a position at a different school with a transformational leader, no mandated curriculum, and opportunities to earn additional stipends. A year later, my complaints were almost entirely different (except for still having a disorganized classroom).

The Essential Question

Using the spheres of control and influence as a framework through which to explore our complaints, current realities, and the wanted and unwanted changes in our lives helps us decide what to do. First, this framework shows us that we can't *control* everything, but we do have great influence over how we feel about and respond to what happens. Our response to circumstances is the only thing truly within our control.

Just about everything else lies within your influence. You *could* have a big influence on teacher salary if you wanted, you *could* influence federal education policy, curriculum, assessment, or hiring decisions. The essential question to ask yourself is, *Where do I want to put my energy?*

This question becomes all the more important to ask ourselves when we're dealing with unwanted and unexpected events. Let's explore where this question fits into the process of managing the kind of change that makes us want to freeze, flee, or fight.

Implications for Leaders

- It's really helpful to keep this concept of the spheres of control and influence at the forefront of your mind when you're dealing with upset people. Listen carefully for where they put their attention and energy and for whether those issues are inside or outside their sphere of control. Coach them in their awareness of the choices they're making about where to put their energy. Keep a copy of Figure 11.1 posted on your wall, as well as copies to give to others, to help them understand this concept.

How to Deal with Unwanted Change

There have been moments in my life when tsunamis of change swept through, and I found myself saying, *How will I get through this?* or *Can I survive this?* In a sense, these phrases of self-doubt were part of a story I was telling about an event that happened to me. Yet this particular mindset was problematic. When we focus just on survival, we see limited options for action, our perception narrows, and we focus on basic needs. When change hits, if we shift the question to *How might this change help me thrive?* or (this is how I think about it) *Is there any way that I might emerge from this shit stronger than before?* then we're far more likely to uncover a wider range of options for action.

A partial disclaimer: I'm not suggesting that when really, really bad things happen you should look for a silver lining or simply ask yourself how the experience will help you thrive. Sometimes really terrible things happen (as when a beloved school leader or your spouse or parent or best friend dies of cancer at a young age), and, in those moments, it's appropriate and normal to cry a lot and get good sleep. In times of excruciating pain, it helps to hold an awareness of the long term and the big picture while focusing on the day to day.

There are different grain sizes to the unwanted changes we experience. Throughout the course of our lives, most of us will deal with lots of the small- to medium-size changes and a few of the massive ones. As you ride the waves of these changes, consider what might be possible if you aim to thrive, not just survive. Whether thinking about your first year as a principal or adjusting to a change in leadership or programming or teaching assignment, keep your eyes on the potential for becoming more resilient. That is possible. The four principles that will help you manage unwanted change and possibly thrive in its aftermath are (1) to slow down, (2) to evaluate and analyze the situation, (3) to use your energy where it counts, and (4) to be open to outcomes. Let's examine these four elements.

Slow Down

On a Monday afternoon one spring, administrators from the central offices came to our staff meeting and announced that our principal and assistant principal were going to be moved to a different school, our campus would be merged with another, and we'd all have to reapply for our teaching positions. We were devastated. Within three hours, committees had formed to oppose the changes, lawyers and union leaders were called, and teachers created long lists of things to do.

Mary was a veteran teacher whom I admired and respected. She was always calm, thoughtful, and good humored. Her students made tremendous growth while under her tutelage, and Mary consistently delivered engaging, organized, rigorous lessons. And almost every day, Mary left school by 4:30 p.m., heading to the gym or yoga or to a book club with friends. Mary had helped start our school, so I was surprised when we talked after the meeting and she said she was going to sleep on the news; I had imagined she'd be up into the wee hours of the morning organizing. "I just need to let this sink in and think about what I want to do," she said.

Many people move too fast and do too much, which is a typical fear response. Yes, when the unexpected occurs, some people also hide under the covers in denial.

Others attack. So this is the first rule when change happens: Slow down so that you can think clearly and assess the situation. It's unlikely that you need to take immediate action. Here's what to do at this stage:

- Get real about your feelings. Notice them. Name them. Accept them. And spend a little bit of time exploring them, especially if you're having strong feelings.
- Give yourself 24–48 hours to think before you take action or make a decision. The following steps in this section will guide you through this process.

When responding to changes in school, it's almost always a good thing to slow down and think.

Evaluate and Analyze the Situation

The following day, when I stopped by Mary's class before school started, I asked her what she was thinking. I was envious of how well rested she looked, as I'd been up late writing angry letters about the district's decision. "I have some clearer thoughts about how I can use my skills to respond to what's happened," Mary said. "I also realized that there are a lot of questions I have and for which I need more information."

I must have looked disappointed, because Mary smiled and said, "I am definitely going to fight this; I'm clear about that. I just want to be intentional and strategic about what I do. This could be a long battle, and I'll need to sustain my energy." I nodded, remembering that Mary had taught in our district for 28 years. "This ain't my first rodeo," she said lightly.

When change hits, take the time to ask yourself these questions:

- What else do I need to know in order to have a more complete understanding of what's going on? Who might be able to provide that information?
- What's the story I'm telling about this change? How could someone else see this change? Who might be able to share another perspective on it?
- What are the ways that this change might affect kids and the community I serve?
- What is within my influence?
- What am I free to choose right now? What do I want?
- What resources do I have available to me? What can I draw on to cope with this situation?
- What might be possible if I challenge this change? What will happen if I sit it out and wait for it to pass?

One strategy that I've found useful for evaluating change is what I think of as switching lenses. Especially when I'm feeling like a victim of a change, I imagine looking through three lenses to help me gain perspective. First, I look at the change through a macro lens, seeing all of the elements close up. Sometimes this helps me see positive aspects that I'd overlooked. Then I put on a long lens and ask myself, *How might I see this situation in six months? In two years?* Then I switch to a wide lens and ask myself, *What other factors are at play? Who else is impacted? What is their experience of this change? How do they see this situation, and how are they experiencing the change?* Changing lenses often helps me gain insight into how I can better respond to what's happening.

Use Your Energy Where It Counts

Time is finite, and our energy is limited. We can manage our energy so as to maximize it, and we can refuel our energy, but, in the end, there's only so much time in a day and only so much energy to expend. If you say this to yourself and accept it, you'll feel better.

Further, when you can accept those limits, then the focus of your energy shifts, and you can use it in a way that counts—a way that is meaningful, resonant, productive, and aligned to your core values. How do you figure out what counts? Return to our first habit, Know Yourself. What really matters?

It is hard to figure out what matters when things that don't matter drain our energy. This confusion occurs when our ego is bruised or we take something too personally. We deny or resist a change because it feels like a personal affront. We push back because we want to be right. Yet we must explore that big gray zone between what *feels* personal and what *is* personal.

I coached Maggie, a teacher deeply committed to the students in her community and loved by both kids and their parents. She was an effective teacher by many measures. After she had been at her school for two years, a new principal was appointed with whom Maggie had a tumultuous history at a previous school. The following March, the new principal dismissed Maggie and made her ineligible for rehire anywhere in our district. Maggie was angry. It was no secret that the new principal didn't like her at all and left grossly ineffective teachers untouched. Maggie rallied colleagues, previous administrators, coaches, and parents; she enlisted union support, spoke to lawyers, and went to school board meetings. Although at times it felt as though Maggie had dug in her heels with her intent to stay at her school, her dismissal did feel personal.

Maggie's circumstances beg the question: How do you know when to walk away? As the school year ended, Maggie had a choice about whether to keep fighting. Over and over, I asked her the same question, "What really matters?" She wanted to keep her job, stay in the community she'd built, and have the option—at the very least—to stay within the school district. Then one evening, Maggie also said, "I want to prove that she was wrong, that she can't do that to me." Maggie had every reason to feel hurt, but, in her pursuit of justice, she was expending a tremendous amount of energy at a cost to her health, relationships, and well-being.

"Maggie," I said, "I know this feels personal, but she's doing what she's doing for who knows how many reasons. Disliking you is just one piece. You can't control what she thinks or feels right now, but you have a choice about where you put your energy. You've challenged her decision, and you could keep challenging it if you want. But if you think about the upcoming school year and look down from 10,000 feet above the situation, what really matters?"

"I want to teach," Maggie said without hesitating. "That's what's most important to me. I want to teach and feel that joy of teaching again. Since she came, I haven't felt much joy."

"So why would you want to stay here?"

"Because I can outlast her. Principals come and go, and she's already gotten herself in trouble. She'll be gone in a year."

"Even if she's here for one more year," I said, "if you're here, what's the likelihood that you'll enjoy teaching?"

Maggie shrugged her shoulders.

I pressed on. "What choices do you have right now?" Maggie shrugged again. "Then what really matters?"

"I want to teach," she said. "So I should probably start looking for a new job. I can keep fighting to stay in the district, but I can also look elsewhere." And that's what she did. In the middle of the summer, the school board ruled to allow her to take a job at a different district school, but, by that point, Maggie had found a position that was a great fit for her and that she came to love, and, sadly, our district lost a committed teacher.

Often it is not clear where to expend our energy. When change comes along, we can feel afraid and uncertain about what "counts." Ask yourself over and over, *What really matters?* and listen to your own responses. Write them down. Ask yourself every day. Return to that first habit, to knowing yourself, and get grounded enough in yourself to be able to look at your situation objectively.

"Who are you?" said the Caterpillar . . .
"I—I hardly know, Sir, just at present," Alice replied rather shyly, "at least
I know who I was when I got up this morning, but I think I must have
changed several times since then."
LEWIS CARROLL

Be Open to Outcomes

The bottom line is this: You have a choice in how you expend your energy. If you decide you want to fight a change—fight it. Intentionally. Direct your energy to what matters most and is most within your sphere of influence, using your most refined skills and making sure that you're not acting out of ego. And then give it your all. Make sure you're checking in with yourself about how much energy you're using (it's rarely a good idea to use all of your energy to manage one change) and check in on the cost of fighting this fight.

At the same time that you challenge an unwanted change, you also need to do something challenging: You need to find a way to be open to outcomes. This is a paradox: Work with vision and commitment, leverage your resources and energy to reach that vision, and, *at the same time,* be open and be unattached to what you're envisioning.

Here's why: Being open to outcomes allows us to be flexible and adaptable. Even if we're well informed and pushing back on an unwanted change in collaboration with others, we still can't know everything. Remain open to possibilities. If a proposal or solution is put forward, consider it even if it isn't exactly what you want. Keep talking and listening to everyone and anyone.

When my school was threatened, we rallied and organized and resisted. Then we were approached with an idea that we'd never considered: Our campus would merge with another; class sizes would increase somewhat, but we'd have double the support staff, more prep time, and others who taught the same content with whom we could collaborate. We had to make some compromises, and there were some minor annoyances, but we not only eliminated the threat of obliteration but also ended up with something far better than what we'd had before the threat.

What makes it hard to be open to outcomes is that we have to manage our uncertainty and live with the unknown. Uncertainty is a shade of fear that unsettles us and makes us want things to stay the same. The habits discussed in this book will help you manage that fear. You can also ride the uncertain waves of change by holding an immense picture of life—which includes recognizing that there's a lot you don't and can't know. The ability to hold that perspective emerges in part from trust, which is a disposition we'll consider in Chapter 12.

Equanimity (which I discussed in Chapter 8) is a mental and emotional state that is invaluable when we're dealing with change. It can allow us to be open to outcomes, to look at a situation and say, "Right now, this is how things are," even if we don't like it or we wish it were different. Equanimity makes room for a fuller perspective on things. It isn't about repressing feelings or being indifferent or resigned;

it is about accepting whatever is happening in a particular moment. By cultivating a state of equanimity, our attachment to outcomes gets a little looser. We can simultaneously remain open to outcomes and take action to stop or lead a change.

The story in Exhibit 11.2, "Maybe," Said the Farmer, is a favorite of mine when navigating uncertain waters. It not only acknowledges that dealing with unwanted change is complex and hard but also reminds us to be open to outcomes and hold an expansive perspective. After you read it, you might find yourself saying, "Maybe" whenever a change rolls in.

Exhibit 11.2 "Maybe," Said the Farmer—A Zen Parable

Once upon a time, there was an old farmer who had worked his crops for many years. One day, his horse ran away.

Upon hearing the news, his neighbors came to visit. "Such bad luck," they said sympathetically. "Maybe," the farmer replied.

The next morning, the horse returned, bringing with it three other wild horses.

"How wonderful," the neighbors exclaimed. "Maybe," replied the old man.

The following day, his son tried to ride one of the untamed horses, was thrown, and broke his leg.

The neighbors again came to offer their sympathy for his misfortune. "Maybe," answered the farmer.

The day after, military officials came to the village to draft young men into the army. Seeing that the son's leg was broken, they passed him by.

The neighbors congratulated the farmer on how well things had turned out. "Maybe," said the farmer.

The Secret to Leading Change

If we can navigate unwanted change, we may arrive at a place where we can be proactive and lead change that benefits others. The following suggestions apply to you whether you're a teacher wanting to change classroom culture, a principal trying to guide a staff in whole-school change, or a coach aspiring to help your clients become aware of their unconscious biases. Let's jump straight to the secret.

Deal with Fear

Deal with fear. That's the biggest secret. Many leaders don't recognize, acknowledge, or manage fear when they're trying to lead change—not their fear or that of others. We humans are fearful creatures, and we're poorly equipped to deal with it.

In my first full-time role as a literacy coach, I aspired to change the teaching practices at the middle school where I worked. When I visited classrooms, I observed teachers sitting at their desks reading while students worked on grammar exercises in silence; there were no agendas or outcomes shared with students, and teachers told me they didn't write lesson plans; eighth graders read from fourth-grade texts; and lessons rarely correlated to state standards. Furthermore, when I reviewed the school's data, I found that our students' literacy skills dropped steadily during the years they attended our school. When our eighth graders graduated, their skills would be lower than when they had arrived as sixth graders. Only 3% of eighth graders read on grade level.

When I began advocating for learning targets, lesson planning, relevant curriculum, and engaging instructional practices, I received pushback. This made me push harder. The resistance got stronger. I become more resolved. Have you ever been in this kind of situation? It was tiring. There was unnecessary suffering. In the end, it didn't really work; in some classrooms, instruction and outcomes improved, but not consistently and not across the school.

At the time, I didn't recognize how afraid the teachers were when I suggested they change their practice. They were afraid they wouldn't be able to do what I was asking them to do, and they were afraid of being publicly exposed for what they didn't know or didn't want to do. Unconsciously, they were also afraid of losing their identity. Many of these teachers had spent years becoming the teachers they were, and I was insinuating that they needed to abandon that identity and become someone new—someone they couldn't imagine. Not only is that scary, but inherent in my demands was the notion that they weren't doing a good job.

Fear and the threat of shame are limited tools. Sometimes they generate compliance, but they're not sustainable, and they aren't transformational. Fear and shame wear all of us down—both those leveraging the tools and those on the other end. I felt intense urgency to change things at this school, but I didn't manage my urgency well. Peeling back the layers of emotions, I recognized my sadness for the students, my fear that I wouldn't be able to improve their experience, my anger at a dysfunctional system and the people who upheld it, my impatience with those who weren't acting on the timeline I thought they should act on, and my own ego and ambition to change things. The secret to leading change is to recognize these emotions while we're experiencing them (not 10 years later), to recognize the emotions that others experience, and to have strategies to deal with what we see.

If you have a tiny inner dictator (as I'm afraid I do), you might believe that it brings some value to your practice. I wish I could tell you that club-wielding urgency produces results or that holding people accountable is the magic that's needed to make them do what you want them to do. I wish I could share tracking tools, short feedback scripts, and examples of teachers who changed because I gave them clear directions, but I can't. I have a list of at least two dozen transactional approaches I used to try to get people to change—and none of them worked. There were moments of compliance, and then there was resistance, sabotage, and more of the same ineffective teaching. Nothing changed for kids. And I felt depleted and depressed.

These ineffective tactics danced around the underlying emotions. The secret to change is to deal with emotions (our own and those of others) and especially to deal with fear, because what many of us have tried in an effort to produce quick results has not worked. Yes, it takes time to deal with emotions, but there is no other option.

Remember That Change Is About Learning

In Chapter 9, we explored the feelings that arise during different stages of learning, the concept of gaps, and the conditions necessary for learning. Leading change most often includes learning; in order for people to do something different, whatever it is that you want them to do, you need to address skill, knowledge, capacity, will, cultural competency, and emotional intelligence.

When you are leading change, the Conscious Competence Ladder and the Mind the Gap framework will provide useful guidance. They will remind you that people need a lot of encouragement when they reach conscious incompetence. You might reflect on how you can boost people's will and commitment to engage in a change initiative. You will need to articulate the skills and knowledge that people will acquire, and you'll need an understanding of the skills and knowledge with which they're starting.

If you want people to change, you're asking them to grow. If you're asking for growth, you're asking for learning. As the facilitator or leader of this effort, you are responsible for creating the optimal conditions for learning and for thoughtfully guiding them through the learning.

Understand the Backfire Effect

Often we aspire to lead schools in change that involves getting people to do something different and thus changing their beliefs about something. Whether we are conscious of it or not, all of our actions emerge from beliefs. If we want to change behaviors, we have to surface and explore, and perhaps shift, underlying beliefs. And, in that process, we're going to confront fear again.

Adam was a novice elementary principal I coached who was concerned about the high numbers of students who were sent to the office and suspended. He wanted teachers to adopt a management approach in which students would receive warnings and be given opportunities to get back on track before immediately being sent out of the classroom. He also wanted teachers to use strategies to de-escalate situations with frustrated students and to "give kids chances" and "not be so rigid and controlling."

At an August staff meeting, Adam rolled out the school's new management plan and tried to make a strong case for why it was necessary. He shared data on the correlation between suspending kindergarteners and dropout rates for high schoolers. He'd synthesized five years of office referral data from his school, showing that students who were suspended were more likely to do poorly on state tests. He showed graphs, statistics of all kinds, and slides of brain imaging. He referenced university-sponsored research and longitudinal studies around the world. As I watched teachers listen to this 90-minute presentation, I noticed their brows furrow, their arms cross over their chests, and their bodies recline.

When Adam finally stopped and asked for questions, he faced a barrage of objections. "You're asking me to lower my expectations for our students," said one teacher, her voice shaking. Another slammed her hand on the table and added, "We have to be firm with them *from day one* so that they learn how to behave!" A kindergarten teacher stood up and loudly said, "You should praise me when I send students out. I'm holding them to our code of conduct," which got a round of applause. A respected veteran said, "I've been teaching here for 26 years, and my students' parents have always appreciated that my management matches theirs at home. We believe in being strict with our kids so that they'll learn to stay out of trouble. You're not even a parent. What do you know about raising kids here?" During all of these statements, there were angry murmurings around the room. Adam calmly listened to their reactions and then said he had a lot to think about and that they'd continue the conversation the following week.

Back in his office, Adam collapsed in his chair and said, "What the hell happened back there?" What happened, I explained, was what's called the *backfire effect,* a term coined by political scientists Brendan Nyhan and Jason Reifler in 2010. This effect occurs when someone shares information with you that contradicts a strongly held belief, and your fear causes you to hold on to your belief even more tightly than before. The information backfires. Let's look more closely at this phenomenon.

When you are surprised with information that challenges your beliefs, your brain responds as if you'd come across a grizzly bear in the forest. Your adrenaline pumps as your system prepares to fight or flee. Your brain doesn't differentiate between the threat of physical harm and the threat to a mental model. So when the teachers at Adam's school listened to his presentation, what was threatened? Not just their "beliefs" about classroom management but their mental model of themselves as educators. This "self" includes personal identity, the psychological self, and their political beliefs. They didn't hear Adam challenging their ideas or management practices; they heard a challenge to their very identities, identities they'd built and fortified for decades.

It was even bigger than this, however, because a person's political beliefs and sense of self are usually connected to a larger social network—to a family, neighborhood, organization, religious community, or geographical region. In the case of Adam's school, the teachers' identities were tied to each other, as well as to the community in which they worked, and, for some, the community in which they were raised. Adam's critique of the way they managed their students was an indirect critique of the way they were raised and how they raised their own children. Many of us already feel defensive about where we come from, but we're especially unlikely to change a belief if it could put us at risk of being alienated from our community. So a threat to a belief is a threat to our social self. This is precisely why it's hard to change people's political beliefs, even in the face of mounds of contradictory evidence.

The situation is not as dire as you might think. Remember: The biggest secret to leading change is to deal with fear. We instinctively and unconsciously protect our beliefs when we're *confronted* with information that doesn't match up to our beliefs. When information comes at us, when it blindsides us or is pushed in our face, it will backfire. If you are a leader, create an experience in which the people whose minds you are trying to change feel comfortable and safe. You don't need to confront them. You don't need to shove the information in their face.

That's what researchers are finding: We are *prone* to choosing information and data that support our worldview, while diminishing or dismissing evidence that contradicts it. However, we *can* expand and change our beliefs and heed corrective information if we don't fear that our core identity will be crushed. *Beliefs can change*—even strongly held political beliefs that form key parts of our individual and social selves. (For more on this, see research by political scientists Tom Wood and Ethan Porter.)

"I wanted to shock them," Adam confessed as we finished up our coaching session. "I don't know if they know what they're doing to kids," he said. "But, clearly, my approach didn't work."

It took Adam a lot of work that year to repair his relationship with teachers, and it was several years before teachers agreed to a new management program.

How you get people to change their minds and consider different practices is beyond the scope of this book, but here are some things you can do that mitigate fear and help change beliefs.

- **Create opportunities for teachers to reflect on why they do what they do.** Teachers need to recognize that we do what we do because of the resources and skill sets that we have.
- **Humanize the need for change.** Invite current and former students (and their parents) to talk about their experiences in school.
- **Set up structures for listening.** We all need to refine our ability to listen to others.
- **Talk about and normalize emotions, especially fear.**
- **Collectively envision new realities.** Guide people in creating alternate futures to see how things could be different for themselves and kids.

Acknowledging Context: When Do We Fight the Good Fight?

First they came for the Communists, and I did not speak out—
Because I was not a Communist.
Then they came for the Trade Unionists, and I did not speak out—
Because I was not a Trade Unionist.
Then they came for the Jews, and I did not speak out—
Because I was not a Jew.
Then they came for me—and there was no one left to speak for me.
MARTIN NIEMÖLLER, GERMAN PASTOR, 1892–1984

Pastor Niemöller initially supported Adolf Hitler, but became disillusioned and led a group of German clergymen in opposition to Hitler. For this, Niemöller spent eight years in a concentration camp. His haunting words evoke the dangers of political apathy and the cataclysmic impact of indifference on other communities, as well as the danger we might face ourselves.

The question *When do we fight the good fight?* is a personal one anchored in deeply held values, morals, and our sense of responsibility toward others. We have to make choices about how we spend our energy. There is so much that we can't control and on which we have minimal influence. At the same time, there are moments when we are morally called to speak up, stand up, and do what is right.

In this chapter, I have invited you to think about what matters, to consider what you can influence, to use your energy with discretion, and to be open to outcomes. I have suggested that you be cautious in how you present people with information that will clash with their beliefs and social identities. But I am also advocating for change. I am hoping, in fact, that the strategies presented in this book will boost your resilience so that you have a surplus of energy, strength, and confidence to get out there and lead change. When we've moved out of survival and into thriving, we can create conditions in which others can also thrive.

These are times when we need to reflect on which changes matter most to us and ask ourselves about the cost of being complacent, silent, and afraid. These are times when we need to look at facts from a range of sources, even facts and information that could threaten our social selves and put us at odds with our own families and communities. These are times when we need to recognize our privilege and consider how we can use that privilege on behalf of those with less privilege. We must manage uncertainty and learn how to preserve relationships, because the costs of not acting may be too high.

> *We ourselves feel that what we are doing is just a drop in the ocean.*
> *But the ocean would be less because of that missing drop.*
> MOTHER TERESA

 ## *A Dive into Patience*

I trusted Liz, my coach, tremendously, so I didn't recoil when she brusquely said, "You are too impatient. You have got to work on that, or you're always going to feel frustrated as a teacher. Your impatience is a problem." She had set down her pen, leaned forward, and fixed her steady gaze on me through her glasses. In that moment, I recognized her experience and wisdom and knew she was speaking truth.

I'm often dissatisfied with the rate of change. When I have a vision for what a student needs to learn or how a school should function or how my life should be—I want to see it manifest *now!* My impatience makes me irritable; I want more control over timelines. Yet I don't make clearheaded decisions about what to do or say when I'm feeling impatient. High levels of impatience make me feel perpetually dissatisfied. That's not an effective or powerful place from which to build relationships or to lead and inspire others. It's also exhausting and wears down my resilience. Because our emotions are complex, what we feel or see on the surface is usually only one layer of the story. We're responsible for recognizing the outer layer and accepting it, but we must also explore the layers underneath.

Below my impatience as a teacher was a lot of anxiety. I worried about my students' futures. I worried about whether they'd learn what they needed to learn. I worried about whether I'd be able to do a good enough job teaching them. I worried about whether their parents would approve of and appreciate what I was doing. I worried about whether my colleagues and principal would think I was doing a good job. I worried that I wasn't enough.

Anger also lurked beneath my impatience. One year when I worked in my school district's central offices, I had a leader who didn't do things the way I thought they should be done. He also worked very slowly. I constantly felt frustrated with him, but, honestly, it was more fear that I felt. I was anxious that my work would be ineffective if my supervisor didn't do what I thought he should do or wasn't who I needed him to be. I worried that I'd fail in my efforts and that my time would be wasted.

Patience is an emotion and a skill. Impatience is often triggered by events outside our control, ones we think should be different. Patience begins when we accept ourselves and the way things are. To do this, we need courage, equanimity, and trust (or what some might call faith). Patience is not passivity or resignation; it doesn't prevent us from drawing boundaries around how people treat us. Patience is a kind of power. It can increase your compassion, and help you see the big picture and get clarity on when to act. Patience is about being honest with yourself—recognizing your underlying anger or fear and then letting go of the stories that you hold about others. Patience calls on us to be fully present and to pay attention to exactly how things are in the moment. It opens the field of awareness and possibility.

I work a lot to cultivate a state of patience. Maintaining a broad perspective and being able to see the bright spots are useful. Practicing meditation (see Chapter 5) is essential—I am far more patient when my mind is settled. Engaging in contemplative activities also helps (see Chapter 12). Patience can fuel tenacity, which is a key trait of resilient people. When remaining open to what happens, when accepting things as they are, when holding a long view, I have more energy to persevere without clinging to desired outcomes.

Disposition: Perseverance

The highlight of my teaching life was when I helped start a new school in Oakland. One of our core values was perseverance, and when I taught sixth grade that first year, I worked hard to cultivate this disposition in our students. In the spring, we took our sixth graders to the Grand Canyon. On the afternoon that we hiked back up the canyon, Veronica said, "Now I know why you guys talked about perseverance and why we read *The Little Engine That Could* so many times!" She stopped to catch her breath, and her friends began chanting, "I think I can, I think I can!"

Later Veronica said, "I realized on the hike that I just had to put one foot in front of the other, and not care about how sweaty I looked. I just thought about how I'd feel at the end. Every time I felt like my legs were going to give out, I said to myself, *I CAN do this*. I didn't need to 'think it'; I just had to do it. I remembered times when school was hard, and I reminded myself that I'd done hard things before. And I've never felt as proud as when I got to the top of the canyon."

Resilient people are tenacious, and completing challenges strengthens this disposition. That's why when the storms of change knock us down or we come to a mountain that we want to climb, we are strengthened by the journey of ascent and recovery. We thrive in the aftermath; we bask in the internal reservoirs of resilience with which we have reconnected and that we have filled up, because resilience is always within us, and it often needs to be replenished.

Yet, in order to cultivate perseverance and tenacity, you must look beyond short-term concerns and toward long-term goals. You need to put off immediate gratification and manage your impatience. You also must venture beyond your comfort zone and take on challenges of different sizes so that you can learn and can increase your confidence. As you work on boosting your tenacity, you'll have to view setbacks as opportunities for growth. And you'll need strategies, such as the behaviors and habits discussed in this book, for dealing with the obstacles that show up on your path. More than anything, you'll need to move—to take thoughtful, intentional actions and keep moving until you get to where you want to be.

Next time you're facing a challenge, in order to access your tenacity, remind yourself of what matters and why you're doing whatever you're doing. Acknowledge your fear and tell yourself that you *can* do whatever you're trying to do. And then put one foot in front other the other and move.

Waves Can Be Fun

My son, who loves the ocean, took his first surfing lesson at age 13. I watched as he caught wave after wave, gracefully standing up on the board and riding the waves to shore. It seemed effortless. At the end of his lesson, Ian, his Hawaiian instructor, complimented his skills. "He's a natural," Ian said. "He's focused, determined, and has good judgment in the water." For his third lesson, Ian (who had been a competitive surfer) decided that my son was ready for "real waves," and took my child about a mile out into the Pacific Ocean, farther than we could see with the naked eye. When they returned a couple of hours later, my son was beaming. "It was awesome!" he said over and over. I grilled him on the experience: Were the waves big? Did he get knocked down? Was he scared? Did he fall? Was it deep? Were there sharks?

"It was fun, Mama," he said, reorienting my questioning. "Some of the waves were big and I felt nervous, but I trusted Ian. So I stayed calm and focused, and if a wave was really big, I went under it. Then it would get too calm and boring, so I'd ride out to get a wave. And when I got up on my board and I felt the breeze and the rush of the water, it was totally awesome."

It's good to spend time with kids because they remind us that age and experience can narrow our perception of events. Change doesn't have to be terrifying. If we find a way to coast through tumultuous moments, if we cultivate trust in others and in uncertainty, and if we stay calm and focused, we might experience grace and joy while we're riding the waves of change. We might even find that we are drawn to change when we feel confident in our ability to navigate its waters, and that we are happier and more resilient when we return to dry land.

CHAPTER REFLECTION

- How did the ideas in this chapter affect your feelings about change?
- Which sections of this chapter were most useful to you?
- What implications for action are there for you from the ideas in this chapter?
- How could you apply these ideas to something that's happening for you now?

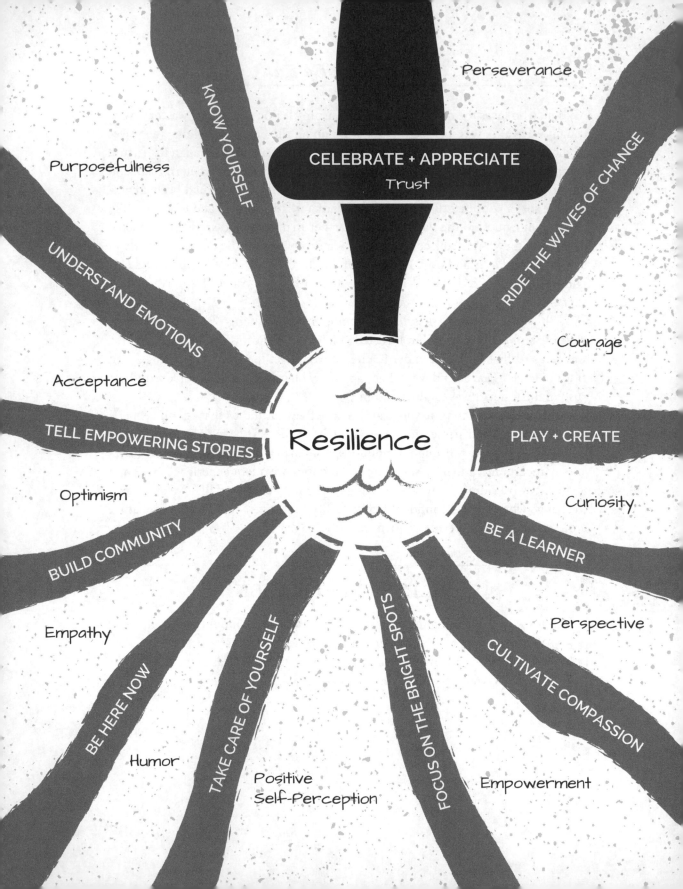

CHAPTER 12

Celebrate and Appreciate

Individual and collective celebration, as well as the practice of gratitude, is the capstone to the habits in this book. Even during hard moments, if we can shift into a stance of appreciation, we'll build our resilience. Appreciation cultivates our trust in ourselves, in a process, and perhaps in something greater, which helps us respond to the inevitable challenges of life.

May: Endings are times for celebration and appreciation, which lay the foundation for resilience in the days ahead.

❧ ❧

On the final day of school, we all squeezed into my portable—my partner teacher, Keiko, and I, and our eighth-grade students. This group of 45 kids would be the first to graduate from ASCEND, the small K–8 school that we'd started three years before. I'd taught these kids for three years and felt deeply bonded to them.

We all had mixed feelings about this graduation. These students had had a positive middle school experience, but weren't naïve about the challenges facing them in high school. As we stood in my portable on that final day, their faces reflecting a gamut of emotions, we marked the end of our journey together with an activity. I tossed a ball of red yarn across the room into a pair of open hands. "We will always be connected," I said. As the yarn made its way around the room, each student wrapped the yarn around one of his or her hands and spoke about what it had meant to be a part of our community. "We will always be connected," I said again as we took in the symbolic the web we'd formed.

I looked at my kids, thinking about their struggles and about how far they had come individually and together. I knew in that moment that what I shared with this group was something unique, something I might never experience again. Those final moments in that portable were magical.

Endings are logical opportunities for celebrations; they are critical junctures for rituals that mark transitions and accomplishments. Our social and emotional selves need opportunities to acknowledge what we've done and to honor the relationships we've built with others. Celebration boosts our resilience, because, in looking back, we select the strands of story that we weave into a narrative of our strength. We edit our memories, selecting those that align with our core values and reflect who we want to be in the world. And, in creating the narrative of who we are, we become more resilient.

My three years teaching these students at ASCEND were the highlight of my teaching career. Had you asked me midway through my time with them how I felt about the experience, I'm not sure what I would have said. There were some difficult and exhausting moments. However, on the day they graduated, the story I began telling was that those were the best years of my teaching life. Yes, there were struggles, but the rewards were greater. How you tell the story of your life matters.

I lean on my story of those three years when facing seemingly insurmountable tasks. I remember where my students were when I met them in sixth grade: Their literacy levels were far below grade level, their critical thinking skills were nascent, and they were often unkind to each other. And then I remember them at their graduation and how much they had changed, learned, and bonded with each other. There were many factors that contributed to their growth—learning and maturity were two obvious ones—but I also allowed myself to acknowledge the role that I played. Many of us could benefit from learning how and when to be humble and how and when to take ownership of our successes; and at my students' graduation, I needed to say, *I played a big role in the positive changes these kids have made.* By honestly and humbly acknowledging our successes, our inner reserve of resilience builds.

Every season, every week, and every day there are opportunities for celebration and appreciation. We humans love ritual and marking transitions. All of our religious traditions have calendars of celebration, secular society has added its own, and our planet offers its own cycles with which we can align celebrations. At the end of every day, as night falls, we have an opportunity to give thanks; as spring sweeps across our hemisphere, we can appreciate new beginnings. As we close every meeting or PD session or class, we can take the last 60 seconds to appreciate our contributions and those of others. Regardless of when you're reading this chapter, you'll find times to apply these ideas. If your resilience is an underground well, an internal reservoir of strength, then celebrations are like a heavy rainstorm that effortlessly tops off your reserves.

The Benefits of Appreciation

To be honest, I was skeptical about all the fuss around gratitude. It seems like you can't turn a corner without bumping into a gratitude journal or an article on appreciation. Maybe this is a legacy of my cultural and family background in which critical feedback and worry were our central narrative, overshadowing praise and appreciation. Or maybe it was just a general, healthy skepticism about what I perceived as fluffy, pseudopsychological self-help directives. But, after doing a ton of research, I've concluded that appreciation is a transformative lever for improving our well-being, so much so that it is the 12th of 12 resilience-boosting habits.

There were several reasons behind my shift in attitude about gratitude. First, I like to know the science of things; if someone is going to tell me to do something (such as take a nutritional supplement or adopt a mindset), I want to know the neuroscience and social science that back up that admonition. Second, I am a learner, and I'll try just about anything if it might be helpful. This stance has uncovered many truths that have enriched my life and made me healthier and happier—among which is practicing gratitude. I know that cultivating appreciation is valuable because I've personally experienced its positive impact.

Try something right now. Close your eyes and take 30 seconds to think about something you're feeling grateful for in this moment.

What did that feel like? What did you notice?

Let's build some knowledge around why appreciation works, and the many ways we can practice it.

ช.ช.

Appreciation is like a secret sauce. You need only a few drops of it every day—in combination with other key habits and dispositions—to create a rich resilience. That's because feeling and expressing appreciation strengthens social connections, deepens our emotional intelligence and self-confidence, and heightens our ability to focus on the positive.

For two years at ASCEND, I had the best partner teacher ever. I taught English and history, and Keiko taught math and science to the same group of 45 middle schoolers. Together we planned units that integrated our content, strategized support for individual students, and led field trips to visit colleges. We also learned from and inspired each other; I was a far better teacher because of Keiko. As if that weren't enough, teaching was simply more enjoyable because of her partnership. Our conversations at lunch or after school provided the emotional respite, laughter, and connection that all teachers need and that make it much easier to show up every day.

During those years, I reflected often on how grateful I was for Keiko. Previous relationships with colleagues had not been as successful, in part because, prior to working with Keiko, I had not been an easy collaborator. When I started teaching with Keiko, I learned about a gratitude practice that's become my favorite. At the end of the day, you identify three things that went well and your role in making them happen. In my gratitude notebook, I wrote things like: "Our advisory lesson went really well and students were deeply engaged. This happened because when Keiko and I were planning this unit, I was open to her suggestions and ideas."

When these waves of gratitude for Keiko hit, I'd ask myself: *How did I get so lucky?* Maybe there was some luck, and, sure, sometimes you just hit it off with someone, but there was also intention and effort on my part. When I collaborated with Keiko, I was more thoughtful, considerate, and reflective than I'd been in previous partnerships. Gratitude practices highlighted the connection between my personal growth and this positive partnership, which then made me feel more committed to managing my uncomfortable emotions, addressing minor conflicts, and maintaining open communication. Gratitude practices helped me see my own growth and potential for growth, and that propelled my commitment to being a better person.

Research backs up my experiences. When people practice gratitude, their social bonds strengthen and they feel more supported, which fuels confidence in their ability to tackle big challenges (Layous et al., 2017). Furthermore, feeling grateful motivates us to do kind things for others. When people receive help and feel grateful, they are motivated to help those who had helped them, as well as total strangers (Bartlett and DeSteno, 2006). Gratitude also shifts the focus off of ourselves and helps us recognize that our successes are due, in part, to the actions of others. This humility makes us want to help others, improve ourselves, and reciprocate support to those who have helped us.

Feeling appreciative can bring up unsettling feelings. When we reflect on how much people have helped us, we might feel obligated to reciprocate or uncomfortable that we needed the help in the first place. We could also feel guilty for not adequately expressing our gratitude earlier. Sometimes these feelings can prevent us from feeling or expressing gratitude. I think this is the nature of life: There are layers of emotions in every experience. Gratitude can make us feel both uplifted and indebted, which may motivate us to reciprocate the good that others have shown us.

Gratitude helps us strive for our goals and inspires us to be better. It prompts us to feel more connected to others, to feel humble, and to feel a sense of responsibility for others, which can prompt us to invest more into work, community, relationships, and even goals we otherwise thought weren't possible. In recent years, some critics and skeptics have argued that gratitude breeds self-satisfaction and acceptance of the status quo, that it makes people feel satisfied with where they are and disinterested in pursuing bigger goals or helping others. However, a growing number of studies have concluded the opposite: That gratitude is an activating, energizing force that may lead us to pursue our goals, become more socially engaged, and improve ourselves and our communities (Layous et al., 2017).

Gratitude is far from being a passive emotion that lulls us into complacency or makes us sit back, marveling at the wonders of our own lives. Instead it can fuel our own emotional resilience, and with the increased energy we have when we're resilient, we can help others.

How to Practice Gratitude

> *Gratitude is like a flashlight. It lights up what is already there.*
> *You don't necessarily have anything more or different, but suddenly*
> *you can actually see what it is. And because you can see, you no*
> *longer take it for granted.*
> M. J. RYAN

Expressing gratitude is a mental habit we can develop—we just need practice. Imagine what our days would be like if we were all practicing gratitude individually for a few minutes in the morning and a few in the evening, and if there were structures built into our workday to express gratitude to others. Imagine how different we'd feel about being at school every day.

If we feel more positive in our school environment, if it's a place where we know others recognize the best parts of ourselves, we will want to be at work. We will then, in turn, be more patient with our students and with colleagues. We may speak to each other more kindly. We might listen to each other more deeply. Expressing gratitude allows us to engage in deeper, more positive work together.

Appreciate Others

It feels good to be appreciated. I suspect that all of us wish we were appreciated more often—so appreciate others! Do it more often: Appreciate colleagues, supervisors, students, their parents, the front office staff, and the custodians; notice little things that people do every day that go overlooked—and acknowledge those things. A few tips when offering appreciations:

- Be genuine. An inauthentic appreciation is disconcerting.
- Speak from the heart. This requires vulnerability, so recognize your emotions.
- Talk about the impact the other person's actions have had on you. For example: "I appreciate how, every time I arrive at school, you welcome me with such warmth. It makes me feel happy to be here."
- Stay focused on the recipient. Twisting an appreciation into a way to get your own emotional needs met takes away from the appreciation. For example, this is not a true appreciation: "I wanted to thank you for bringing in my kids after recess when I wasn't out there; I was stuck in the office trying to finish making copies, and if this school functioned at all, I wouldn't have been late." A true appreciation would be, "Thanks so much for bringing in my kids after recess. It was a relief to know that they weren't outside waiting for me."

Appreciations can be offered individually and in a group setting. You can end a class or meeting with appreciations, which can leave everyone feeling good, or you can open meetings with appreciations, which can help people bond.

Public appreciations can be powerful—it can feel great to give and receive recognition in front of your peers—but they can also be tricky. When offered and received verbally, in front of others, there's a risk that a member of the group won't receive an appreciation. This undermines the health of the whole group. Furthermore, some people are extremely uncomfortable receiving appreciations in front of a group, and that means they won't get the benefit of the appreciation and could actually end up feeling worse. Finally, sometimes people use appreciations as a passive-aggressive way to give someone feedback. For example, I remember a staff meeting after a big event when almost everyone extended appreciations to all who had helped with event, but Jack was left out. He didn't receive any appreciations—and it felt awkward and obvious that it was an indirect way for the staff to express their frustration at Jack for his lack of participation in the event. Be mindful of how public appreciations are expressed.

By using different structures for handing out appreciations, you can mitigate some of the potential challenges. Here are some options:

- **Public appreciations.** With the whole group, in front of everyone, people are invited to offer an appreciation to anyone they want.
- **Pulling a name.** At varying intervals, pull one community member's name out of a hat (a team member or student). Then invite people to share an appreciation for that person. Each time you meet, pull another person's name so that, after some time, everyone has received appreciations.
- **Written appreciations.** Invite group members to jot down appreciations on sticky notes or paper and then hand them to the recipient. This makes the giving and receiving less public, but you still run the risk of missing someone. If you have a small group, you can ask each team member to write a note of appreciation for every member.
- **Silent appreciations.** To explain this strategy, I'll need to describe how I use it. At the end of a class or PD session, I ask all participants to close their eyes or bring their attention inward. Then I ask everyone to first appreciate themselves, then their community and students. I continue by suggesting they think of someone else in the room who has positively contributed to their day, week, work, or life, and telepathically send that person a message of appreciation. I say, "Tell them in your mind exactly what you appreciate about them and how they've enhanced your life." Finally, I invite everyone to send appreciations to anyone else who is not in the room. The primary reason for practicing gratitude is for our own mental and emotional well-being. Silent appreciations accomplish that goal.

Appreciate Yourself

For years, Teacher Appreciation Day surfaced complicated emotions for me. I'd anticipate the day hoping that I'd be acknowledged by students, their parents, and my administrators, that I'd be appreciated in a way that matched the effort I invested. I was often disappointed. I'd get a few meaningful cards from kids, and the bagel breakfast was nice, but these appreciations didn't equate the effort I put into my work.

Teachers deserve and need to be appreciated. And it's true that the ways in which students, parents, and administrators do this needs some refinement.

Teacher appreciation needs to be offered more than just once a year and in more meaningful ways than a breakfast. In addition, appreciation for teachers should be reflected in education policy that values teaching and should be evidenced in teacher salaries. At the same time, the only person who knows how much you put into your teaching is you. Self-appreciation may not sound as if it would be as rewarding as external appreciation, but you'd be surprised by its benefits. Here are a few ways to appreciate yourself.

Think of Three Things

At the end of each day or week, select three things that went well, and describe your role in making that happen. Here are some examples:

- My lesson on understanding character development in the novel we're reading went really well, and Mica, who usually never talks, was really engaged. My role in making that happen was that I spent a lot of time planning this lesson and used a new discussion structure.
- Another teacher dropped off some supplies that I can use for a science lesson, and now I can actually teach the unit. My role in making that happen was that I sent out an email asking for supplies.
- Miguel was calm and focused today. It was the first day in two weeks that I didn't have to send him to the office. My role in making that happen was that I was really aware of how he can trigger me, I used strategies to calm myself down, and I responded to him in a way that kept him calm.

This activity can be a mental contemplation, perhaps as you lie in bed, but to get the most out of this, write. As you gather evidence for how you've made good things happen, you build your confidence. Having a written record of this makes it all the more powerful.

Set an Alarm

Set an alarm a few times a day. When it goes off, take a moment to appreciate yourself for whatever you're doing right then. You might be surprised to catch yourself doing something really valuable, for which you otherwise wouldn't have taken stock.

The first time I engaged in this practice, at the urging of my coach, my phone alarm went off as I talked to a grandmother about her fears that her grandson—an eighth grader—had a learning disability. She'd caught me in the hallway, during a prep period. I did things like this all the time, but I had never registered those moments as ones in which I was doing something worthy—and I was. When my alarm went off, I swiftly and silently took in the moment, acknowledged myself for talking to the grandma, and continued the conversation.

Write a Letter of Appreciation

At the end of each day or week, write yourself a letter of appreciation. Here are a couple sentences that I wrote to myself during a particularly difficult year teaching: "I appreciate that you weren't really frustrated today with your first period. I know they are challenging and push your buttons, but you stayed calm and patient with them." No one else could appreciate how hard it was for me to manage this group of students, but when I started appreciating myself, I felt different. These words were what I wished someone would say, but saying them to myself was cathartic.

Send a Text-Message Appreciation

As you appreciate yourself, if you are compelled to appreciate others, go ahead and do so! Then you can also appreciate yourself for sending that quick email or text. I just took a break from writing and sent Keiko a message. I haven't seen her in six or seven years. Writing a quick note to her felt really good, as did her appreciative and warm response. Tonight, when I lie in bed and review my day, I'll remember this moment and experience another wave of gratitude.

Gratitude fuels more gratitude and well-being. After I sent Keiko a message, I started thinking about people in my life now who are collaborators and partners. I thought about how much better my work is because of these people, how much happier my days are. I recognized what I'd done to make these relationships effective, and also acknowledged that luck and chemistry play a mysterious role, and I'm grateful for that too.

❧❧

Teachers: You have a right to be appreciated by others *and* you need to appreciate yourself. You will feel better if you do, and, with that energy, you'll be better able to advocate for the respect, rights, and salary that you deserve.

Try it. Right now. Appreciation really feels good.

Relax and Take In the Appreciation

Receiving appreciation can feel awkward. If you feel you don't deserve it, you might downplay the compliment with something like, "Oh, it wasn't a big deal, and I didn't do it that well anyway." You might turn it back on them: "But *you* helped *me* so much! I couldn't have done it without you." Or you might just squirm uncomfortably. If your cultural background or family places great value on humility, or believes that pride is a deadly sin, appreciations can be even more challenging.

Appreciations can also be complicated by power dynamics. A principal can say, "I appreciated your hard work today" to a teacher more easily than a teacher can say that to a principal. Sometimes you might receive an appreciation that feels slightly condescending, or you might want to appreciate someone, but feel as though she could receive it as condescending. It's likely you'll sometimes feel uncomfortable with appreciations for many reasons. Learn to manage your discomfort, and you'll find ways to navigate and respond to whatever happens.

Often when I receive an appreciation, I feel vulnerable. I sense my connection with the other person and recognize layers of emotions: I'm grateful to receive the appreciation, but what if I let this person down in the future? What if I lose her appreciation? And did I really deserve it? She's helped me just as much. Noticing all this mental chatter rumbling through my mind, I take a deep breath, let the other's appreciation sink in, and I simply say, "Thank you." Like all other habits, this gets easier with practice.

Next time someone gives you an appreciation, just smile and say thank you. And that's it. If discomfort bubbles up, recognize it. Pledge to understand it, but don't argue, interrupt, or downplay. If someone appreciates you, he's giving you a gift. It's *his choice* to give you a gift, and you need to humbly receive it. It's unkind to toss back the person's gift and essentially say, "I don't want it." See what happens when you let an appreciation sink in.

Implications for Leaders

- Across the United States, in all sectors, the top reason why people quit a job is that they don't feel appreciated: According to the US Department of Labor, 64% of people who quit their jobs say they do so because they don't feel appreciated or valued (Robbins, 2007).

- Also according to the US Department of Labor, 65% of people in the United States say that they receive no praise or recognition in the workplace. Interestingly, researchers suspect that of those 65%, it's possible that many do receive praise, but aren't able to hear it, or it isn't delivered in a way and with language they can register (Robbins, 2007). Employees who receive praise are more productive and more engaged with their colleagues, and stay with their organizations longer.

- New teachers in particular really need their successes and contributions to be acknowledged to build resilience (Sumsion, 2004).
- Be mindful of the subtle difference between appreciation and praise. When offered by a superior, praise can have a slightly condescending tone or can feel paternalistic, depending on the phrasing. For example, this statement could sound condescending if an assistant principal were to say it to a teacher: "Good job getting your attendance in on time." By contrast, the same sentiment might be communicated as appreciation through a statement like, "I appreciate receiving your attendance on time so that I can now file our attendance report for the day."
- Giving appreciations does not preclude offering feedback. A certain amount of constructive feedback is necessary and productive. Research conducted by John Gottman (1999) recommends five instances of praise or positive reinforcement for every one piece of feedback or negative reinforcement. Emphasize the positive and offer feedback.

Perhaps this story will compel you to institute appreciation routines with your staff: Karina was a second-year principal whose staff complained of not feeling appreciated. When the new school year began, she asked each staff member how he or she wanted to be appreciated. Some requested affirmation in private, others preferred public acknowledgment, and some wanted appreciation in writing. And a few staff members said that chocolate made them feel appreciated.

As Karina became more intentional about appreciating her staff's actions and behaviors, she also structured opportunities for staff to appreciate each other, their students, and their students' parents. Every meeting or PD session ended with a few minutes saved for expressions of gratitude. Teachers incorporated this routine into classes and parent meetings, in which parents appreciated each other, the school staff, and their children. On the end-of-year survey, 94% of Karina's staff said that within the prior week, someone in their school had appreciated their work; this was a remarkable increase from the previous year and an indicator of a healthy staff culture. Furthermore, that year, Karina only lost one staff member out of a total of 47, which was the lowest turnover for her school in a decade. Although there were many factors that may have contributed to the high staff retention rate that year, it also made sense: The school felt like a place where people wanted to be.

Sometimes the process of appreciation causes you to gain insight into changes you need to make or jobs you need to leave. I am committed to reducing teacher turnover and creating stable learning environments for kids, and I hope the strategies in this book help you manage the stressors at your school. This doesn't mean, however, that you should stay indefinitely in a position in which you are suffering. There are times when you may want to leave a position, a school, or an organization—and it's okay. The need to leave might have to do with the working conditions, the organizational culture, or personal and professional circumstances. Endings are new beginnings and might lead you onto a path where you can thrive.

I'd taught for a decade when I experienced a wave of intense burnout. I recently came across the following journal entry from my last year at ASCEND:

> I want to quit. I feel ineffective. Like nothing I do matters. The systemic problems impacting our kids are so tremendous that it feels like my efforts are an insignificant blip in their lives. I am so tired and drained from kids and all their needs and it's not their fault, there are just too many of them. And the bathroom for staff is usually dirty and there are rarely paper towels and I can't even get someone from HR to sit down with me and talk. It's not teaching I am sick of; it's the dysfunction in this district and feeling like I'm never doing enough and I'm tired of feeling hopeless.

When I read this now, considering what I know about resilience, what strikes me most are the first and final statements—I wanted to quit because I didn't feel that I was making a difference, and I didn't have hope. I suspect I may have been clinically depressed for a chunk of this year; I found little joy or satisfaction in my work, and this was exacerbated by the real challenges of my position, which wasn't a good fit for my strengths and personality. I used many of the resilience habits I've described in this book, and some of them helped me gain clarity and find the energy to take action. But I still didn't feel content or fulfilled.

I remember recognizing what I was experiencing as burnout and feeling fear and shame. Since I'd started teaching, I'd been warned about burnout. It was talked about in hushed voices, as if it was something to feel ashamed of if you let yourself get there. My greatest fear was that this marked the end of the road for an educator. I thought, *If I'm burned out in one school, is this a reflection of my permanent state of being? Will I be burned out, hopeless, and cynical somewhere else too?*

I contemplated other professions and considered graduate school programs, but, in the end, I left ASCEND for a position as a coach in another school. I'd dipped my toes into coaching at ASCEND, and I loved it. When I was coaching teachers, I'd felt the most curious, fulfilled, and even joyful. I registered gratitude for those moments. Paying attention to the bright spots, noticing when I felt that I was fulfilling my purpose, and cultivating gratitude helped me find a path through the burnout. It was painful to leave ASCEND, a community that I cared about deeply, but it led me to what I consider my calling—the world of coaching.

Practicing gratitude can help you gain clarity when you are conflicted. You might recognize, for example, that even though you love your students and are grateful for them every day, you aren't able to offer them your full potential as a teacher because you're in an environment that's obsessively focused on test scores. Or practicing gratitude might help you see that your appreciation for your colleagues at your school overrides the stressful demands from the central office that make you want to quit. Or practicing appreciation for yourself can help you see that you deserve to be treated better and that you need to join an organization where you can contribute your unique skills and gifts.

Context, say researchers who study workplace happiness, might be the most powerful and most often ignored catalyst for changing your life. If you are unhappy, you might just need to get out of the place you're in. Find a different job. It's possible that your unhappiness could have to do with the people around you. Psychologists have observed that bad habits can spread through an office like a contagious disease. Employees tend to mirror the bad behaviors of their coworkers. If you suspect that you're surrounded by people whose habits you don't want rubbing off on you, leave. And when you consider another job, take a long look at the people you're going to be working with—because the odds are you're going to become like them. But especially if you've implemented every strategy in this book and you've diligently worked through the workbook, and you're not feeling a lot better able to deal with the challenges at work, it might be that you need to leave. Consider this your permission to do so.

Acknowledging Context: Spirituality

A desire to kneel down sometimes pulses through my body, or rather it is as if my body has been meant and made for the act of kneeling. Sometimes, in moments of deep gratitude, kneeling down becomes an overwhelming urge, head deeply bowed, hands before my face.
ETTY HILLESUM

We stood in front of a memorial to T.J., a 17-year-old student who had been shot. He was well known and adored in this school. I asked the principal how he was dealing with a recent bout of violence in the community he served, and he described using a particular form of Buddhist meditation. "I couldn't get through these days without that," he said. A teacher approached us; she'd known T.J. since he was a child. I gave her a hug and asked her how she was doing. "God has a plan, and he must have wanted this angel back by his side," she said, tears running down her cheeks.

As I read about resilience and teachers, I noticed a trend. Social scientists, when conducting research, frequently made comments like this one: "Although not solicited by the interviewers . . . teachers and teacher leaders pointed to their personal spirituality as a source of resilience. Irrespective of the nature of the spirituality, whether it was mainstream religion or metaphysical beliefs, these teachers reported turning to a higher power for strength on difficult days" (Patterson, Collins, and Abbot, 2004, p. 8). With this in mind, when exploring how we deal with and understand adversity, we must consider the role of spirituality.

This subject makes me uncomfortable. I was born in London, England, and, until I was 10, I attended British schools. In England, there is no separation of church and state, and every morning, students attended an assembly during which we sang Christian hymns and prayed. Now, my family was not Christian, nor were some 70% of the children at my school; they were Hindu, Muslim, and Sikh. For me, the assembly felt like a daily reminder that I did not belong, that my family's practices and beliefs were not acceptable. My belief that religion should be kept apart from secular society, and my respect for the rights of everyone to practice as he or she wishes, causes me to feel unsettled about having this discussion in this book.

But, for the majority of us, spirituality is a central part of our lives. The quest to understand what it means to be human, to connect with a greater power, to find meaning beyond what we can see, hear, and touch is a hallmark of being a human being. Sometimes the highs and lows of life—death, injustice, unfathomable beauty, amazing coincidence and luck—can bring spiritual questions to the surface. Most relevant to our current endeavor, spirituality can be a key resource for resilience. For that reason, I will set my discomfort aside and aim, as thoughtfully as possible, to guide us through an exploration of the connections between spirituality and resilience.

The Connections Between Spirituality and Resilience

First, let's define two terms that are sometimes used interchangeably. *Spirituality* is a search for meaning and the sacred beyond the individual self. *Religion* involves a spiritual search, but within a formal, institutional context.

Some people consider themselves spiritual, but not religious. You do not have to believe in God to sense that ordinary things are sacred. If you feel that your body is holy or that love is eternal or that your work is a calling or that your life is blessed, you are imbuing aspects of your life with sacred or divine qualities. That kind of sanctification can provide motivation, meaning, and satisfaction (Lyubomirsky, 2007). You don't have to belong to a religious institution to benefit from a spiritual life.

Research on the well-being of religious people finds that they are happier and healthier, and recover better after traumas than nonreligious people (Ellison and Levin, 1998). This is likely due in part to social support, as well as to the meaning a religious doctrine can ascribe to tragedies. Religious organizations provide a sense of identity and belonging to a close-knit community, which in turn provides social, emotional, and material support. People gather for activities and share basic assumptions and beliefs, as well as social values. The finding that religious people are happier than the nonreligious may have more to do with the benefits of community than with their spiritual beliefs and the substance of their religion. However, there's also research concluding that spiritual people are relatively happier than nonspiritual people. They have better mental health, cope more effectively with stressors, have more satisfying marriages, use drugs and alcohol less often, are physically healthier, and live longer (Pargament and Mahoney, 2002). Even beyond the contributions of community, which we know are essential to living a good life, there's something of value in having a spiritual or religious life.

For many, whether they are spiritual or religious, having a sense of a relationship with the divine can be a tremendous source of comfort; it helps us craft an overarching story about our lives and existence that can help mediate a great deal of our experiences in life. A belief in a higher power helps people feel unconditionally loved, cared for, and valued. Believing that an omnipotent entity may intervene in a challenging situation also provides a kind of security. It can be reassuring to think that a higher power ascribes a purpose for everything, including unexpected changes and turmoil. Whether people experience illness, job loss, breakups, or school upheaval, their having a sense that there is a broader divine plan or that "God has a reason" helps them cope. We yearn for our lives to have purpose, and we crave a sense of control over our fates—and, for many, spirituality provides those experiences.

Religious or spiritual faith can also give rise to a number of positive emotions and experiences that are associated with happiness, such as a disposition to forgive or to trust in a higher power. The habits and practices of religion—private prayer, spiritual pursuit, and collective worship—can engender hope, gratitude, love, awe, compassion, and joy. Whether from singing with a choir on a holy day or riding your beloved horse in a field under the full moon, the feelings of connection, communion, and something greater than just you on this planet fuel emotional resilience.

When Spirituality Evokes Gratitude

If the only prayer you ever said in your whole life was
"Thank you," that would suffice.
MEISTER ECKHARD, THIRTEENTH-CENTURY THEOLOGIAN AND MYSTIC

As I stood in front of T.J.'s memorial, stifling tears, I acknowledged the threads of gratitude weaving their way into the sadness. Students stopped in front of the collectively assembled memorial and shared recollections of T.J. They remembered his humor and kindness, telling stories of how he'd bring levity to tense moments; of his antics in kindergarten; and of the way he cared for his younger siblings. On construction-paper hearts, they wrote notes to T.J., conveying these memories: "You were a good friend even when I wasn't good to you," "I'll never forget how you helped me when my mom was sick," "You've made me a better person." They taped these up on the wall, a patchwork of appreciation surrounding photos of the young man.

At the core of this spiritual commemoration was gratitude—for T.J., for each other, perhaps for something greater than what we all could see and know. Parallel to the intensity of the sadness, I couldn't help but feel an odd mix of hope and joy. I saw community gathering—and an interfaith community at that. The Buddhist principal stood with his arm around a Baptist teacher; Catholic students crossed themselves and prayed with a rosary while a Muslim student chatted about how much she'd admired T.J.'s skills in debate. One young woman said to her friend, "I just thank God for letting me meet T.J. I'll be a better person because I did." Another teacher said, "I don't know why this happened, I don't believe in a God that takes kids, but it definitely has made me feel like I need to be more appreciative of people and tell them how much I love them now, while they're here."

It seems as though the moments in which we crave knowledge of and connection with the divine are those that evoke the most intense emotions—fear, loss, appreciation, love. It is perhaps in moments of great loss that our most intense feelings of gratitude are activated as we take stock of what we no longer have and appreciate the mystery of the universe.

Implications from the Research

Researchers have found that resilience is strongest in those who seek to experience a sense of the divine in their day-to-day experience. These are people who cultivate feelings of awe, inspiration, and wholeness by fostering a sense of the vastness of a divine love, nurturing a belief in a power greater than themselves, and developing a connection with the transcendent. A handful of referenced practices were repeatedly touted as having the strongest potential for positive impact on resilience; meditation and prayer were at the top of that list. Meditative prayer that focused on experiencing a sense of a divine presence was found to be more effective at boosting levels of happiness than prayer in which people petitioned for relief or asked for forgiveness (Poloma and Gallup, 1991).

Among the frequently mentioned activities most likely to cultivate resilience were contemplative activities. These may include religious or spiritual activities, but they can also be more expansive. In my research on resilience, when I asked educators how they dealt with difficult events and the daily strain of the work, the answers included the following: Coloring in a meditation coloring book, watching the sunset every evening, playing the cello, walking through a labyrinth on the weekend, reading poetry, and spending focused time petting a cat or dog. When people talked about these experiences, their reflections meandered back and forth between the sacred and the secular. The activities provoked contemplation, which helped them quiet their minds, provided perspective, and connected them with something nourishing outside themselves. In those moments, their wellsprings of resilience filled up.

What do you already do that helps you connect with your spirituality? What could you do more consistently? Which of these activities could you do with others—so that you also reap the benefits of being with community? A big takeaway from my research is that engaging regularly in spiritual habits strengthens your spiritual muscles for use when you come up against hard times.

A Disclaimer

It would be irresponsible to include this discussion about religion without acknowledging that religious institutions, at certain times and in certain places, have dehumanized others and denied them basic rights. This continues today, where, in some religious communities, groups of people are made to feel that they don't belong, that they are not loved by that version of the divine, or that they'll be condemned to hell for being who they are. Clearly, these are not communities that cultivate resilience but ones that severely undermine happiness and well-being. Use your critical judgment about whether a religious tradition or community is a source of strength, affirmation, and support. And remember that many people pursue a healthy spiritual life outside the bounds of a religious tradition.

Toward Conversations with Colleagues

I wonder if, or how, this conversation about spirituality could take place among adults in secular organizations. Could we establish ground rules for how we share our beliefs and how we listen to others speak about theirs? It would need to be voluntary; we'd need to grant people the right to pass. There would have to be skilled and effective facilitators. With that in place, I wonder what these conversations might sound like. I wonder what might come from them. Perhaps we could start small by talking about the sacred in ordinary life, the holiness in everyday experiences.

Maybe a key to having this conversation is our emotional intelligence. Even just thinking about discussing spirituality with others makes me feel very uncomfortable. But could I manage my discomfort if it improved my life and my community? Maybe. There might also be an opportunity to cultivate community resilience, because if we had this conversation about spirituality together and we struggled or fell, perhaps we could learn how to get back up—and then we'd be stronger.

Small wonder, then, that teaching tugs at the heart, opens the heart,
even breaks the heart—and the more one loves teaching, the more
heartbreaking it can be. The courage to teach is the courage to keep
one's heart open in those very moments when the heart is asked to hold
more than it is able.
PARKER PALMER

A Dive into Awe and Wonder

As I've said a few times now, our schools would be healthier, happier places for all if we had more conversations about emotions. Throughout this book, I've prompted you to reflect on your experiences of sadness, fear, shame, and anger, as well as on your positive emotions, including love and joy. And, maybe, if we explored and talked about positive emotions more, instead of focusing on the challenging ones, we'd all be healthier, happier people. For this final dive into an emotional state, I'm exploring awe and wonder. These states can emerge from experiences of gratitude or can lead us to appreciation. Either way, they are worth honoring as emotional experiences in and of themselves.

Ordinary life is filled with moments that can be awe inspiring and full of wonder. I've felt awe when listening to music, while watching a lightning storm, and when I managed to grow tomatoes for the first time. I've experienced awe during an incredible meal. My relationships with a few of the cats and dogs I've lived with have also been transcendent. I've felt awe and wonder many times when watching my child; his existence alone makes me marvel.

I've also experienced awe and wonder, and intense gratitude and delight, during celebrations. One year, a student I'd taught in third grade invited me to her high school graduation. From the moment I started teaching, I always told my students, "I will be at your high school graduation if you invite me." When I went to Marilu's graduation, I didn't realize that in her class were many students whom I'd taught my first year. As these young men and women walked across the stage and offered poignant words about their journeys through school, I was flooded by memories of them as seven- and eight-year-olds.

And then Esau crossed the stage, and tears streamed down my face. Esau was a second grader when I met him, but, having been retained one year, was approaching his ninth birthday. Although I was a new teacher and felt as though I knew nothing, I knew that something was wrong. He reversed letters, he couldn't spell his own name, and he was a gifted artist. He was a sweet, kind, gentle child, loved by his peers. I spent months speaking to his mother about getting Esau tested for learning differences, but she adamantly refused. She told me that as a child, in rural Mexico, her husband had been labeled "retarded" and had been ostracized and physically abused by teachers. I explained the process in our school and took her to meet the resource teacher. I promised to stay with Esau for the entire time he was tested and invited her to observe the testing. I connected her to other mothers whose children received services, and she listened to their assurances. Finally, she granted permission for us to test Esau. The results were that he had severe learning differences and was at prekindergarten levels in most areas. We did what we could do while he was in our elementary school, but I worried about him when he headed off to a huge, chaotic middle school.

At his high school graduation, Esau made a short speech thanking his parents and his teachers, tears pouring from his eyes the whole time. He spoke of his struggles with learning and of his passion for art—he was headed off to an art institute for college. He was the same sweet boy I'd met 10 years earlier, and I experienced a wave of intense gratitude and wonder at what the universe had orchestrated. As I recalled the struggle of that first year of teaching, the exhaustion and insecurity I'd experienced, I felt that seeing Esau graduate made it all worthwhile.

When you think about awe and wonder, what comes to mind? Take a moment to explore a memory or two. Close your eyes if you'd like and reexperience one. How does it feel to remember those times? My prediction is that it feels good. And, remember, things that make you feel good, including memories, strengthen your resilience.

Disposition: Trust

Wrapped into the act of celebration is the act of reflection; you look back at a journey, identifying the peaks and valleys. You see yourself plodding along, the moments when sweat ran down your face and obscured your vision; you see the muscles in your calves strengthening. You remember thinking, *I don't know if I can make it up this hill,* and then you see that you did. You recall those moments of feeling triumphant—and the process of recollection makes you stronger.

I didn't think I would get through my first year teaching.
I didn't think I'd hold it together during my student's funeral.
I didn't know how I could teach and have a baby.
I couldn't imagine returning to that toxic school for a second year.
I had no idea how I'd deal with the reorganization of our department.
I thought I'd never finish writing this book.

As you reflect, you see that you made it. You did it. You see the confluence of factors that played a role, the way that others helped you, and you recognize what you did to make it. With that, your confidence is fortified. You can do hard things.

It took me a long time to learn this final lesson: To trust the process, to trust myself, to trust perhaps in something bigger (and beyond) and unknowable. Many times I've faced a challenge and thought, *I don't know if I can do this.* This has taught me a lesson about patience, about holding off on making judgments, about being open to outcome. I've also increased my self-acceptance and gotten much better at not being too hard on myself.

Trust the process—it always works is my mantra for writing, coaching, leading teams, and facilitating PD. I take this confident stance because I've seen the evidence to support it. It's not naïve or a way of evading responsibility for my actions; it's tried and tested, and it results from learning how to celebrate and appreciate. Without the looking backwards, the reflection and compassionate assessment, I wouldn't have reason to trust the process.

Celebration can cultivate a disposition of trust, of believing in something bigger and more powerful. Perhaps that something bigger and more powerful is simply the passage of time; perhaps it's something else. As I've learned how to reflect, to celebrate, to appreciate and give thanks for my own efforts and those of others, my trust has grown exponentially.

I'm calling this final disposition of an emotionally resilient person "trust." As I read the research, as I reflected on my experiences, as I spoke with friends and colleagues, this trait emerged clearly and undeniably. Resilient people trust themselves, and they trust a process. But this disposition is talked about indirectly and vaguely—perhaps because it verges into the realm of the spiritual, where words are woefully insufficient to describe such a state of being. What I'm calling trust might be better known as faith. I'm apprehensive about using a term so closely associated with religion, so I use "trust." I invite you to select the word that resonates for you to describe this disposition.

Here's how I call on this disposition. When I'm feeling most fragile, vulnerable, or uncertain of my own capacities, when I have to take a risk or I've chosen to take one but am apprehensive, I activate this disposition. *Trust the process,* I tell myself. The anxieties peel away like a skin that I've outgrown, and I feel more myself but also more something else. I feel less alone because I know that I can only do whatever it is I'm doing. I can only offer whatever I'm offering, and I know that there are more factors at play than what I can see or control. I let go. I give what I can give. And then I appreciate myself, which builds more trust and more resilience.

> *When a man is singing and cannot lift his voice, and another comes and*
> *sings with him, one who can lift his voice, the first will be able to lift his*
> *voice too. That is the secret of the bond between spirits.*
> HASSIDIC SAYING

Underground Rivers

Celebrations can open the floodgates for awe, wonder, and gratitude; they can cultivate trust and hope and optimism; and they can make visible the webs of connection in our communities. By using the other habits in this book, such as practicing mindfulness, being in the present moment, building community, and focusing on the bright spots, we will find more to celebrate than we imagine. Celebrations can be grand—such as a graduation or an exposition of student learning. Or they can be minor—such as appreciations delivered at the end of a meeting. Celebrations and appreciations—collective and private, grand and miniscule—open up underground rivers of resilience that fill our individual reservoirs and those of our community.

CHAPTER REFLECTION

- How were your thoughts and feelings about appreciation and celebration affected or changed by this chapter?
- Of the different ideas and practices that were raised in this chapter, which are you interested in exploring further?
- What role does your spirituality, a sense of awe and wonder, and the ability to trust play in your resilience?

CONCLUSION

Onward to Freedom

I hope that your journey through this book has enabled you to discover your internal pool of resilience. I hope that you have recognized the skills you already possess to deal with adversity, as well as new ways to manage stress, prevent burnout, and bounce back from challenges.

I also hope that as you've taken this journey, you've become aware of the larger role that resilience can play in transforming our schools and world. Resilience is the key to our own ability to thrive and, therefore, our ability to help others thrive.

On Freedom

The resilient are purposeful. The resilient find meaning in every moment, and exercise whatever power and agency are available—including the power to choose their attitude. There is a thin line between agency and victimhood: We may feel as though we can affect a situation only up to a point, and then we feel like a victim. Freedom lies in the space between agency and victimhood—where we can recognize our power and can recognize the larger context of power that we're in. We recognize where our power ends.

Viktor Frankl's book *Man's Search for Meaning* (2006) offers profound lessons on being resilient in dire situations, and as a Holocaust survivor, Frankl is an authority on this subject. In *Man's Search for Meaning,* he writes that purpose is found in every moment of living. Life never ceases to have significance, even in suffering and death:

> We who lived in concentration camps can remember the men who walked through the huts comforting others, giving away their last piece of bread. They may have been few in number, but they offer sufficient proof that everything can be taken from a man but one thing: the last of the human freedoms—to choose one's attitude in any given set of circumstances, to choose one's own way. (2006, pp. 65–66)

This is the deepest level of freedom, one that is hard to imagine when located inside Nazi death camps. It is the kind of freedom from which forgiveness and compassion flow, the kind that Nelson Mandela wrote about in his memoirs of imprisonment during South African apartheid, the kind of freedom about which the Dalai Lama speaks.

I have long been fascinated by those who have found this kind of freedom while enduring unimaginable horror. It is the distant backdrop for many of the little moments in which I feel powerless, helping me gain perspective and clarity of thought. This kind of macro context helps me remember my own power in the onslaught of daily frustration.

❧❧

I arrive at school an hour early to prepare for the day. I'm organized and everything is set, and I dash over to the office to make a few copies of the Do Now. The machine is broken. I curse under my breath. I huff and puff. I blame others— I'm sure it's someone's fault. I'd slept well; I'd meditated and felt centered. Now all that calm is slipping away, and the day stretches ahead of me with a shadow cast over it.

And then an inner voice speaks: *You have a choice. Right now in this moment. You can choose how you respond to this event. This is your freedom.*

Then I curse at myself a little bit. Perspective hits me with a jolt—it's just a copy machine, not a Nazi separating me from my mother. I can modify the Do Now. I am resourceful, and my resilience reserves are full; I've been tending to them. This doesn't have to throw my whole day off. And there—in that shift in my stance, in my attitude, in my emotion—there is my freedom. I unlocked that door.

Having dusted off my knees—that broken copy machine took me down for a minute—I can return to my purpose, which is to serve children. My resilience allows me to be my best: I'm not thrown by the barrage of everyday challenges that sprout up in my path. Those will always be there! I can go around them, over them, under them, through them. Sometimes they trip me, but I rebound faster than ever.

My resilience serves a purpose far greater than simply managing the everyday adversities of work and life: My resilience allows me to uncover my potential, my unique skills and abilities, and to contribute those to the world. In doing so, I thrive. In doing so, I find joy and meaning. In doing so, I alchemize my joy and potential into an offering that helps others find their joy and potential.

This is why we cultivate resilience: So that we can thrive and contribute to helping others thrive and unlock their freedom. The goal is freedom of the mind, of the spirit—for us as individuals, and for our communities. Our joy and freedom are bound with those of every other living creature on this planet. Our very survival is intertwined. I cultivate my resilience through dozens of behaviors and habits every day, and I strengthen my dispositions that feed my resilience so that I may experience joy and equanimity every day, and so that I may help others find their freedom.

There is a great deal each of us can do, individually, to boost our resilience and manage stress. There is a great deal that leaders can (and must) do to create conditions in which educators thrive. Even the most resilient educator will not stay in a school or district that's toxic and dysfunctional. This book is not intended to be dropped on the desk of a tired and stressed-out teacher with the suggestion that all of her problems will be solved if she'll just do something about her attitude, if she'll just get a good night's sleep and boost her resilience.

Let me remind you that as you cultivate your individual resilience, you'll have more physical, emotional, cognitive, and spiritual energy to challenge injustices and inequities. We can do both simultaneously. We'll have the energy to fight the good fight—to elect the officials who will fund public education, organize against policies that dehumanize educators, and push back on punitive assessment practices and scripted curriculum that turn teachers into robots. We'll have the energy to lead and engage in PD that explores equity in schools and that holds space for us to examine our own biases. As we cultivate individual resilience, we'll have energy to build PLCs in which we can take risks, be vulnerable, look at student work together, challenge each other's thinking, and have uncomfortable conversations about race, class, gender, privilege, and so on.

It is also incumbent on us to examine and do something about the macro political and economic context in which we live and work—a context that until we change it, will profoundly undermine our resilience. These macro conditions are not conducive to retaining resilient, effective educators. Funding structures must change so that teachers are not buying classroom supplies for their students, so that they can afford to purchase a home, and so that they can take time off work when they have a baby. We need to talk about government spending, taxation structures, whom we elect to political office, who votes, and whose right to vote is being taken away. We need to have these conversations as well as conversations about our individual attitudes and responses to stress. They are connected. To sever these connections is to slash the Achilles tendon of our collective, interconnected body.

These efforts will take energy; some will be lengthy battles. We need tremendous reserves of resilience in order to create the just and equitable society for which so many of us yearn. We are each responsible for discovering the cenote that lies within us, our own internal spring of resilience, and lovingly replenishing it.

Onward: The Movement

Let's take up this endeavor to cultivate individual and collective resilience as a movement—a social, political, cultural movement. For centuries, our societies have been dominated by a mindset of individualism and greed. Emotions have been pathologized, suppressed, dismissed, and relegated to the domain of women and children, and therefore seen as less important, less valuable, less trustworthy. The rational, analytical mind has been elevated to supreme master, our bodies and hearts being secondary and subservient. But our emotions, however denigrated, refuse to be repressed. They have spilled out in messy ways at times, and have remained a source of power. Our bodies have also been required to submit to our minds, to ignore their need for rest and nutrition. But many of us are waking up to the unsustainability of pushing ourselves to the point of physical illness.

In asserting our desire to experience, explore, express, and discuss emotions—with each other and with our students—we claim a human right, for *humans have emotions.* In insisting that we care for our bodies—that we have time to go to the bathroom during the day and to eat lunch, and for our kids to have recess and clean drinking water—we are reclaiming a right to physical well-being and even pleasure, which is also our human right. The personal is political; to cultivate resilience is to take political action.

Movements have manifestos, declarations of purpose and values, principles under which they operate. I offer the Resilience Manifesto, which follows the introduction, in the hopes that it can unify us to make changes in our schools and our world.

&⬥&

I am writing this conclusion during a period that feels like the most politically fragile, volatile, and terrifying of my life. It requires daily effort to stay above the swamp of fear and anger that threatens to pull me in. I find myself using resilience-boosting strategies more often than ever. The list of things that scare me includes the rise in overt white supremacy and nationalism, climate change, and a political system that might be broken beyond repair. I have never felt such urgency to protect the planet, my African American son's future, the civil liberties that many have enjoyed in the United States, and the honorable democratic ideals on which this country was founded. Our public schools face a constant threat as transactional leadership sweeps our education system, mandating how teachers teach and what they say, undermining a teacher's ability to know a child and make decisions based on that child's needs in that moment. The economic divide between the haves and the have-nots has never been greater. Securing funding for public schools feels like a daily battle.

Yet I have no choice but to forge onward.

I will wrap my stories around my shoulders like a cloak, sensing the resilience that runs through my veins; I will strengthen my compassion for myself and for others every day; I will rest and dance and eat delicious, nutritious food. I will name and honor my feelings: *Hello, fear. Greetings, anger.* I will accept them and know that they will visit from time to time, but that they do not have permanent residency in my being. I will pull closer my community that upholds me, and I will be here now, in this miraculous present moment—basking in the warmth of the morning sun on my skin and relishing my teenager's sharp sense of humor. I will float when I can in my internal cenote, my reserves of resilience, and then I will proceed onward.

I know that I am not alone. I hope to see you on this journey, to link our arms and inspire each other and break bread together and tell stories of love, sadness, healing, and resilience. Also, I love board games and music and making drip castles on the beach, so let's play and have fun as well.

Onward, ever onward.

APPENDIX A

The Habits and Dispositions of Resilient Educators: A Self-Assessment

Resilient educators effectively and regularly engage in 12 habits and demonstrate 12 dispositions. Assess how regularly and strongly you feel that you engage in these habits and dispositions.

The Habits of Resilient Educators		
Habit	**Description**	**On a 1–5 Scale, How Strong I Feel in This Habit**
Know Yourself	I know my values, personality type, skills and aptitudes, and social identities and how these impact my work as an educator. I use this understanding to make decisions and to deal with obstacles.	
Understand Emotions	I recognize and understand my emotions, and I have strategies to respond to them. I recognize and understand other people's emotions and have strategies to respond to them.	

(continued)

The Habits of Resilient Educators		On a 1–5 Scale, How Strong I Feel in This Habit
Habit	**Description**	
Tell Empowering Stories	I am aware of the way I interpret events, and I make choices about those interpretations.	
Build Community	I know how to build strong and healthy communities in which I feel nurtured. I have a community that supports me.	
Be Here Now	I use strategies to manage worry and regret and to keep me in the present moment so that I can make clearheaded decisions.	
Take Care of Yourself	I value and prioritize my own physical self-care and know how to give my body what it needs so that it will be healthy.	
Focus on the Bright Spots	I direct my awareness and attention to strengths, assets, and things that are going well. When I face challenges, my ability to identify bright spots helps me respond.	
Cultivate Compassion	I have compassion for myself and for others; I can activate my compassion for myself and for others when I want.	
Be a Learner	I am regularly in the mental stance of a learner, seeing challenges as opportunities for learning. I know how to guide and direct my own learning so that I can improve my skills or craft.	
Play and Create	I understand how playing, creating, and appreciating art helps me deal with challenges and stress, and I engage in these activities.	
Ride the Waves of Change	I have strategies to deal with change, and I use them to manage or lead change.	
Celebrate and Appreciate	I understand how gratitude and celebration contribute to my resilience, and I engage in appreciation practices.	

What, if anything, surprised you after doing this self-assessment?

Based on this self-assessment, what implications are there for how you engage with this book?

In which habit do you most want to make growth?

≈ ≈

Resilient educators demonstrate these 12 dispositions. Assess how strongly you feel these dispositions in yourself.

The Dispositions of Resilient Educators		
Disposition	Description	On a 1–5 Scale, How Strong I Feel in This Disposition
Purposefulness	I know what I'm doing and why I'm doing it. This sense of direction guides me in making decisions and facing challenges.	
Acceptance	I am not resigned, but I'm able to recognize what I can and can't change in a situation, and I can accept that.	
Optimism	I know that I can increase my optimism and maintain a positive outlook in the face of adversity, without denying the current reality. I take the long view, accept that life has ups and downs, and search for root causes of challenges.	

(continued)

The Dispositions of Resilient Educators		
Disposition	**Description**	**On a 1–5 Scale, How Strong I Feel in This Disposition**
Empathy	I can put myself in other people's shoes and feel their pain.	
Humor	I can use humor to lighten difficult moments, help me be in the present moment, explore difficult emotions, and connect with other people.	
Positive Self-Perception	I value myself. I have solid self-esteem. I am self-confident. I accept myself as I am. I'm not overly critical of myself, I don't strive for perfection, and I forgive myself for mistakes and take responsibility for my choices and actions.	
Empowerment	I believe I can influence my surroundings and the outcome of events, and this contributes to my feelings of confidence and competence.	
Perspective	I can see events from many different sides, and this insight helps me respond productively to situations and emotions.	
Curiosity	I am open to new ideas, I question my assumptions, I view obstacles and challenges as opportunities for growth, and I have many questions about many things.	
Courage	I am not afraid to try new things, to make mistakes, or to take a risk. I can identify my reserves of courage and draw on them when I need to.	
Perseverance	I am tenacious when dealing with challenges. I can put off short-term concerns and gratification for the sake of long-term success.	
Trust	I trust myself, and I trust something bigger outside myself: the passage of time, a process, or possibly something spiritual.	

What, if anything, surprised you after doing this self-assessment?

Based on this self-assessment, what implications are there for how you engage with this book?

In which disposition do you most want to make growth?

APPENDIX B

How to Make Lasting Change

The information in this appendix will help you implement all of the strategies in this book and in the *Onward Workbook*. You can use it as a reference and guide.

❧❧

Think about a behavioral change you want to make. What thoughts and feelings come up? I often experience a wave of self-doubt when I imagine a change I want to make. My mind goes to, *I won't be able to do that . . . I'll fail . . .* And I notice yearning: *If I could, it would be so good . . . I really want to . . .*

To make lasting change, you need to build new habits. Habits are behaviors that are so deeply ingrained that we no longer have to be intentional about them. Wouldn't it be a relief if we could get up and just meditate without all the mental drama and struggle to sit on the pillow? Or if we would prepare materials for a lesson the prior afternoon, rather than scrambling around that morning?

Most of us go about making behavioral changes all wrong. But there are people who have spent decades researching how to effectively make change. The conclusions they share aren't complicated, and their findings work. Here are 15 lessons about change that are based on research by psychologists, economists, neuroscientists, and sociologists. Use these to guide your behavior change and habit building.

1. Start at the end. Start with a vision of yourself having made the changes. If you want to be an organized teacher, imagine yourself in your classroom, doing the things an organized teacher does. Maybe you want to be more social with colleagues; visualize yourself talking with them in the hallways. Want to start running? Close your eyes and see yourself running on trails or a treadmill. Paint vivid pictures of whatever it is you want to do, and pay attention to how you feel in your visualizations. Sink into those feelings.

We've been taught to create goals, but many of us are not motivated by goals, or get quickly discouraged as we struggle to meet them. Visualize yourself engaging in the habits you want to build, and you'll be on the path.

2. Plan backwards. What might you need to do or learn in order to adopt a new habit? You might need to find a book, or someone who has the habit down whom you can observe. In this step, you narrow in on the specific behaviors you need to enact.

3. Make little tweaks. Very few people are successful at making major behavioral shifts in one massive swoop. Sustainable new habits are built slowly, over time. The authors of *Switch* urge us to *shrink the change* (Heath and Heath, 2010). If the habit you aspire to build seems monumental, you're likely to feel demoralized if you don't shrink the change. Make the change you're enacting something small enough that you're almost guaranteed to do it. That accomplishment will generate enough enthusiasm and confidence to make the next little tweak. In this way, you engineer your own success small step by small step.

For example: If you're trying to cut sugar out of your diet, start by cutting out sodas, don't drink sodas on the weekdays, or limit yourself to half the amount you currently drink. Shrink the change until it is something you can do without tremendous willpower. Once you've been engaging in that new behavior for a period of time, then implement another tweak. *Note:* This lesson applies to dealing with *behaviors* and not addictions or other dangerous or unhealthy situations.

Small is best. Set bite-size goals. When you accomplish them, you're going to feel happy and motivated to set another little goal. We've been brainwashed that we have to think big, that if we don't set high expectations for ourselves, we're not ambitious. This fallacy undermines our ability to make sustained behavioral changes. We set huge goals, feel quickly demoralized, and quit. Our brains love frequent rewards, so think small—ridiculously tiny.

4. Fire up emotions. Emotions motivate us to do things, and the most useful emotions when making behavior changes are positive emotions—hope, optimism, excitement, joy, and passion. Ignite these emotions by exploring your motivation to make change. Why do you want to change? How will your life be different? How will you feel? How would your behavioral change and new habit affect others?

5. Monitor your mindset. Do you *believe* you can change? Struggle and failure are part of learning. Hold a growth mindset; you'll stumble along the way, so don't get discouraged. At the same time, look for the indicators that you are changing. As you train your mind to acknowledge and focus on the changes, you'll gain confidence to move through rough patches and setbacks, and you'll gain insight into managing challenges.

6. Activate autonomy. Think *want to* or *get to* rather than *have to* or *should.* Tell yourself, *I* want to *take a walk,* rather than *I* should *take a walk;* or *I* want to *grade these essays and see how my students are doing,* rather than *I* have to *read 50 papers.* Create "want-to" goals rather than "have-to" goals, which are usually externally imposed or come from your own sense of obligation or desire to avoid shame. You can choose to eat more healthfully because of fear, shame, or anxiety about your appearance, or you can choose to eat healthfully because you *want to* feel good and enjoy life more.

Have-to motivation can enable you to make positive changes for a while, but willpower and determination have their limits. Have-to motivation can intensify temptation because it makes you feel deprived, which undermines your self-control. Think *I want to turn off the TV and go to sleep early because when I get up at 5:30, I will be rested.*

7. Identify choice points. By identifying a "choice point," you can prime yourself to form good habits (Thaler and Sunstein, 2009). If you want a peaceful wake-up routine, but as soon as you open your eyes, you reach for your phone and read email, then the choice point is to leave your phone in another room. New habits are built around dozens of miniscule choice points that we can set up in our daily life to send us in the direction we want to go. By identifying those choice points, you can create the conditions that will help you be successful.

A choice point establishes an environment that encourages and supports the changes you want to make. If you want to exercise first thing in the morning, leave your shoes and exercise clothes within arm's reach of your bed. If you know that the Internet sucks you in every time you work on lesson plans, turn your Wi-Fi off. By identifying choice points, you can also create action triggers such as checklists, routines, and other specific, visible, and intentionally created triggers that lead to new behaviors. Identifying choice points helps us make change and new habits inevitable.

8. Build a routine. When does this new behavior you want to undertake happen? Where does it happen? How does it start? How does it end? Our brains love repetition and routine. You will get much more out of the habit—whether it's meditating or journaling or painting—and the habit will be much easier to sustain, if you engage in it at the same time, in the same place, every day.

9. Make it easy. The easier, the better. Shawn Achor, author of *The Happiness Advantage* (2010), suggests using a "20 second rule." If you can make the positive habit you're trying to build 3 to 20 seconds easier to start, your likelihood of doing it rises dramatically. Trying to make one positive phone call home every afternoon to a kid's parent? Have the student punch his or her parent's number into your phone so that all you have to do is dial.

10. Piggyback behaviors. Build new behaviors by tacking them on to an existing habit (Thaler and Sunstein, 2009). Want to start taking vitamins every day? Identify the already existing habit, such as eating breakfast, and attach that vitamin taking to it. As your brain learns to associate the two behaviors, the new behavior becomes unconsciously integrated. Think of a new habit as an add-on to something you already do routinely.

11. Make a precommitment. Anticipate obstacles and prepare for them with "if-then" strategies. If you suspect you won't want to walk after school because you'll have too much grading to do, then in the morning as you're packing for the day, take your walking shoes and leave them somewhere visible. Remind yourself that if you walk, your thinking will be clearer and you'll have more energy to grade. Say to yourself, *If I take a walk, then I'll feel much better all evening*. When you anticipate obstacles, and problem-solve them before they arise, you create mental pathways with better options. When you encounter one of those obstacles, your mind already has a plan.

12. Gather your people. Surround yourself with those who are doing what you want to do. Often the people you associate with determine the type of person you become. To improve your health, hang out with other healthy people (and perhaps exercise and eat with them). You need backup, role models, cheerleaders, and friends on this journey. Rally your support systems and make a literal precommitment with someone else. If you promise a colleague that you'll walk after school, that commitment will make you much more likely to follow through.

13. Stop thinking and act. An abundance of research suggests that the most efficient way to change our minds is to change our behaviors. If you want to feel happier in the classroom and more connected to your students, smile at your kids as they arrive. Say "Good morning, it's nice to see you." Your mind and emotions are likely to follow along behind your behavior change.

14. Reward yourself. Rewards can be tricky motivators over the long run, but in the early stages of cementing a habit, they can be a powerful reinforcer. In an interview with Eric Barker (2015), Charles Duhigg, author of *The Power of Habit*, explains: "The research shows that every habit has three components. There's the cue, which is a trigger for an automatic behavior to start. Then, a routine, which is the behavior itself. Finally, a reward. The reward is really important because that's how your brain essentially learns to latch onto a particular pattern and make it automatic . . . What matters is that if you want to make a behavior into a habit, you need to give yourself something you enjoy as soon as that behavior is done." Rewarding yourself doesn't have to mean eating a big chocolate chip cookie. It can be taking the satisfaction of having a clean desk or empty inbox, or the reward of a minty fresh cleanliness in your mouth after you brush your teeth.

15. Soak in the satisfaction. As you begin building new habits, you must pause after implementing one of the behaviors you're aspiring to build and then bask in the afterglow. Acknowledge yourself for your new behaviors, for surmounting obstacles, and for navigating a rigid mindset. Register the rewards in that moment and notice your positive emotions. Recognize that you're making progress toward your vision.

❧❧

These 15 lessons about habits offer a map to change behaviors. You can use these to change your own behaviors and build new habits, as well as to guide your students to change theirs. In the workbook, you'll find a template to help you create your own Change Plan.

Implications for Leaders

- Your business as a leader is to lead change. Which of these 15 lessons do you use when trying to get staff on board with a new initiative or when introducing a new goal? Which do you need to incorporate?
- Change is hard, and educators experience a lot of change. It's one of the external factors that can most deplete resilience. If you are committed to retaining staff and boosting their ability to manage stress, then use this research on creating new behaviors to reflect on how you've led change and what you could do differently.

APPENDIX C

The Core Emotions

Core Emotion	Fear	Anger	Sadness	Shame
Common Labels for This Emotion	Agitated	Aggravated	Alienated	Besmirched
	Alarmed	Agitated	Anguished	Chagrined
	Anxious	Annoyed	Bored	Contemptuous
	Apprehensive	Antagonized	Crushed	(of self)
	Concerned	Bitter	Defeated	Contrite
	Desperate	Contemptuous	Dejected	Culpable
	Dismayed	(other than for	Depressed	Debased
	Dread	self)	Despairing	Degraded
	Fearful	Contentious	Despondent	Disapproving
	Frightened	Contrary	Disappointed	Disdainful
	Horrified	Cranky	Discouraged	Disgraced
	Hysterical	Cruel	Disheartened	Disgusted
	Impatient	Destructive	Dismayed	(at self)
	Jumpy	Displeased	Dispirited	Dishonored
	Nervous	Enraged	Displeased	Disreputable
	Panicked	Exasperated	Distraught	Embarrassed
	Scared	Explosive	Down	Guilty
	Shocked	Frustrated	Dreary	Hateful
	Shy	Furious	Forlorn	Humbled
	Tense	Hateful	Gloomy	Humiliated
	Terrified	Hostile	Grief-stricken	Improper
	Timid	Impatient	Hopeless	Infamous
	Uncertain	Indignant	Hurt	Invalidated
	Uneasy	Insulated	Insecure	Mortified
	Worried	Irate	Isolated	Regretful
		Irritable	Lonely	Remorseful
		Irritated	Melancholic	Repentant
		Mad	Miserable	Reproachful
		Mean	Mopey	Rueful
		Outraged	Morose	Scandalized
		Resentful	Neglected	Scornful
		Scornful	Oppressed	Sinful
		Spiteful	Pessimistic	Stigmatized
		Urgent	Pitiful	
		Vengeful	Rejected	
			Somber	
			Sorrowful	
			Tragic	
			Unhappy	

Core Emotion	Jealousy	Disgust	Happiness	Love
Common Labels for This Emotion	Competitive	Appalled	Agreeable	Acceptance
	Covetous	Dislike	Amused	Admiration
	Deprived	Grossed out	Blissful	Adoring
	Distrustful	Insulted	Bubbly	Affectionate
	Envious	Intolerant	Cheerful	Allegiance
	Greedy	Nauseated	Content	Attached
	Grudging	Offended	Delighted	Attraction
	Jealous	Put off	Eager	Belonging
	Overprotective	Repelled	Ease	Caring
	Petty	Repulsed	Elated	Compassionate
	Possessive	Revolted	Engaged	Connected
	Resentful	Revulsion	Enjoyment	Dependent
	Rivalrous	Shocked	Enthusiastic	Desire
		Sickened	Euphoric	Devoted
		Turned off	Excited	Empathic
			Exhilarated	Faithful
			Flow	Friendship
			Glad	Interested
			Gleeful	Kind
			Glowing	Liking
			Gratified	Passionate
			Harmonious	Protective
			Hopeful	Respectful
			Interested	Sympathetic
			Joyful	Tender
			Jubilant	Trusting
			Lighthearted	Vulnerable
			Meaningful	Warm
			Merry	
			Optimistic	
			Peaceful	
			Pleasure	
			Pride	
			Proud	
			Relieved	
			Satisfied	
			Thrilled	
			Triumphant	

Source: Adapted from Erin Olivo, *Wise Mind Living* (Louisville, CO: Sounds True, 2014).

APPENDIX D

Depression and Anxiety Scales

Self-Rating Depression Scale

Read each statement and decide how much the statement describes how you have been feeling **during the past week.** Circle the appropriate number for each statement.

	None or a little of the time	Some of the time	Good part of the time	Most or all of the time
I was bothered by things that usually don't bother me.	0	1	2	3
I did not feel like eating; my appetite was poor.	0	1	2	3
I felt that I couldn't shake off the blues, even with help from friends or family.	0	1	2	3
I felt that I was just as good as other people.	3	2	1	0

(continued)

	None or a little of the time	Some of the time	Good part of the time	Most or all of the time
I had trouble keeping my mind on what I was doing.	0	1	2	3
I felt depressed.	0	1	2	3
I felt that everything I did was an effort.	0	1	2	3
I felt hopeful about the future.	3	2	1	0
I thought my life had been a failure.	0	1	2	3
I felt fearful.	0	1	2	3
My sleep was restless.	0	1	2	3
I was happy.	3	2	1	0
I talked less than usual.	0	1	2	3
I felt lonely.	0	1	2	3
People were unfriendly.	0	1	2	3
I enjoyed life.	3	2	1	0
I had crying spells.	0	1	2	3
I felt sad.	0	1	2	3
I felt as though people disliked me.	0	1	2	3
I could not get going.	0	1	2	3

Source: This depression questionnaire is adapted from the Center for Epidemiologic Studies Depression Scale, or CES-D (Radloff, 1977). It is commonly used with the general public.

Add up all of your scores. Total: _____

The lowest score you can get is 0; the highest is 60. Psychologists use the cutoff score of 16 to differentiate depressed persons from nondepressed ones. If your score is 16 or higher, you would be classified as depressed. Depression can range from mild (a score of 16–20) to moderate (a score of 21–25) to severe (a score of 26–60). This is not a diagnostic tool. Please speak with a mental health expert about any questions that arise from using this screening tool.

Depression scales are acutely sensitive to your mood and your general mental state, so you could obtain different depression scores at different times, even as close as two weeks apart.

If you scored above 16, I encourage you to seek out the expertise of a licensed counselor, a clinical psychologist, or a psychiatrist with whom you can discuss options for treatment. Depression is an illness, and there are many ways it can be treated.

Self-Rating Anxiety Scale

Read each statement and decide how much the statement describes how you have been feeling **during the past week**. Circle the appropriate number for each statement.

	None or a little of the time	Some of the time	Good part of the time	Most or all of the time
I feel afraid for no reason at all.	0	1	2	3
I feel more nervous and anxious than usual.	0	1	2	3
I get upset easily or feel panicky.	0	1	2	3
I feel as though I'm falling apart or going to pieces.	0	1	2	3
I feel that everything is all right and nothing bad will happen.	3	2	1	0
My arms and legs shake and tremble.	0	1	2	3
I am bothered by headaches and neck and back pains.	0	1	2	3
I feel weak and get tired easily.	0	1	2	3
I feel calm and can sit still easily.	3	2	1	0
I can feel my heart beating fast.	0	1	2	3
I am bothered by dizzy spells.	0	1	2	3
I have fainting spells or feel faint.	0	1	2	3
I can breathe in and out easily.	3	2	1	0

(continued)

	None or a little of the time	Some of the time	Good part of the time	Most or all of the time
I get feelings of numbness and tingling in my fingers and toes.	0	1	2	3
I am bothered by stomachaches and indigestion.	0	1	2	3
I have to empty my bladder often.	0	1	2	3
My hands are usually warm and dry.	3	2	1	0
My face gets hot and blushes.	0	1	2	3
I fall asleep easily and get a good night's rest.	3	2	1	0
I have nightmares.	0	1	2	3

Source: This questionnaire is adapted from the "Zung Instrument for Anxiety," published by the American Psychiatric Association (1971).

Add up all of your scores. Total: _____

A score of 16 and over suggests the need for further assessment of anxiety. This is not a diagnostic tool. Please speak with a mental health expert about any questions that arise from using this screening tool.

This book, and the workbook, will help you cultivate resilience—not address depression or anxiety. If you struggle with depression or anxiety, please get help.

Common Problematic Core Beliefs

Problematic Core Belief About Self	Description	Sounds Like . . .
Worthlessness	• A general sense that one is inferior, inherently flawed, or incompetent. • Most common. • Drives many problematic behaviors. • Often behind depression.	I'm worthless. I'm not good enough. I can't get anything right. I'm stupid. I'm useless. I'm a failure. I'm always wrong. There's something wrong with me. Other people are better than me.
Unlovability	• Assumes that others don't understand them and won't accept or approve of them. • Often reflects an overemphasis on status, beauty, money, and achievement.	I'm always left out. I'm not wanted. I'm unwelcome. I'm alone. I don't fit in anywhere. I'm not interesting. I'm going to be rejected. It's important to be admired. I'm only worth something if people like me.

(continued)

Problematic Core Belief About Self	Description	Sounds Like . . .
Lack of Trust	• Typically rooted in abandonment. • Assumes that anyone to whom an emotional attachment is formed will be lost. • Can overlap with core belief about being unlovable.	People are untrustworthy. I can't trust or rely on another person. People I love will leave me. I will be abandoned if I love someone. I'm not important. People will let me down.
Helplessness	• Results in people assuming they lack control and cannot handle anything effectively or independently. • Making changes is very difficult. • A sense of powerlessness can cause people to try to overcontrol their environment or completely give up control. • Can see themselves as victims.	I can't handle this. I can't do it. I'm powerless. I'm trapped. I'm needy. I can't change. Other people are trying to control my life. Bad things happen all the time. The world is a dangerous place. People will hurt me if I let them.
Superiority	• Leads to a sense of entitlement, which can lead to rule breaking, resentment of others' success, and unreasonable demands. • May come from compensating for feeling defective or socially undesirable.	If people don't respect me, I can't stand it. I deserve a lot of praise and attention. If I don't excel, then I'm inferior and worthless. If I don't excel, I'll just end up ordinary. I'm a very special person, and others should treat me that way. I don't have to be bound by the rules that apply to other people.

Problematic Core Belief About Self	Description	Sounds Like . . .
		People should satisfy my needs. People have no right to criticize me. Others don't deserve the good things they get. People don't understand me, or get me, because I am special/brilliant/etc.
Self-Sacrificingness	• May produce the kind of caretaking behavior that puts the needs of others ahead of their own. • May feel guilty and compensate by prioritizing the needs of others, believing they are responsible for the happiness of others. • Excessive apologizing is an indicator.	My needs are not important. It's not okay to ask for help. I have to do everything myself. If I don't do it, no one will. If I care enough, I can fix him/her/this. I shouldn't spend time taking care of myself. When I see others who need help, I have to help them. I'm only worthwhile if I'm helping other people. I have to make people happy.
Perfectionism	• Can look like conscientiousness and a strong work ethic, but they are taken too far. • Sense of self-worth is overly tied to external praise and accomplishments. • A tendency to think in black-and-white terms, hold rigid standards, and quickly discount positives.	I have to do everything perfectly. If I make a mistake, it means I'm careless/a failure/etc. People who make mistakes should have consequences. People should follow the rules or be punished. I have extremely high standards for myself and others.

(continued)

Problematic Core Belief About Self	Description	Sounds Like . . .
	• Perfectionists believe they must strive to act and be at their best all the time in order to prove they are capable, worthy, and loveable.	
Negativity	• Pessimists. • The glass is always half empty—whether looking at the world, themselves, or others.	Life inherently sucks. Life is meaningless. Nothing ever works out for me. The world is falling apart. Nothing ever gets better. I'm not a pessimist; I'm a realist.

APPENDIX F

Resources for Further Learning

The following is not intended to be an extensive list, but rather a selection of places that you might begin to continue your learning. Please consider buying books from a local independent bookstore. They can usually order anything you want. Local bookstores are essential resources for resilience! Spend a couple hours in one, get to know the sellers, and you'll find out why—if you haven't already made this discovery.

General

Books

Goldstein, Dana. *The Teacher Wars: A History of America's Most Embattled Profession*. New York, NY: Doubleday, 2014.

> Whether you're a new or veteran teacher, this fascinating and thorough book provides a rich historical context for those of us in the field of education.

Intrator, Sam, and Megan Scribner. *Teaching with Fire: Poetry That Sustains the Courage to Teach*. San Francisco, CA: Jossey-Bass, 2003.

————————. *Leading from Within: Poetry That Sustains the Courage to Lead*. San Francisco, CA: Jossey-Bass, 2007.

————————. *Teaching with Heart: Poetry That Speaks to the Courage to Teach*. San Francisco, CA: Jossey-Bass, 2014.

These three books have the best collection of poems that speak to every habit and disposition in *Onward*. They're essential additional resources on the journey to resilience.

Other

- The *On Being* podcast (www.onbeing.org), with Krista Tippet, is an exploration of the "big questions of meaning." This is my favorite podcast, and I always discover new ideas, people, and books through it, as well as a lot of inspiration and hope.
- *Greater Good Magazine* (https://greatergood.berkeley.edu/) is an invaluable resource for information, news, activities, and so much more.

Chapter 1: Know Yourself

Books

Block, Peter. *The Answer to How Is Yes.* San Francisco, CA: Berrett-Koehler, 2002.

Brown, Brené. *Daring Greatly.* New York, NY: Portfolio, 2014.

Buckingham, Marcus, and Donald Clifton. *Now, Discover Your Strengths.* New York, NY: Free Press, 2001.

Cain, Susan. *Quiet.* New York, NY: Random House, 2013.

McKee, Annie, Richard Boyatzis, and Frances Johnston. *Becoming a Resonant Leader: Develop Your Emotional Intelligence, Renew Your Relationships, Sustain Your Effectiveness.* Cambridge, MA: Harvard Business Review, 2008.

Seligman, Martin. *Authentic Happiness.* New York, NY: Atria, 2002.

Other

- CliftonStrengths: www.gallupstrengthscenter.com/home/en-us/strengthsfinder
- Free Myers-Briggs test: www.16personalities.com
- Free Myers-Briggs test: www.humanmetrics.com
- "The Holstee Manifesto." Google it. Read it. Post it somewhere that you can see every day.

Chapter 2: Understand Emotions

Books

Bradberry, Travis, and Jean Greaves. *Emotional Intelligence 2.0.* San Diego, CA: TalentSmart, 2009.

Brown, Brené. *The Gifts of Imperfection.* Center City, MN: Hazelden, 2010.

Foster, Rick, and Greg Hicks. *How We Choose to Be Happy.* New York, NY: Perigree, 2004.

Goleman, Daniel, Richard Boyatzis, and Annie McKee. *Primal Leadership.* Boston, MA: Harvard University Press, 2002.

Lyubomirsky, Sonja. *The How of Happiness.* New York, NY: Penguin, 2007.

_____. *The Myths of Happiness: What Should Make You Happy, but Doesn't, What Shouldn't Make You Happy, but Does.* New York, NY: Penguin, 2013.

Olivo, Erin. *Wise Mind Living.* Boulder, CO: Sounds True, 2014.

Rosenberg, Marshall. *Nonviolent Communication.* Encinitas, CA: PuddleDancer Press, 2003.

Seligman, Martin. *Flourish: A Visionary New Understanding of Happiness and Well-Being.* New York, NY: Simon & Schuster, 2012.

Other

- Dr. Martin Seligman's website: www.authentichappiness.sas.upenn.edu, has a number of free quizzes you can take to build self-awareness.
- Here's an emotional intelligence quiz that I really like: greatergood.berkeley.edu/quizzes/take_quiz/ei_quiz
- The Yale Center for Emotional Intelligence has created a very useful tool called RULER: http://ei.yale.edu/ruler/ RULER is an acronym that stands for **r**ecognition, **u**nderstanding, **l**abeling, **e**xpressing, and **r**egulating emotions. It is a research-based approach for integrating social and emotional learning in schools.

TED Talks

- Brené Brown, "The Power of Vulnerability"
- Neil Hughes, "Walking on Custard: How Physics Helps Anxious Humans"
- Alison Ledgerwood, "Getting Stuck in the Negatives (and How to Get Unstuck)"
- Kelly McGonigal, "How to Make Stress Your Friend"
- Andrew Solomon, "Depression, the Secret We Share"
- Guy Winch, "How to Practice Emotional First Aid"

Chapter 3: Tell Empowering Stories

Books

Frankl, Viktor. *Man's Search for Meaning.* Boston, MA: Beacon Press, 2006.

Haidt, Jonathan. *The Happiness Hypothesis: Finding Modern Truth in Ancient Wisdom.* New York, NY: Basic Books, 2006.

Hutchens, David. *Circle of the 9 Muses: A Storytelling Field Guide for Innovators and Meaning Makers.* Hoboken, NJ: Wiley, 2015.

Kegan, Robert, and Lisa Lahey. *Immunity to Change.* Cambridge, MA: Harvard Business Press, 2009.

Seligman, Martin. *Learned Optimism.* New York, NY: Vintage Books, 2006.

Solnit, Rebecca. *Hope in the Dark* (2nd ed.). Chicago, IL: Haymarket Books, 2016.

TED Talk

- Chimamanda Ngozi Adichie, "The Danger of a Single Story"

Chapter 4: Build Community

Books

Abrams, Jennifer. *Having Hard Conversations.* Thousand Oaks, CA: Corwin. 2009.

Abrams, Jennifer, and Valerie A. von Frank. *The Multigenerational Workplace.* Thousand Oaks, CA: Corwin. 2014.

Aguilar, Elena. *The Art of Coaching Teams.* San Francisco, CA: Jossey-Bass. 2016.

Coates, Ta-Nehesi. *Between the World and Me.* New York, NY: Spiegel & Grau, 2015.

Delpit, Lisa. *The Skin That We Speak: Thoughts on Language and Culture in the Classroom.* New York, NY: New Press, 2002.

DiAngelo, Robin. *What Does It Mean to Be White? Developing White Racial Literacy* (rev. ed.). New York, NY: Peter Lang, 2016.

Fleischman, Paul. *Seedfolks.* New York, NY: Harper Trophy, 2004.

A beautifully written short story that's incredibly inspiring.

Kegan, Robert, and Lisa Lahey. *How the Way We Talk Can Change the Way We Work: Seven Languages for Transformation.* San Francisco, CA: Jossey-Bass, 2001.

Schein, Edgar. *Humble Inquiry: The Gentle Art of Asking Instead of Telling.* San Francisco, CA: Berrett-Koehler, 2013.

Scott, Susan. *Fierce Conversations.* New York, NY: Berkley, 2002.

Showkeir, Jamie, and Maren Showkeir. *Authentic Conversations.* San Francisco, CA: Berrett-Koehler, 2008.

Tatum, Beverly D. *"Why Are All the Black Kids Sitting Together in the Cafeteria?" and Other Conversations About Race* (updated ed.). New York, NY: Basic Books, 2017.

Wheatley, Margaret. *Turning to One Another: Simple Conversations to Restore Hope to the Future.* San Francisco, CA: Berrett-Koehler, 2009.

Wise, Tim. *White Like Me: Reflections on Race from a Privileged Son.* Berkeley, CA: Soft Skull Press, 2008.

Chapter 5: Be Here Now

Books

Baraz, James. *Awakening Joy: Ten Steps to Happiness.* Berkeley, CA: Parallax Press, 2012.

Boorstein, Sylvia. *It's Easier Than You Think: The Buddhist Way to Happiness.* New York, NY: HarperCollins, 1997.

Dalai Lama, Desmond Tutu, and Douglas Abrams. *The Book of Joy.* New York, NY: Penguin Books, 2016.

Gunaratana, B. H. *Mindfulness in Plain English.* Somerville, MA: Wisdom Publications, 2002.

Hanson, Rick. *Hardwiring Happiness: The New Brain Science of Contentment, Calm, and Confidence.* New York, NY: Random House, 2013.

Hanson, Rick, and Richard Mendius. *Buddha's Brain: The Practical Neuroscience of Happiness, Love, and Wisdom.* Oakland, CA: New Harbinger, 2009.

Kornfield, Jack. *No Time Like the Present.* New York, NY: Atria Books, 2017.

Nhat Hanh, Thich. *How to Eat.* Berkeley, CA: Parallax Press, 2014.

_____. *How to Walk.* Berkeley, CA: Parallax Press, 2015.

_____. *Peace Is Every Step.* New York, NY: Bantam Books, 1992.

hooks, bell. *Teaching to Transgress: Education as the Practice of Freedom.* New York, NY: Routledge, 1994.

Rankine, Claudia. *Citizen.* Minneapolis, MN: Graywolf Press, 2014.

Srinivasan, Meena. *Teach, Breathe, Learn.* Berkeley, CA: Parallax Press, 2014.

Steele, Claude. *Whistling Vivaldi and Other Clues to How Stereotypes Affect Us.* New York, NY: Norton, 2010.

Tolle, Eckhart. *The Power of Now.* Novato, CA: New World Library, 2004.

Articles

Devine, P. "Long-Term Reduction in Implicit Race Bias: A Prejudice Habit-Breaking Intervention." *Journal of Experimental Social Psychology,* 2012, *48*(6), 1267–1278.

Djikic M., E. J. Langer, and S. F. Stapleton. "Reducing Stereotypes Through Mindfulness: Effects on Automatic Stereotype-Activated Behavior." *Journal of Adult Development,* 2008, *15,* 106–111.

Hafenbrack, A. C., Z. Kinias, and S. G. Barsade. "Debiasing the Mind Through Meditation: Mindfulness and the Sunk-Cost Bias." *Psychological Science,* 2014, *25,* 369–376.

Kang Y., J. R. Gray, and J. F. Dovidio. "The Nondiscriminating Heart: Lovingkindness Meditation Training Decreases Implicit Intergroup Bias." *Journal of Experimental Psychology: General,* 2014, *143,* 1306–1313.

Richeson J. A., and N. Ambady. Effects of Situational Power on Automatic Racial Prejudice. *Journal of Experimental Social Psychology,* 2003, *39,* 177–183.

Audio Recordings

- Rick Hanson, *Meditations for Happiness: Rewire Your Brain for Lasting Contentment and Peace*
- Rick Hanson and Richard Mendius, *Meditations to Change Your Brain: Rewire Your Neural Pathways to Transform Your Life*

Other

- Mindful Schools (www.mindfulschools.org) is a fantastic resource for educators that offers online and in-person courses.
- A wealth of podcasts on mindfulness, meditation, compassion, and more is available at www.beherenownetwork.com
- The Heart Wisdom podcast, with Jack Kornfield, is my favorite podcast on Buddhist philosophy.
- Sounds True, www.soundstrue.com, is a multimedia publishing company that has podcasts, books, audiobooks, and much more.

Mindfulness Apps

- **Insight Timer** is one of the most popular free meditation apps out there. It features more than 4,000 guided meditations—on such topics as self-compassion, nature, and stress—from over 1,000 teachers, plus talks and podcasts. If you don't want to listen to a meditation, you can always set a timer and meditate to intermittent bells or calming ambient noise.
- With the **Aura** meditation app, every day you get a new, personalized, three-minute meditation. To personalize the experience, Aura initially asks about your age and how stressed, optimistic, and interested in mindfulness you are. The daily meditation that appears also depends on your mood. On Aura, you can also listen to relaxing sounds or try its Mindful Breather feature, where you synchronize your breath to an animated circle that gently expands and contracts.
- **Headspace** is a very popular app that is free to download, but to access all the lessons, you'll need to pay for a subscription. The guided meditations are based on Buddhist mindfulness, but are completely secular. Lots of people love this app. If you want guided meditations, this is a good option.

Chapter 6: Take Care of Yourself

Books

Ackerman, J. *Sex Sleep Eat Drink Dream: A Day in the Life of Your Body.* New York, NY: Mariner Books, 2008.

Blackburn, Elizabeth and Elissa Epel. *The Telomere Effect: A Revolutionary Approach to Living Younger, Healthier, Longer.* New York, NY: Grand Central Productions, 2017.

Buettner, Dan. *The Blue Zones of Happiness: Lessons from the World's Happiest People.* Washington, DC: National Geographic, 2017.

Medina, John. *Brain Rules: Twelve Principles for Surviving and Thriving at Work, Home, and School* (2nd ed.). Seattle, WA: Pear Press, 2014.

Pick, Marcelle. *Is It Me or My Adrenals?* New York, NY: Hay House, 2013.

Roach, Mary. *Gulp.* New York, NY: Norton, 2013.

Ross, Julia. *The Diet Cure.* New York, NY: Penguin, 2012.

Movies

- *Cooked,* Netflix documentary with Michael Pollan
- *Chef's Table,* Netflix documentary series
- *Supersize Me*

Chapter 7: Focus on the Bright Spots

Books

Baumeister, R. *Willpower: Rediscovering the Greatest Human Strength.* New York, NY: Penguin, 2012.

Cooperrider, David L., and Diana Whitney. *Appreciative Inquiry: A Positive Revolution in Change.* San Francisco, CA: Berrett-Koehler, 2005.

Gottman, John. *The Seven Principles for Making Marriage Work.* New York, NY: Harmony Books, 2015.

> Gottman's research is applicable to making all kinds of relationships better—not just marriages.

Hammond, Sue A. *The Thin Book of Appreciative Inquiry.* Bend, OR: Thin Book, 1998.

Whitney, Diana, and Amananda Trosten-Bloom. *The Power of Appreciative Inquiry: A Practical Guide to Positive Change.* San Francisco, CA: Berrett-Koehler, 2010.

Websites

- For resources on appreciative inquiry: https://appreciativeinquiry.champlain.edu/
- A site that'll just make you feel good: www.1000awesomethings.com

Chapter 8: Cultivate Compassion

Books

Jinpa, Thupten. *A Fearless Heart: How the Courage to Be Compassionate Can Transform Our Lives.* New York, NY: Avery, 2015.

Manson, Mark. *The Subtle Art of Not Giving a F*ck.* New York, NY: HarperOne, 2016.

> If you care too much about what others think and you need compassion for yourself, then you'll find this an amusing read.

Neff, Kristin. *Self-Compassion: The Proven Power of Being Kind to Yourself*. New York, NY: HarperCollins, 2011.

This is a more serious reflection on self-compassion.

Ricard, Matthieu. *Altruism: The Power of Compassion to Change Yourself and the World*. New York, NY: Little, Brown and Company, 2015.

Salzberg, Sharon. *Lovingkindness: The Revolutionary Art of Happiness*. Boulder, CO: Shambhala Press, 1995.

———. *Real Happiness at Work: Meditations for Accomplishment, Achievement, and Peace*. New York, NY: Workman, 2013.

Sutton, Robert. *The Asshole Survival Guide: How to Deal with People Who Treat You Like Dirt*. Boston, MA: Houghton Mifflin Harcourt, 2017.

If you have a hard time drawing boundaries with others, and if you work with difficult people, this is an insightful, wise, and useful resource.

Videos

- Amma and Dr. James Doty, "Conversations on Compassion with Amma"
- Paul Ekman, "The Roots of Empathy and Compassion"
- Thupten Jinpa, "The Science of Compassion: Origins, Measures, and Interventions"
- Dacher Keltner, "The Evolutionary Roots of Compassion"
- Daniel Siegel, "Interpersonal Neurobiology: Why Compassion Is Necessary for Humanity"

Chapter 9: Be a Learner

Books

Heyck-Merlin, Maia. *The Together Teacher*. San Francisco, CA: Jossey-Bass, 2012.

———. *The Together Leader*. San Francisco, CA: Jossey-Bass, 2016.

Holmes, Jamie. *Nonsense: The Power of Not Knowing*. New York, NY: Crown, 2015.

Hubbard, Ruth, and Brenda Power. *The Art of Classroom Inquiry: A Handbook for Teacher Researchers*. Portsmouth, NH: Heinemann, 2003.

Leslie, Ian. *Curious: The Desire to Know and Why Your Future Depends on It*. New York, NY: Basic Books, 2014.

McGonigal, Jane. *Super Better: A Revolutionary Approach to Getting Stronger, Happier, Braver, and More Resilient*. London, England: HarperCollins, 2015.

It's also worth checking out McGonigal's 2010 TED Talk, "Gaming Can Make a Better World."

Newport, Cal. *Deep Work*. New York, NY: Grand Central Publishing, 2016.

Rock, David. *Your Brain at Work: Strategies for Overcoming Distraction, Regaining Focus, and Working Smarter All Day Long*. New York, NY: HarperCollins, 2009.

Chapter 10: Play and Create

Books

Barry, Lynda. *What Is*. Montreal, Canada: Drawn and Quarterly, 2008.

———————. *Syllabus*. Montreal, Canada: Drawn and Quarterly, 2014.

Brown, Brené. *Braving the Wilderness*. New York, NY: Random House, 2017.

Brown, Stuart. *Play: How It Shapes the Brain, Opens the Imagination, and Invigorates the Soul*. New York, NY: Penguin, 2009.

Cameron, Julia. *The Artist's Way* (25th anniv. ed.). New York, NY: Penguin Random House, 2016.

> See also *The Artist's Way Workbook*. New York, NY: Penguin, 2006.

De Botton, Alain, and John Armstrong. *Art as Therapy*. New York, NY: Phaidon, 2013.

Edwards, Betty. *Drawing on the Right Side of the Brain* (4th ed.). New York, NY: Penguin, 2012.

Gilbert, Elizabeth. *Big Magic: Creative Living Beyond Fear*. New York, NY: Penguin Random House, 2016.

Kaufman, Scott, and Carolyn Gregoire. *Wired to Create: Unraveling the Mysteries of the Creative Mind*. New York, NY: Perigee, 2015.

Kleon, Austin. *Steal Like an Artist*. New York, NY: Workman, 2012.

Krahula, Beckah. *One Zentangle a Day: A 6-Week Course in Creative Drawing for Relaxation, Inspiration, and Fun*. Beverly, MA: Quarry Books, 2012.

Palmer, Parker. *The Courage to Teach* (20th anniv. ed.). San Francisco, CA: Jossey-Bass, 2017.

Movies

- *Cave of Dreams,* about prehistoric art
- "Power of Art—Picasso's Guernica": https://www.youtube.com/watch?v=tI4OABAP4Is
- *Waste Land,* about garbage pickers in Brazil
- *A Strong, Clear Vision,* about Maya Lin making the Vietnam Memorial

Other

- Sketchbook Skool (www.sketchbookskool.com) has really fun, engaging online courses; so does Skillshare (www.skillshare.com).
- Look for Neil Gaiman's 2012 commencement speech at Philadelphia's University of the Arts, "Make Good Art," on YouTube: https://youtu.be/plWexCID-kA
- "The Art of Emotional Healing" (https://www.expressiveartworkshops.com/). This site offers an extensive list of therapeutic and reflective art-related courses.

Chapter 11: Riding the Waves of Change

Books

Chödrön, Pema. *Comfortable with Uncertainty.* Boulder, CO: Shambhala Publications, 2002.
_____. *When Things Fall Apart* (20th anniv. ed.). Boulder, CO: Shambhala Publications, 2016.

Day, Laura. *Practical Intuition.* New York, NY: Broadway, 1996.

Duhigg, Charles. *The Power of Habit.* New York, NY: Random House, 2012.

Heath, Chip, and Dan Heath. *Switch: How to Change Things When Change Is Hard.* New York, NY: Broadway Books, 2010.

Horton, Myles, and Paulo Freire. In Brenda Bell, John Gaenta, and John Peters (Eds.), *We Make the Road by Walking: Conversations on Education and Social Change.* Philadelphia, PA: Temple University Press, 1990.

Kegan, Robert, and Lisa Lahey. *Immunity to Change.* Cambridge, MA: Harvard Business Press, 2009.

McGonigal, Kelly. *The Willpower Instinct: How Self-Control Works, Why It Matters, and What You Can Do to Get More of It.* New York, NY: Penguin Books, 2013.

Ryan, M. J. *How to Survive Change You Didn't Ask For.* San Francisco, CA: Red Wheel, 2009.

Sinek, Simon. *Start with Why: How Great Leaders Inspire Everyone to Take Action.* New York, NY: Penguin, 2011.

Thaler, Richard, and Cass Sunstein. *Nudge: Improving Decisions About Health, Wealth and Happiness.* New York, NY: Penguin, 2009.

Wheatley, Margaret. *Perseverance.* San Francisco, CA: Berrett-Koehler, 2010.

Wood, Thomas, and Ethan Porter. "The Elusive Backfire Effect: Mass Attitudes' Steadfast Actual Adherence," August 5, 2016. Retrieved from https://ssrn.com/abstract=2819073

Chapter 12: Celebrate and Appreciate

Books

Emmons, Robert. *Thanks! How the New Science of Gratitude Can Make You Happier.* Boston, MA: Houghton Mifflin Harcourt, 2007.

Kaplan, Janice. *The Gratitude Diaries: How a Year Looking on the Bright Side Can Transform Your Life.* New York, NY: Dutton, 2017.

Loeb, Paul Rogat. *The Impossible Will Take a Little While.* New York, NY: Basic Books, 2004.

Pasricha, Neil. *The Book of Awesome.* New York, NY: Putnam, 2011.

Robbins, Mike. *Focus on the Good Stuff: The Power of Appreciation.* San Francisco, CA: Jossey-Bass, 2007.

Tippet, Krista. *Becoming Wise.* New York, NY: Penguin Press, 2016.

Article

Emmons, Robert, and Anjali Mishra. *Why Gratitude Enhances Well-Being: What We Know, What We Need to Know,* 2011. Retrieved from http://emmons.faculty.ucdavis.edu /wp-content/uploads/sites/90/2015/08/2011_2–16_Sheldon_Chapter-16–11.pdf

Other

- With the free app Gratitude 365 (gratitude365app.com) you can capture a photo a day that reflects what you're grateful for.

ACKNOWLEDGMENTS

These acknowledgments feel woefully limited, as so many people have contributed to my personal resilience as well as to my understanding of resilience that there is no way I can thank them all. What follows is a very partial recognition of the people who made this work possible.

This book is dedicated to my maternal grandparents, Lil and Frank, who are my role models for living a resilient, joyful life that is of service to others. Their example guides me on a daily basis, and their love—which was enormous—will last me a lifetime. I don't know who I would be without my ancestors, and I aspire to live up to the dreams they had for me.

Friends have boosted my resilience like nothing else. I am grateful to Kathy MacKay and Kristen Guzmán for 30 years of friendship and for helping me to stay true to who I am. Kristen, for buoying me through the roughest year of my life and Kathy, for being my go-to resource on questions related to the natural world and helping me arrive at the metaphor of the *cenote*—and so much more. For their friendship, colleague-ship, and overall wonderfulness, I'm so grateful to Dara Wolochow, Shannon Carey, Lettecia Kratz, and Lisa Jimenez.

The following people have profoundly influenced the way I think about resilience and transformation: My uncle, Walter Umaña Aguilar; Sylvia Boorstein; Pema Chödrön; His Holiness the Dalai Lama; Ram Dass; Jack Kornfield; Rabbi Michael Lerner; Thich Nhat Hanh; Sharon Salzberg; Rebecca Solnit; Archbishop Desmond Tutu; and Margaret Wheatley. I am grateful to have gleaned so much wisdom from these courageous leaders.

Meaningful conversations with the following people sparked connections, insights, and inspiration on the topic of resilience: Drea Beale, LesLee Bickford, Javier Cabra, Rebecca Crook, Davina Goldwasser, Bessie Goodman, Prentis Goodman,

Tina Hernandez, Raiza Lisboa, Tiffany Cheng Nyaggah, Carol Owala, Steve Sexton, Ricardo Toro, and Huber Trenado. I am grateful for their presence in my life.

The following colleagues and students offered me unique lessons about kindness, compassion, and resilience: Eileen Barerra, Brenda Castro, Angela Parker, Keiko Suda, Kathryn Suyeyasu, and Christina Wildhagen. I have learned from each of these powerful women.

There are a group of people who uniquely support me. I couldn't do my work without Magdalena Dittmer, Ryn Speich, David Rittenger, and Josh Lowitz. I am deeply grateful to Eloiza Jorge, my coach, for her wisdom, guidance, and presence. Maia Heyck-Merlin's friendship got me through many rough days in the last couple of years. Zaretta Hammond has been a generous friend, offering camaraderie, resources, and a sounding board.

My fantastic team at Bright Morning Consulting contribute tremendously to my ability to write and share my work in myriad ways. What a gift to work with Jeanne Carlson, Noelle Apostol Colin, Jessie Cordova, Maya Haines, and Lettecia Kratz. I have so much appreciation for their energy, brilliance, and friendship.

As for preparing this book, there are also many to thank. Judith Wolochow provided meticulous editing of the first draft, as well as many kind words of encouragement. Caitlin Schwartzman offered extensive feedback on several drafts and on the graphics; this is the second book she's coached me through, and now I can't imagine writing anything without her eyes. Cheryl Beeson read this manuscript with careful attention toward what leaders might need. Michele Reinhart and Jessie Cordova provided a final round of critical feedback pushing me to refine the ideas, language, and concepts. This book is much stronger because of the feedback from these readers.

For help pulling *The Onward Workbook* together, I am very grateful to Laurelin Whitfield and Stacey Goodman. It may not have been completed on time without their assistance and encouragement.

Kate Gagnon, my editor at Jossey-Bass, has championed my ideas and writing for many years now. She is relentlessly positive and encouraging, she offers resources and connections, and she makes the whole (sometimes excruciatingly difficult) process of writing a book as easy as it could possibly be.

There's no way I could have written this book without the love of my husband, Stacey Goodman, and my son, Orion. Their support and encouragement are so tightly woven into the everyday fabric of my life that it's impossible to point out their precise contributions. When it comes to the love from these two or the way in which they allow me to be me and do what I do, I am rendered wordless and humbled beyond description.

Without my father, Gilbert, and my aunt, Jeanne, it's hard for me to imagine the last few years or decades. Their importance in my life continues to expand, and their love, encouragement, and support has filled some big holes. I am grateful for who they are and for our ever-evolving relationship.

My mother's enduring love nurtures, anchors, and guides me every day. I could not do what I do without her; I would not be who I am without her. I am infinitely grateful for the 30 years of unconditional love that she gave me and for the eternal reverberations of that love. I hope that my life might be a testament to the love she gave me.

ABOUT THE AUTHOR

Elena Aguilar is the author of *The Art of Coaching* and *The Art of Coaching Teams*. She has also been a longtime contributor to *Edutopia* and *EdWeek*. She is the founder and president of Bright Morning Consulting, an educational consulting group that works around the world supporting educators to meet the needs of children. Bright Morning offers dozens of workshops each year where educators dive deep into the ideas presented in Elena's books. You can learn more about Bright Morning at www.brightmorningteam.com. Elena lives in Oakland, California, with her husband and son. When she's not writing, coaching, or teaching, she enjoys being in nature, reading fiction, making art, and traveling abroad.

REFERENCES

Achor, S. *The Happiness Advantage.* New York, NY: Crown, 2010.

Adichie, C. N. "The Danger of a Single Story." *TED Global,* 2009. Retrieved from www.ted .com/talks/chimamanda_adichie_the_danger_of_a_single_story

Aguilar, E. *The Art of Coaching Teams.* San Francisco, CA: Jossey-Bass, 2016.

Alliance for Excellent Education. "On the Path to Equity: Improving the Effectiveness of Beginning Teachers," 2014. Retrieved from https://all4ed.org/press/teacher-attrition-costs-united-states-up-to-2–2-billion-annually-says-new-alliance-report/ 2014

American Psychiatric Association. "Zung Instrument for Anxiety." *Psychosomatics,* 1971, *8,* 371–379.

Bandura, A. *Self-Efficacy: The Exercise of Control.* New York, NY: W. H. Freeman, 1997.

Barker, E. "How To Stop Procrastinating: 4 New Steps Backed by Research," 2015. Retrieved from www.bakadesuyo.com/2015/01/how-to-stop-procrastinating/

Bartlett, M. Y., and D. DeSteno. "Gratitude and Prosocial Behavior: Helping When It Costs You." *Psychological Science,* 2006, *17*(4), 319–325.

Beltman, S., C. Mansfield, and A. Price. "Thriving Not Just Surviving: A Review of Research on Teacher Resilience." *Educational Research Review,* 2011, *6*(3), 185–207.

Blackburn, E., and E. Epel. *The Telomere Effect: A Revolutionary Approach to Living Younger, Healthier, Longer.* New York, NY: Grand Central Productions, 2017.

Bradberry, T, and J. Greaves. *Emotional Intelligence 2.0.* San Diego, CA: Talent Smart, 2009.

Briggs Myers, I., and Peter B. Briggs. *Gifts Differing: Understanding Personality Type.* Mountain View, CA: Davies-Black, 1995.

Brown, S. *Play: How It Shapes the Brain, Opens the Imagination, and Invigorates the Soul.* New York, NY: Penguin, 2009.

Bryk, A., and B. Scheider. *Trust in Schools: A Core Resource for Improvement.* New York, NY: Russell Sage Foundation, 2002.

Cano-Garcia, F. J., E. M. P. Muñoz, and M. A. Carrasco-Ortiz. "Personality and Contextual Variables in Teacher Burnout." *Personality and Individual Differences,* 2005, *38,* 929–940.

Carver-Thomas, D., and L. Darling-Hammond. *Teacher Turnover: Why It Matters and What We Can Do About It.* Palo Alto, CA: Learning Policy Institute, 2017.

Chiesa, A., and A. Serretti. "A Systematic Review of Neurobiological and Clinical Features of Mindfulness Meditations." *Psychological Medicine,* 2010, *40*(8), 1239–1252.

Clements, A. "You Could Damage Somebody's Life." *Journal of Social Work Education,* 2013, *31*(4), 91–104.

Collins, S. "Statutory Social Workers: Stress, Job Satisfaction, Coping, Social Support and Individual Differences." *British Journal of Social Work,* 2008, *38*(6), 1173–1193.

Correll, J., B. Park, C. M. Judd, and B. Wittenbrink. "The Influence of Stereotypes on Decisions to Shoot." *European Journal of Social Psychology,* 2007, *37,* 1102–1117.

Dalai Lama, D. Tutu, and D. C. Abrams. *The Book of Joy.* New York, NY: Penguin Books, 2016.

Darling-Hammond, L., R. C. Wei, A. Andree, N. Richardson, and S. Orphanos. "State of the Profession: Study Measures Professional Development." *Journal of Staff Development,* 2009, *30*(2) 42–50.

Davidson, R., and A. Harrington, eds. *Visions of Compassion: Western Scientists and Tibetan Buddhists Examine Human Nature.* New York, NY: Oxford University Press, 2001.

Davidson, R., and A. Lutz. "Buddha's Brain: Neuroplasticity and Meditation." *IEEE Signal Processing Magazine,* 2008, *25*(1) 174–176.

Day, C., P. Sammons, and Q. Gu. "Combining Qualitative and Quantitative Methodologies in Research on Teachers' Lives, Work, and Effectiveness: From Integration to Synergy." *Educational Research,* 2008, *37*(6), 330–342.

Deal, T., and K. Peterson. *Shaping School Culture.* San Francisco: Jossey-Bass, 2009.

De Botton, A., and J. Armstrong. *Art as Therapy.* New York, NY: Phaidon, 2013.

Dweck, C. *Mindset.* New York, NY: Random House, 2006.

Ellison, C. G., and J. S. Levin. "The Religion-Health Connection: Evidence, Theory and Future Directions." *Healthy Education and Behavior,* 1998, *25,* 700–720.

Farber, B. A. *Crisis in Education: Stress and Burnout in the American Teacher.* San Francisco, CA: Jossey-Bass, 1991.

Flook, L., S. B. Goldberg, L. Pinger, K. Bonus, and R. J. Davidson. "Mindfulness for Teachers: a Pilot Study to Assess Effects on Stress, Burnout, and Teaching Efficacy." *Mind, Brain, and Education,* 2013, *7*(3), 182–195.

Frankl, V. E. *Man's Search for Meaning.* Boston, MA: Beacon Press, 2006.

Gibbs, J. *Tribes: A Process for Social Development and Cooperative Learning.* Santa Rosa, CA: Center Source Systems, 1987.

Gilbert, D. *Stumbling on Happiness.* New York, NY: Random House, 2005.

Goldin, P. R., and J. J. Gross. "Effects of Mindfulness-Based Stress Reduction (MBSR) on Emotion Regulation in Social Anxiety Disorder." *Emotion,* 2010, *10*(1), 83.

Goleman, D. *Emotional Intelligence.* New York, NY: Bantam Books, 1995.

Gottman, J. *The Seven Principles for Making Marriages Work.* New York, NY: Crown Publishers, 1999.

Grant, L., and G. Kinman. "The Importance of Emotional Resilience for Staff and Students in the 'Helping' Professions: Developing an Emotional Curriculum," 2013. Retrieved from www.heacademy.ac.uk/system/files/emotional_resilience_louise_grant_march_2014_0.pdf

The Guardian. "The Counted: People Killed by the Police in the U.S.," 2015. Retrieved from www.theguardian.com/us-news/series/counted-us-police-killings

Hanson, R. *Hardwiring Happiness: The New Brain Science of Contentment, Calm, and Confidence.* New York, NY: Random House, 2013.

Heath, C., and D. Heath. *Switch: How to Change Things When Change Is Hard.* New York, NY: Broadway Books, 2010.

Hirschkorn, M. "Student-Teacher Relationships and Teacher Induction: Ben's Story." *Teacher Development,* 2009, *13*(3), 205–217.

Hölzel, B. K., J. Carmody, K. C. Evans, E. A. Hoge, J. A. Dusek, L. Morgan, and S. W. Lazar. "Stress Reduction Correlates with Structural Changes in the Amygdala." Social *Cognitive and Affective Neuroscience,* 2010, *5*(1), 11–17.

Hölzel, B. K., J. Carmody, M. Vangel, C. Congleton, S. M. Yerramsetti, T. Gard, and S. W. Lazar. "Mindfulness Practice Leads to Increases in Regional Brain Gray Matter Density." *Psychiatry Research: Neuroimaging,* 2011, *191*(1), 36–43.

Howard, S., and B. Johnson "Resilient Teachers: Resisting Stress and Burnout." *Social Psychology of Education,* 2004, *7*(4), 399 420.

Huffington, A. *Thrive: The Third Metric to Redefining Success.* New York, NY: Random House, 2014.

Ingersoll, R., L. Merrill, and D. Stuckey. *Seven Trends: The Transformation of the Teaching Force.* CPRE Report (#RR-80). Philadelphia: Consortium for Policy Research in Education, University of Pennsylvania, 2014.

Jennings, P. A., J. Brown, J. L. Frank, S. L. Doyle, R. Tanler, D. Rasheed, A. DeWeese, A. DeMauro, and M. T. Greenberg. "Promoting Teachers' Social and Emotional Competence, Well-Being and Classroom Quality: A Randomized Controlled Trial of the CARE for Teachers Professional Development Program." In C. Bradshaw (Ed.), *Examining the Impact of School-Based Prevention Programs on Teachers: Findings from Three Randomized Trials.* Washington, DC: Symposium presented at the Society for Prevention Research Annual Meeting, 2015. (Submitted for Initial Review).

Jennings, P. A., J. L. Frank, K. E. Snowberg, M. A. Coccia, and M. T. Greenberg. "Improving Classroom Learning Environments by Cultivating Awareness and Resilience in Education (CARE): Results of a Randomized Controlled Trial." *School Psychology Quarterly,* 2013, *28*(4), 374–390.

Jensen, P., K. Trollope, H. Waters, and J. Everson. "Building Physician Resilience." *Canadian Family Physician,* 2008, *54*(5) 722–772.

Jeon, L., C. K. Buettner, and A. R. Snyder. "Pathways from Teacher Depression and Child-Care Quality to Child Behavioral Problems." *Journal of Consulting and Clinical Psychology,* 2014, *82*(2), 225–235.

Keltner, D., J. Marsh, and J. A. Smith. *The Compassionate Instinct: The Science of Human Goodness.* New York, NY: W. W. Norton, 2010.

Kevern, J., and C. Webb. "Mature Women's Experiences of Preregistration Nurse Education." *Journal of Advanced Nursing,* 2004, *45,* 297–306. doi:10.1046/j.1365-2648.2003.02890.x

Lambert, D. "A Changed Perspective: How Gratitude Can Affect Sense of Coherence Through Positive Reframing." *Journal of Positive Psychology,* 2009, *4*(6), 461–470.

Larrivee, B. *Cultivating Teacher Renewal.* Lanham, MD: Rowman & Littlefield Education, 2012.

Larsen, B. "10 Reasons a Sense of Humor Is No Laughing Matter." *Standard-Examiner* [Ogden, UT], March 26, 2015.

Layous, K., K. Sweeny, C. Armenta, S. Na, I. Choi, and S. Lyubomirsky. "The Proximal Experience of Gratitude." *PLOS ONE,* 2017, *12*(7), e0179123.

Lieberman, M. *Social: Why Our Brains Are Wired to Connect.* New York, NY: Crown, 2013.

Louis, K. S., K. Leithwood, K. Wahlstrom, and S. Anderson. *Investigating the Links to Improved Student Learning: Final Report of Research Findings,* 2010. Retrieved from www.wallacefoundation.org/knowledge-center/schoolleadership/key-research/

Lueke, A., and B. Gibson. "Mindfulness Meditation Reduces Implicit Age and Race Bias: The Role of Reduced Automaticity of Responding." *Social Psychological and Personality Science,* 2014, *6*(3), 284–291.

Lutz, A., H. A. Slagter, J. D. Dunne, and R. J. Davidson. "Attention Regulation and Monitoring in Meditation." *Trends in Cognitive Sciences,* 2008, *12*(4), 163–169.

Lyubomirsky, S. *The How of Happiness.* New York, NY: Penguin, 2007.

Maslach, C. *Burnout: The Cost of Caring.* Englewood Cliffs, NJ: Prentice Hall, 1982.

Medina, J. *Brain Rules.* Seattle, WA: Pear Press, 2008.

Mercola, Dr. "The Ultimate Antioxidant: Fight Premature Aging for Free," 2012. Retrieved from https://articles.mercola.com/sites/articles/archive/2012/11/04/why-does-walking-barefoot-on-the-earth-make-you-feel-better.aspx

Moir, E. "Phases of First-Year Teaching." *Newsletter for the California New Teacher Project,* 1990. Retrievable from www.otago.ac.nz/education/otago065978

Mongrain, M., J. M. Chin, and L. B. Shapira. "Practicing Compassion Increases Happiness and Self-Esteem." *Journal of Happiness Studies,* 2011, *12*(6), 963–981.

Morrison, T. *Staff Supervision in Social Care.* London, UK: Pavilion, 2005.

Morrison, T. "No Place for Self-Pity, No Room for Fear," *The Nation,* 2015. Retrieved from www.thenation.com/article/no-place-self-pity-no-room-fear/

Nichols, W. J. *Blue Mind: The Surprising Science That Shows How Being Near, in, on, or Under Water Can Make You Happier, Healthier, More Connected, and Better at What You Do.* New York, NY: Little, Brown, and Company, 2014.

Nyhan, B., and J. Reifler. "When Corrections Fail: The Persistence of Political Misperceptions." *Political Behavior,* 2010, *32*(2), 303–330.

Okonofua, J. A., and J. L. Eberhardt. "Two Strikes: Race and the Disciplining of Young Students." *Psychological Science,* 2015, *26*(5), 617–624.

Olivo, E. *Wise Mind Living.* Louisville, CO: Sounds True, 2014.

Osório, C., T. Probert, E. Jones, A. Young, and I. Robbins. "Adapting to Stress: Understanding the Neurobiology of Resilience." *Behavioral Medicine,* 2017, *43*(4), 307–322.

Pande, N. "The Effect of a Sense of Humor on Positive Capacities: An Empirical Inquiry into Psychological Aspects." *Global Journal of Finance and Management,* 2014, *6*(4), 385–390.

Pargament, K. I., and A. Mahoney. "Spirituality: Discovering and Conserving the Sacred." In C. R. Snyder and S. J. Lopez (Eds.), *Handbook for Positive Psychology* (pp. 646–659). Oxford, England: Oxford University Press, 2002.

Patterson, J., L. Collins, and G. Abbot. "A Study of Teacher Resilience in Urban Schools." *Journal of Instructional Psychology,* March 2004, *31*(1), 3–11.

Patterson, J., and P. Kelleher. *Resilient School Leaders: Strategies for Turning Adversity into Achievement.* Alexandria, VA: ASCD, 2005.

Pease, A., and B. Pease. *The Definitive Book of Body Language: How to Read Others' Thoughts by Their Gestures.* Buderim, Australia: Pease International, 2004.

Poloma, M. M., and G. H. Gallup. *Varieties of Prayer: A Survey Report.* Philadelphia, PA: Trinity Press International, 1991.

powell, j. a. "Understanding Our New Racial Reality Starts with the Unconscious." Greater Good, 2015. http://greatergood.berkeley.edu/article/item/understanding_our_new_racial_reality_starts_with_the_unconscious.

Psychology Today. "Seasonal Affective Disorder," Feb. 1, 2017. Retrieved from www.psychologytoday.com/conditions/seasonal-affective-disorder

Radloff, L. "The CES-D Scale: A Self-Report Depression Scale for Research in the General Population." *Applied Psychological Measurement,* 1977, *1*, 385–401.

Rawlence, B. *City of Thorns.* New York: Picador, 2017.

Robbins, M. *Focus on the Good Stuff: The Power of Appreciation.* San Francisco, CA: Jossey-Bass, 2007.

Rock, D. *Your Brain at Work: Strategies for Overcoming Distraction, Regaining Focus, and Working Smarter All Day Long.* New York, NY: HarperCollins, 2009.

Roth, G. *Maps to Ecstasy: The Healing Power of Movement.* Novato, CA: New World Library, 1998.

Ruch, G. "Reflective Practice in Child Care Social Work: The Role of Containment." *British Journal of Social Work,* 2007, *37*, 659–680.

Safford, V. "The Small Work in the Great Work." In P. Loeb (ed.), *The Impossible Will Take a Little While: Perseverance and Hope in Troubled Times* (pp. 224–230). New York, NY: Basic Books, 2004.

Salzberg, S. *Lovingkindness: The Revolutionary Art of Happiness.* Boulder, CO: Shambhala, 1995.

Salzberg, S. *Real Happiness at Work.* New York, NY: Workman, 2013.

Sarason, B. R., I. G. Sarason, T. A. Hacker, and R. B. Basham "Concomitants of Social Support: Social Skills, Physical Attractiveness and Gender." *Journal of Personality and Social Psychology,* 1985, *49,* 469–480.

Scherwitz, L. "Self-Involvement: A New Risk Factor Heart Disease," n.d. Retrieved from www.empowher.com/heart-disease/content/self-involvement-new-risk-factor-heart-disease

Schwartz, T., and C. McCarthy. "Manage Your Energy, Not Your Time." *Harvard Business Review,* October 2007, 114–125.

Solnit, R. *The Mother of All Questions.* Chicago, IL: Haymarket Books, 2017.

Sumsion, J. "Early Childhood Teachers' Construction of their Resilience and Thriving: A Continuing Investigation." *International Journal of Early Years Education,* 2004, *12*(3), 275–290.

Thaler, R., and C. Sunstein. *Nudge: Improving Decisions About Health, Wealth and Happiness.* New York, NY: Penguin, 2009.

Tippett, K. *Becoming Wise: An Inquiry into the Mystery and Art of Living.* New York: Penguin, 2016.

US Department of Education, Office for Civil Rights. *Issue Brief 1,* March 2014. Retrieved from https://ocrdata.ed.gov/downloads/crdc-school-discipline-snapshot.pdf

Wallace Foundation. *The School Principal as Leader: Guiding Schools to Better Teaching and Learning,* 2011. Retrieved from www.wallacefoundation.org/knowledge-center/school-leadership/effective-principal-leadership/Documents/The-School-Principal-as-Leader-Guiding-Schools-to-Better-Teaching-and-Learning.pdf

Wilks, S., and C. Spivey. "Resilience in Undergraduate Social Work Students: Social Support and Adjustment to Academic Stress." *Social Work Education, 29,* 2010, 276–288.

Wulsin, L., T. Alterman, P. Timothy Bushnell, J. Li, and R. Shen. "Prevalence Rates for Depression by Industry: A Claims Database Analysis." *Social Psychiatry and Psychiatric Epidemiology,* 2014, *49*(11), 1805–1821.

Yost, D., "Reflection and Self-Efficacy: Enhancing the Retention of Qualified Teachers from a Teacher Education Perspective." *Teacher Education Quarterly,* 2006, *33*(4), 59–76.

Zak, P. "Why Your Brain Loves Good Storytelling." *Harvard Business Review,* October 2014. Retrieved from https://hbr.org/2014/10/why-your-brain-loves-good-storytelling

Zolli, A., and A. M. Healy. *Resilience: Why Things Bounce Back.* New York, NY: Simon & Schuster, 2012.

INDEX

Page references followed by *fig* indicate an illustration.